A302

Critical Acclaim for this Book

This is a bold, imaginative book. Robbie Robertson elucidates the origins of globalization and the subsequent paths it has followed, highlighting important lessons for how the present wave of globalization should be understood, and handled. A very stimulating, critical contribution to the contemporary literature.

Stephanie Lawson, Professor of International Relations, University of East Anglia

At last an historian who sees the big picture about globalization and its present manifestation. Robbie Robertson has produced a readable but learned book that will cause anger, debate, even dismay both to those who support and to those who oppose globalization. A must-read for all those who care about our common future and want to know more about the human condition and its evolution and promise.

Mike Moore, World Trade Organization

About the Author

Dr Robbie Robertson teaches History and Development Studies at La Trobe University, Australia. He is the author of several books including:

Government by the Gun: Fiji and the 2000 Coup (with William Sutherland) (2002)
Multiculturalism and Reconciliation in an Indulgent Republic: Fiji after the Coups (1998)
Fiji: Shattered Coups (with Akosita Tamanisau) (1988)
The Making of the Modern World (1986)
The Contemporary Era: An Introductory History (1984)

. . . .

The Three Waves of Globalization
A history of a developing global consciousness

ROBBIE ROBERTSON
. . . .

Fernwood Publishing
NOVA SCOTIA

Zed Books
LONDON • NEW YORK

The Three Waves of Globalization: A history of a developing consciousness
was first published by Zed Books Ltd, 7 Cynthia Street, London N1
9JF, UK and Room 400, 175 Fifth Avenue, New York, NY 10010, USA,
and in Canada by Fernwood Publishing Ltd, 8422 St Margaret's Bay
Road (Hwy 3), Site 2A, Box 5, Black Point, Nova Scotia, B0J 1B0, in
2003.

www.zedbooks.co.uk

Copyright © Robbie Robertson, 2003

Second impression, 2004

Cover designed by Andrew Corbett
Set in Monotype Dante by Ewan Smith, London
Printed and bound in the EU by Biddles Ltd, King's Lynn

Distributed in the USA exclusively by Palgrave Macmillan, a division of
St Martin's Press, LLC, 175 Fifth Avenue, New York, NY 10010.

The right of Robbie Robertson to be identified as the author of this
work have been asserted by him in accordance with the Copyright,
Designs and Patents Act, 1988.

A catalogue record for this book is available from the British Library
US CIP data is available from the Library of Congress
Canadian CIP data is available from the National Library of Canada

ISBN 1 85649 860 3 cased
ISBN 1 85649 861 1 limp

In Canada
ISBN 1 55266 100 8 limp

Contents

Preface and Acknowledgements

Globalization is not a subject renowned for interventions by historians. It has so far remained the realm of sociologists, political scientists and economists. But historians should be as concerned about contemporary issues as other academics. The present is never disconnected from the past. I hope this introductory study demonstrates that historians have something useful to contribute to contemporary debates.

The Three Waves of Globalization deals with matters of inclusion and empowerment. In this regard language is obviously important, and not only for reasons of accuracy. Accordingly I have made three decisions as to usage. The first is gender-related. I do not refer to nations as women. The second is geographical. The world consists of three main continents – Afro-Eurasia, the Americas, and Australia. Thus Europe is not a continent but a subcontinent, and the 'Near East' or 'Middle East' is more properly described as West Asia. The third point of usage relates to the division of time. In a study designed for global and non-religious application, the terms BC and AD are inappropriate. Hence I have followed a newer convention and used instead BCE (Before the Common Era) and CE (the Common Era).

The Three Waves of Globalization is an exploratory history only. It is designed to stimulate debate. It is not intended as the definitive word on the subject, let alone an exhaustive study of all aspects of globalization and its scholarship. Instead I have selected elements of the story that I believe best convey a sense of the processes of change involved, and have focused on a small number of writers whose work is representative of general trends in contemporary scholarship.

Many people assisted in the making of this book, but my family – especially Akosita Tamanisau and Nemani Robertson – require special mention for their support, understanding and patience during a long year of very intense creativity. La Trobe University allowed me leave to work on this project, and the Institute of Social Studies (particularly Professor Martin Doornbos and Professor Mohamed Salih) once again provided a perfect working environment in The Hague to undertake much of the writing. William Sutherland read a draft and provided much welcome criticism and comment. Omissions and errors remain mine, however, and while every effort has been made to attribute sources correctly, no slight is intended in any misattribution or omission.

For Nemani Robertson

PART ONE

. . . .

Globalizing Knowledge

. . . .

CHAPTER I

Developing Global Consciousness

The Historical and Social Context of Globalization

This book is an exploration of the nature of globalization. It takes as its starting point the idea that globalization is not a post-Second World War phenomenon, still less a process of change that followed the collapse of the Cold War. Yet, undeniably, globalization is everyone's favourite catchphrase today. It never enjoyed this currency in the mid-twentieth century or before. Indeed, it has become the *bête noir* of analysts angered at the contemporary power and influence of transnational entities, monsters that they believe are rapidly homogenizing the world, destroying its diversity, and marginalizing its peoples' hard-won democratic rights. For others, transnationals and the new forms of global integration they represent are harbingers of a new order that will enable humans to co-operate more meaningfully with each other. Nations that embrace globalization, we are regularly informed, do not go to war with one another. Instead they compete on the global economic playing field and prosper.

But globalization is more than just McWorld or Westernization. It is about human interconnections that have assumed global proportions and trans-formed themselves. If we focus on globalization simply as a modern strategy for power, we will miss its historical and social depths. Indeed the origins of globalization lie in interconnections that have slowly enveloped humans since the earliest times, as they globalized themselves. In this sense, globalization as a human dynamic has always been with us, even if we have been unaware of its embrace until recently. Instead we have viewed the world more narrowly through the spectacles of religion, civilization, nation or race. Today these old constructs continue to frustrate the development of a global consciousness of human interconnections and their dynamism. Even analytic tools at our disposal are often infected; sometimes they are products of these perceptions.

More commonly however, as knowledge has expanded, academic lines of inquiry have become increasingly distinct disciplines, dedicated to the detailed

studies such knowledge now enables and requires. Unfortunately such specialization tends to separate knowledge from ordinary people. It makes their task
of understanding life more difficult. It also ill equips us for the study of a
subject that is diverse, not only in all its various social, geographical, biological,
political, historical, cultural and intellectual components, but also in the outcomes of their interconnections. Far from being static or one-dimensional,
globalization is the manifestation of extremely diverse dynamic synergies.
This book seeks to provide a historical basis for exploring those synergies.

Its focus is on the past five hundred years, when humans experienced three
distinct global waves of interconnectedness. The first, after 1500, centred on
the globalization of regional trade; the second, after 1800, gained impetus
from industrialization; the third derived from the architecture of a new world
order after 1945. Each wave began with an event – sometimes a war – which
gave space for its burgeoning as a global force for change. Each wave produced
new interconnections and generated new synergies that in time led to its own
transformation. No wave has ever been the creature of one country alone,
although at times hegemons and would-be hegemons have attempted to
monopolize them for their own advantage. No wave has ever been the product
of one 'civilization' or one culture alone. Waves encompass many cultures;
they enable them to interact, although not necessarily as equals. They enable
cross-fertilization. Exclusivity, on the other hand, denies mutual benefit and is
difficult to sustain. It frustrates globalization. It creates instability and makes
war and conquest attractive alternatives. The first wave faltered in the
eighteenth century for this reason; similarly the second wave foundered in the
early twentieth century. It is too early to make a final judgement about the
third wave.

Like earlier waves, the third wave is dynamic but it possesses characteristics
that also make it qualitatively different. Its difference can be summed up in
one word that suggests the emergence of something greater than the accident
of interconnections. That word is globalism, meaning a conscious process of
globalization or a set of policies designed specifically to effect greater global
rather than international interactions. Thus, it has been possible since 1944 to
speak of American globalism. No such globalism existed under British hegemony in the nineteenth century. Britain rode the forces driving globalization
but never pursued strategies designed to engender global relations. Its goals
were always nationally or imperially focused. The same might be said of the
United States, but its globalism set in place institutions capable, in theory if
not in practice, of independently developing global policies. The difference
lay in part in the US desire not to repeat the mistakes of the second wave, but
it lay also in the fact that American hegemony coincided with a remarkable
process of democratization that radically transformed societies and enabled
the emergence of dynamic structures for global co-operation.

To understand globalization then, we need to understand its historical dimension. But we need also to understand its equally important, though usually indirect, social dimension. As interconnections increasingly assumed global proportions, trade prospered and the power and influence of trading classes increased accordingly. Sometimes the nurturing and accommodation of such agents of profitable activity established precedence for social and political reform. Thus human interconnectiveness extended opportunities for human empowerment, although not without contestation and struggle. It promoted social transformation, but without the autonomy that empowerment requires, the result of social transformation became inequality.

Social transformation and interconnectiveness were also influenced by human environments, population sizes and movements, technologies and economies, and cultures. Differences between these factors have always ensured that no one society became identical to another. Consequently, many analysts have sought to explain social inequalities by reference to these differences.

But they have also focused on the strategies adopted by different communities and on the quality of leadership. As social animals, humans have always pursued a range of collective strategies to ensure their survival and well-being; they have migrated, conquered, traded, and technologically innovated. As societies grew larger and more interconnected, the range of strategies adopted tended to broaden. Yet for many societies until a thousand years ago, conquest remained the dominant strategy, and, like most strategies, was ultimately premised on an unsustainable zero–sum understanding about the generation of wealth. In the end, conquering societies always ran out of loot to plunder or societies worth subjugating. Sometimes their exploitation destroyed the very environments they coveted.

Trading societies were not always different in this regard. Their desire to monopolize trade and satisfy the lust for instant fortune frequently destroyed the potential for future market growth. It also attracted the attention of unwelcome predators. This was still a world dominated by elites who regarded any sign of economic success as an invitation for conquest. In time these rapacious classes would be swept aside or incorporated, and conquest subjugated – at least in principle – to the promotion of commerce and industry. Thus merchants and industrialists remained comfortable with slaves and colonial subjects during the first two waves of globalization. As initial beneficiaries of the autonomy and empowerment that the wider global environment increasingly gave space for, traders and industrialists wanted to monopolize their potential. But like conquerors before them, they failed. Democratization, long before it emerged as a global strategy for security and well-being, consistently frustrated all forms of exclusivity. First the struggle of traders, then industrialists, middle and working classes, and more recently of empowered civil societies bear testimony to this constancy.

Some writers give greater weight to the role of technology in stimulating change. They argue that the scope for human action altered dramatically with two paradigm shifts, the first heralding an agricultural revolution over ten thousand years ago, the second an industrial revolution beginning some two hundred years ago. Technological changes altered the way humans produced and transformed the nature of human societies. But what gave these revolutions significance was human interconnectiveness. Agricultural technology, like writing, evolved in only a small number of places. Yet its consequences were profound because it spread. The same is true of industrialization, except that ten thousand years later, greater human interconnectiveness gave it global resonance within a much shorter period of time.

Human interconnectiveness, then, has long been an important feature of human survival and well-being. Indeed, its historical strength has been such that human strategies have changed over time because of human interconnectiveness, especially after the fifteenth century, when it assumed global proportions and developed three very distinct consecutive forms. Globalization changed the nature of human communities accordingly. It also magnified tremendously the forms and scope of exclusionary strategies, thereby generating new dangers and challenges.

But the forms and scope of human co-operation and empowerment have similarly magnified, enabling a nascent global consciousness of the social import of globalization. From the macro level of the global community to the micro level of the family, the same imperative exists. Democratization empowers and enriches people. It transforms them. It fashions space for creativity, new specialisms, and new strategies. It creates scope for positively transforming the human condition. But managing such transformations is a difficult process; indeed globalization has twice faltered because elites sought to frustrate democratization and reorient globalization towards more exclusive ends.

The same prospect may well face our own third wave of globalization if we ignore the social and historical lessons that globalization presents to us. We should not allow globalization to be privatized, to become the privileged agenda of national and transnational entities. People need to reclaim ownership of globalization and democratize the process. The alternative has confronted humans before. Actions that seek to marginalize human agency and creativity, and undermine democratic gains, will not only make societies more vulnerable to economic and political shocks, but will also deny humans the mass global dynamism they now need to address problems that exist in global proportions. Every child that starves is a child denied the ability to contribute to society to the best of his or her ability. Every child refused education represents a loss in social and human potential. In one way or another, all peoples and their societies pay the penalty for such neglect.

Our Exploration

To understand these relationships, we have to develop global consciousness and abandon the narrow perspectives that have imprisoned us in the past. We need to embrace knowledge that helps us in this task. In fact humans have been struggling towards this goal ever since they became conscious of themselves, and in Chapter 2 we explore some of the consequences that struggles for survival and well-being have had in the creation of global consciousness. In particular we focus on the importance of understanding our place in the universe, the nature of that universe, and the evolution of humans as a species. These are all prerequisites for understanding the human condition.

Unfortunately we often put on masks and veils in order to deny our genetically determined desires and our materialism. We claim that intelligence drives human history, rather than our ability to utilize resources and to imitate successful behaviour. We do not want to believe that we are governed by desires no more complicated than that of survival and well-being.

Nonetheless, we are also socially dynamic. We control our desires. We co-operate. We specialize. We have to because we do not live in a vacuum. We are affected by our environments, by our abilities to access and utilize resources, and by the size of our populations. Increasingly also, we are affected by human interconnectedness.

Our examination of early global transformations in Chapter 3 focuses on the interconnections that the human dynamic first generated. Many of these interconnections shared characteristics that are remarkably similar to those of globalization today: lost diversity, new forms of difference, environmental degradation, expanding social, political and economic units and, above all, the gradual development of synergies that had interregional impacts. Behind all these changes lay basic human drives for security and well-being as humans migrated, conquered, traded and innovated. We may regard interconnectiveness as a feature of contemporary globalization, but the records of the past demonstrate its ancient centrality as a motor for human change.

Power based on increased unequal relations became the basis for governance in most agricultural societies. The different weight they gave to strategies for security and well-being produced very different outcomes. Yet none of them could isolate themselves from the consequences of increasing linkages between communities. By a thousand years ago, these linkages had begun to assume continental proportions. But they remained fragile. Indeed, war and a very biological consequence of human interconnectedness swept large parts of the Afro-Eurasian continent and delayed its global emergence until the sixteenth century.

Thus the first wave of globalization, the subject of Chapter 4, assumed a very different form than a reading of human history one thousand years ago might have presumed. Weakened by plague and distracted by the activities of Eurasian warlords, China never fulfilled its early promise. Into the vacuum stepped a number of European states whose fractious competitiveness provided motivation and whose accidental discovery of the Americas and its wealth provided the means to insert themselves into the lucrative intra-Asian trade. During the course of our examination of their fragile commercial imperatives, we will consider how this three-century-long transformation of global relations has been interpreted in the past, and whether Europe's growing pre-eminence suggested a degree of European exceptionalism.

However, at the heart of the matter lay an old human drive, the lust for riches. What drove Europe out of recession and produced the basis for successful commercialism was the sudden wealth that Atlantic and Asian trade networks generated. But while its multiplier impact created new opportunities for growth, it did not guarantee particular outcomes for its participants. The ruling classes of the first wave's protagonists tried to convert their newfound wealth into the basis for hegemony within Europe; in the end power flowed instead to societies that gave space to those who directly or indirectly generated wealth.

Commerce deepened the democratic imperative and made old forms of exclusion less viable. Indeed, the first wave – although less all-embracing than subsequent waves – transformed global dynamics. For the first time some humans operated globally. They transformed intersecting regional markets into global networks and enabled new interconnections, which accelerated the global distribution of plants and animals, spawned rapid population growth, and altered environments. These changes all had far-reaching political, social and economic outcomes. For all countries, the first wave of globalization was highly destabilizing.

As a goal, the attainment of wealth was uncontroversial, but in leading commercial nations it was accompanied by changes in class relations and property laws. Such nascent democratization sometimes threatened the interests of old elites. Commercial classes increased in size and influence. Urbanization expanded. Rural communities similarly changed as commercial activities increased. How those changes were managed not only dictated the success or otherwise of commercial activities but also determined the future character of their societies. During the course of the seventeenth and eighteenth centuries, many European societies sought sustainability through exclusions of class, religion, race, empire or commercial monopoly. But their passage was never easy, and frequently countries resorted to war and conquest. France did both at the end of the eighteenth century, and brought the first wave to an end.

Despite the instability generated by the nascent democratic imperative, the synergies produced by the first wave enabled a remarkable technological transformation. The Industrial Revolution, globalization's industrial child, is examined in Chapter 5. We have not always viewed it thus. Often we have been conscious of industrialization as a late-eighteenth-century process emana-ting only from Europe, or from Britain alone, rather than as a product of the first wave's interconnections and synergies. But there can be no doubting its impact. Industrialization enabled environments to carry larger populations, which in turn generated new social and political dynamics. More than ever before, technology now had the capacity to generate huge profits. It also increased interconnectiveness, enabling its own more rapid diffusion.

But it also generated disadvantage. The societies that initially benefited most from industrialization were those that had been transformed by the first wave of globalization. The Industrial Revolution was the pay-off for empowering more of their citizens and for enabling the creation and integration of diverse and dynamic economic activities. That democratizing process continued during the nineteenth century and heralded a new age of the masses.

Former powerhouses such as China never experienced the same dynamic surge through their economies capable of raising demand as trade had in Europe. Consequently no democratic impulse existed to generate demand also. In that difference lay disadvantage. So too the loss of autonomy. Societies unable to refashion themselves as industrial nations increasingly became im-prisoned as colonies or semi-colonies in the industrial futures of other nations.

But even countries that did manage to retain their autonomy discovered no equality in their advantage. Inequalities between industrializing countries, together with the internal tensions that industrialization generated, tempted their leaders to boost security and well-being by exclusionary alternatives. Pressure mounted in the late nineteenth century as more countries industrial-ized and as a second generation of industrial technology emerged that depended on social transformation and democratization for its success. State systems needed to be more coherent and responsive; they had to become less hierarchical. States had to make huge investments in communications infra-structure and human capital. Industry and finance responded by restructuring, but this simply raised the stakes further. It did not produce mass prosperity, on which industrialization now increasingly depended. Not unnaturally many industrializing countries sought to distract disaffected subjects from their shortfalls by producing colonial successes. Japan turned to empire to offset the impact of unequal development at home and competition abroad. The United States sought empire to symbolize its great-power status, gain access to new wealth abroad, and demonstrate the universal benefits that Social Darwinism created. Russia expanded eastward across Eurasia.

There were many other reasons for colonies: they sustained national con-fidence, they possessed strategic value, they restored competitive advantage, and they demonstrated global reach. But they brought no lasting stability.

Certainly they brought little stability to the peoples they engulfed. Indeed, the nature of colonial transformation often made future autonomous development both tortuous and difficult. The various holocausts and economic reconstructions that accompanied incorporation into global processes of colonial production generated racism and victim mentalities that reduced the ability of their peoples to develop autonomously. In the long run these empires of disadvantage, the subject of Chapter 6, were unsustainable. They created new forms of difference and inequality that denied the key imperatives for successful transformation, autonomy and empowerment. Colonies involved zero–sum strategies. They destabilized communities. They denied inclusion. They suppressed demand. These contradictions never had time to become apparent to most industrializing colonizers; by the early twentieth century they were overwhelmed instead by pressures from their own communities for democratization and by competition among themselves.

The implosion of the second wave (Chapter 7) demonstrated the danger that this scale of globalization now presented. Instead of globalism and the development of mechanisms for co-operation and mutual development, the second wave promoted nationalism and the creation of empires that sought to become worlds unto themselves. Both responses demonstrated a belief that societies now possessed the necessary means to control the multiple transformations and class conflicts rippling through them. Fearing that they might lose out in competition increasingly drawn in Darwinian terms, the leaders of industrializing nations were prepared to go to the brink of war and over in order to preserve their democratically challenged social structures and gain hegemonic status at home and abroad. The First World War cost the fighting nations tremendously, and not only in lives. It cost them the confidence that had at one time energized the second wave.

In a sense nothing changed immediately after 1918; the deck chairs were simply rearranged. Consequently, a brutal depression – born of state indecision and timidity, and symbolic of the second wave's collapse – provoked a second round of bloodletting during the 1930s and 1940s. Inward-looking economic policies simply reinforced the drive to empire and conquest. But the avenging fascist conquerors, who believed that national solutions could only come from baptisms of fire and empire, served only to demonstrate the futility of fostering zero–sum perceptions and denying the democratic synergies that globalization gave space to.

In Chapter 8, we begin an examination of the third wave of globalization, which followed the second wave's implosion. War bestowed on the United States unprecedented opportunity to establish the first global world order. Indeed, American globalism did create a qualitatively different wave. It laid the basis both for domestic political stability in industrialized nations and for international co-operation. Through state planning and social engineering, it facilitated the return to prosperity of its former industrial rivals. It also created new multilateral institutions to manage international trade liberalization and prevent the return of ruinous national economic competition. Both projects incorporated US desires to maintain its hegemony, but in a more globalized world such desires were not always possible to fulfil.

American globalism also created an international environment in which the second wave's empires of disadvantage could be dissolved. Thus decolonization, too, was a child of globalization and its struggles, although not the uncontested Western gift that it is still sometimes presented as. Nor did decolonization guarantee future meaningful participation in the globalized economy for members of the emergent Third World. Nonetheless, it did represent a break with the traditions of the past and held the promise of autonomy for societies that decolonized. Achieving it proved more difficult.

Colonialism left most independent countries poorly equipped to survive in a more globalized world. In addition, residues of the past lingered in the modernization policies that more powerful industrial nations imposed as a condition for development assistance. They lingered also in the perceptions people held of globalization at a time when the term was barely recognized. Neither the policies nor the perceptions gave weight to the democratic imperative. Instead they encouraged the segregation of economic sectors, denied social reform, and reinforced dependence on export production. Consequently the promise of decolonization was not always realized. Dictatorships emerged. Development faltered. Neocolonialism prospered. A global divide emerged that still holds the potential to destabilize the third wave.

Residues of the past also lingered in the war of globalisms that erupted between the two victors of the Second World War, the United States of America and the Union of Soviet Socialist Republics. Instead of peace and global harmony, the third wave began with a new global ideological division, an unprecedented arms race, and a destructive Soviet–American rivalry that spilled over into East European occupations and Third World wars. It was not an auspicious start. In the end both globalisms died, one more dramatically than the other.

The victor was transnationalism. Large corporations and their allies exploited popular fears when post-war prosperity ended in the 1970s. They deregulated domestic economies and transformed global regulatory systems to their advantage. As transnational capital became more active, it harnessed a third generation of technological change to fashion new global production networks. These networks often exploited Third World vulnerabilities, but their primary purpose was to promote corporate survival and find new avenues for profit. By the close of the twentieth century, the corporate vision of globalism held centre stage.

But transnationalism threatened many of the achievements of democratization, the subject of Chapter 9: Globalizing Democracies. Industrialized societies sometimes like to claim ownership of certain features of globalization, such as democracy. This too is a form of exclusion. Democratization is the process of social empowerment that makes modernity attainable. It too is challenging and destabilizing, not least to existing elites and powerholders who have a vested interest in declaring democracy 'a foreign flower'. Not surprisingly, the process of democratization has historically been exceedingly slow, at least until the third wave.

Recognition of the symbiotic relationship between economic growth and democratization has been similarly slow in emerging. Nonetheless, economic health demands a balance of power that better favours previously subordinate classes. Such a situation was never achieved until the third wave. In many respects the Great Depression and the Second World War were wake-up calls. Only a strong civil society could generate the social harmony and confidence necessary to breed dynamism.

The decades that followed sent shock waves of unprecedented empowerment rippling through the industrialized world. They reached deep into societies to transform working and domestic lives, as well as family and social relationships. As democracy deepened, it also radically transformed gender and race relations. These latter transformations, although incomplete, demonstrated the possibilities inherent in democratization and indicated the dynamic character of the third wave, in particular its ability to generate among people new ways of thinking and new forms of action quite independent of the more hegemonic tendencies exhibited in American, Soviet and transnational globalisms.

These new synergies demand from us new globalizing perspectives, the subject of our concluding chapter. The dynamics of globalization have changed, but the dangers they now present are not dissimilar to those of the late eighteenth century or the early twentieth century. The third wave could falter; it could collapse. Three challenges stand out; first, the challenge of extending and deepening democratization globally and enhancing the centrality of civil society. The attempted privatization of the third wave has strengthened short-term profit-maximizing strategies and forms of monopoly control at the expense of investment in human capital and infrastructure. The resulting increase in inequalities, exacerbated by war and debt, has cost the third wave much of its former popular legitimacy. It has also increased the scope for corruption and for new policies of exclusion at a time when human expectations for empowerment have never been higher. Like the empires of old, the First World, the industrialized world, cannot survive as a world unto itself. Human interconnectivity makes that impossible.

Second, there exists the environmental challenge of addressing issues of sustainability globally. Just as democracy cannot survive in a sea of poverty, it cannot survive in an environmentally damaged and disease-ridden world. Transnational corporations are not always helpful in this regard. Their drive for short-term profit contributes to many environmental and health disasters. So too the quest by many states for big-power status or industrial might. Of course many problems are both cumulative and global, and can be addressed only by co-operatively developing global strategies that employ technology in environmentally sensitive ways. The machinery for developing and implementing such strategies barely exists.

The third challenge is the multicultural one that human diversity now globally presents to all societies that once defined themselves exclusively as homogeneous nations. In an age in which global strategies for security and well-being still include human migration, albeit on a scale that is both greater and more rapid than at any time in the past, national exclusions are unsustainable and generate instability.

All three challenges represent divides that have the potential to cripple the third wave and its human dynamic. In the short term, however, it is the refusal of many societies to accommodate diversity, one of the most important consequences of globalization, that may immediately prove most destabilizing. The creation of effective strategies to handle the reality of human diversity is one of humanity's most pressing challenges, as recent wars, ethnic cleansings, genocides and the restless tide of refugees and displaced persons demonstrate. But the first task is not an ideological one. Rather, steps need to be taken to relieve tensions by generating social equity.

Institutions already exist that can help to transform the third wave to meet these challenges. New ones can be created. War and depression should no longer be the only circuit-breakers. But for transformation to occur, we need to enhance our global consciousness in order to develop the necessary framework for future growth and change. Faith in a future technological revolution to resolve all our environmental, economic and social problems is not enough. Revolutions do not guarantee equality and harmony.

The key lies instead in continued democratization, and relentless individual and collective empowerment. Empowerment transforms class structures. It reduces barriers and broadens the scope for wealth generation. It encourages equity and the devolution of authority. It creates skills to manage complex societies, and makes possible diverse solutions and new ways of understanding ourselves. But empowerment also involves consciousness of our global history, and understanding that our very basic human drives require equally basic material solutions. Accordingly, our nascent global consciousness needs to be harnessed in material and institutional ways in order to manage the human condition more positively and to effect global solutions based on an inclusive rather than exclusive reading of human history. It is to that end that this book seeks to make a contribution.

. . . .

CHAPTER 2

Struggles for Survival and Well-being

§ THE one common factor in the history of globalization is people, and it is in the drives and strategies of people that we often seek explanations for the human condition. Humans have not always been aware of why they act in certain ways, let alone of the nature of the world they inhabit. Nonetheless, during the past ten thousand years, understanding our place in the scheme of things has been a dynamic process. This chapter examines some central features of that process – the nature of our universe, the origins of life, the evolution of human beings, and our own interpretations of the human condition.

To that list we must now add the changes that human societies have experienced in the last hundred thousand years, and more particularly during the past ten thousand years. Many scientists believe that some of these changes have their origins in our genetic make-up, while others see their origins in the human propensity to co-operate. But neither explanation accounts for the great diversity of human experience. Hence we need also to consider environmental circumstances, the availability of resources, the nature of technology, and pressures exerted by population densities. Human societies developed a mix of strategies to deal with these possible constraints on their survival and well-being, but increasingly they also came to be influenced by the extent to which they were connected with each other. Interconnections, as we shall see, provided a powerful dynamic long before it developed global proportions.

Rare Earth

When in the late twentieth century NASA finally pieced together all the images of Earth's solar neighbours received from its various unmanned flights, its scientists confirmed that no one planet or moon was alike. We live in an extremely diverse solar system, they concluded, which has also experienced extreme instability in the past. Our solar system might not differ in this regard from many other solar systems, but the Earth can at least take comfort from some of its own very special features.[1] It contains large amounts of metals conducive to life. It is well positioned to avoid the freezing temperatures of Mars and the scorching heat of Venus. It even possesses a guardian, the distant giant Jupiter, which draws to it comets that might otherwise spell the end of life as we know it on Earth. Even our relatively large moon serves a purpose beyond stimulating the daily ebb and flow of our tides. It keeps our axis stable. It stops the Earth wobbling chaotically and endangering life.

We enjoy stability of another rare kind also. Our very small planet moves around a very small sun situated on the spiral arm of a disc-shaped galaxy of some hundred billion suns that we call the Milky Way. Spiral arms are a product of size; they signify that the galaxy lacks the kind of gravity that in many other galaxies produces black holes at their centres. In the early history of the universe, these black holes became giant cosmic vacuum cleaners sucking in the mass of billions of stars and emitting intense radiation. They became violent quasars.

The recent search for planetary systems like ours paints a similar picture. Stars with planetary systems capable of sustaining life appear to be rare. Nine out of ten planetary systems that form from dust on the fringes of gas clouds find themselves overwhelmed by emerging stars that blow away the very particles that give the systems existence. Very few planets are sufficiently distant from stars to allow collected rock and dust to add to their bulk. So far only 5 per cent of all stars are estimated to have planetary systems, and of these only one has been found to have the potential for life.[2]

It is of course early days, and we need to remind ourselves that it is only four hundred years since Galileo Galilei first used a fairground toy to discover the moons of Jupiter and the rings of Saturn, and thereby revealed a universe that required fresh perspectives.[3] Ever since then, new technologies have expanded our knowledge and produced ways of thinking that often seem bizarre.

Humans have always been able to stare up at the one thousand or so stars visible at night through the Earth's atmosphere and glimpse things that were not of their own immediate world. They based cosmologies around what they believed they saw – the movement of stars, the cycles of the moon, and later the movement of the more constant sun. Humans in arid lands gave particular weight to the heavens as the source of life and salvation. As the influence of these people spread, so too did the idea of nature as passive and subject only to heavenly direction.[4] Structures of power utilized such beliefs to garner legitimacy, and fiercely resisted new ways of thinking that might challenge their authority.

Nonetheless, by the start of the seventeenth century, technological innovations did begin to transform the way some people viewed the wider universe. This was no revolutionary transformation because it impacted little on people's daily lives and left largely untouched people's perceptions of themselves and nature. Certainly we were now no longer at the centre of the universe but part of a solar system whose planets circled a sun, that was itself one of a vast number of suns in the universe. Yet even this new understanding could not conceive of a dynamic universe. The seventeenth-century scientist Isaac Newton interpreted the universe as a gigantic clockwork mechanism whose future could be rationally determined by its present state.

In the past century such comforting views have been swept aside. The Milky Way is no longer the universe. Instead we have learned that it is but one galaxy among a seemingly infinite number of galaxies that possess awesome chaotic phenomena, such as white dwarfs, which are so dense that even a spoonful of their matter would weigh tonnes, and x-ray stars ten billion times brighter than our sun. The Hubble telescope, launched into orbit around the Earth in 1990, has enabled us finally to remove the distortions created when viewing space through the Earth's atmosphere, thereby opening up hitherto unseen vistas. In 1996 the telescope focused on one dark spot in the sky where no stars could be seen. When images taken over ten days were finally assembled, they revealed some two thousand galaxies over ten billion light years away. Soon, with newer technologies, we will be able to see back to the beginning of time.

In 1929 the astronomer Edwin Hubble – after whom the orbiting telescope was named – measured the light that emanated from stars and conceived the idea that the universe was not static. In fact it was expanding. The stars were moving away from each other in much the same way as dots on a balloon move away from each other as it is filled with air. Here then was an infinite universe with infinite possibilities, not Newton's finite, static universe.

In 1944 the physicist George Gamow provided an explanation that was at once plausible and preposterous. The universe expanded because it resulted from a massively powerful single explosion some 13.5 billion years ago. Indeed, in the 1960s, scientists discovered exactly the kind of background cosmic microwave radiation that one might expect from such an explosion. In the 1990s, mathematicians such as Stephen Hawking and Neil Turok argued that the universe was originally a tiny pea-like point of energy suspended in a timeless void. Then, for reasons unknown, it inflated and exploded, forming a universe of atomic particles that rapidly cooled to form the matter of galaxies and stars. These galaxies and stars continue to hurtle through space away from their point of origin and will presumably, in hundreds of billions of years, end up as mere specks in an increasingly dark void. The transition from the infinitesimally small to the infinitely large still remains difficult for most of us to comprehend.[5]

The Big Bang theory has some serious problems which await explanation, in particular the contradictory evidence that the universe as a whole is younger than many of the stars in our own galaxy appear to be. There is also less matter visible in the universe than there should be, but new forms of matter have since been discovered that offer some explanation. Nonetheless, quantum theory expects that we suspend disbelief about things that we cannot see, indeed that we accept that what we can see may only be a small facet of physical reality, a multiverse made up of many universes.[6] These difficulties aside, the Big Bang theory has transformed our understanding of our place in the scheme of things. Certainly it has removed any sense we once assumed of our own centrality; it has left us at once belittled and special.

This unpretentious galaxy of ours, then, is but one of an estimated forty billion galaxies in one of possibly many universes that some scientists estimate to be five million light years wide. A light year represents the distance covered by light in one Earth year, approximately six trillion miles (9.46 trillion kilometres). That means that our universe might be nearly thirty million trillion miles (47 million trillion kilometres) wide, assuming that such earthly dimensions hold for a universe with as yet undiscovered dimensions.

The Chaos of Life

Developing global consciousness has always involved much more than coming to terms with the minuteness and isolation of the human realm. It has also involved accommodating the history of that realm itself, in particular its strange mixture of chance and evolution. Our universe began some 13.5 billion years ago when the hydrogen and helium created by the Big Bang gradually cooled and coalesced into stars. Around five billion years ago one exploding supernova began with great violence over the next one billion years to condense slowly into our solar system. By 3.5 billion years ago our earth had cooled sufficiently for single-celled microbes bearing DNA molecules to emerge and diversify. Life had begun, and for some two billion years it took the form of blue-green algae, which released low levels of oxygen into the atmosphere as a by-product (toxic to it) of photosynthesis. As oxygen levels increased, new oxygen-consuming plant forms emerged that simultaneously increased oxygen levels. Consequently the era of blue-green algae passed, plants invaded the land, and life diversified. Insects and reptiles emerged to dominate the planet.

The land itself also changed over the next 1.5 billion years. By 300 million years ago two large continental masses dominated the Earth's surface. As the Earth's atmosphere reached its current level of oxygen over the next hundred million years, new mammals evolved. The restless landmasses merged, then broke apart, reaching their current positions only about twenty million years ago.

In many respects the Earth became a symbiotic planet.[7] Its life thrived on symbiosis as niches emerged and expanded. But the unexpected also happened. A comet six kilometres wide slammed into the Earth 250 million years ago and wiped out 90 per cent of all marine species and 70 per cent of all land species. It created the necessary space for reptiles to gain the ascendancy.[8] A similar catastrophe occurred 65 million years ago, when another giant meteorite plummeted into the Gulf of Mexico, severely disrupting climatic patterns and creating vast volcanic disturbances. The maelstrom ended the reign of dinosaurs and allowed new players to dominate, among them birds and mammals. Sometimes disasters were regional in scale. Severe winter temperatures wiped out nearly 90 per cent of all sea creatures along the Gulf coast of North America 34 million years ago.[9]

Many writers argue that life has a natural tendency to evolve towards higher life forms and eventually intelligence.[10] So far our account suggests a more cautious assessment. Most global environments are hostile. Even where life exists, intelligence is rare. Our Earth alone has experienced some four billion species during the course of its existence, but only one has evolved the capacity for global intelligence.[11] In addition most environments, including our own, have been subjected to massive catastrophes. Inevitability assumes a different meaning under these circumstances.

Knowledge about our expanding, infinite and unpredictable universe has affected our thinking in a number of different ways, perhaps the most significant being the notion of chaos. In 1963 the physicist Edward Lorenz ran computer simulations of weather systems which most people then believed followed Newtonian principles of mechanical predictability and determination. What he found disturbed him. You could run the same simulation over and over again, but very small deviations at any stage in the simulation could produce dramatically different results, despite the fact that each simulation appeared to be identical. Thus was born the idea of chaos, and with it died determinism and predictability. Chaos explained changes observed not only within climatology but also biology, epidemiology, ecology and a host of social sciences like history and economics, which previously evaluated and measured past and present actions as if they conformed to deterministic equations.[12]

Chaos has also affected notions about ourselves. We are all familiar with cartoons depicting humans evolving along a single path from monkeys. This of course is a very deterministic portrayal of what actually happened. It suggests – as determinism naturally does – that we are now what we were meant to be. It rationalizes our superiority. It was our fate to be at the end of the chain, and, as we will see later in this book, many people have developed ideas which similarly suggest that they have become superior sub-species of *Homo sapiens*.

The truth is much more complicated, just like the truths concerning our place in the solar system and universe. In fact the origins of humans can best be illustrated by reference to a tree in which there are many different hominid branches and no one creature progressing by itself until extremely recently. Even fifty thousand years ago, *Homo sapiens* were not alone; their history – like that of all species – is the product of symbiosis and opportunity.

Evolving from Diversity to Diversity

More than seven million years ago, long after most dinosaurs had been reduced to fossils, the descendant of a chimpanzee common to the vast Afro-Eurasian continent began to evolve differently in the central African rainforest. We do not know why, but small, isolated communities can change significantly in response to environmental pressures. If self-selection was the cause, it suggests at the very least that a stronger sense of self-consciousness played a role in determining the fate of some animals.

Four million years later there existed a number of human-like species derived from this ancestor of today's chimpanzees, among them East African Australopithecines, who thrived in one of the few parts of the world not gripped by an ice age and which still enjoyed abundant rainfall. But resources were not plentiful and climates were changing. The Australopithecines had not only to compete among themselves for survival but also to adapt to environments beyond the shelter of their shrinking forests. They learned to walk upright and to forage over wider areas. They became meat-eaters, and their bodies (particularly their brains) adjusted accordingly to the increased intake of protein. Hunting required new skills and new forms of intelligence. One of their descendants, with brains still only half the size of our own, developed stone tools. For 800,000 years *Homo habilis* scavenged for an existence before being edged out by the much more intelligent and archetypal Palaeolithic hunter–gatherer, *Homo erectus*. These people were very much like us. They lived in small communities. They possessed a sense of ritual. They buried their dead. In all probability they communicated with each other through language.

Homo erectus's success produced a still more competitive environment. Warmer weather, together with new hunting technologies and an ability to manipulate the environment by use of fire, enabled these humans to make better use of the resources around them. Their numbers expanded. By two million years ago, population pressures had already forced them to move in search of sustenance. By one million years ago they had reached into Asia, by 500,000 years ago Europe, and 100,000 years ago the Indonesian archipelago.[13] One school of thought contends that *Homo erectus* evolved into modern humans, interbreeding with later waves of descendants from Africa, and – as

Java 'Man' – making it across the then smaller sea distances to Australia.[14] However, the evidence, such as it is, does not yet support the idea of sustained interbreeding.[15]

In much cooler Europe and Central Asia, the smaller and very scattered population of *Homo erectus* is known to us as Neanderthals, after the German valley in which their remains were first discovered in the mid-nineteenth century. Neanderthals had larger brains than humans today and were heavily muscled, powerful hominids, well adapted for the harsher conditions imposed by ice-age Europe. Herein lies a possible clue as to their eventual disappearance. Their physical size, and the protective sedentary lifestyle that the climate possibly also encouraged, may have made it more difficult for Neanderthals to survive competition from leaner *Homo sapiens*, descendants of *Homo erectus* who expanded out of Africa some 100,000 years ago for the same reasons as their distant ancestors. In addition, some 30,000 years ago – perhaps coinciding with the development of the warm Gulf Stream alongside Europe – temperatures rose rapidly, by as much as 15 degrees within the space of two decades. This was certainly to the advantage of *Homo sapiens*. Perhaps it disadvantaged the Neanderthal ice-age specialists.

The zoologist Matt Ridley reminds us that specialization as grassland animals most distinguished *Homo sapiens* from other human species. Not surprisingly, wheat and rice grasses are still our staple foods. We are, he says, ideally built for the sun-scorched savannah of Africa: the way we walk, our shade-maximizing posture, our sweat glands, bare skin, special blood vessels to cool the brain, and hands free to carry weapons and other objects.[16] But grasslands also enable large animals and all their very social predators, including hunting humans, to survive. *Homo sapiens* had to be great hunters. Their complex brains and the power of speech enabled them to be well organized and mobile. As they followed the seasonal movements of animals, they planned, specialized, innovated, shared and traded with each other. This strategic lifestyle gave *Homo sapiens* an advantage.[17]

The *Homo sapiens* expansion began around 200,000 years ago as a new ice age deepened. Sea levels fell, climates dried. Rainforests shrank and grasslands expanded, and with them vast populations of huge animals – mammoths, rhinoceroses, horses, bison, deer, lions, wolves, bears, elephants and sabre-toothed cats. As this new environment expanded, so the hunting *Homo sapiens* spread out.[18] They had no choice if they wished to survive and prosper. By 100,000 years ago they were poised to break out of Africa. As tribes expanded and split into new tribes and moved on, they gradually spread across much of the globe. Coastal routes were probably the most accessible;[19] nonetheless, they still took some 50,000 years to reach Australia. As the ice age eventually retreated, they advanced further north – into Europe 30,000 years ago, Siberia 20,000 years ago, and, for the first time for any human, North and South

America 11,000 years ago. For many of those years of very gradual expansion in Eurasia they lived alongside other hominids.

The biologist Jared Diamond believes that the smaller size of *Homo sapiens* and their better use of tools for hunting enabled them to expend as much energy as other hominids but without requiring as much food. Hence their populations grew faster. But technology also enhanced communications and social skills for survival. This did not necessarily mean warfare or genocide, despite the appalling human record in both since. Warfare was not always a wise strategy. It carried too many risks of death and injury for small hunter–gatherer communities. Rather, the simple monopolization of resources could drive out rivals.[20]

In Europe, Neanderthals were squeezed out within a thousand years, although they lingered for a time in Spain and south-east Europe. Some scientists now believe that Neanderthals may have coexisted with *Homo sapiens* for 10–15,000 years, perhaps even longer in West Asia.[21] Nonetheless, by the time *Homo sapiens* reached Siberia, they were the sole surviving descendants of those East African apes who had pioneered the human trajectory some five million years ago. Small differences, sparked by competition for survival, had produced a very different beast.

Alone, *Homo sapiens* spread out around the world, living in small tribes and family groups, and delicately balancing the need to trade with one another with xenophobic hostility to outsiders.[22] By the time they completed their occupation of South America, their numbers had probably quadrupled to four million since their departure from Africa. Humans were globalizing themselves, but at the same time something quite different was also occurring. They were fragmenting. As they separated from each other, they confronted different environments and different pressures. Their appearances altered. Their cultures and languages changed.

Today science enables us to understand something of the initial fragmentation process that transformed *Homo sapiens* in the last 100,000 years, after they left Africa. Some forty years ago scientists discovered the structure of DNA[23] and transformed our understanding of inheritance and the role of genes (sections of DNA code) in determining the physical attributes of people. Through DNA testing we now know that Europeans are more closely related to one another, and Asians to other Asians, Amerindians to other Amerindians, and so on, than Africans are to each other. This is as we might expect. The further we move from the source of humans, the smaller the gene pool, and hence the smaller the variation in genetic make-up. A recent study of Pacific Islanders confirms this pattern. As the ancestors of Polynesians moved further and further away from the starting point of their migration – Taiwan – their gene pool, and hence the differences between them, became smaller and smaller.[24]

Similar tests make the same point about our earlier ancestors. Some twenty billion years ago we separated from the ancestors of monkeys (with whom we share 93 per cent of our genes). Nine billion years ago we separated from the ancestors of gorillas (with whom we share 97.7 per cent of our genes). Seven million years ago we separated from the ancestors of chimpanzees (with whom we share 98.4 per cent of our genes). But the difference among humans is much smaller – no more than 0.1 per cent, largely affecting superficial features.

Diamond reminds us that it used to be stressed that these differences between people – their skin colour, eyes, hair, body shape and facial hair – were due to natural selection. In other words, these differences evolved as humans adapted to their environments. The people of the Andes developed large chests the better to extract oxygen from very thin air. Inuits developed compact shapes to preserve heat, the Sudanese slender bodies to lose heat, North Asians slit eyes to protect against the cold and sun glare. Skin colour also enables people to receive doses of vitamin D appropriate to their climate. Without fair skins, people in temperate zones might suffer from rickets; without dark skins, people in the tropics might absorb too much vitamin D and suffer kidney disease.[25]

But these theories do not entirely explain some important inconsistencies. Not all hot places are sunny, and of course people move and intermingle. For example, aboriginal Tasmanians had dark skins but lived in a temperate zone. Aboriginal Americans and south-east Asians live in tropical regions but have lighter skins. People who live in the world's most dimly lit places (with less than 3.5 hours of sun per day) – such as Scandinavia, south China, and West Africa – have quite varied skin colours. The nineteenth-century naturalist Charles Darwin always argued that natural selection could not really explain what people often called 'racial' distinctions; instead he believed sexual preference to be the most likely explanation. In other words people self-select by tending to be attracted to people like themselves.[26] There are scientists who now claim that this is how social ideas about beauty began.

Interpreting the Human Condition

To what extent has our past shaped human history? We should remember the scale of that past. We evolved from chimps over seven million years ago. Only in the last 500,000 years have we been identifiable as *Homo sapiens*. 'For most of our history', Diamond notes, 'we were not mighty hunters, but skilled chimps, using stone tools to acquire and prepare plant food and small animals'.[27] We have no consciousness of this enormous period in which we evolved as people, but does that mean it was without effect on our behaviour as social animals?

This is of course a highly contentious issue. Are we simply machines whose basic drives are genetically determined? To what extent do we control our destiny? Does that long past about which we know so little really tell us anything about ourselves? And if it does, is such knowledge in any way useful for understanding our more recent past and present, of which we know so much more, but which we still find hard to place in perspective?

The genius of humans came from a highly developed sense of consciousness, initially triggered perhaps by sensations that indicated dangers or threats to survival. Such consciousness 'confers spectacular survival advantages', according to one interpretation. 'The ability to make the present congruent with the past and to imagine future scenarios carries vast dividends'. Strategies that can be tested in the mind reduce the risk of injury or death.[28]

In fact the brain is the natural technology that makes this possible. It constantly cycles information from its right hemisphere to its left, transforming novelty into routine.[29] One by-product of that action was that humans learned to scrutinize the process of thinking itself. Intelligence, says neurologist Antonio Damasio, is the ability to manipulate knowledge so successfully that novel responses can be planned and delivered. But such intelligence has a downside. Judgements can also be self-directed. And consciousness is ephemeral: 'You are the music as long as the music lasts'.[30]

Much of the drama of the human condition, says Damasio, comes from knowing this. And it is all the more dramatic because subconsciously we do not want to believe that we are governed by desires no more complicated than that of survival, or that in the end we are simply fated to die. We put on masks and veils. We deny what sounds too cold and clinical and argue instead for passion. We use emotion to hide from the realities of life and its unpleasantness. We turn envy into desire for justice. We use religion to shelter from death. We falsify history to remove inconvenient truths, or we simply forget.[31] We employ the well-being of a larger group to disguise our own desires for fame and fortune.[32] We laugh at people who tell us that really we are no more than programmed machines, or who themselves behave without regard to our well-contrived pretences. Indeed we believe our masks to be evidence of our humanity.[33]

We employ other strategies to deny our materialism as well. Political scientist Graeme Donald Snooks cites our insistence on giving primacy to ideas as the motor of change or progress in human society. As societies have grown larger, the activities people undertake have become more specialized, and knowledge generation – in a variety of forms – has become increasingly important. Like all specialists, knowledge generators have a vested interest in arguing that their professions are central to human survival and well-being.[34] To that end, they have transformed the history of the world into a history of ideas, a history that gives primacy not only to intellectuals but also to the cultural heritage of leading societies. Civilizations have become their focus, flowering first with the Classical Greeks, gaining a wider audience under the Romans, being lost when barbarians overthrew the Roman Empire, but recovering to flower again as the Rise of the West. Whole periods have been so routinely described in this manner that we embrace these descriptions without even appreciating how they have distorted our understanding of history. They have become the stepping stones of linear progress: the Classical Age, the Dark Ages, the Renaissance, the Enlightenment, Modernity.

But for Snooks the elevation of ideas is simply another way by which we deny our genetically determined desires.[35] Since the seventeenth century, when the philosopher René Descartes drew a line between our minds and our bodies, many philosophers have argued that our minds have a reality of their own. What creates this illusion of mind–brain difference is our ability to scrutinize our own processes of thinking.[36] Its consequence is to distance us further from reality. Reason shields us from the unpleasantness that is part and parcel of its manufacture. We divorce reason from money and power, or from any other manifestations of self-interest. Yet any form of knowledge generation, such as science, is a human activity that suffers from the same passions and desires as other human activities.[37]

If we believe in the centrality of ideas – in other words, of intelligence – then clearly we believe also in inequalities among humans. We may base those inequalities on the superficial appearances that have differentiated *Homo sapiens* ever since their dispersal from the savannahs of East Africa. We may argue that those differences are short-cuts to identifying communities with different intellectual configurations. Or we may simply use the success of contemporary communities in achieving wealth and power as the basis for determining the capabilities of their people. Both interpretations hold that intelligence is inherited, a belief which sustains the modern fetish for IQ tests,[38] but whose corollary is that human history is driven by genetic fitness.

But if ideas do not drive human activity, if intelligence is not the motor of development, then it stands to reason that all communities potentially have the same ability to create, to learn, and to prosper. But of course they do these things in different ways. What makes for difference is not intelligence but the ability of members of different communities to utilize resources. Sometimes, as Jared Diamond highlights, difference results from the uneven distribution of resources around the world. Communities are not equal in their ability to access resources.[39] On other occasions, as Snooks argues, communities might lack the competitive incentive to move in certain directions, or else possess alternatives that meet their basic drives.[40] But with greater interaction among human communities, a further cause for difference also becomes important.

In the 1990s, scientists under the direction of Michael Marmot completed a study of some ten thousand British civil servants. They found a dramatic fourfold difference in disease rates between those at the top of the civil service and those at the bottom. Even people one step down from the top had rates twice as high as those above them. The reason, says former Berkeley epidemiologist Len Syme, is simply control of destiny. 'The lower down you are in social class standing, the less opportunity and training you have to influence the events that impinge on your life'.[41] Stratification meant that, within societies, people were increasingly denied opportunities to perform simply because of the class or caste they belonged to. With increased world interconnectiveness, whole societies similarly lost the ability to control their own destinies and became imprisoned in the futures of other communities. It became an important determinant of difference that we shall consider much later in this book.

Ideas, then, are not the central determinant of human destiny. They may help to facilitate change, as Snooks concedes, but usually long after change has begun. In fact, knowledge is exceedingly slow to develop. Training people takes decades. We are not clones; each generation has to relearn what other generations already know, and that may consume 60 per cent of the average lifespan. This is not to say that the way we organize ourselves to learn is unimportant. But innovation itself is dependent upon much more than intelligence. Products of knowledge do not generate their own demand.

Nor do societies use knowledge as the basis for order. They impose laws for that purpose.[42] Nor do they necessarily use knowledge as the basis for decision-making. Economists may tell us that we do, that decisions are rationally determined on the basis of all available knowledge, but in most instances – from the buying of clothes to buying shares, from national investments in information technology to the creation of specialized manufacturing sectors, from the privatization of state functions to colonization – most decisions are largely imitative and self-interested. We follow fashion. We copy behaviour that has demonstrated success. We are driven by desire and want, not reason. We are consumed by energy, passion and imagination, not information.[43] People, says Snooks, have no model of the world in their heads except very fundamental ones such as conspiracy theories that target certain minorities, religious models that offer divine justification, or self-serving explanations such as altruism.[44] Today, in the world's most advanced industrial society, 44 per cent of citizens still believe in creationism.

Our penchant for mimicry has not stopped humans from theorizing about the human condition. The philosopher Plato was not alone in believing that life must have been better at some time in the distant past. The occupants of environmentally challenged lands often dreamed of past golden ages and gardens of Eden that preceded the fall of humankind. Such beliefs formed the basis for faith in human or tribal salvation after a day of judgement.[45]

But not all humans viewed themselves so pessimistically. Aristotle thought humans were progressing towards a more perfect state, not away from it. Life, after all, did have a purpose. In our more contemporary era, these contradictory perspectives have continued to manifest themselves.[46]

The seventeenth-century philosopher Thomas Hobbes argued that the basic human condition was nasty, brutish and competitive. Only strong authoritarian government could enable society to progress. In 1776 the philosopher Adam Smith similarly described human society as dominated by the self-interest of individuals. But instead of demanding a strong ruler or unforgiving laws, Smith argued for governance by the invisible hand of the market. Since only the best survived competition, competition enriched society.

Smith's novel assumption had its doubters. Some years later the writer Thomas Malthus asked why only the best would survive? Might not the least successful also survive? Could we not imagine a situation in which the rapidly growing populations of less competitive peoples swamped society, and famine and poverty became widespread. All would suffer as a consequence.

Despite Malthus's gloom, Smith's notion of self-interest caught the public's imagination, and it was not long before new applications were found for the theory. Indeed in 1859 Charles Darwin's *The Origin of Species* described nature in much the same way – hierarchical, self-interested, and dominated by competitive struggles for survival. In turn, Darwin's natural selection and Adam Smith's self-interest were joined together and popularized as Social Darwinism in the late nineteenth century by the philosopher Herbert Spencer. Self-interest led to the struggle for survival, and the survival of the fittest represented a social meritocracy. The rich were rich because they were the best, the most fit of their societies. They were an elite, the best of the best, the future of the human race. In an age of industrial and imperial expansions, such ideas lent moral comfort and ideological support to new elites. They demonstrated a way by which humans might rationally or scientifically transform their societies.

Thus was born the science of eugenics. A successful society required that the best dominated, that only the fittest should breed. The less fit should put social good ahead of self-interest by not breeding. Only by this means could the human stock be improved. In Sweden the less fit were sterilized – even into the 1970s. In Australia the more genetically fit were forcibly separated from parents considered less genetically fit, again until the 1970s. They became the 'stolen generations'. In Germany, Hitler's genocidal tribalism in the 1930s and 1940s went much further, but the principles were the same. On this occasion ethnic cleansing came via gas chambers.

The drive for a future perfect did not always neglect a past lost. In the middle of the eighteenth century, French philosopher Jean-Jacques Rousseau fervently believed that modernity corrupted humanity. When European explorers chanced upon the island of Tahiti in the Pacific in 1768, they thought they had found Rousseau's paradise of noble savages. But it was an idea that could not long survive power politics; within decades missionaries were girding their loins and sailing forth to convert and civilize savages now considered bereft of nobility.

Nonetheless something of Rousseau's vision of modernity resurfaced in the early twentieth century, when anthropologists argued that culture, not genes, determined social fitness. The idea was not new, but in an age of renewed ethnic cleansing it won many converts across a surprisingly diverse range of fields. Humans, the psychologist B.F. Skinner told us in the 1960s, were born with a blank slate – a *tabula rasa*. They learned solely through association with people and with their environment.

Of course there was an unfortunate corollary to this, just as unfortunate as that which arose from Smith's self-interest: if people learned through association, they might be perfected – not by means of genetic manipulation or by weeding out the unfit, but culturally through education, propaganda and force. When revolutionaries seized power in Russia and China in the twentieth century, they reinterpreted modernity and declared themselves its future. Communist societies, they claimed, demanded a new consciousness – a 'new man', to use the shorthand of the times – a new, postmodern communist human nature. Unfortunately, refashioning society by cultural dogma produced its own horrors, among them Stalin's gulags and Mao's appropriately named Cultural Revolution.

In the late twentieth century the noble savage has enjoyed a second coming, this time promoted as much by modernist alienation and discontent as by postcolonialism's angst. And it has returned as ecological wisdom. 'Modern society', says one environmentalist, Jonathon Porritt, 'will find no solution to the ecological problem unless it takes a serious look at its lifestyle'.[47] Human nature must change. And, like Rousseau before us, we believe that our condition is a modern condition, that in the past things were different. 'We [even] treat aboriginal peoples with ... condescending sentimentality', says Matt Ridley. We claim that they are at one with nature – noble savages. They possess the virtues we lost in our rush to modernize, the wisdom we failed to recognize during our rush to colonize. We even bowdlerize nature. We cleanse it of what we do not want to see. We recognize dolphins as animals of virtue, but rarely as ferocious sea killers who hunt down porpoises. 'We eliminate the negative and sentimentalize the positive', Ridley asserts.[48] We do the same to our past. We do not wish to face what we are.

Eleven thousand years ago *Homo sapiens* crossed the Bering Strait and entered North America. Within one thousand years they had reached Patagonia in the south and their numbers had expanded to around ten million. Within that time also the Americas lost 75 per cent of their animals: giant bison, wild horses, short-faced bears, lions, mammoths, mastodons (elephants), sabre-toothed cats, giant sloths and armadillos, wild camels, ant-eaters the size of horses, rodents the size of bears.[49] Most of these animals had never seen humans before and were relatively tame – easy pickings for tribes on the move and rapidly expanding in number.[50] But the slaughter restricted the future resource base of these people, as we shall see later.

The Americas were not an isolated instance. When Austronesians colonized Madagascar fifteen hundred years ago, seventeen species of lemur (a relative of monkeys), bats, mongooses, two species of giant land tortoises, a pigmy hippopotamus, and something called an elephant bird disappeared. When, as Maoris, they colonized New Zealand some seven hundred years ago, they ate their way through twelve species of giant moa birds. At one site in Otago alone, 30,000 moas were killed for a feast.[51] Of course the rampage could not last. Moas did not breed fast enough. Nor did half the country's land birds; 16 species became extinct, including ducks, geese, pelicans, swans, and eagles.

In Hawaii, seventeen hundred years ago, the same thing happened. Within a few years half the islands' bird population had gone – some fifty species, including some flightless ones and some with no close relatives. Slaughter or the destruction of habitat by fire, grazing or the introduction of dogs and pigs: the result was always the same. In Australia also, at the time humans arrived over fifty thousand years ago, a whole swathe of animals disappeared – marsupial rhinos and lions, giant wombats, giant kangaroos, and moa-type birds.[52]

As we noted earlier, when humans first left Africa one hundred thousand years ago and followed the grasses into Eurasia, they discovered many edible animals. The sheer size of Eurasia and the relatively small numbers of humans reduced the impact of their arrival compared with our earlier examples. Nonetheless, within twenty thousand years mammoths and woolly rhinos were also extinct. In the eastern Mediterranean pigmy hippos, giant tortoises, dwarf elephants and dwarf deer met the same fate.

Human societies, Diamond tells us, have always undermined their own subsistence by exterminating species and damaging environments.[53] Says Ridley, 'there is no instinctive environmental ethic in our species – no innate tendency to develop and teach restrained practice. Environmental ethics … do not come naturally',[54] whether in the past or today. Sir Peter Scott, founder of the World Wildlife Fund, once argued: 'We've spent millions and millions of pounds trying to save endangered species and wild animals and I've come to the conclusion that if we'd put all that money into condoms, we'd have ended up saving more wildlife'.[55]

What Drives Humans?

In the distant past, the slow rate of genetic change dictated the pace of human development. But during the last hundred thousand years human development has surpassed the achievements of the previous million years; in other words human development has been faster than anything that genetic change can explain. Cultural evolution, says science writer Robert Wright, has replaced natural selection.[56] This explanation does not satisfy sociobiologists such as Richard Dawkins. People's vanities have always exceeded reality, he claims. Once they thought they existed at the centre of the universe; then it turned out that the world is but 'a little speck of cosmic dust on the edge of some galaxy'. Darwin told us that we were close cousins of apes;[57] now evolutionary psychologists assert that we are no more than cave people cast adrift in a modern environment, with all the desires of our ancestors intact.[58]

What drives those desires? In the 1970s Dawkins argued that we are the product of selfish genes. Humans 'are survival machines – robot vehicles blindly programmed to preserve the selfish molecules known as genes'.[59] Not surprisingly, some writers have gone one step further and declared that humans are consumed by the drive for reproduction. Even rape has been proposed as a male reproductive strategy.[60] Less provocatively, Roger Short and Malcolm Potts argue that

> The great cuisines of the world, for example, were built on our need to eat in order to replenish the cells which carry our DNA, which will reproduce itself in our offspring. ... Fashion in clothing is based on attracting a mate; men dress to show off their material success, proof of their ability to provide a secure home for a woman's child; women dress to show their youth and beauty, proof they are good breeding stock for a man's genes.[61]

This was always the way, according to some archaeologists. One study of artefacts in Central Europe claims that 27,000 years ago women wore low-slung frocks, fine string skirts, and wrapped fabric around their chests.[62]

There are scientists who regard this kind of reductionism as dangerously misleading. Biologist Steven Rose believes that it creates a kind of 'Flintstone' view of the past, which causes us to lose faith in our ability to transform our societies and ourselves, to be social engineers.[63] Similarly, Snooks suggests that genes determine only our basic drives and our capacity to respond to stimuli. Like environmental factors, they influence our tastes, our personalities, and the way we learn. But in themselves they do not explain why we are different from other animals, who are also influenced by similar genetic drives. To give primacy to genetics is to deny social dynamism, to deny the capacity of humans to control and redirect their desires, and to use their skills to extend their physical and intellectual capabilities. Genetic primacy makes human society static.[64] Not surprisingly, more sophisticated sociobiological views have emerged. These tend either to stress the importance of cooperation or to focus on a variant of the selfish gene concept – the meme.

Human beings are individuals but they tend to congregate in groups.

Undoubtedly this allows the selfish gene to survive and to reproduce. But it also produces co-operation of two different kinds – with individuals genetically related, and with individuals who are not. The first kind of co-operation involves kin selection, and is often held to be the more important. Snooks is contemptuous of such thinking. We tend to invest time and effort in individuals to whom we are genetically related simply because they are our first associations. For Snooks, it is economic distance, not genetic association, that matters. When economic distance with non-family members decreases, co-operation outside the family increases.[65] These matters are not genetically fixed, but are the function of social and economic change.

The second form of co-operation is called reciprocal altruism. We co-operate with non-family members because we expect something in return. It may be a form of insurance on our part, but altruism is also – according to Wright – a survival strategy employed by the selfish gene. In many forms of competition, only one person or one group benefits. This is known as a zero–sum result. But if both sides win or benefit, the result is non-zero–sumness. Life, says Wright, is simply a series of non-zero–sum games.[66] Non-zero–sum games drive human history. As life evolves it becomes more complex. The number of people with whom you have to co-operate increases. Consequently, non-zero–sumness – co-operation for mutual benefit – is logical.[67]

Matt Ridley believes that humans have been built to be trustworthy and co-operative. Humans, he says, have social instincts.

> They have come into the world equipped with predispositions to learn how to co-operate, to discriminate the trustworthy from the treacherous, to commit themselves to be trustworthy, to earn good reputations, to exchange goods and information, and to divide labour. ... We owe our success as a species to our social instincts; they have enabled us to reap undreamt benefits from the division of labour for our masters – the genes. They are responsible for the rapid expansion of our brains in the past 2 million years and hence for our inventiveness. Our societies and our minds evolved together, each reinforcing trends in the other.[68]

To counter self-interest we impose taboos on greed and selfishness, and stress co-operation for the greater good. We divide our work in such a way that we have no choice but to depend upon each other for survival. We specialize like no other animal, says Ridley. The larger societies are, the greater the possibilities of specialization. And the greater the possibilities of specialization, the greater the number of people able to specialize at the level of society, rather than just at the individual level.[69]

Changes in the division of labour – particularly their results – attracted the attention of Adam Smith in his *Wealth of Nations*. He believed that the division of labour was one way in which society became greater than the sum of its parts. A specialist craft pin-maker, Smith argued, could hope to make only twenty pins a day. But if he divided the task into a number of simple repetitive tasks, each performed by a separate person, then the number of pins his factory could produce would increase. In fact, ten people in a pin factory could produce 48,000 pins a day. Twenty pins would cost only 1/240th of a person's day compared with a whole day previously. This understanding, he believed, produced the Industrial Revolution in the late eighteenth century.

Specialization has always been a feature of human society. In 1991 a 5,300-year-old corpse of a Neolithic hunter was found frozen in the Italian Alps. With him was found a woven grass cloak, a stone dagger with a wooden handle, a copper axe, a bow, quiver and arrows, tinder for lighting fires, and two wooden containers, one of which once held the hot embers from his last fire. In addition, he carried other tools and a medicine kit containing, among other things, antibiotic fungus. 'People lived their lives steeped in technology', says Ridley.[70] Even a hundred thousand years ago, people specialized. Hunting required co-operation, and its consequence – meat – was always shared. But if individuals chose not to share, society had ways to enforce the value of co-operation – ostracism being one mechanism.[71]

Of course, one of the earliest forms of specialization was that between men and women. Such co-operation undoubtedly assumed many forms, but one possibly common form resulted in men scavenging or hunting rare but protein-rich meat while women gathered plentiful but protein-poor fruit. It is unlikely that this sharing had anything to do with patriarchy, at least to begin with. Humans needed to survive. Women gathered plants and fruits while they tended to their children close by. Men supplemented community diets by hunting. Hunting was dangerous, dependent upon chance, and not necessarily successful. The Neolithic hunter in the Italian Alps met his fate with an arrow through his left shoulder. Hunters and gatherers needed each other. Such co-operative specialization was a form of insurance.[72]

Women developed other forms of insurance also. Natalie Angier argues that women's emotional and material need for each other is a vestigial legacy of the importance of women's ancient support for one another and each other's children, particularly that given by post-menopausal women.[73]

These newer interpretations suggest that we co-operate instinctively. We share. We give gifts to create an obligation to reciprocate. We hope that good behaviour will elicit trust and motivate virtue for mutual benefit. Co-operation requires social skills, not brute strength; it adds a new dimension of intelligence to human society.[74]

This new dimension has enabled a new version of the selfish gene to prosper, this time in the guise of memes. Memes are really just ideas, but according to Susan Blackmore they are what really distinguishes humans from animals. Only humans have two replicators – genes and memes. The great leap for humans came when they learned to imitate each other. With the human brain a form of computer, information could be selected and copied or varied. It could be taught and passed on to future generations. In fact Blackmore describes our brains as meme machines, mere copying devices. 'I am nothing but a society of memes', Dawkins echoes.[75]

Memes exist because of human intelligence. But human creativity, Blackmore warns, is a kind of selection process that takes place in a very competitive environment. Some people are better at using memes or putting them together than others.[76]

But is this telling us anything new – that we are driven by ideas and that our capacity to use ideas is driven by intelligence? Since memes are only one of two replicators influencing human behaviour, might it not also be suggested that intelligence is affected by genetic factors? In the memes debate we may have come full circle. Certainly we are still left not knowing what drives society. Ideas are only a means to an end; they are organizational tools useful for shaping consciousness, but they do not drive it.[77]

Struggles for Survival and Well-being: the Historical Consequences

Human social life remains defined by an unceasing struggle for survival and well-being. This is the principal causal force in human life, according to sociologist Stephen Sanderson. Certain behavioural characteristics have evolved to assist humans in this common struggle, for example heterosexual preference designed to ensure the reproduction of life. The same drive also produced competition between men for women and intimate carers, and similarly between women for men and resource providers. In addition it promoted the family as a mechanism to enhance reproductive success. Both parents needed to co-operate if they wanted their children to survive.[78]

Involved in this competition for resources and to pass advantage to future generations is the desire for comfort and prestige. Sometimes people seek rank for its own sake, or success for the pleasure of success. Usually, we have no conscious recognition that we are driven by such motives.[79] Nonetheless, some of us are better endowed to compete than others – bigger, more intelligent, aggressive, ambitious, deceitful. Some of us co-operate better in order to achieve the same goals. There is no equality at the individual level in this struggle.

Certainly in the distant past, as humans evolved from their animal ancestors, male physique was an important indicator of a person's ability to survive and raise a family. Indicators were important, and here may well lie the origin of the male fetish about his penis. Over thousands of years, natural selection resulted in men developing the physical characteristics needed to be hunters, competitors for women, and perhaps also community leaders. Women developed differently; hence their longer lifespan, hence the female menopause to guarantee that longer lifespan. Childbirth was dangerous, both for the mother and for the future of her existing offspring.[80]

But at some point, also in the distant past, intelligence and personality came to be just as important as physique. We might speculate that the development of language transformed communication between individuals, and bestowed new value to social and emotional skills unassociated with brute strength. But sex remained of course, a kind of social cement, the inducement for both sexes to co-operate.[81]

Since human fertility rates are so low, sex is unlikely ever to have been tied solely to conception. Hence sexual jealousy or accusations of infidelity that often lie behind conflicts between individuals or families, and even wider groups. Some writers suggest that in the dual purpose of sex lay the origins of marriage. Men subjugated women to ensure their paternity; but issues of control also played their part. Of course we know of many other actions that subsequently reinforced subjugation: laws defining adultery on the basis of female activities only, female confinement, chaperoning, foot binding, and female circumcision.[82]

The development of patriarchy suggests that something other than simply natural selection was at play here. Humans are social animals, and although many human activities have animal precursors and may originally have helped survival and gene transmission, they eventually acquired uniqueness and served different purposes. Take the arts as an example. Some sociobiologists believe that art evolved as a signal of status in the struggle to pass on our genes. Dance and music were preludes to sex. But even if this interpretation is correct, they certainly had other functions as well. They helped to define groups and their cultures, to build camaraderie, group spirit, and to feed our xenophobia, our fear of strangers. Nothing distinctively human here, of course, but music, dance, and art assisted social survival in other ways also. They passed on knowledge and skills to future generations. In addition they channelled energy into useful, non-destructive activities that also became economically valuable. And they provided pleasure. In these ways, human culture constantly transformed itself and acquired new goals. It also specifically enabled us, to quote Diamond again, 'to pursue ethical goals which can conflict with the goals and methods of the sexual content. Having that choice … represents one of our most radical departures from other animals'.[83]

We have basic drives, which are genetically determined, and they affect our behaviour. But we have evolved also the intelligence to control those drives and to transform their consequences. This is in part the result of co-operation, as Ridley claims; of the rise of non-zero–sumness, in Wright's parlance. However, co-operation as an important feature of the human condition does not explain why human societies have changed in the way they have or how they have changed.

Sanderson's answer is to link basic human drives with access to resources. Rising populations increase pressure on available resources and make land relatively scarce:

> [I]ncreased land scarcity leads to increased competition and struggle for the control of land, and ... at some point land begins to be controlled in an unequal fashion. Differential access to resources has emerged. Some people can now compel others to begin producing economic surpluses and to relinquish them. Technological advance is also part of this process, being dictated to a large extent by population pressure. All of these variables move together as a package. Technological advance allows increased economic productivity, and thus bigger and bigger surpluses can be extracted from the primary producers. Underlying the whole chain is the insatiability of human wants. As people get more, they want more, and so stratification feeds on itself over time and becomes both self-perpetuating and self-enhancing. As the lid gets lifted, the possibilities become greater and greater. People can never have enough wealth or enough status.[84]

The relationship between population, resources, technology and human drives is much more complex than this statement suggests. Indeed many societies develop mechanisms to temper the destabilizing impact of insatiable human wants.

In hunter–gatherer societies sharing was and is an insurance policy. They made a fetish of giving. It became central to their way of life. Status became dependent on how well one gave things away, not on hoarding. This distributive mechanism minimized economic inequalities (but not necessarily social ones) and reduced the human impact on limited resources. Today, in many recently transformed hunter–gatherer societies or more sedentary horticultural societies, remnants of these distributive mechanisms linger to contrast sharply with what is mistakenly regarded as Western individualism.[85] But even so-called Western societies employ mechanisms to reduce the impact of economic inequalities. They are certainly different in form from those employed by small hunter–gatherer societies, but their intent is much the same. Indeed, as we shall see in Part Four of this book, they have come to assume a central place in popular reactions to globalization.

The trajectories of human societies assume a chaotic pattern. We know that all humans possess the same basic drives, and that genes alone do not dictate human responses. We know also, as Sanderson suggests, that the resources societies enjoy and the pressures they confront influence human responses.[86] Neither resources nor pressures have ever been the same over time or place. Even where conditions seem similar, small differences in response can have vastly different results. There are also occasions when unexpected catastrophe simply overwhelms societies.[87]

For social scientists these parameters are frustratingly vague when accounting for change. Hence the social scientists' explanations range from Sanderson's package of variables focusing on resource scarcity and population growth to those of historians who follow the rise and fall of civilizations as steps to higher orders. Sometimes each step is regarded as having its own logic ('the past is a foreign country') and is superseded only because of changes to institutions or because growth in knowledge motivates change.[88] Often the end result of such analyses is the rise of Western Civilization as the motor for global change. Sometimes a sense of inevitability is assumed. Sociobiologists are certainly not alone in claiming that social evolution is natural, and that human society was somehow destined to evolve in the way that it has.

Some contemporary analysts avoid these tendencies by simply dividing the world into two eras: a comparatively static traditional era and a dynamic modern one. But again the pathway from one to the other often comes in the form of stages, each of which is prescribed, as is the ideal end result. Stages, like the stepping stones of civilizations, describe states of equilibrium rather than dynamic disequilibrium. In these analyses it is capitalism which is said to drive change: private capital accumulation most corresponds with the human desire for wealth and status.

Snooks does not deal in stages, although his analysis bears some similarities. He argues that human society has experienced three major technological paradigm shifts.[89] The first involved the Palaeolithic development of hunting technology some two million years ago by *Homo erectus*, and subsequently pursued more competitively by *Homo sapiens*. Hunting technology transformed human existence in a way that would not be repeated until 10,000–13,000 years ago, when a Neolithic agricultural revolution began. Since that time, humans have experienced only one further paradigm shift: the Industrial Revolution, which ushered in a new age of industrial technology in the late eighteenth century.

Paradigms describe the parameters within which people operate, the limits that the technologies associated with each paradigm prescribe. Like stages, paradigms possess their own logical coherence. Consequently, population sizes, nutritional standards, the nature of services consumed, leisure, and even religions are shaped by the paradigms they belong to.[90] This does not mean that societies are static or that changes to technology, living standards, religion, nutritional standards, or population are impossible. However, it does mean that there are limits beyond which they cannot go, although Snooks does suggest that humans may be able to overcome the constraints of their present industrial paradigm.[91] It is a point we shall pick up much later in the book.

To a certain extent, all societies pursue strategies designed to overcome existing paradigm constraints. Snooks lists four major strategies: family multi-plication, conquest, commerce, and technology. During Palaeolithic hunter–gatherer times, family multiplication strategies dominated. This did not prevent trade occurring across large distances and between many communities. Un-doubtedly conquest also occurred, but given the low standards of living common to most communities and the dangers that war presented for small group survival, conquest probably never assumed the importance it did once wealthy centres emerged as sources for plunder.[92] In addition, the tremendously skilled Palaeolithic hunters became increasingly adept at creating tools to help them hunt. On the eve of the Neolithic Agricultural Revolution, they had added bows and arrows, fishhooks, nets, and various forms of traps to their inventory of technology.

But technology did not exist as the basis for an alternative strategy to family multiplication. Wherever lands provided good sustenance to *Homo erectus* and *Homo sapiens* families, their numbers grew. But if populations grew too large, if environments were degraded, or if competitive neighbours restricted access to the limited resources that their hunting technology permitted them, sections of the community moved on. Migration did not necessarily involve the huge distances that many Austronesians later crossed; often migrants simply moved into neighbouring regions. Nonetheless the effect was the same. Over long periods of time, humans populated the world.

The family multiplication strategy was not confined to Palaeolithic times. It finds echoes in the vast migration of peoples during the past three thousand years within the Afro-Eurasian continent, and across the Atlantic and Pacific Oceans. But in most instances, unless societies were relatively isolated and faced little competition, it never again assumed strategic dominance.

Nonetheless, for hunter–gatherer societies, the strategy enabled a good life with substantial time for leisure. Their societies were more egalitarian, and their members probably received more protein from animals than the farming communities that often succeeded them. Nor did they suffer the decline in nutrition and diet that came with protein-reduced grasses and population pressure. They were not vulnerable to crop failures like farming communities, although they lacked the resources to withstand major catastrophes. Often environments made rivalry for scarce resources incredibly intense; with the result that infanticide sometimes became a means to maximize the warrior base for competition.[93]

In general, however, hunter–gatherers did not suffer the economic in-equalities and increased workloads that greater specialization and stratification brought to agricultural societies, nor the diseases that spread rapidly among densely populated communities or which crossed over from the very animals that agriculturists domesticated. The anthropologist Marshall Sahlins once described hunter–gatherers as the original affluent society. Their average life span was 31 years. Sanderson asserts that early agricultural peasants, having lost the individuality and opportunities for self-realization possessed by their ancestors, probably had the lowest standard of living in global history. Even during the affluent Roman era, their average life expectancy rarely exceeded 37 years; during the European 'Middle Ages' it was only 34 years.[94]

In many respects both hunter–gatherers and agriculturists seem trapped by their respective paradigms. Their distinctive technologies did not permit living standards to rise above a low level. Nor did they permit infant mortality to decline. In making this comparison, we need to remember that in most instances people were not necessarily in a situation where they felt they had a choice, at least not one between two sharp contrasts. The transition from hunter–gathering to agriculture was slow and incremental, and people did what they have always done – imitate and innovate. Yet clearly we know today of many instances where the transition from one way of life to another is presented both suddenly and sharply. Pastoralists have conquered agriculturists, and agriculturists have driven out hunter–gatherers. Similarly, during and after the nineteenth century, mechanized farmers drove out agriculturists and others. The huge migration of people from rural communities to cities in the twentieth century, or from poor countries to wealthier ones, represents what people will do when faced with choices.

Hunter–gatherers, when presented with alternatives that they believed they controlled and which had the potential to sustain their lifestyle, would in all probability have admitted change. Even more so if it permitted living standards to rise (particularly for elite decision-makers), increased the overall numerical strength of their community, and opened the way for new strategies to enhance survival and well-being. Demand for innovations that might have these consequences was greatest in areas whose natural fertility acted as magnets for shifting populations. The Nile Valley was one such attraction, at first for pastoralists, but increasingly for people retreating from the expanding North African deserts. Sometimes river systems, such as those in and around the Fertile Crescent from the Levant to the Euphrates, also acted as natural migratory funnels. Under such conditions family multiplication was no longer possible. Pressure on resources and competition between communities became intense. Here also the advantages of even small changes could be quickly realized, and equally quickly imitated. Warfare was one such option.

It is no coincidence then that the agricultural transformation became a global one, within the space of 4,000–5,000 years and in at least seven quite separate regions. From West Asia (the Levant, Mesopotamia, Anatolia) 8,000–10,000 years ago, it spread to Egypt, North Africa, Central Asia, India, and into Europe – reaching Britain and Scandinavia 5,500 years ago. From China around 10,000 years ago, it spread east to Korea and Japan and south to South-east Asia. From West and Central Africa 6,500 years ago, it spread east and south. And it occurred independently in Central America 10,000 years ago, in Ethiopia and New Guinea some 6,000 years ago, and in eastern North America 5,000 years ago.

This then was no sudden transformation, and in all probability was precipitated by ecological factors that we have so far not explored. Humans respond to technological change, population pressure, and the availability of resources. But these factors are in turn often deeply influenced by environmental changes, such as the end of the last major ice age thirteen thousand years ago. A sudden but brief return to ice-age conditions two thousand years later possibly made more urgent changes already begun.[95] Warmer climates and more regular seasons presented new opportunities for hunter–gatherers. To start with, most changes were small. In many communities hunter–gatherers had long altered their environments in order to manage game herds to their advantage. They also accumulated considerable knowledge about the wild plants that they collected. They smoked meat. They ground seeds. Together with food processing, they developed new means to store food, particularly grains. Storing reduced further the risk of starving. It enabled communities to become more sedentary (one village excavated near the Euphrates contained some 157 species of plants).[96] These factors combined to enable larger populations. Births no longer had to be paced to accommodate seasonal movements. And those larger populations competed more intensively for land and resources, which they began to monopolize in a way that hunter–gatherer societies could not. Once the transformation had begun, it was unlikely to stop. Each change fed upon itself.

The first crops ten thousand years ago were edible grasses such as wheat, barley and peas in West Asia, or squash in Mexico. Many plants such as turnips and oats probably began as weeds. Invariably, cropping coincided with animal husbandry or more intensive game management. As people followed the seasonal movements of animals, particularly slower-moving animals, they learned how to manipulate their breeding and to improve herd yields. Across the Fertile Crescent, increasingly sedentary populations experimented with mixtures of different grasses and animals – goats, sheep, pigs, and, less successfully, gazelles.[97] Five thousand years ago their skills were such that nuts and fruits such as grapes and olives could be exploited. More difficult fruit such as apples and pears were cultivated later. But in all cases plants and animals changed either because of natural selection or because humans selected according to their own preferences. The pressure of expanding populations on resources made the extra effort of agriculture worthwhile in terms of maintaining living standards for larger populations. Towns emerged, among the first in West Asia being Jericho, a huddle of clay buildings for humans, their animals, and their stored foods. Significantly it lay behind four-metre-high walls,[98] an indication perhaps that even at the onset of the agricultural transformation, strategies for survival and prosperity had broadened. Conquest would become the dominant strategy employed by agricultural societies in the millennia to come.

The transition from hunting to agriculture was a global phenomenon, just as significant as the shift to hunting that first globalized human communities. Both were driven by the same basic human desires for survival and well-being, and both provided humans with a new capacity to draw greater value from the resources around them. In both instances, also, changing climates helped to make those opportunities and resources available. Success – even in very small ways – always bred imitation, and in a comparatively short time the particular very rapidly became universal.

This is, of course, a common description of globalization. It emphasizes interconnectedness.[99] Human transformations – or at least their consequences – have always been global. This does not mean that people were conscious of interconnections: transformations were always indigenized. Nor does it mean that all societies became the same. Pressures on societies differed. Some societies remained sheltered or geographically isolated from the competition that drove change in more densely populated parts of the world. And the resources available to communities differed widely.

There are scientists who believe that biogeographical differences on the eve of the Neolithic Revolution explain why technological and political developments seem to have been fastest on the landmass of Eurasia and slower in Africa, the Americas, and Australia. Jared Diamond describes three main influences – the global distribution of animals, the global distribution of plants, and the lie of the land.

Diamond's first biogeographic factor concerns the global distribution of animals. Animals are obviously important as a source for protein, and their availability is a factor in determining human population densities. Eurasia possessed the largest number of wild mammals – 71 species; sub-Saharan Africa 51; the Americas 24; and Australia 1. Given the size of Eurasia and its ecological diversity, this is not unexpected. But the early extinction of animals when humans first moved across the globe also played an important role, particularly in the Americas and Australia. There, humans removed animals that might in the future have provided stock for domestication. Animals fared better in Africa and Eurasia because they co-evolved with humans and wisely learned to fear them.[100]

Just as important as the availability of animals was the availability of animals capable of being domesticated. Only a small fraction of animals can be domesticated. Invariably they are animals that live in hierarchical herds and are instinctively submissive. They have also to be able to breed in captivity, have diets that are not too demanding on resources, and dispositions that are not unpleasant or panicky. Out of 148 wild vegetarian animals, only five major species meet these criteria – sheep, goats, pigs, cows and horses – and nine minor species – Arabian camels, Bactrian camels, llama–alpacas, reindeer, donkeys, yaks, water buffalo, gaurs (India's bison) and their relative, bantengs. These animals were not spread evenly over the globe. Again Eurasia possessed the largest proportion –18 per cent; the Americas only 4 per cent, of which the llama was the most important. But it existed in only two areas, it never yielded milk, carried riders, pulled a cart or plough, or became a source of power generation. Similarly Africa's big animals were never domesticated at all, let alone used for these further purposes.[101]

Much the same situation existed for plants. There might be some 200,000 wild plant species globally, but humans eat only a few thousand of these and domesticate only a few hundred. Of those few hundred, only twelve account for more than 80 per cent of today's crops: wheat, corn (maize), rice, barley, sorghum, soybean, potato, manioc (cassava), sweet potato, sugar cane, sugar beet, and banana. In other words, only a very small number of plants are capable of domestication. And their global distribution was far from equal. Australia had few. This did not mean stagnation for Australia: in the south-east of the continent, people developed winter villages and farmed fish.

In contrast, the Americas had corn, potatoes, tomatoes and squash. Corn was difficult to domesticate and slow to develop. In its wild state, corn's advantages as a food were less obvious. It had to be sown and harvested individually; its kernels had to be scraped. But once it was established in Mexico, its usage increased and spread. Before it could flourish in different conditions, the plant had to be transformed, and that took time. But once it had been, it became the basis for new intensive settlements, such as those that grew along the Mississippi river a millennium ago. Today corn is the most important global crop after wheat, but wheat has always been easier to domesticate and possesses more protein than corn or rice.

West Asia had self-pollinating varieties that were easy to select and maintain. West Asians were probably settled and collecting large quantities of wild cereal seeds long before they began cultivation. Domestication was probably an unintended consequence of people preferring some wild plants to others and accidentally spreading their seeds. In time, preferences led to larger seeds developing. Mild wet winters and hot dry summers suited cereals; it created the food surpluses on which the first cities in the Fertile Crescent (at one time incorporating Mesopotamia, in today's Iraq and Iran) were built. In fact the whole of western Eurasia possessed the world's largest zone with a Mediterranean-type climate. This encouraged a greater diversity of plants. In addition the wide range of altitudes and topographies in small areas enabled harvest seasons to be staggered, thereby enabling larger populations to be sustained. This, combined with a wider range of animals to depend upon, bestowed advantage.

By contrast, agriculture in Africa was delayed by the paucity of native plants (and domesticated animals). In part, Diamond argues, this explains why today Eurasia possesses four billion people and Africa only seven hundred million. The situation for South-east Asia is similar. For most of its history, it has been a region of dense forest and water. Accordingly, population densities were low. Few suitable foods existed to sustain large populations. Tropical diseases – particularly malaria – also exacted a toll. Only at the start of the second millennium CE did that situation change, when a vast migration of people from the north brought with them rice-growing technology.

New Guinea also had no large native animals to domesticate, but it did have a very diverse topology and was rich in plant and animal species. Six thousand years ago its farmers cultivated sugar cane, bananas, nuts, taro, breadfruit and yams. But they possessed no suitable cereals and no domesticated animals, except those that came via South-east Asia, and these never penetrated the highlands. Many of the plant foods they cultivated do not grow well in cool climates, but sweet potatoes do and once they had penetrated the highlands, they enabled a massive population explosion.[102]

In addition to the availability of plants and animals, Eurasia enjoyed one further advantage, says Diamond: the lie of the land itself. Not all areas might have indigenous plants or animals, but they could always receive them from areas that did. Diffusion in Eurasia was easier and much faster because its main axis lies east and west. This is important because climate zones flow east and west, along latitudes. Day lengths, seasonal variations, temperature regimes, rainfall, even diseases and vegetation are similar within climate zones. Plants and animals spread easily within climate zones, but outside them plants need to evolve into new varieties with different climate tolerances.

But we must not overlook the physical obstacles to diffusion. Barriers constrained movement between north and south India, within Indonesia and New Guinea, and between south-west and south-east Australia. Eurasia had other barriers. China was separated from West Asia by desert and high mountains and by seasonal variations in rainfall. Despite this, Eurasia still possessed the largest land mass within the same latitude, and opportunities abounded for many forms of exchange.

The Americas also constitute a vast continent, but its axis lies north–south, with its two main components separated by thousands of kilometres of tropics. This is why the llamas and alpacas never moved north, why potatoes did not spread beyond the Andes and why sunflowers were unknown outside the north. Corn did spread, but it took thousands of years for suitable varieties to evolve outside Mexico. Other barriers existed also, in particular the dry plains between south-eastern and south-western North America.

Africa is half the size of the Americas and it too lies north–south. Between southern Africa and Ethiopia lie more than three thousand kilometres of dense tropical landscape. Between North Africa and Central Africa lies a similar distance of desert. Climate and landscape conspired to reduce movement across the continent. Egypt's wheat and barley never reached the Cape in the south. The spread of livestock was similarly impeded, in part also by tropical illnesses.[103]

Diamond's biogeographical differences are significant. They serve to remind us of the importance of human interconnections. All humans imitate if imitation assists them to survive and prosper. But imitation and experimentation are possible only if people have access to animal and plant resources and if their environments are able to support such resources. Population pressures might promote change. Technology might create the scope for further changes. But increasingly, even in this very early stage of human existence, interconnectivity assumed a vital part in shaping the human story. Indeed, as we shall see next, it drove early global transformations.

Notes

1. Peter Ward and Donald Brownlee, *Rare Earth: Why Complex Life is uncommon in the Universe*, New York, Copernicus, 2000; see also the *Australian*, 14 February 2000, p. 10.

2. *The Economist*, 9 June 2001, pp. 97–8. Despite its fortune, Earth very nearly did not survive the turbulence of its birth. During the early years of the solar system another large planet the size of Mars collided with Earth. Fortunately the result of that collision was not disintegration but the formation of the Earth's moon.

3. Richard Planck, *Seeing and Believing: The Story of the Telescope, or how we found our place in the Universe*, London: Fourth Estate, 2000.

4. Brian Griffith, *The Gardens of their Dreams: Desertification and Culture in World History*, Nova Scotia, London and New York, Fernwood Publishing and Zed Books, 2001, pp. 50–55.

5. *Australian*, 25 February 1998, p. 13.

6. David Deutsch, *The Fabric of Reality: The Science of Parallel Universes and its Implications*, London, Allen Lane, 1998. Quantum theory's approach is not too dissimilar to that held by many religions and faiths. It is worth remembering that even as late as 1991, a Gallup poll in the United States revealed that 52 per cent of people still believed in astrology, 35 per cent in ghosts, 46 per cent in ESP, 42 per cent in communication with the dead, and 22 per cent in aliens on earth (Margaret Wertheim, 'Science, Magic, and the Kitchen Sink', *Australian*, 1–2 January 2000, p. 27).

7. Lynn Margulius, *The Symbiotic Planet: A New Look at Evolution*, London, Weidenfeld and Nicolson, 1999.

8. *Australian*, 24–25 February 2001, p.4; *Guardian Weekly*, 4–10 January 2001, p.22.

9. *New York Times*, 18 October 2000.

10. Robert Wright, *NONZERO: The Logic of Human Destiny*, New York, Pantheon Books, 2000, pp. 7, 243.

11. Colin Tudge, *The Variety of Life: The Meaning of Biodiversity*, Oxford, Oxford University Press, 1999.

12. James Gleick, *Chaos: Making a New Science*, New York, Penguin, 1987.

13. Graeme Donald Snooks, *The Dynamic Society: Exploring the Sources of Global Change*, London and New York, Routledge, 1996, pp. 44–52.

14. D. Schulz, 'The first bronzed Aussie?' *theage.com.au, 26. June 2001;* D. Smith, 'In the Beginning', *Sydney Morning Herald* (smh.com. au), 12 August 2000. One theory suggests that Aborigines are a 60,000-year-old mixture of *Homo Sapiens Gaciles*, who had migrated south from China, and Javanese Robusts (*Australian*, 10 January 2001, p. 13). Another theory suggests that modern Aborigines arrived only some 4,000 years ago from southern Asia. With them came new hunting weapons and dingoes (Peter James, 'The Indigenous Dilemma', Ockham's Razor, Radio National, abc.net.au, 4 March 2001).

15. DNA samples from Neanderthals do not support the idea that they interbred with *Homo sapiens*. But isolated cases may have occurred; the 25,000-year-old body of a 'Neanderthal sapiens' found in Portugal in 1999 may yet demonstrate that some interactions occasionally occurred.

16. Matt Ridley, *The Origins of Virtue*, London, Viking, 1996, p. 106.

17. Ibid., pp. 107–10.

18. Ibid., pp. 106–7.

19. This is the view of Professor David Harris of the Institute of Archaeology, University College, London (Science Show, Radio National, abc.net.au, 15 July 2000).

20. Jared Diamond, *The Rise and Fall of the Third Chimpanzee*, London, Vintage, 1992, pp. 34–48.

21. Deborah Smith, 'In the beginning', *smh.com.au*, 12 August 2000.

22. Ridley, *The Origins of Virtue*, pp. 199–202; Diamond, *The Third Chimpanzee*, pp. 206–7.

23. The human genome comprises over three billion pieces of information written into molecules of DNA or deoxyribonucleic acid. Each strand of DNA, or gene, carries about five thousand pieces of coded information, and is itself carried in one of twenty-three pairs of structures called chromosomes.

24. Dr Peter Chalmers, Institute for Molecular Systematics, Victoria University of Wellington, *Fiji Times*, 26 April 2001, p. 7.

25. Diamond, *The Third Chimpanzee*, pp. 96–7.

26. Ibid., pp. 100–5.

27. Ibid., p. 34.

28. Dr Derek Denton, *Australian*, 3–4 February 2001, pp. R 4, 5 and 8.

29. Oliver Sacks, 'Full Frontal', *Australian Review of Books*, May 2001, pp. 19–20, 27 (Review of Elkhonen Goldberg, *The Executive Brain: Frontal Lobes and the Civilized Mind*, New York, Oxford University Press, 2001).

30. Antonio R. Damasio, *Body and Emotion in the Making of Consciousness*, New York: Harcourt, Brace and Co., 1999.

31. Emma Paris, *Long Shadows: Truth, Lies, and History*. London: Bloomsbury, 2001.

32. John Elster, *Alchemies of the Mind: Rationality and the Emotions*. Cambridge: Cambridge University Press, 1999.

33. Henri Berson and John Cleese quoted in 'No Laughing Matter' *Australian*, 26–27 1998, p. R3.

34. Snooks, *The Dynamic Society*, pp. 172, 202.

35. Graeme Donald Snooks, *The Ephemeral Civilization: Exploding the Myth of Social Evolution*, London and New York, Routledge, 1997, pp. 1, 122–6.

36. Jaeg won Kim, *Mind in a Physical World*, Cambridge, Mass., MIT Press, 1999; Colin McGinn, *The Mysterious Flame: Conscious Minds in a Material World*, New York, Basic Books, 1999; *The Economist*, 1 May 1999, p. 86.

37. Freeman Dyson, 'The Scientist as Rebel', *Australian*, 7 June 1995, pp. 22, 28; see also J. Cornwell (ed.), *Nature's Imagination*, Oxford, Oxford University Press, 1995.

38. Bryan Appleyard, 'IQ Tests', *Australian*, 30–31 October 1999, p. R5.

39. Jared Diamond, *Guns, Germs and Steel: The Fates of Human Societies*, London, Jonathan Cape, 1997, p. 25.

40. Graeme Donald Snooks, *The Laws of History*, London and New York, Routledge, 1998, pp. 194–5.

41. Len Syme, quoted in Norman Swan, 'Mastering the Control Factor', Radio National's Health Report, *abc.net.au*, 9 November 1998.

42. Snooks, *Ephemeral Civilization*, p. 46; *The Dynamic Society*, p. 93.

43. Snooks, *Ephemeral Civilization*, p. 39.

44. Ibid., p. 36.

45. Griffith, *The Gardens of their Dreams*, p. 87.

46. Ridley, *The Origins of Virtue*, pp. 249–65; see also Snooks, *Laws of History*, pp. 249–65.

47. Jonathon Porritt, quoted in Ridley, *The Origins of Virtue*, p. 214.

48. Ibid., p. 215.

49. Diamond, *Guns, Germs and Steel*, pp. 42–7; *The Third Chimpanzee*, pp. 285–325; see also Tim Flannery, *The Eternal Frontier: An Ecological History of North America and its Peoples*, Melbourne, Text Publishing, 2001. Flannery claims there are 12 sites of mammoth slaughter in North America. In Arizona tools and spears were found among the remains of 9 mammoths.

50. Some scientists argue that the megafauna simply caught diseases from humans or their accompanying animals and deny the overkill thesis ('Mammoths killed by Germs', *Guardian Weekly*, 8–14 February 2001, p. 24).

51. Ridley, *The Origins of Virtue*, p. 219; Diamond, *The Third Chimpanzee*, pp. 287–95; David Bellamy, Brian Springett, and Peter Hayden, *Moa's Ark: The Voyage of New Zealand*, Auckland, Viking, 1990, pp. 135–45; Peter Crawford, *Nomads of the Wind: A Natural History of Polynesia*, London, BBC Books, 1993, pp. 243–5.

52. Ridley, *The Origins of Virtue*, p. 219; Diamond, *The Third Chimpanzee*, p. 295; Tim Flannery, *The Future Eaters: an Ecological History of the Australasian Lands and People*, Chatswood, Reed Books, 1994.

53. Diamond, *The Third Chimpanzee*, p. 285.

54. Ridley, *The Origins of Virtue*, p. 225.

55. Sir Peter Scott, quoted in Miriam Cosic, 'What's it all about?', in *Australian Magazine*, 13–14 February 1999, p. 34.

56. Wright, *NONZERO*, p. 296.

57. Richard Dawkins in 'The Moral Animal', Part 1 of *The Descent of Man*, The Science Show, Radio National, abc.net.au, January–February 2000.

58. Steven Pinker in 'Stone-Age Minds', Part 2 of *The Descent of Man*, The Science Show, Radio National, abc.net.au, January–February 2000; Steven Pinker, *How the Mind Works*, London: Penguin, 1998.

59. Richard Dawkins, *The Selfish Gene*, Oxford: Oxford University Press, 1976; cited in Ridley, *The Origins of Virtue*, p. 19.

60. Randy Thornhill and Cray Palmer, *A Natural History of Rape: Biological Bases of Sexual Coercion*, Cambridge, Mass., 2000.

61. Roger Short and Malcolm Potts, *Ever since Adam and Eve: the Evolution of Human Sexuality*, Cambridge, Cambridge University Press, 1999.

62. *Australian*, 27 December 1999, p. 1.

63. Steven Rose in *The Descent of Man*, Parts 1 and 2, The Science Show, Radio National, abc.net.au, January–February 2000. In the 1960s, an American cartoon company produced a television series called *The Flintstones* which set contemporary suburban America in the 'stone age'.

64. Snooks, *Ephemeral Civilization*, pp. 110–12, 122–3.

65. Ibid., pp. 125–6, 29.

66. Wright, *NONZERO*, pp. 264, 1.

67. Ibid., pp. 323, 330.

68. Ridley, *The Origins of Virtue*, p. 249.

69. Ibid., pp. 37–50.

70. Ibid., pp. 48–9.

71. Ibid., pp. 81, 89–92.

72. Ridley, *The Origins of Virtue*, pp. 115–116.

73. Natalie Angier, *An Intimate Geography of Women*, London, Virago Press, 1999.

74. Ridley, *The Origins of Virtue*, pp. 118–120.

75. Sarah Blackmore and Richard Dawkins in 'Is Anyone in There?' Part 3 of *The Descent of Man*, The Science Show, *Radio National*, abc.net.au, January–February 2000; Susan Blackmore, *The Meme Machine*, New York: Oxford University Press, 1999.

76. Blackmore in 'Is Anyone in There?'

77. Snooks, *The Dynamic Society*, p. 103.

78. Stephen K. Sanderson, 'Synthetic Materialism: An Integrated Theory of Human Society', Paper to the American Sociological Association, San Francisco, 21–25 August 1998, pp. 19–20.

79. Sanderson, 'Synthetic Materialism', p. 20.

80. Diamond, *The Third Chimpanzee*, pp. 58–71.

81. Ibid., p. 71.

82. Ibid., pp. 65–6, 72–83.

83. Ibid., pp. 152–61.

84. Sanderson, 'Synthetic Materialism', p. 49.

85. Ibid., pp. 27–33; Ridley, *The Origins of Virtue*, pp. 118–23.

86. Sanderson, 'Synthetic Materialism', pp. 35, 47.

87. There are many such examples, but recently evidence has emerged of huge floods caused by the expansion of the Mediterranean into the Black Sea some 7,000 years ago. A palaeoecologist has also suggested that the Earth suffered devastating

famines when a swarm of comet fragments struck around 540 AD, reducing temperatures sufficiently to cause harvests to fail.

88. Snooks, *The Laws of History*, p. 138; *The Dynamic Society*, pp. 124–6.

89. Snooks, *The Laws of History*, p. 206.

90. Ibid., p. 209.

91. Ibid., pp. 214–216. Snooks gives examples of superficial regularities in human experience and also describes certain historical patterns that emerge within specific paradigms. But it is the paradigms themselves that most encapsulate the eternal regularities of human existence (pp. 186–7).

92. Snooks, *The Dynamic Society*, p. 54.

93. Ibid., p. 228; Snooks claims that up to 40 per cent of female Inuit infants were regularly killed for these reasons.

94. Stephen K. Sanderson, *Social Transformations: A General Theory of Historical Development*, Oxford, Blackwell, 1995, pp. 21, 338–41; see also Diamond, *Guns, Germs and Steel*, pp. 104–5.

95. Melinda Zeder and Bruce Smith, Smithsonian Institution, 'Are Goats our Oldest Crop?' The Science Show, Radio National, abc.net.au, 3 March 2001.

96. Wright, *NONZERO*, p. 75.

97. Bruce Smith, curator National Museum of Natural History, 'The Domestication of Plants', The Science Show, Radio National, abc.net.au, 15 July 2000.

98. Snooks, *The Dynamic Society*, p. 52.

99. Robert J. Holton, *Globalization and the Nation State*, London, Macmillan, 1998, pp. 7–8, 192.

100. Diamond, *Guns, Germs and Steel*, pp. 137–63.

101. Ibid., pp. 168–75.

102. Ibid., pp. 131–56.

103. Ibid., pp. 176–90. J.R. McNeill argues that Diamond overstates the axis case. At the very least, 'Eurasia's East–West axis could not have been much help in the spread of cattle and goats', he maintains. Despite a common latitude, Eurasia enjoys 'an extreme variety of climatic conditions'. Hence, 'the role of geography is much more complex than the axes suggest' and human factors must not be neglected. After all, 'Along the East–West axis of Eurasia, cattle became important in Europe, fundamental in India, yet inconsequential in China. This is not because Chinese environmental conditions were inhospitable to cattle, but because Chinese social and economic conditions were'. (J.R. McNeill, 'The World According to Jared Diamond', *The History Teacher*, 34: 2, February 2001, (historycooperative.org/journals/ht/34.2/mcneill.html).

. . . .

PART TWO

The First Wave of Globalization

. . . .

CHAPTER 3

Early Global Transformations

Civilizations

Between the ziggurats of Mesopotamia and the rocket spires of Cape Canaveral lie more than just six thousand years of ambition. Both achievements demonstrate how quickly the capabilities of humans would be radically transformed. At one level, their origins lie in the development of farming and in the utilization of fossil fuels. The technologies that these activities involved extended the realm of human activities far beyond anything previously experienced. Sanderson believes that this dynamic also transformed human adaptiveness into a new social confidence that soon found expression as a drive for mastery and became a determining feature of human societies.[1]

The new technologies enabled old boundaries to be transcended. Military might or monopoly access to resources enabled wealth, power and population concentrations to exceed by far the technological basis on which most societies ultimately depended. But privileged access could be challenged, resources could run out, and rivals could thwart ambition. In growth based on exclusion and conquest lay an apparently new feature of human existence – the rise and fall of civilizations.

The term 'civilization' requires a brief explanation because it denotes a sense of discreteness that is unhelpful in understanding the interconnections of globalization. It carries the baggage of past empires which used 'civilization' to convey a sense of cultural and racial superiority. Even today it is often used to describe societies that have successfully adapted themselves to the demands of a new industrial paradigm. Since this paradigm is also held to be the product of West European societies, Westernization and 'civilization' are often said to be one and the same thing.

In reality, the grand cultures that civilizations are said to represent were never discrete. We cannot declare cultures independent and place them within an evolutionary hierarchy. In fact, what made cultures distinctive and gave them lasting meaning and significance was their interconnectedness. 'There is no unitary process to global history', sociologist Robert Holton reminds us, no singular thrust of civilization. 'All we need to sense is interchange and interdependency'.[2] To understand global history, it is counter-productive to exaggerate the role of particular cultures or to describe them as discrete 'civilizations'. By themselves societies did not drive human history. Only when societies became part of something bigger did they achieve prominence, as this brief survey of early global transformations seeks to demonstrate.

Accordingly, when we talk of civilizations, we are usually describing societies that became significant because they connected with other peoples and created something greater than themselves. As such they are but one element in a globalizing process that emanated from the transformation of hunter–gatherers into larger and more settled communities of agriculturists. That process itself took several thousand years and, although influenced by resources at hand and the lie of the land, came increasingly to depend on interactions between communities. Thus farming spread and the achievements of one community became the traditions of another.[3] By this means any fragility inherent within the complex changes involved was overcome by the human propensity to imitate and to indigenize anything that might be useful in the drive for security and well-being. Hence, technology alone did not drive human change any more than civilizations did. Also of importance was human interconnectivity.

Sociobiologists, as we saw in the previous chapter, sometimes suggest that the human propensity to copy is generated independently of human control. 'Useful memes replicate themselves en masse insuring the planet against regional crashes', Wright argues in the contemporary language of information technology. Back-up copies always exist to thwart global setbacks.[4] But the world is not the single planetary brain that Wright describes,[5] and humans are not its data processing machines.[6] Humans possess no innate global consciousness; for the most part they have lived extremely local and parochial lives.[7] But they were lives that became increasingly interconnected, and as a consequence gained new significance.

Interconnections drove the transition to farming. Increased pressure on resources demanded human responses that were quickly disseminated. Agriculture represented a new technology for humans to exploit resources at hand. It enabled larger populations to be sustained and new communities to coalesce as villages, towns, cities, and states. Indeed over a three-thousand-year period, states emerged from interconnected agricultural societies all over the world. Five thousand years ago a highly centralized city-state system developed in Mesopotamia. Similar developments occurred also in Egypt, along the Indus in present-day Pakistan, in central and northern China, in Nubia and Ethiopia, in Central America, southern Europe, and in West and southern Africa. Faced with rising populations competing for scarce resources, communities employed state organizations as coping mechanisms. This became part of their strategy for survival and well-being.

Irrigation is a case in point, representing at one level the development of communal means to raise production. But irrigation in Egypt also represented a survival mechanism employed when desiccation and reduced flows of water from the Nile threatened whole agricultural communities. The same was probably true of irrigation initiatives in the Indus Valley and in northern Mesopotamia, where shrinking resources made warfare and conquest an additional strategy for survival.[8]

Around the world, the dynamics of human societies were similar. Where communities differed, however, was in their ability to transform those dynamics. In theory, the larger the community, the greater the potential for specialization and stratification. Specialization enabled improved productivity through new farming practices or irrigation. Intensified food production often made labour demands more seasonally defined, thereby enabling labour to be organized for public works or military service after harvests. Intensified food production also produced larger food surpluses that could be used to free more people to specialize outside food production in craft activities or in politics and administration. In other words, food production and stratification reinforced each other.

Certainly more sedentary and larger populations, living virtually on top of each other and depending upon each other for an ever-expanding range of tasks, incorporated greater risk of internal conflict and breakdown. Old communal forms of decision-making were no longer effective. Hence decision-making and conflict resolution became more centralized. Space had to be treated differently and laws made to define how resources could be used. Older procedures no longer worked. Herein lay opportunities for elites to feather their own nests. Herein also lay new dangers. More centralized authority placed a greater emphasis on leadership. Inevitably the future welfare of states depended on the quality of leadership and on mechanisms in place for orderly succession. But it also depended on how societies managed their relations with other societies, particularly predatory ones.

In their focus on civilizations, historians have often lost sight of the importance of such interconnections. Indeed there exists a tradition in history that emphasizes climate as a significant factor in determining the nature of societies. We have already examined biogeographical features that placed limits on social developments, at least while societies remained isolated from each other. But could climate have had a similar and perhaps longer-lasting effect? Economic historian David Landes certainly believes that it did. He is less concerned with continental differences than with differences within defined geographical entities such as Eurasia.

At the heart of his contention is the difference between communities that rely on rivers for their water needs and those which receive adequate rainfall. Western Europe, he says, is blessed by the Atlantic Gulf Stream, which brings warm water from the Caribbean and bestows on the region mild temperatures and evenly distributed rain all year round. Adequate, even rainfall enables more crops to be produced, dense hardwood forests to develop, and larger livestock to be bred. In times past this was an important factor. Stronger and larger horses reduced workloads for people; they also provided alternatives for transport, and helped to fertilize land, which in turn produced better crops and larger populations. Yet for all this, Landes is forced to concede that these benefits never allowed Europe to sustain populations as large as those in China or India.[9]

Nonetheless, Landes is determined to find historical and contemporary difference in geography. In contrast to West Europeans, the Chinese focused less on the use of animals. Little space existed for animals in the intensive agriculture of south China. Instead the Chinese fertilized their soil with human wastes, risking higher worm infestations among their people. What political or social consequences this produced, Landes does not tell us. His attention switches to the huge water schemes the Chinese developed to satisfy rice production. These were so labour intensive that they encouraged both population growth and ever-larger government machinery for water management. Herein lay the seeds of Chinese despotism. Western Europe's future differed, Landes claims, because it did not need such government machinery to maintain water supply. It possessed adequate rainfall. Thus Western Europe focused instead on smaller households and smaller political units.[10]

Most Eurasian societies did depend on rivers for their water needs. They had to learn how to use their rivers if they were to prosper. Not unnaturally water control became a central feature of societies that developed around the Nile in Egypt, the Tigris and the Euphrates in West Asia, the Indus in South Asia, and the Huanghe and Yangzi Jiang in China. In the long run, Landes argues, such centrality enabled Asian authorities to retain a high degree of control over the lives of their citizens. In contrast, West Europeans enjoyed more decentralized control. Thus they could respond more flexibly and differently to new demands and challenges, an advantage that eventually enabled Western Europe to steal a march on all other societies. Political decentralization, competition, tolerance and openness, says Landes, made Western Europe adaptive.[11]

Climate undoubtedly impacts on societies, but rarely in the direct and civilization-bound manner Landes suggests. Across North Africa, south-east Europe, and in West, Central and South Asia huge swathes of desert began forming or expanding between four and six thousand years ago as rainfall patterns changed. Human agricultural and pastoral practices contributed to the changes. Overgrazing, deforestation and irrigation turned once fertile lands into arid dustbowls or saline deserts. These changes were as profound as those that had confronted migratory hunter–gatherers after the mass destruction of native fauna. Ridley focuses on several examples as a way of demonstrating that ancient peoples did not possess an ecological wisdom since lost. Polynesians turned the once lush Easter Island into a treeless, birdless, poverty-stricken grassland. Maoris did much the same to the eastern plains of New Zealand's South Island. The Mayans reduced the Yucatan Peninsula to scrub. The Anasazi transformed their Chaco Canyon into a treeless, waterless desert.[12]

These were not isolated examples, but it was on the Afro-Eurasian continent, where the bulk of humanity lived, that human activities and climatic change combined to effect dramatic environmental consequences. Through burning and overgrazing, humans altered their landscapes. As tree covers declined, rainfall levels fell. Across the Fertile Crescent, salination and erosion reduced the benefits once derived from extensive irrigation. The land could no longer support its population.[13] Migration became one solution, but migrants did not venture into new lands ecologically chastened. The Harappans invaded the Indus Valley, cut down its trees, allowed goats and sheep to erode the landscape, and permitted irrigation to waste its soils. Later Indo-European invaders similarly destroyed the lush forests of the Ganges Plain further east. Warfare and overgrazing had the same effect on much of North Africa. On the steppes or grasslands of Central Asia, desertification drove nomadic tribes to turn on their eastern neighbours for relief.[14]

War and plunder also created opportunities for environmentally challenged peoples to survive and prosper. In North Africa, Carthaginians demanded half the crops produced by Berber farmers; in northern China the Qin took up to three quarters of their farmers' produce. The Shang had been no different when they established control in northern China in 1760 BCE, or the Macedonians in Egypt, the Dorians in Greece, the Romans in Italy, and the Qidan and Nuzhen tribes in north China after the tenth century CE. Desiccation begat warlords, writes author Brian Griffith, and warlords begat desiccation.

There were environmental costs associated with pushing the people so hard, and these costs were especially high in fragile semi-arid farmlands. To meet imposed annual production quotas, farmers often had to sacrifice fallow years for their fields. The land was then forced into constant use without let-up. Between the requirements of the military and the survival needs of the farmers' families, any reinvestment in the land was often squeezed out.[15]

The rulers of all the great empires (civilizations) – the Akkadians, Assyrians, Persians, Macedonians, Romans, Qin, Mongols, Mughals, and Manchus – were semi-nomadic warlords or their descendants whose responses to climatic constraints were to subjugate farmers and treat their lands as rewards for conquest. 'The whole rise of sedentary civilization and nomadic empires', writes Griffith, 'can be viewed as a concentration of resources in the hands of competing warlords'.[16] It is this environmental background that informs early global transformations. But it produced interconnections, not distinctive, climatically responsive and tyrannical civilizations. Across Afro-Eurasia – and in particular in Europe, North Africa, and Asia – the vast migrations of nomadic tribes transformed the populations and cultures of societies, and generated new interconnections.

Migration as a Strategy for Security and Well-being

Migration involves the expansion of growing populations into virgin territory or into land occupied by hunter–gatherers, horticulturists and agriculturists who can be conquered, absorbed or pushed on to less sustainable land. Like all strategies, it usually formed part of a mixed package that also included conquest, trade and technology.

Migration has transformed human societies globally ever since Palaeolithic times. Long after the agricultural revolution made other strategies more viable, migration continued to exert a powerful influence, so much so that writers such as Diamond see in its early manifestations many of the features that we now regard as common to contemporary globalization. The most important of these is loss of diversity, and in particular linguistic diversity, and the losses were felt most keenly in South-east Asia, Europe, and Africa. Today 90 per cent of the world's people speak languages derived from those once confined to West Asia and China.[17]

Let us look first at Europe. We can trace something of the peopling of Europe by examining language. In all likelihood Europe once possessed a diverse range of languages, but today few of these survive, with the exception perhaps of the Basque language (now known as Euskera) and Finno-Ugric. All Europe's other languages derive from a single language spoken some seven thousand years ago and known today as proto-Indo-European. Migrations of Indo-Europeans divested Europe of much of its linguistic diversity, yet it needs also to be acknowledged that these migrants generated new forms of diversity and hybridity. English is a case in point, as Holton argues: an Indo-European language, developed by German immigrants, fused with Latin and French, and using Phoenician letters and Indian numbers.[18] Diversity, then, is a feature of globalization – an unexpected one perhaps, but nonetheless one that has important implications, as we shall see later.

As Indo-Europeans spread over Europe and into West and South Asia, their language split into different branches. Today Europe is home to the second-largest branch of proto-Indo-European, a branch which contains some 300–500 million speakers of 144 Indo-European languages grouped into three main sub-branches: Germanic (including English), Italic (including French and Spanish), and Slavic (including Russian). Each of these sub-branches has twelve to sixteen languages. Some of these languages – for example, Greek, Albanian,

Armenian, Baltic, and Celtic – are very small in terms of the number of speakers, often because they represented early Indo-European migrants who were themselves overwhelmed by later ones. Baltic-speaking peoples were once widely distributed across Russia, before later arrivals of Goths and Slavs restricted their language to present-day Latvia and Lithuania. Similarly, three thousand years ago the Celtic language was widely spoken across Europe, but by 500 BCE, after incursions of new Indo-Europeans, it survived only in the west among the Irish, Scots, Welsh, and Bretons. At the same time Rome's expansion had the same effect on other languages, among them the Etruscan language of northern Italy.[19]

Yet when Rome collapsed, the relative isolation of peoples caused dialects to transform into distinctive languages. Hence the departure of French, Italian, Spanish, Portuguese and Romanian from Latin, although many of these languages did not derive their present currency until very recently. On the eve of the French Revolution, only about one quarter of the French population spoke French, at one time the language only of the court. (The rest spoke regional languages and dialects such as Alsatian, Basque, Breton, Catalan, Flemish, Occitan and so on.) This suggests something of the complexity of language formation, especially in the most interconnected of the world's continents.

The largest branch of the original proto-Indo-European language today is Indo-Iranian, which contains some ninety languages and 700 million speakers.[20] One of those languages is Romany, the language of the misnamed gypsies, who hail not from Egypt, as the British among others once thought, but from India. They were derived from three Rajastan tribes, taken in bondage to Afghanistan to provide a ready source of slaves for their Muslim kidnappers. When, much later, the Muslims conquered north India, they became redundant and were set free. But the gypsies regarded themselves as unclean outcastes, and refused to return home. Instead the 50,000-strong group moved westward, reaching Constantinople on the eve of the fourteenth-century plague epidemic. To escape blame and persecution, they kept moving.[21] The gypsies, then, were later migrants westward, but their movement was not unique among Eurasians. The Finno-Ugric Magyars spent two thousand years travelling from the Ural mountains down the Volga basin before finally settling on the Hungarian plains.[22] Certainly the desire for a new homeland featured strongly among the many Indo-Europeans who moved south into India – the speakers of Sanskrit, which forms the basis for Hindi, today's dominant language in India.

In the nineteenth and early twentieth centuries, it was sometimes argued that Indo-European languages derived from the Caucasus, between the Black and Caspian Seas, and that Indo-Europeans were blond-haired, blue-eyed 'Aryans'. But if Hitler's Aryan supermen ever existed, says Diamond, they were most likely to have been dark-haired, swarthy Indo-Iranians who either intermingled with the original inhabitants of Europe or dominated them sufficiently to transform their languages. Many of those early Europeans belonged to tribes of blond, light-skinned hunters, among them the Finno-Ugric peoples (ancestors of today's Finns, Estonians and Hungarians). The result was a mixture of peoples and languages. Diamond suggests that German might well have begun as a kind of pidgin or creole language when Indo-Europeans first settled among Baltic tribes and traded.[23] Not all movements of peoples came in the form of invasions or massive migrations over long distances. As we saw in the case of Palaeolithic migration, the gradual movement of new and more numerous generations achieved the same result.[24] Nonetheless, it is from the steppes of Eurasia that the most dramatic early forms of global transformation emanated.

The Russian steppes, north of the Caucasus, stood at the end of a funnel, several hundred kilometres wide, that stretched all the way to the Caspian Sea and thence to China. Here, between five and seven thousand years ago, early Indo-Europeans lived and farmed, but under conditions that steadily worsened. Changing climates caused the Black Sea to shrink, tree cover to decline, and hunting to become more difficult. Domesticated animals provided some relief in the form of meat, hides, milk and wool, but to sustain herding many tribes were forced to become nomadic.

Further east on the Kazakhstan steppes and north of the Black Sea in the Ukraine, Indo-European tribes domesticated the horse. Horses eventually bestowed new wealth and power on their owners; they enabled larger herds to be managed over longer distances. Increasingly also, they enabled surprise raids on near and distant neighbours to garner plunder or tribute.

This combination of pastoralism and technology revolutionized Indo-European societies. It expanded their populations and bestowed upon them a kind of power that farming and herding alone could never have achieved, especially on the vast steppes where distance did represent a form of tyranny. The proto-Indo-Europeans did not require intensive agriculture to support a growing population. Instead they relied on conquest, and as long as they remained mobile and open to new ideas and technology, they were for a time able to remove the disadvantages imposed by their degraded landscapes.[25] But there were always winners and losers in the steppe battles, with losers such as the Celts and Dorians fleeing into Europe to become conquerors themselves.

For five thousand years this package of strategies enabled Indo-European tribes to dominate the steppes. But beyond that their technology was less suitable. Once they reached the forested landscape of Western Europe or the rich farmlands of southern China and North Africa, survival dictated a new lifestyle.[26] Invariably the adaptable invaders settled and intermingled with local tribes, although not always easily. In India, the emergence of caste revealed something of the contempt the Indo-Europeans felt for the darker-skinned aboriginal Dravidians, and their desire to use birth as a means to retain leadership in their own hands.[27]

The desiccation of Central Asia initially impacted most on China. Its first dynasties were formed from semi-nomadic peoples who used their power to establish themselves as tax farmers. The border state of Qin, which first united China in 221 BCE, differed little in this regard. In its quest for total power, Qin warlords so bled their people that their peasants rose up in revolt when a major famine struck fifteen years later. The following Han dynasty learned the lesson, but they also consolidated the Great Wall of China as a new defence against nomads. The walls had once protected China's warring states from each other. But the Xiongnu – the Turkic-speaking Huns who then made up the largest body of nomads menacing China – were desperate for food and had only their promise not to attack the Chinese to trade. At the start of the Han dynasty's rule, the Chinese paid the Xiongnu to keep the peace, sometimes even employing them as border guards. On other occasions they plotted to weaken the Xiongnu by allying with their enemies, and by establishing their own effective cavalry.

The invention and initial monopolization of the stirrup in Central Asia around 300 CE gave Huns renewed advantage – fast, highly mobile cavalry armies. For the next thousand years they exploited that advantage over sedentary peoples as much as they could. They attacked China and partitioned it into states, even building the 1,900-kilometre Grand Canal to bring rice from south China to feed their northern armies. In Eastern Europe, they overthrew the Ostrogoths and the Visigoths (many of whom were now settled farmers) and pushed them and the Vandals westwards against the Romans. The Goths spread into Germany, driving the Franks into France. Ostrogoths and Lombards moved into Italy; Visigoths into southern France and northern Spain.[28] Attila the Hun unsuccessfully attacked the Romans in Gaul in 451 CE and a little later in northern Italy, before retreating north of the Black Sea. In the late seventh century one Hun group founded Bulgaria, although like the Swedes, who later founded Russia, the bulk of their conquered peoples re-mained Slav speakers. Other Huns moved into north-west India, the ancestors of today's Rajputs. After the Huns came Turkish Tartars. In the tenth century, Qidan (Khitan) Tartars seized a large part of northern China and established the state of Liao. It is from these Eurasian nomads that one name for China derives. The Russians called them Kitai; the English Cathay. In the thirteenth century CE, Nizhen (Jurchen) tribes from Manchuria carved out their own state of Jin in north China.[29]

Perhaps the most famous of the Tartars were the Mongols, who under Temuchin (Genghis Khan) built up a confederation of tribes at the beginning of the thirteenth century. His hordes spread across the whole of the steppes and created a vast empire stretching from the Pacific in the east to Iran, Iraq and Burma in the south, and to the Danube in the west. Unlike the Huns, they produced a united empire that brought together cultures previously isolated from each other. But the Mongol Empire did not last.

Like most nomadic rulers, they were harsh tax farmers. During their reign over China, war, famine and plague reduced China's population from one hundred million to sixty million. The Mongols were themselves weakened by plague, but by the time they recovered, the spread of firearms across Eurasia had destroyed their military advantage. By the end of the fourteenth century, Indo-European-speaking Russians began a counter-invasion of the steppes from the north-west. After 1368, a new Ming dynasty expelled them from China.[30]

But the Mongols' defeat did not end China's exposure to nomads. When harsh weather conditions again produced famine in the north, semi-pastoral Manchu warlords from Manchuria moved south and overthrew the Ming in 1644. They ruled China until 1911.

Despite this history of foreign governance, China – unlike many other parts of Afro-Eurasia – is not a melting pot of migratory peoples. Nor does it harbour the remnants of aboriginal languages to the same extent as India, with some 850 languages, or Indonesia, with 670. China is different. It has only one writing system (compared with dozens of modified alphabets in Europe). Two thirds of its people speak one language, Mandarin, and nearly one quarter speak one of seven related languages.[31]

China was once much more diverse. The remnants of that diversity are still visible in the differences between northerners and southerners, and in the pockets of minorities which remain with their 130 languages linked to languages now spoken more widely in Tibet, Vietnam, Cambodia, Malaysia, Thailand, Burma, and Laos. These linkages should not surprise us, for many of the people of South-east Asia came originally from China, often moving south as Han Chinese moved down from the north. Others were absorbed into larger groups or into the Han people themselves. The people on the move did the same as they travelled south, pushing out darker-skinned existing populations of hunter–gatherers who retreated into less hospitable mountainous regions. In China such movements were geographically unproblematic. The country's north–south axis was smaller than America's, and long rivers flowed eastward into the sea. The culture of the sizeable Han became extremely influential; to the east it provided much of the basis for Korean and Japanese culture.[32]

Also pushed out from southern China via Taiwan (where they survive today as the country's aborigines) were some of the ancestors of today's Pacific islanders. These people were Austronesians, and about 5,500 years ago they moved south only to find the lowlands of South-east Asia already occupied by earlier farmer populations derived from China. Consequently they moved down into the Philippines, Vietnam, Malaysia and Indonesia where they displaced local populations. Groups of Austronesians also moved along the northern coast of New Guinea, intermingling with dense local farming and trading populations (who were also expanding eastwards into Timor). In a series of waves the Austronesians reached the Solomon Islands 3,500 years ago; Fiji, Tonga, Samoa, Vanuatu and New Caledonia about 3,000 years ago; Tahiti and the Cook Islands 2,000 years ago; Hawaii to the north 1,500 years ago; and New Zealand to the south about 800 years ago.

Today, Pacific-island Melanesians and Polynesians carry the physical signs of their passage through New Guinea (and, in the case of Fiji, of passage through the Solomons and Vanuatu). But their languages remain Austronesian, as do their predominant foods – taro, yams, bananas, coconut and breadfruit. The one exception is the sweet potato, almost certainly the product of Polynesian contact with South America. Pacific island interconnections ensured its widespread use. Even less well-known is the fact that one group of Austronesians left Borneo between 1,200 and 1,700 years ago and travelled 6,000 kilometres across the Indian Ocean to occupy the large and then unpopulated island of Madagascar, 400 kilometres off the east coast of Africa. They brought with them their familiar crops of yams, taro and bananas.[33] Human global migration had come full circle.

With one quarter of the world's languages, five different language families of over 1,500 languages, Africa is of course the cradle of humanity. It is a continent of great physical diversity, ranging from fertile Mediterranean lands to deserts, highlands and dense rainforests. Here also exists the greatest diversity among peoples. It includes African blacks, North Africans (whose Semitic languages spread into West Asia), Austronesians, pygmy hunter–gatherers of Central Africa, and the southern African Khoi (South African Hottentots) and San (Namibian hunter–gatherers). These last three groups once occupied most of central and southern Africa, but were displaced as a result of the eastward and southward expansion of West African blacks from the Cameroon–Niger region, which began three thousand years ago. They were farmers. The people they displaced lacked their access to plants and animals capable of being domesticated. Although West African agriculture developed independently, its animals came mostly from North Africa or West Asia via Egypt and Ethiopia. But geography treated them less kindly when they began to expand southward. Dense tropical jungle, tropical diseases, hostile hunter–gatherers, and climates unsuitable for their predominantly West African summer-rain crops made their trek south a two-thousand-year affair. When the Dutch arrived at the Cape in 1652, they found only the small Khoi-San population enjoying its Mediterranean winter-rain conditions.[34]

Migration north of the Sahara was much more rapid, because of North Africa's access to Europe and West Asia. The lands of the aboriginal peoples of North Africa, the Berbers, were conquered and occupied by Phoenicians around 814 BCE, and later by Romans. War and economic exploitation turned much of the Maghreb into semi-desert, transforming Carthage's wheat belt into dry lands fit only for olives, dates and pasture. Thereafter it was variously occupied or ruled by Vandals, West Asians from Constantinople, Arabs and finally Ottoman Turks. In many respects North Africa's history mirrors that of Eurasia.[35]

Conquest as a Strategy for Security and Well-being

Migration may have been one of the most pervasive of the strategies pursued by societies under stress, but nothing quite generated the same rush of well-being for the protagonists as conquest. Conquering prosperous neighbours provided an unprecedented influx of massive profits that stimulated economic growth far beyond anything agricultural technology, pastoralism or migration alone could provide. The difficulty, of course, was to sustain a constant flow of loot. In the end that goal eluded even the empires with highly specialized war machines dedicated to the task.

Societies never wholly focus on one strategy. They expand, they conquer, they trade and they innovate. In Mesopotamia, competition between cities over shrinking resources – in particular land and access to water – led to war, with the victorious Sumer profiting most. But Mesopotamian societies limited warfare to ritual fighting between elites. Once they had gained advantage over similarly matched cities, they could sustain prosperity only by means of commerce or technological innovation.

Nonetheless, Sumer demonstrated what was possible. By investing in a military elite, it obtained loot, tribute, territory and slaves to the sudden benefit not only of that elite, but also substantially of the society as a whole. Conquest enhanced Sumer's infrastructure and enabled the population to expand.[36] Invariably what draws us to civilizations such as Sumer are the impressive social and cultural achievements that their infrastructure and populations allowed. Yet while such communities demonstrated the synergies that amalgamations and interconnections could produce, they also demonstrated the disturbing fragility of the strategy on which such expansion was based.

To sustain conquest as a viable strategy, societies placed themselves at the mercy of leaders whose qualities could never be guaranteed from one generation to the next. In a manner of speaking, these societies were also hostage to the ability of their conquered territories to continue delivering tribute, which invariably they could not, or at least not to the initial extent. Thus the conquering state had few options open to it. It could reorganize itself to seek fortune further afield. Or it could risk atrophy by trying to sustain itself with existing resources. These usually shrank, because rulers gave little thought to reinvesting the wealth they had plundered. In these moments of transition, conquering societies were always vulnerable to opportunists seeking to enjoy for themselves the same heady pathway to well-being. Thus Sumer's elite soldiers fell victim to more ruthless and heavily armoured Akkadians, who in turn fell victim to the first of the Indo-European conquerors, the Assyrians, whose military specialization and technology eventually founded an empire that incorporated the eastern Mediterranean, Mesopotamia and Egypt.

The conquest strategy ensured that the most professionally organized and technologically innovative military organization would succeed, but only for as long as leadership qualities remained high and conquered territories delivered. The Assyrians constantly pushed out the boundaries of their empire in order to gain new sources of plunder as old sources were depleted.[37] Sometimes success came too rapidly for organizational weaknesses to be addressed. Thus Macedonia's far-flung empire – built initially on the wealth of its conquered Greek territories, and briefly incorporating its Persian model and stretching into north India – rapidly collapsed after its warlord Alexander died. War technology by itself could not sustain the strategy.

More successful, however, were the Romans, who sustained expansion for some 450 years. The Romans, like the Macedonians, were Indo-European tribal pastoralists who had settled in Italy around 750 BCE and seized Rome from native Etruscans about 140 years later. Roman expansion began gradually under the auspices of wealthy landowners employing part-time peasants as the basis for military force. Roman success led eventually to the establishment of a professional army to undertake full-time engagement, and to the consolidation of a vast bureaucracy to manage a society growing rapidly in size and complexity.

But the costs were high. Rome's wars with Carthage devastated North Africa and southern Italy. Larger estates employing slave labour emerged as a solution to Rome's food shortages. After Carthage was defeated in 146 BCE, the entire 400,000-strong Carthaginian population was transported to southern Italy as agricultural slaves. Slaves and absentee landowners (often former army commanders) cared little for the land they farmed, only for what it brought them. Consequently, deforestation and erosion forced Rome to depend increasingly on colonies to supply the food needed to feed its rapidly expanding population (at its height Rome contained over one million people), its armies, and expatriate populations. In conquered North Africa, Rome established some six hundred towns, each containing between sixty and one hundred thousand inhabitants.[38]

Inevitably Rome's dependence on its military brought with it a political price, which was paid when the military seized control under Caesar. Thereafter its commanders became its emperors, with power increasingly devolving to the large Danube army, which confronted the massive movement of Indo-Europeans into Europe. Like the Chinese northern army, its size increased as the pressures from nomads increased and as frontier peoples were absorbed into the army in order to buy peace. Others, like the forces of Alaric the Goth, were grudgingly hired to protect the Empire from Huns and Ostrogoths. Vandals were similarly hired to protect North Africa from the Berbers.[39] But the costs of these engagements burdened the Empire, and inevitably Rome ran out of profitable societies to conquer and thereby sustain military expansion. Unable to maintain itself by taxes, and too large to be ruled centrally, the Roman Empire fragmented into feudal components that best reflected the true state of its productive technology. These soon became targets for rival German and Persian conquerors.[40]

The conquest strategies played out by Eurasian empires were present also in the Americas, particularly in Central America, where more than two million people lived in fiercely competitive cities and villages. Here too conquest brought windfall profits to conquerors such as the Teotihuacans (150 BCE–150 CE), and Mayan city dwellers (600–830 CE) which could never be sustained in the long term. The same fate undoubtedly awaited the Mexican Aztecs, whose massive 200,000-strong city of Tenochtitlan on Lake Tetzcoco commanded an empire built from the ruins of the former Tepanec Empire.

The Aztec Empire was raised on tribute and loot, but the peasant nature of its agriculture, its part-time military, and the high cost of transport typically limited its size. Lacking animals and carts, it relied instead on over 100,000 porters to sustain its 200,000-strong army on forays of up to 900 kilometres. Despite high campaign casualties (often as high as 17 per cent), the rewards were such that the strategy was never doubted. On the eve of its second expansion, this time against more distant Mayan cities, the Aztecs developed the capacity to field armies double the former size and to reach further into Central America than ever before. Despite its obvious dynamism, the Aztec Empire too had no solution to the long-term weakness associated with the conquest strategy – its unsustainability. Strange as it might seem, that problem also dogged societies that pursued commerce as their dominant strategy.

Commerce as a Strategy for Security and Well-being

No society survives on warfare alone. People have to be fed, clothed, housed; desires for luxuries met. The Mayans possessed rich cities like Cancún on the Pasión river that acted solely as trading centres and possessed no temples or defence systems.[41] What distinguished urban communities from smaller, mainly hunter–gatherer or horticultural societies, was the degree of specialization that existed to meet those fundamental needs. Trade and the specialization it came to entail, Matt Ridley argues, were the precursors of politics. Trade – like warfare – required management, and management generated further specialization and stratification. In time, states emerged as a form of social management. Their elites controlled the production and trade of prestige goods, and they used that control selfishly. It became a demonstration of their power and influence.[42]

Early cities like Çatal Hüyük in Anatolia nearly nine thousand years ago produced a diverse range of commodities, many of which were traded with nearby communities.[43] In northern and southern Mesopotamia, a cluster of highly urbanized societies traded among themselves and conducted long-distance trade with Indus and Egyptian communities, although transportation difficulties made long-distance trade viable only for luxury commodities. Nonetheless these were highly productive cities, whose wealth (like that of Egyptian communities) was based in part on trade and on the technologies they employed – irrigation, the plough, the pottery wheel, wagons, and ships. But by themselves these activities could not sustain economic growth, particularly not in a highly competitive environment with shrinking resources. Consequently the temptation always existed to reach for the conquest card, as Sumer eventually did.

Trade presented a viable alternative to conquest only if it could produce the same result, namely vast profits that demonstrably increased living standards. As Snooks argues, the sudden discovery of new resources could have that effect on societies. Phoenician trade was spurred on by the discovery of precious metals in Spain, that of Athens by its access to the wheat lands of the Black Sea, Persian by its use of the Silk Road, and much later that of Spain by its discovery of gold and silver in the Americas. If these advantages could be monopolized, then even greater profits were possible. If innovations in transport and communications made trade more viable or extended its scope, then so much the better.[44] But in most instances, trade could not sustain economic growth, and interconnections between agricultural societies could just as easily encourage zero–sum strategies that sought plunder or exclusion instead.

Commerce transformed Greece from a land of subsistence farmers into a wealthy community of two hundred cities. Made up of native Pelasgians and their conquerors, the Indo-European Dorians, the Greeks had stripped their environment of its forests for farmland and timbers for ships. As erosion and desiccation set in, trade and colonization became necessary for survival. What made the strategy work initially for Greece was its monopoly of trade within the Aegean Sea, its colonies in West Asia and around the Mediterranean, its navies, and its access to food supplies from the Black Sea and to silver. But the wider environment in which Greece existed threatened all of these advantages. What it possessed, rival traders and conquering states coveted. Eventually it lost access to its colonies in Corsica, Spain and Sicily, and nearly suffered defeat at the hands of Persia in 479 BCE. The danger prompted Athens to transform itself into both a military and an imperialist power. So too Sparta. Sparta had always remained a Dorian state, militaristic and contemptuous of

Athens's cosmopolitanism. In the struggles that followed, the very weakened Greek states fell prey to neighbouring Macedonia in 338 BCE.[45]

The same fate awaited the Phoenicians, whose wealth was based on trade, access to precious metals, and the mass production of luxury goods and cloth. Around its cities hung Assyrian, Babylonian and Persian vultures, which no amount of tribute could keep at bay for long. Eventually its cities were incorporated into Persia and it too fell victim to marauding Macedonians.

Carthage also faced the same difficulty, despite possessing military forces and alliances with Etruscans to protect itself from rivals such as the Greeks. But ultimately nothing could save Carthage from the military might of Rome. Conquering societies and commercial societies could not coexist.[46] Much later the Venetians learned the same lessons.

Venice's wealth initially derived from its commercial dominance of the Adriatic Sea, but it was consolidated massively by the huge profits earned from its monopoly of European trade with Constantinople, bestowed on it by a grateful Byzantine emperor in 1082 CE for helping to defeat the Normans. Similar windfall profits came from its monopoly of trade with the Levant, earned from its involvement with Crusaders thirteen years later. Its role as a trader took off. But its privileged access to markets and trade routes could never be guaranteed, and in the twelfth century Venice faced greater competition from rival Italian cities. In response it hijacked the Fourth Crusade in 1203, which it had underwritten as a commercial venture, and directed it against Constantinople in order to win back its monopoly rights. In addition to seizing many of Byzantium's ports to consolidate its advantage, Venice secured loot that would have satisfied any conquering state. But it still could not guarantee its monopoly access to markets. Indeed, within two hundred years it had again lost its privileged access to West Asia and faced renewed threats from rival trading centres such as Genoa. Like Greece, it tried unsuccessfully to reinvent itself as a conquering state, but simply lacked the size and resources to make an impact on neighbouring countries such as France and Spain or the new eastern Ottoman Empire.[47] Instead it turned to craft production and integrated its economy more fully with its hinterland, a solution which – as we shall see much later – pointed the way to a very different strategic future.

The Technological Impulse

Migration, conquest and commerce represented three common strategies employed by agricultural societies in their self-interested pursuit of security and well-being. Invariably all three strategies were employed in various mixtures, but increasingly societies specialized, always hopeful that the investment they made would pay off massively.

At first this latter feature does not seem at all prominent in the fourth common human strategy, technological innovation. Technological innovation assisted humans through the millennia of hunter–gathering and provided the basis for the new, unstable world of agriculture. Despite its centrality to this process, it remained a poor third to conquest and commerce as a strategy for survival and well-being.

Nonetheless, technology remained immensely valuable. It offered the prospect of sustaining larger populations, harnessing rivers, extending trading capabilities, and transforming fighting capacities. But not until the eighteenth century did it begin to offer societies a new strategy by which to generate windfall profits, without the damaging consequences that always accompanied conquest and commerce, the very zero–sumness that Wright claims always doomed societies that surrendered to it.[48] However, until then, technology tended to act as a supportive strategy only.

The various mixes of strategies employed by agrarian societies derived from and in turn intensified human connectivity, either directly or indirectly, violently or peacefully. One obvious consequence, as Holton concedes, is that it has made our history far more syncretic than we realize. Nothing demonstrates this point more than the way in which technology has consistently diffused, particularly across that most populated part of the world where the lie of the land most assisted diffusion, namely Eurasia. 'No human group could invent by itself more than a small part of its culture and technological heritage', he states, quoting the historian Philip Curtin.[49]

The sociobiologist Robert Wright agrees, but argues that, since the process of innovation is not unique, certain technological breakthroughs were bound to occur anyway. Practical technology always spreads. The more useful an idea, the more likely it is to spread or be reborn. Even communities isolated from the mass of humanity in Afro-Eurasia still underwent technological change. Despite its isolation, says Wright, Central America 'began to resemble a single social brain testing memes and spreading useful ones'.[50] No one community was more capable of technological development than another. Wright cites the example of Eurasian nomads, long dismissed as barbarians. They and their descendants were just as innovative or receptive to technology as anyone else, especially when it came to technology that assisted their desires for conquest; the stirrup, horse archery and the short sword are three obvious examples.[51]

However, as Wright concedes, they at least had the advantage of being able to borrow technology as they saw fit. The Mongols used Chinese iron technology and siege warfare against the very people who developed them. The Chinese invented the harness, which tripled the weight a horse could pull and reduced the reliance of farmers on slower oxen. Without it the north European heavy plough, which transformed old Roman farming practices, might never have come into existence to enable a substantial increase in agricultural productivity.[52] Had Europe not formed part of the Afro-Eurasian landmass, its history would have been vastly different. Communities like those of the Americas were disadvantaged by not being able to draw on the culture and technology of more distant communities, by not being connected.

Writing is a case in point. Wright argues that practicality and diffusion ensured its survival. Yet we have to acknowledge the process's fragility. Writing is such a difficult process to begin that there are only four known independent instances of its development ever recorded: in the Fertile Crescent about 6,000 years ago, in China about 3,500 years ago, in Central America 2,500 years ago, and in Easter Island over 1,000 years ago. Of these four instances, only two have had lasting global significance. All other writing systems developed as a result of diffusion from these sources. It is easier to copy than to start afresh. But in order to imitate, societies have to be sufficiently connected with other peoples to learn of the existence of a thing and to understand its significance. Once again geographical factors affected literacy.

Writing developed long after the rise of agrarian communities because initially it had very limited uses. Technology requires demand to transform invention into innovation. In the Fertile Crescent, in cities such as Tell Hamoukar, the first examples of writing have been found on seals used to mark possessions. Writing was a product of socially stratified societies with highly centralized bureaucratic structures. It was associated with trade and with authority. In Sumer it developed to facilitate trade transactions, to help the state to tax its citizens, and to systematize the application of justice in urban communities. Not unnaturally, scribes occupied very important positions in Mesopotamian society.

Yet it took a long time for the symbols that Sumerians used to evolve into representations of sounds. Once they did, writing's usefulness increased and the practice spread more widely. The Semitic alphabet derived from Sumer and it in turn produced the Arabian, Hebrew, Indian and South-east Asian scripts. Another Sumer derivation spread from Phoenicia to the Greeks and then to the Romans. But even with its spread, writing remained confined to bureaucratic accounts and matters of religion and state propaganda. It was not designed as a tool for creativity or mass communication. Nor was it a tool that drove human history. Writing did not increase the security and wealth of societies, no matter how passionate individuals later became about its creative products.

The agricultural society that came closest to employing technological innovation as a principal strategy was China. Scholars have long criticized China for 'unplugging' itself from the world and contributing to its own backwardness at the very moment that global interconnectedness most demanded greater competitiveness.[53] Yet here was a society that comprised nearly one fifth of humanity, and had managed to overcome the petty squabbles of its warring states and institute a system of governance based on scholars rather than aristocratic warriors. With education and competitive examinations the basis for entry into its civil service, China possessed 'a body of like-minded men who could confidently anticipate and intelligently carry out decisions of superiors because each would have undertaken the same decision himself'.[54]

But China's innovations went far beyond institutional structures. It developed 50,000 kilometres of canal and river networks for transportation, invented paper and many associated technologies – wood-block printing and mobile type. It produced gunpowder and water-powered spinning machines, and cheques to make commerce easier. In many parts of the country, commercialized peasant agriculture enabled some 10 per cent of its population to live in cities of over 100,000 people, the highest rate of urbanization for any agricultural society.

In many respects China was the most successful agricultural society in the world, especially during the Song Dynasty from 960 to 1279 CE. It did not rely on conquest to sustain itself, perhaps – as Snooks suggests – for the simple reason that no rich urban peoples temptingly surrounded it.[55] Instead it focused on internal migration, commerce, and technological change to generate the surpluses required to sustain its large bureaucracy and armies. This was especially the case when Xia Xia and Nizhen tribes robbed the Song of its important northern peasant tax base and forced it to promote southern trade as an alternative tax source.[56]

Too often our view of China is coloured by later events and in particular by the puzzle presented by the most technologically driven society when it fails to anticipate the revolutionary changes occurring at the opposite end of Eurasia. Yet this is a misreading of history. China's failure to initiate an industrial revolution is undeniable, but this should not detract either from China's incredible technological achievements within the agricultural paradigm or indeed from its very significant role in making possible the transition to a much more industrial age.

The signs were already there by the start of the second millennium CE; and what made the difference was China's size. It created a huge market that enjoyed increasing linkages with Japan and South-east Asia. Although distance and physical barriers hindered communications with the bulk of Afro-Eurasia, the size of that market and its specialization in craft production acted as a magnet, even if for much of the time Europe remained only dimly aware of China. But its presence in the markets of West Asia, courtesy of Baghdad Silk Road traders or Arab Indian Ocean fleets, was keenly felt, and made Constantinople and the Levant even more desirable as prizes in the quest for wealth. Trade created the linkages for this embryonic world economy, but China's technology made it possible. Again, a different mix of strategies produced a different result, and again it was one that no connected community could ignore, even after the Black Death and the collapse of the unifying presence of the Mongols ended its brief flowering.[57]

In fact, useful technologies were never ignored and diffusion occurred through trade, espionage, migration and war. Silkworms were smuggled out of China. The Huguenot diaspora took their glass and cloth manufacturing skills and technology with them when they fled persecution in France at the end of the seventeenth century. In 751, warring Arabs captured Chinese paper-making technology. The harder way was painstakingly to replicate existing technology. Europeans spent several centuries attempting to copy Chinese methods for porcelain production.

But technology always had to meet a perceived demand to be successful. Mexicans independently invented the wheel. But without animals, the wheel offered no advantage over human porters, and it was used simply as a toy. Similarly 3,500 years ago words were first printed in Crete using clay type. But without paper and a mass audience, printing had no practical application.[58] It was easier and cheaper to write by hand. And so it remained for 2,500 years, until China independently developed the technique using paper and moving type. David Landes argues that because China did not have an alphabet, printing was used mostly for drawings. China's script, with its thousands of ideographs, did not enable movable type to reduce costs of production and hence raise circulation. Another 600 years would pass before the technique reached Europe. There all the ingredients missing in Crete and China existed: an alphabet, paper, moving type, metallurgy, presses, ink, a growing literate market, and a political need, spurred on by Europe's religious divisions.[59]

The link between invention and innovation is a crucial one for any form of technology. Inventions like the phonograph and the combustion engine in the nineteenth century had no immediate use. Sometimes early models of items such as typewriters, cameras and televisions were just too rudimentary to be useful. Invariably also, inventions were the result of cumulative research going back hundreds of years. Rarely were they the result of genius. Watt's steam engine is an important example, as are Edison's lightbulbs, Morse's telegraph, and the Wright brothers' aeroplane. The same was true of iron ore metallurgy. It grew from thousands of years of human experience with natural outcrops of pure metals, such as copper and gold, capable of being hammered into shape without heating, and thousands of years of simple furnaces making pottery and bronze objects.

Technology develops cumulatively. New technology always requires an advantage over existing technology to be adopted. It must also be compatible with contemporary interests and needs. When typewriters were first invented in the 1870s, they were notorious for jamming. Consequently a cumbersome layout for keys was designed specifically to slow typists down. It was called the QWERTY system, after the first letters on the top row of keys. Once typewriters had improved, all attempts to reform the layout failed. Too many vested interests existed to frustrate the development of an improved keyboard. And so the inefficient QWERTY system remains to this day the industry standard. Transistors offer another example. They were invented by Western Electric but sold to Sony in 1954 because US industry did not want competition with their existing highly profitable vacuum tubes.[60]

Technology can also conflict more fundamentally with social structures. When the Japanese first acquired guns from the Portuguese in 1543, they quickly armed themselves. But firearms were not compatible with the exclusive samurai culture of Japan's feudal elites. And in the hands of non-samurai they threatened class privilege and the whole structure of society. Consequently, guns were banned. For a time, the relative isolation of Japan permitted such a response. Social organization, as well as interconnectivity, plays a role in receptivity to technology.

Chinese technology permitted it to explore the Indian Ocean in the early fifteenth century and contact over thirty countries, including Kenya and Somalia. Between 1405 and 1433, Admiral Zheng He crossed the Indian Ocean seven times, commanding a fleet of 27,000 men and some seventy ships, each ship being 150 metres long and weighing five times the vessels used by the Portuguese later in the century. But expenditure on such expeditions conflicted with the Ming dynasty's more pressing concerns with new Mongol incursions. In addition, China had recently suffered costly setbacks in its military ventures in Vietnam, and had little taste for projecting its power more widely. The development of locks on the Grand Canal made China less reliant on pirate-vulnerable ocean-going ships to transport goods north. Consequently, even expensive navies were now less necessary. In any case, pursuing new possibilities for trade beyond South-east Asia was never high on the Ming's agenda. They were less commercially adventurous than the Mongols and regarded China as principally a continental power. The use of technology for maritime purposes promised few benefits that interested the Ming or justified its huge cost at a time when nomadic movements on China's northern borders posed fresh dangers. China's decision not to focus on international trade was entirely rational, even though in the long term – by creating space for Europeans in Asia – greater human interconnectivity made the strategy counter-productive.[61]

The Agricultural Record

This account of almost ten thousand years of agrarian existence is intended to do no more than highlight features that explain the general thrust of history. Its subject matter has not included all societies; to do so would add little to the picture we have painted. Nonetheless, certain patterns have emerged. All societies are driven to maximize their potential for security and well-being. How they achieve this varies according to circumstance. But all societies share certain characteristics basic to the strategies that they pursue. They imitate what they believe will be successful. At one level that may mean something as simple as farming techniques; at another, writing systems. Where strategies are most successful, in other words where they result in an almost instant rise in wealth and living standards, the effects on whole societies can be overwhelming. Institutions are formed to promote these strategies or to ensure their continuation. This may seem logical enough, but too often, accordingly to Snooks, we tend to argue that the institutions themselves initiate the changes or that the culture a particular society comes to represent shapes the particular mix of strategies it pursues.[62] This is not so.

Rome was a conquering machine whose institutions promoted that goal precisely. Its gladiatorial sports acted out the strategy of conquest before its urban masses, and the sports continued for as long as they remained an effective means of engaging people and engendering confidence in its strategy. According to Griffith, these diversions also became a substitute for war when Augustus demobilized 60 per cent of the Roman army in order to reduce the potential for rebellion against his rule.[63] The Aztecs also practised huge sacrifices of their captives both to symbolize the power of the conqueror and to celebrate the death that yet awaited all warriors. Religion and social practices supported the strategies pursued by the state.[64] If strategies changed, so did the institutions and their practices. When Rome's conquering thrust became exhausted, new religions designed to console in times of uncertainty became prominent, chief among them Christianity, the Persian bull cult of Mithras, and the old Egyptian nature religion of Isis.

Religions are usually bound to the fortunes of states. Rarely do they arise independently. Christianity spread within the Roman Empire, initially on its margins in West Asia and North Africa. Hence it spread among Gothic tribes before they migrated to Europe, and among Roman armies in the east. For lower classes, Christianity presented itself as a mystery cult of the Madonna and Son, but for the military forces its attraction lay instead in the cult of victory inherent in its struggle of good against evil. Not surprisingly, Christianity gained Roman ascendancy only when Constantine courted Christians in order to win military backing for his struggle to become Emperor.

Similarly, Islam spread with the military and later commercial influence of Arabs, but it began as a means to unite fractious Bedouin tribes against domination and exploitation by Persia and Constantinople. Both Christianity and Islam provided cross-cultural networks of shared belief and behaviour not otherwise possible in a preliterate world.[65] To large parts of Eurasia they gave a West Asian patriarchal view of life, born of nomadic struggles against nature and for the loyalty of the tribe.[66] Such associations demonstrated the continued power of regional and class characteristics in relation to geographically expansive religions. Even Confucianism and Buddhism in China became fused with the legalist traditions of nomadic rulers. But they also absorbed the older Daoist forms of nature worship practised by its peasantry. Interconnectivity did not deny indigenization and diversity.

Commercially oriented societies had their own particular mix of institutions and cultures, all serving to maintain and maximize social strategies. Rome had its warrior-based games, but in Greece athletic competitions engendered civic pride and confidence. It is no coincidence that contemporary societies have resurrected their Olympic games; they too seek to engender pride and confidence in non-violent national accomplishments.

There are other contemporary similarities as well. In commercially oriented societies, power tends to be more decentralized than in societies based on militarism. In the case of Greece, this feature has been read as the origin of democracy. But democracy was never possible in an age of patriarchy and slavery, and certainly never became the basis for economic growth that it is today. Our democracy is not based on classical scholarship or precedence, but on the emergence of increasingly democratic economies that responded to the opportunities that interconnectivity presented. If commercially oriented societies such as Greece possessed features that we recognize within our own, it is because they derive from strategic similarity.

Unlike conquering societies which glorified chaos and disorder (our most recent examples of these are the European fascist states of the early twentieth century), commercially oriented societies required order and certainty to maintain business confidence and investment. Their religions and scholarship focused on understanding human desires, rather than glorifying military prowess. They sought to comprehend a fragile world, always delicately balanced between opposing forces: warriors and merchants, civilized and barbarians, west and east. Today both Greece and Venice are particularly remembered for this aspect of intellectual life that their trading strategies made possible. In Venice's case, it produced a great burst of intellectual and artistic creativity that the city's wealth paid for, and which later historians described as a Renaissance, the first in a series of intellectual steps that carried Europe into modernity. Religion also paid homage to the source of social well-being and success. In the annual Wedding of the Sea festival, the Venetian leader, the Doge, married the sea to reinforce publicly the city's dependence on commerce.[67] In much the same way, ancient Mesopotamia celebrated its fertility by annually honouring the sacred marriage of its sky-king and earth-queen in purpose-built ziggurats.[68]

China shared an interest in order. Its tolerance of religions, its development of a very secular code of social behaviour (Confucianism) and its scholarship demonstrated an even stronger emphasis on social stability. No great cultural divide separated China from the rest of humanity, although many Eurocentric histories imply a difference based on inscrutability or size. Certainly, China's experience differed from Europe's or West Asia's, but it also had much in common. A recent study of early science in China, Greece and Babylon by Geoffrey Lloyd, Cambridge professor of ancient philosophy and science, makes exactly this point.

The three societies each possessed high levels of literacy and communication and were able to transmit the work of each generation to the next. Scientists in Babylon and China received state support, and while this always carried the potential to stifle innovation it did not prevent scientific data being collected, particularly in astronomy. In Greece, scientists received no state support. Consequently they sustained themselves as teachers, and had no choice but to endure the lack of security and sustained effort that state support could bring. And although the Greek hothouse of debate ensured high standards of justification, their obsession with proof bordering on certainty inhibited the presentation of many discoveries and their application to areas such as medicine. In the end such obsession undermined not only scientific consensus but also public confidence in scientific inquiry.[69]

We should not assign cultural superiority to any one of these three societies. Nor should we simply dismiss them all as unscientific. Each society possessed significance through the interconnections an increasingly globalized humanity made possible. But science awaited a more technologically driven age in which to make an impact. Until then it could do no more than hint at the potential humans might achieve.

There is one final consequence of agricultural societies that perhaps more dramatically than any other demonstrated humanity's increased global dimension. Jared Diamond recently made it a central feature of his study of human differences. I refer to the second component of his title, *Guns, Germs and Steel*. Many germs flowed directly from the biogeographical factors that encouraged agricultural development in the first place: the axes of the continents and the availability of animals. Many of the diseases that afflict people do so because they are diseases common to animals that humans domesticated. Influenza is perhaps the most common, many of its varieties being associated with chickens and pigs. Some of these strains can be deadly. A flu epidemic in 1918 wiped out 21 million people globally within a matter of months. Measles similarly evolved from cattle, yellow fever from monkeys, and tuberculosis from dogs, cattle and pigs.[70]

The ways in which lifestyle diseases are transmitted vary. Typhoid, dysentery, diarrhoea and cholera are digestive tract disorders transmitted through contaminated foods and water. Smallpox, diphtheria, tuberculosis, measles, influenza, and pneumonic plague are airborne diseases that can be transmitted easily from person to person simply by coughing. Syphilis, venereal diseases and AIDS are sexually transmitted, whereas the plague, typhus and yellow fever require blood transfusions or bites from fleas, lice or mosquitoes for humans to become infected.[71]

Human lifestyles and behaviour certainly influence the transmission of diseases. Farmers often lived and worked with sewage. Not only did this risk infection, but agricultural practices invariably attracted rodents and a host of insects, including mosquitoes. In China, one such disease was the bubonic plague, whose microbes were carried by fleas. Many variables are involved in the creation of epidemics such as those associated with the plague: the size and density of human populations, the mobility and immunity of host rat populations and their distance from humans, and the parasitic intensity of fleas.[72] Variants of the plague had already reached southern Europe and West Asia after 541 CE, but remained largely contained. Eight hundred years later the more interconnected communities of Eurasia presented an entirely different scenario. In the mid-thirteenth century, Mongol armies ended the plague's isolation in Yunnan and Burma; by early in the next century their horses had transported it to the rodent communities of the steppes, leaving in their wake over 12 million Chinese dead. In the 1330s the highly mobile Mongols inadvertently spread it across Eurasia, and used it as a weapon of war in the Crimea in 1346 against the Genoese.[73]

Within five years of its introduction in 1347 into Sicily by Genoese traders infected in West Asia, the bubonic plague had swept through Europe, killing twenty-five million people in the first two years alone. Thereafter it recurred with nightmarish frequency at least once every eleven or thirteen years over the next three centuries. Since nearly everyone who contracted the disease died, immunity could never protect Europe from the scourge, as it did centuries later with smallpox. Why it eventually retreated in the eighteenth century is unknown, but it is likely that improved measures to quarantine ships, to cordon off infected areas, and other public health measures assisted. Improvements in hygiene and living standards may have helped, but other diseases associated with filth and squalor, such as typhus (another Asian import into Europe), survived and flourished.[74]

Many diseases that afflict agricultural societies do so because people live in densely populated communities. They are crowd diseases; they survive only within large populations. An epidemic of measles, for example, could probably not survive in populations under half a million. It requires a constant crop of susceptible children. On the other hand, small communities might be afflicted by diseases such as yellow fever because these diseases are maintained by animal hosts rather than humans, or those such as yaws and leprosy, which are naturally long-living and do not kill their victims quickly. But plague, smallpox, mumps and polio do kill quickly and therefore require substantial host populations in order to survive. Agricultural society provided exactly what they required. It is a problem we still live with today.

Every year at least two previously unknown viruses are identified. These viruses are not necessarily new, but they may be new to humans. Today there are greater opportunities for viruses to jump species as expanding populations clear rainforests and as human communications enable their rapid transmission globally. HIV–AIDS (from monkeys), lassa fever (from rats), ebola (from chimpanzees or bats), equine morbilli (from bats), the chicken flu in Hong Kong in 1997 and the pig virus in Malaysia in 1999: these are but a few recent examples.

Many of these diseases have the potential to become epidemics, all the more so if they are introduced into communities with no immunity. That knowledge has often been used as a weapon by warrior communities against their enemies. Mongols catapulted plague-infected bodies into Caffa to weaken the Genoese defence of their West Asian trading port in 1347. Consequently Europe lost one third of its population (60 per cent of those losses being in north Europe).[75] It took two centuries to recover. When Spanish warriors and settlers entered the Americas at the end of the fifteenth century, the diseases they inadvertently brought with them (especially smallpox, measles, influenza, diphtheria, mumps and TB) very quickly killed 95 per cent of its peoples. The populations never recovered. Hispaniola's Carib population fell from 8 million in 1492 to zero in 1535.[76]

Most of the large concentrations of people within Central America, and to a lesser extent along the Mississippi to the north and the Andes in the south, were probably too recent in formation for crowd diseases to become established among them. In any case, they possessed few domesticated animals. Nonetheless, Spanish soldiers returning from Central America are thought to have brought syphilis and yellow fever back with them, and Europe's endless wars soon saw the former spread rapidly across the subcontinent. In general, isolation and the lack of domesticated animals also made many other peoples susceptible to sudden and dramatic epidemics whenever isolation ended. Hawaii's population fell from half a million to ten thousand by the mid-nineteenth century because of disease. In Fiji, one flu epidemic alone wiped out a quarter of the population in 1875; in Australia, aboriginal peoples similarly suffered huge population losses from diseases in the early nineteenth century. It made confronting the spread of agricultural communities all the more difficult.

Early global transformations bore heavy costs, but in all the instances that we have examined in this chapter the most determining feature has been the interconnectivity of human communities. Today we tend to regard this as a feature of contemporary globalization only, but the records of the past clearly demonstrate its ancient centrality as a motor for human change. From the

Welcome to SOAS
CheckOut Receipt

05/05/08
03:27 pm

The three waves of globalization : a history
of a developing global consciousness/
Robbie Robertson.
1805344267

Due Back By12-05-08

Thank You for using
the 3M SelfCheck System!

fifteenth century, however, interconnectivity began to assume new global forms that generated new pressures for individual societies to respond to.

Notes

1. Stephen K. Sanderson, *Social Transformations: A General Theory of Historical Development*, Oxford, Blackwell, 1995, p. 396.

2. Robert J. Holton, *Globalization and the Nation State*, London, Macmillan, 1998, p. 28.

3. John C. Langdon, *World History and the Eonic Effect: Civilization, Darwinism & the Theory of Evolution*, New York, Xlibris Corporation, 1999, p. 204.

4. Robert Wright, *NONZERO: The Logic of Human Destiny*, New York, Pantheon Books, 2000, p. 146.

5. Ibid., p. 51.

6. Graeme Donald Snooks, *The Ephemeral Civilization: Exploding the Myth of Social Evolution*, London and New York, Routledge, 1997, p. 34.

7. David Held, Anthony McGrew, David Goldblatt and Jonathon Perraton, *Global Transformations: Politics, Economics and Culture*, Oxford: Polity Press, 1999, p. 340.

8. Brian Griffith, *The Gardens of their Dreams: Desertification and Culture in World History*, Nova Scotia, London and New York, Fernwood Publishing and Zed Books, 2001, pp. 62–63; There is some suggestion of a global mini-ice age dramatically reducing rainfall around 2,200 BCE (news.bbc.co.uk, 26 July 2001).

9. David Landes, *The Wealth and Poverty of Nations: Why some are so rich and some are so poor,* London, Little Brown and Co, 1998, pp. 19–21; China sustained a population 30–40 times that of Europe.

10. Ibid., pp. 20–25.

11. Ibid., p. 28.

12. Matt Ridley, *The Origins of Virtue*, London, Viking, 1996, pp. 220–21; David Bellamy, Brian Springett, and Peter Hayden, *Moa's Ark: The Voyage of New Zealand*, Auckland, Viking, 1990, p. 139; see also Jared Diamond, *The Rise and Fall of the Third Chimpanzee*, London, Vintage, 1992, pp. 285–303.

13. Griffith, *The Gardens of their Dreams*, pp. 18–20, 62–3, 67.

14. Ibid., pp. 137–40, 178.

15. Ibid., p. 75.

16. Ibid., pp. 63, 66, 166–70, 75.

17. Jared Diamond, Australian Museum Lecture, Science Show, *Radio National*, abc.net.au, 28 November 2000.

18. Holton, *Globalization and the Nation State*, p. 28. Holton also makes the observation that its books would come to be produced by moveable type invented in China.

19. Diamond, *The Third Chimpanzee*, pp. 225–35, 240.

20. Ibid., p. 229.

21. Roger Moreau, *Rom*, Sydney, University of New South Wales Press, 2000.

22. Griffith, *The Gardens of their Dreams*, p. 246.

23. Diamond, *The Third Chimpanzee*, pp. 147; 245–7.

24. Massimo Livi-Bacci, *The Population of Europe*, Oxford: Blackwell, 2000, p. 27.

25. Griffith, *The Gardens of their Dreams*, pp. 246–50; Diamond, *The Third Chimpanzee*, pp. 242–9.

26. Diamond, *The Third Chimpanzee*, p. 245.

27. Ibid., pp. 141–3.

28. Ibid., p. 283.

29. Ibid., p. 173.

30. William H. McNeill, *The Pursuit of Power: Technology, Armed Forces and Society since AD 1000*, Oxford, Blackwell, 1982, p. 60.

31. Jared Diamond, *Guns, Germs and Steel: The Fates of Human Societies*, London, Jonathan Cape, 1997, pp. 322–3.

32. Ibid., pp. 323–9.

33. Ibid., pp. 336–53.

34. Ibid., pp. 377–89.

35. Griffith, *The Gardens of their Dreams*, pp. 215–19.

36. Graeme Donald Snooks, *The Dynamic Society: Exploring the Sources of Global Change*, London and New York, Routledge, 1996, pp. 272–8.

37. Griffith, *The Gardens of their Dreams*, p. 74.

38. Ibid., pp. 267–70.

39. Ibid., pp. 274–9.

40. Snooks, *Dynamic Society*, pp. 292–9.

41. *Guardian Weekly*, 14–20 September 2000, p. 34.

42. Ridley, *The Origins of Virtue*, p. 202.

43. Snooks, *Dynamic Society*, p. 53.

44. Ibid., pp. 339–44.

45. Snooks, *Ephemeral Civilization*, pp. 210–32; Griffith, *The Gardens of their Dreams*, pp. 256–64.

46. Snooks, *Ephemeral Civilization*, p. 206.

47. Ibid., pp. 239–65.

48. Wright, *NONZERO*, p. 135.

49. Holton, *Globalization and the Nation State*, pp. 27–8.

50. Wright, *NONZERO*, pp. 146, 108, 115.

51. Ibid., pp. 125–8.

52. Ibid., pp. 161, 145.

53. Ibid., p. 163.

54. Robert Elegant, 'Gorfu, Anyone?' *Far Eastern Economic Review (FEER)*, 15 April 1999, pp. 66–70.

55. Snooks, *Dynamic Society*, p. 319.

56. John Fitzpatrick, 'The Middle Kingdom, The Middle Sea and the Geographic Pivot of History', *Review*, Fernand Braudel Center, XV (3: 1992), pp. 499–501.

57. Janet L. Abu-Lughod, *Before European Hegemony: The World System AD 1250–1350*, New York, Oxford University Press, 1989, p. 342.

58. Diamond, *Guns, Germs and Steel*, p. 241.

59. Landes, *The Wealth and Poverty of Nations*, pp. 51–2.

60. Diamond, *Guns, Germs and Steel*, pp. 248–9.

61. McNeill, *The Pursuit of Power*, pp. 46–7; Abu-Lughod, *Before European Hegemony*, p. 342.

62. This is one of Snooks's main points in *Ephemeral Civilization*, but see pp. 25–70 for a detailed discussion of the role of institutions.

63. Griffith, *The Gardens of their Dreams*, p. 273; Snooks, *Ephemeral Civilization*, pp. 167–8.

64. Snooks, *Ephemeral Civilization*, p. 191.

65. Held et al., *Global Transformations*, p. 332.

66. Griffith, *The Gardens of their Dreams*, pp. 77–92.

67. Snooks, *Ephemeral Civilization*, pp. 221–32, 252–65.

68. Griffith, *The Gardens of their Dreams*, pp. 48–9.

69. Geoffrey Lloyd, 'Watching for the eclipse', *Times Literary Supplement (TLS)*, London, 18 February 2000, pp. 3–4.

70. Diamond, *Guns, Germs and Steel*, pp. 195–214.

71. Livi-Bacci, *The Population of Europe*, p. 64.

72. Ibid., p. 71.

73. Abu-Lughod, *Before European Hegemony*, p. 174.

74. Livi-Bacci, *The Population of Europe*, pp. 76–80; see also S.A.M. Adshead, *China in World History*, London, Macmillan, 1995, pp. 148–52; Abu-Lughod, *Before European Hegemony*, p. 94. Europe's population took a long time to recover. Europe had approximately 80 million people in 1340. One hundred years later it had only 50 million.

75. Livi-Bacci, *The Population of Europe*, p. 81.

76. Diamond, *Guns, Germs and Steel*, pp. 210–13.

CHAPTER 4

Fragile Commercial Imperatives

§ DURING the sixteenth century, human societies experienced a fundamental change in the nature of their interconnections. Previously isolated communities suddenly found themselves dangerously exposed to new global forces. Many societies were transformed by the experience; others were enslaved. Many peoples did not survive.

But the first wave of globalization was deeply destabilizing in other ways also. Human interconnectivity on a global scale transformed the global distribution of plants and animals, accelerated population growth, and altered environments. Even its protagonists were unsettled by the sudden wealth that globalization generated. New trading and agricultural classes expanded, but their commercialism also brought to the fore a democratic imperative that had rarely found expression in the past, but which now challenged the interests of old elites.

This was a world that did not understand itself, let alone possess global consciousness. Global interconnectivity presented a means to achieve greater security and well-being, but humans still sought sustainability through exclusion – in particular by class, religion, race, empire, and commercial monopoly. These exclusions generated tensions that brought instability, and eventually doomed the first wave.

Reading Backwards

We have viewed this past with something of the same sense of exclusivity. We have transformed it into a European triumph, and made the year 1500 a divide. It has become a time of so many beginnings; an age of discovery in which Europeans journey to the Americas, pioneer a new sea route to India and to the Spice Islands of South-east Asia, and circumnavigate the world. It is an age that lays the European foundations of modern global trade and finance, and enables science and reason to flourish. It is also an age of global European empires and the start of new global systems of production.

In short, the first wave of globalization foreshadowed the superiority that

Europe would demonstrate with such dazzling effect in the centuries to come. A resurgent Europe, fully recovered from the disasters that followed the break-up of the Roman Empire nearly a millennium before, and newly invigorated by the cultural achievements of the Renaissance, broke from its feudal strait-jacket, strutted the world stage as a new capitalist force, and formed a world economy around itself.

Here lies the origin of so many of the problems confronting contemporary global analysis. It takes as its starting point the inevitability of a Western-dominated present and traces its roots accordingly. It reads history backwards and assumes the mantle of the modernist prophet. It takes for granted that the origins of contemporary globalization are to be found within Europe, that those origins are based on European exceptionalism – the demise of feudalism, the creation of capitalism and nation states, and the development of global trading networks. In this exceptionalism, we are told, lies the real significance of the first wave of globalization.

There is nothing particularly new in this approach. The nineteenth-century philosopher Karl Marx gave weight to the early maturity of Western Europe's bourgeois classes and their ability to strike a blow against the tyranny of feudalism. In the end, Marx argued, feudalism simply collapsed under the weight of its own internal contradictions. The demand by lords for status, often in the form of luxury goods, required money, which meant pressuring peasants to produce more surplus. Sometimes peasants rebelled or sought sanctuary in the increasingly independent towns that expanded as long-distance trade flourished. Only across the rest of Eurasia did 'oriental' despotism continue to hold sway.

World Systems theorists such as Immanuel Wallerstein argue that because feudalism was unable to generate the kind of wealth now expected by its upper classes, nobles were increasingly disposed to compensate by adopting labour-saving or more productive agricultural techniques. In this sense they under-mined their own existence. They were also inclined, in the case of Europe, to look to expansion abroad to acquire additional wealth, especially once internal expansion faltered in the fourteenth century, and changing weather patterns, depleted soils, and epidemics ravaged the continent.[1] Thus European feudalism fell and capitalism expanded, its trading networks eventually globalizing.

David Landes approaches from another angle. In Europe, the conditions for transition were initially laid by the collapse of Rome's authority over the subcontinent after 500 CE. The result was political fragmentation. Even five hundred years later, Europe remained divided into one thousand or more different principalities, their isolation and fragmentation reinforced by Europe's continued vulnerability to nomadic attacks – Norse incursions from the north, Arab invasions from the south, and Magyar (Hungarian) attacks from the east. From this insecurity arose feudal society.[2]

With subcontinental communication networks collapsing, and new post-Roman identities and allegiances coalescing with intense insecurity, periodic efforts to resurrect Roman-type unity, most notably through the chief surviving institution of the late Empire, the Roman Catholic Church, failed. The power of the Church frustrated the emergence of empire in the twelfth century, but was never strong enough itself to provide an alternative.[3] Even Christianity fragmented as it transformed itself into a popular religion with texts translated into vernacular languages.

Feudalism undermined conformity. Certainly its fractured, decentralized noble and regal authorities undermined the assertion of Papal interests. But it also created an environment in which emerging trading towns could win political and economic concessions and transform themselves into self-governing centres.

Decentralization, says Landes, created 'room for multiple initiatives from below as well as above'. During the relative peace from external aggression that Europe enjoyed after the eleventh century, decentralization served Europe well. It assisted adjustment to the devastation wrought by the disastrous Black Death during and after the mid-fourteenth century. In essence, multiple centres of authority and influence enabled multiple initiatives, and from that wider range of experiences, something different began to emerge.[4]

Farming became more intensive, productive and co-operative. A new German plough made it possible for the first time to farm heavy clay soils using dray horses for power. A three-fold system of crop rotation increased food production by one third, and allowed greater herds of livestock, which in turn helped to make soils more fertile and productive. Forests too were cleared and land was reclaimed; the windmill became a technologically important innovation for farming otherwise unproductive lands.[5]

Urban centres provided the intellectual and political basis for change, but their significance lay also in the linkages they forged with rural communities. Landes considers this important. Trade alone did not account for the rise of capitalism. Most early trade concerned luxury goods and was insufficiently connected with domestic economies to have a dramatic impact on them,[6] although some analysts believe that such trade at least provided a basis from which expansion could begin.[7]

Certainly more people became dependent on markets for food and clothing, and on non-agricultural employment. Often rural and urban labour competed for employment opportunities. In England during the fifteenth century, half the woollen cloth produced came from private homes in small rural villages. Landes cites this as an example of how changes occurred from below as well as from above. It enabled a mercantile class to manipulate different centres of authority and to prosper.[8]

One of the more common explanations for the collapse of feudalism is the demographic one. Part of this we have already rehearsed. As Europe's population grew after the start of the first millennium CE, more marginal land came into production and yields declined. Famines and diseases during the late thirteenth and fourteenth centuries contributed to a dramatic decline in labour and production. One solution was capitalist agriculture, emphasising efficiency rather than subsistence techniques. Peasants either became waged farm labourers or were empowered by the scarcity of employment to migrate to towns. Either way, feudalism faltered. According to this argument, what most stimulated capitalism was underpopulation.

Sanderson believes population to be significant only with regard to urban growth. Urbanization created large pools of workers, enabled further economic specialization, and increased the size of markets available to traders. But he also argues that the countries that eventually made the transition from feudalism to capitalism were all relatively small, and did not require the same scale of resources to manage as did large empires like China. Empires tended to stifle trade because traders ultimately threatened the monopoly that rulers enjoyed to exact tribute from subjects. The decentralized structures of England and the Netherlands made it harder for any one authority to contain merchants; in fact, rivalry between different authorities created a niche that merchants could exploit. Eventually, Sanderson claims, commercialization achieved a critical density, in that enough people were profiting from it to ensure that it kept going. In essence, once urban networks and trade densities became extensive, commercialization could not be stopped.[9]

Both Landes and Sanderson see significance in the fact that the first 'capitalist' nations were maritime countries. Trade by sea was always easier than trade over land. Nations rose to prominence by monopolizing small seas. Greece monopolized the Aegean, Venice the Adriatic, and the Netherlands the North Sea. Yet not all maritime nations benefited, and among those that did, advantage was not always sustained. Other factors were also involved, as we saw earlier in the cases of Greece and Venice, but these have little to do with Landes's and Sanderson's suggestion that temperate climates also influenced capitalist development.[10]

Another very different explanation for change came from the sociologist Max Weber in 1904. He claimed that capitalism was a unique West European phenomenon that benefited immensely from entrepreneurial skills promoted by sixteenth-century Protestantism. Protestant individualism combined with urbanization, free wage labour, and the emergence of rational, legal states to end feudalism. But does this extremely influential theory, now referred to as the Protestant Ethic, accord with the evidence? Wallerstein believes that the link between Protestantism and capitalism is accidental; it arose from the fact that the Counter-reformation, the Roman Catholic Church's attempt to roll back the expansion of nationally based dissident churches, failed in several places where capitalism coincidentally triumphed. In northern France, the Low Countries, southern German states and Switzerland, Protestants were disproportionately represented in trade, banking and finance. But in England, dissenters rather than orthodox Protestants were more important.[11]

Weber's argument leaves unanswered a number of important questions. First, does capitalism reflect Calvinist values? Frugality, hard work and sobriety might assist capitalist endeavours, but capitalism is also endowed with the spirit of adventure, risk and speculation. Much of the wealth it generates goes into conspicuous displays of status and power, including country estates.

Second, the involvement of particular communities in capitalist activities hints not at the importance of any one particular faith but at the role of outsiders and migrants in fostering new attitudes to work and wealth generation. Migrants lack the encumbrances of local obligations and ties; they also lack the security that those ties provide. The common feature then might be not a Protestant ethic but social tolerance, openness, and interconnectedness.

Certainly the Counter-Reformation caused closure and censure. Whether intended or not, it sometimes produced societies dedicated to conformity rather than knowledge. On the Iberian peninsula, books were banned. Students were forbidden to study abroad. The Roman Catholic Church took four hundred years to forgive Galileo for questioning its view of the universe. Meanwhile dynamic market centres such as Sicily declined rapidly after Rome forced them to expel Jewish traders. Spain expelled 90,000 Jews after 1492 and 310,000 Muslims (Moriscos) in 1609. Some 150,000 Protestants (Huguenots) fled French persecution after 1685.[12] They took their skills and networks to the Low Countries and England.

Third, as we noted in Chapter 3, religions do not drive society; they reflect the state of society. In Britain, Henry VIII's move against the established church reflected the desire of the middle classes for a less hierarchical and feudal church, and for a religion that provided them with assurances against the uncertainties that the old order represented. Religion changed in response to the strengthening of commercialism; it did not drive capitalism or cause its emergence.[13]

Weber himself remained uncertain as to whether his Protestant ethic did explain anything, and later he stressed instead the development of nation states as a pre-eminent cause of capitalism. Today this remains a more common explanation for Europe's exceptionalism. In England's case, Robert Holton centres the rise of the nation state on its mid-seventeenth-century civil war. Parliament's struggle against the crown ended any potential drift back to despotism, and enabled England to establish a constitutional monarchy and give fiscal control to its parliament. This, Holton believes, created a post-feudal structure conducive to capitalism.[14] It enabled a process of national integration that saw authority centralized within increasingly bureaucratic but more diverse structures than existed previously. Holton does not suggest that any particular type of nation state is important. England happened to become a constitutional monarchy; Prussia – also a successful innovator – remained avowedly absolutist. The key lay in state centralization and rational political coherence.

It is in the setting of fiscally secure centralized states that the role of agriculture assumes more importance. Landowners wanted to preserve their estates, and their power and status. Agriculture was still a critical source of capital and labour during the sixteenth and seventeenth centuries, and rural communities were important markets for commodities. In contrast, cities were often hostages to the fortunes of agriculture. Rising food prices or harvest failures could produce massive urban crises.

Holton argues that just as there was no one model of state development in Europe, so there was no one model of agricultural change. In France, the state secured property rights for its peasants, and created a vast peasant population scratching a living from small plots of land. Food production remained inefficient and peasants had no incentive to end their subsistence mode and enter the market, become wage labourers, or form a home market that could become the initial basis for expanding consumer production. The French nobility, deprived of land as a source of wealth, depended instead on state offices for income.[15]

In Britain it was very different. The landed aristocracy and gentry dispossessed the country's small peasants, enclosed land, introduced improvements, developed mineral resources and rural manufacturing, and invested in roads and canals. They became agrarian capitalists, and transformed the British countryside into a market for pottery and textiles, and a source of wage labour. Much the same thing happened in Prussia.

Exceptionalism Denied

These theories accept at face value that the origins of change occurred in Western Europe, that here we find the first rumblings of capitalism and democracy, and that what happens in Western Europe matters most. Other theories are more measured; certainly Landes and Sanderson concede that Japan contradicts the concept of European exceptionalism. Its demographic patterns could not have been more different from Europe's. Instead of declining and stagnating, Japan's population doubled to 18 million between the twelfth and sixteenth centuries; by 1750 it stood at 30 million. No relative shift in power to peasants occurred, as population theorists claimed in the case of feudal Europe, and yet Japan's agriculture commercialized.

Japan's feudal structures were also transformed, though in a very different way. As imperial rule fractured in the twelfth century, assisted by the country's fragmented geography and the growing authority of its local warlords (*daimyos*), Japan was ravaged by civil war. These wars ended at the start of the seventeenth century, when an alliance of warlords backed a powerful military commander (the Tokugawa Shogun), who set in place a system of government that promoted greater national coherence. Military power became the preserve of a samurai elite, and an elaborate system of governance reduced the influence of competing *daimyos*. The Alternative Attendance System forced all *daimyos* or their families to spend time in the capital, Edo (Tokyo), effectively as hostages. This extremely expensive undertaking dramatically increased *daimyo* costs and spurred the commercialization of agriculture and the growth of trade. Even at the start of the Tokugawa shogunate, exports comprised 10 per cent of Japan's GDP. In the following decades, Japan expanded its trade in silver and copper, and sent increasing quantities of tea, rice, camphor, *sake*, lacquer and furniture into South-east Asia and China. In the wake of this expansion came national road networks and a wealthy class of merchants and financiers. With as many as 15 per cent of its people living in cities, and with Osaka, Kyoto and Edo holding over one million residents each, Japan was as urbanized as north-western Europe at the end of the eighteenth century.[16]

Globalization has always been much more than the story of Europe writ large. Europe did change and for many of the reasons quoted above. But it was not Europe's uniqueness that gave it advantage. Two factors most stand out. First, its connectedness – the nature and consequences of its linkages to the rest of the world; second, the ability of some of its polities to subsume conquest to commercial goals and transform class relations as a consequence. In this regard, two countries stand out – England and the Netherlands.

The speed of their transformation lends weight to the idea of newness. Here were countries that seemed suddenly to have greatness thrust upon them. Like Greece and Venice before them, they experienced the rush of rapid success and used the wealth they generated to remake their societies and create dazzling cultures that resonated long after the rush had passed. But we tend to forget that, like their predecessors, these new commercial nations faced the same constraints. Commerce was a zero–sum strategy. It depended on new markets to survive. And success always risked provoking the descent of conquering vultures.

We tend to forget these constraints because – reading history backwards – we know that England later successfully transformed its dominant strategy into an industrial one. But this outcome was by no means ordained. Let us briefly revisit Europe in the years before the sixteenth century to remind ourselves of those constraints.

Like the entire world, Europe operated within the same paradigm that Neolithic agriculturists had begun ten thousand years before. Much had happened in those ten thousand years. Agricultural technology itself had improved. It supported much larger populations, but living standards were not significantly higher than they had been during Roman times. Average life expectancy still fluctuated between twenty-five and thirty-five years; indeed during periods of pestilence and war it struggled to exceed twenty years.[17] Only during the nineteenth century would advances brought by industrial technology allow life expectancy to exceed forty years. Until then the agrarian age ruled and all societies confronted the same paradigm constraints.

Nearly two thirds of England's feudal economy at the start of the second millennium CE was based on subsistence farming.[18] The market economy dominated the rest, spurred on by the overwhelming need of England's fractious warrior lords for cash. They had taxes to pay to their king. They had armies, estates, and lifestyles to maintain. Consequently they produced for the North Sea market, shipping textiles, wool, metals, salt and horses to Scandinavia, Flanders and southern Europe. If new technologies helped to increase the surpluses they could gain from their estates, they were adopted. Over the next five hundred years a constant process of small but significant improvements occurred, involving the heavy plough, waterwheels, windmills, horseshoes, stirrups and horse harnesses. Forests were cleared, marshes drained, fertilisers applied and the three-field rotation system was adopted. But as far as England's warrior lords were concerned, these commercial and technological strategies were never ends in themselves.

In Europe conquest was the norm. The Normans had invaded England in 1066, and subsequently Sicily and Italy. In the following centuries the crusading lust diverted many of Europe's warring adventurers eastward into West Asia. In each instance the goal was the same: wealth, with the wealth of victors quickly becoming the target for new generations of aspirants. Europe was littered with the remnants of such ambitions. Not surprisingly, its leaders were quick to invest in technologies that gave them an edge in warfare: in the fourteenth century, pikes and longbows; in the fifteenth century, cannon. They were also quick to reorganize their economies in order to pay for such technologies.

In any conquering strategy, the quality of leadership is crucial. Nothing beats failure for testing loyalties and creating scope for division, as England's King John discovered when he imposed new taxes to raise an army that he hoped would recover the Norman territories he had lost in France owing to his own incompetence. At Runnymede in 1215 his nobles imposed conditions on their support. After 1258, John's lacklustre successors confronted a more disciplined council of barons keen to exercise greater control over their expenses. By 1295 this council had become a model parliament, which soon also incorporated a commons of other important taxpayers: traders and gentry.

But the conquering strategy remained. If anything, declining trade and the plague in the fourteenth century increased its attractiveness. Indeed, for over one hundred years English monarchs continued to seek their fortunes in

France, for a time with success. By 1360 they controlled one third of France and reaped huge profits, including a massive ransom for releasing a captured French king. But the social costs of war were high too: it disrupted trade; living standards fell; taxes rose. When subsequent kings again lost their French possessions and sought to regain them with fresh injections of capital and soldiers, English peasants revolted (in 1381) against the hardships that the taxes imposed. Success at Agincourt in 1415, and the capture of Paris in 1420, proved fleeting. By 1453, the English had been driven back to Calais, and the divisions that this failure created among its warrior nobles lasted for decades, until the Tudors seized power in 1485.

The Tudors eventually abandoned the conquering strategy. They turned instead on the old feudal aristocracy and church, and confiscated their wealth and lands. With the ravages of war and plague dissipating in Europe, commerce again appeared to offer better certainties. The Baltic grain trade had revived. So too North Sea trade. The Dutch prospered. The revival of Central European silver and copper trade whetted European appetites for consumer expansion after more than a century of decline. The Tudors saw new opportunities for wealth generation. So did the gentry and yeoman farmers on whom they now relied for support.[19] Elizabeth I consolidated the shift, doubling the size of the Commons to 600 and reducing the Lords by one third to a mere 40 members.[20]

What caused England to change? Certainly not technological innovation. Technology changed, but its goal had been to make more sustainable England's strategy as a conqueror. Certainly not its drift to nation state status. That was simply the outcome of England's need to rationalize the way in which it operated as a conquering state. Certainly not power sharing. Nobles had always exercised power, and rulers had always consulted councils of nobles.

Undoubtedly failure weakened the position of kings *vis-à-vis* nobles, but the growing importance of commerce dictated a change in the nature of decision-making bodies, as it had in Greece and Venice. These changes neither heralded the inevitability of deeper democracy in the future, nor determined the sustainability of commerce as a strategy. But they did ensure a wider class basis for decision making, and property laws that sustained class autonomy and created greater scope for private security and well-being. In the long run these changes had consequences not only for Britain's traditional rulers but also for the uses to which Britain's new-found wealth would be put.

Nonetheless, the same desires drove the English in the sixteenth century as 500 years before: the lure of massive profits to secure survival and well-being. What now also differed, however, were the opportunities to secure those desires. In the past England had tried to satisfy them by continental expansion. But Europe's states were too evenly matched for easy conquest and sustained profits.[21] Empowered traders and gentry were eager for alternatives. In 1492, the Genoan Christopher Columbus provided the model.

With Spanish backing, Columbus set out to find a way across the Atlantic to reach directly the products of eastern Asia. Since the Mongols had disrupted Genoan access through the Black Sea as well as Baghdad's Levant connection, Venice virtually monopolized this trade with Arabs in Cairo.[22] Columbus believed that he could create an alternative route to Asia, and thereby destroy Venice's monopoly. But instead of reaching the Orient, Columbus found the Americas. Six years later, driven by fear of Spanish advantage, the Portuguese explored the possibility of their own route to the East; Vasco da Gama rounded Africa and opened up the vast Indian Ocean to European adventurers. The first wave of globalization had begun.

The Lure of Riches

'If you look only under the European street light you won't see much beyond Europe', political economist Andre Gunder Frank remarks. 'It confines us to parochialism'.[23]

It is ironical that many of the theories produced today to explain the first wave of globalization routinely exclude reference to what is being interconnected. To the historian Fernand Braudel, Europe simply created its own world around itself.[24] But Europeans in the sixteenth century had no world-view to confirm, as later analysts do. They saw the potential that globalization offered and seized it. Despite all Europe's achievements – and they were considerable – nothing they possessed compared with the scale of the networks they now found laid before them. They needed to link into them and, if possible, control them. Wealth provided the motivation, and from its realization flowed cultural achievements that again demonstrated the timeless human capacity to respond creatively whenever so empowered. From the Dutch arose the image of comfortable bourgeois townhouse domesticity;[25] from the English, Queen Bess and Shakespeare. During the sixteenth century, England's per capita GDP rose 1.2 per cent per annum, compared with 0.6 per cent during its last period of significant growth, 1000–1200. Its living standards now exceeded those of Augustan Rome; by 1700 twice over. By 1650, England's 5.5 million people were nearly three times as prosperous as they had been in 1300.[26] But such wealth also generated envy, and old conquering ambitions were easily revived within Europe. The first wave of globalization was deeply unsettling.

Europeans had long sensed the potential that Greater Asia offered. But until the sixteenth century their connections had been limited to West Asia. Despite intermittent access difficulties, profits and demand for Asian products sustained the trade and had a powerful influence on the well-being of the entire European region. This was true also for much of Afro-Eurasia, even if members of its main regions were not conscious of it. The largest region was China. Despite being the despotic empire of later analysts, China's economic influence lay in the fact that it was the world's first large nation, in which nearly one fifth of humanity conducted commerce without the kinds of barrier that beset Europe. China flourished under the Song Dynasty; so too the regions it traded with. It is probably no coincidence that Europe's long expansion at the start of the second millennium CE coincided with the fortunes of the Song. Nor that its decline in the fourteenth and fifteenth centuries reflected the disruptions that Mongols and disease caused to China and its Eurasian linkages. A similar decline in the mid-seventeenth century also reflected the difficulties that China experienced as the new Manchu Qing dynasty extended its control over the country after 1644.[27]

It is Gunder Frank's contention that long before the sixteenth century a nascent Afro-Eurasian economy existed. Traders moved goods from one region to another, often organizing themselves into guilds to assist their activities. Across Asia remittance banks, money shops, credit and insurance facilities thrived. Strong town–country relations existed, regions specialized in production for intra-country and international trade, and international networks grew.[28] Maritime trade around Senegal and East Africa complemented and stimulated internal African trade. Ivory, gold and silver were exchanged for Indian textiles and grain, Arabic earthenware and Chinese porcelain. Admiral Zheng He's voyages around the Indian Ocean in the early fifteenth century all included East African ports such as Mogadishu and Zanzibar. Gold and silver also travelled from West Africa, the Balkans, Egypt, and Syria, much of it ending up in China, the only country in the world then running a constant trade surplus. Marco Polo had tried to awaken a European 'sense of wonder'[29] in the distant world in which he had moved at the end of the thirteenth century, where north Chinese trade alone was ten to fifteen times greater than Europe's thriving Baltic trade.[30] But even if Europe had been able to access China directly, it had nothing to exchange for the commodities it wanted. Until it did, Europe had no choice but to rely on the intersection of regional trade networks.

Only the discovery of silver and gold in the Americas provided Europe with the means to plug directly into the huge Asian economy and transform the intersecting regional trade networks into global networks. Never before had people at the end of the trade chain of regions been able go directly to the source. But once merchants had globalized their activities in this way, nothing stayed the same: not the societies providing the much-needed raw materials, not the traders and societies now excluded from the new trading deals, and certainly not those communities that once provided goods for exchange at different points along the trade chain. Everything was forever changed. Not surprisingly, in the intense competition that this new round of globalization generated, confusion reigned. There were no international rules of engagement.

The sudden wealth that America and Asian trade provided drove Europe out of recession and produced the basis on which commercialism could again thrive. Internal reforms could never have generated similar wealth. In 1600, Portugal exported from Brazil sugar worth twice the value of all Britain's exports. Handled correctly, this tremendous expansion in commercial activity could have a multiplier effect within economies and promote new oppor-tunities for growth. But this was not a universal outcome.

Spain at the end of the fifteenth century had only recently divested itself of Muslim control, and the result, according to Landes, was a warlike society whose energies had to be directed externally to prevent self-destruction.[31] Columbus's discovery of the Americas proved fortunate. Spain was keen to go west to grow sugar cane, for which a large market already existed. The Americas now offered a different range of possibilities. With no indigenous labour left in the Caribbean owing to colonization and disease, and no gold to maintain interest, the Spanish abandoned the Caribbean for cattle farms on the mainland and set about plundering Mexico and Peru for gold and silver. Consequently the French, Portuguese, Dutch and English filled the void and began farming sugar on the islands. Because they lacked the labour and the technology for intensive agriculture, they turned instead to slavery. Over the next three centuries, ten million slaves were bought in West Africa and shipped across the Atlantic. The kind of societies that slavery produced were harsh and unforgiving. Since slaves died faster than they could reproduce, the trade flourished and became part of a vast triangular trade involving the production of goods to exchange for slaves, and the production of raw sugar for export to Europe for refining and sale. Soon coffee, cotton and cocoa joined the trade, and Britain and France established new plantation and trading colonies in North America. This new, regionally integrated system of transatlantic trade stimulated European craft manufacturing and agriculture, particularly in England.

The Spanish decision to abandon the Caribbean benefited others. Spain made other mistakes also. Massive wealth flowed through Spain because of its conquests, but Spain did not use it productively. Instead it was squandered on war and luxuries. Spain, says Landes, 'was a poor school for patience and hard work, partly because the crafts and tasks of industry and agriculture were long associated with despised minorities such as Jews and Muslims'.[32] Once the inflow of bullion had dried up, Spain had nothing to replace it with. It had bought products from England and the Netherlands rather than learn how to produce those products itself. It had exported its bullion to north-west Europe for manufactured goods, to the Baltic for furs, and to Asia for the luxuries it could now afford. Easy money made for short-term gains, but produced little on which future growth (except English and Dutch growth) could be based.

Spain was not the only nation that sought to globalize previously regional trade networks for its own benefit. In the fifteenth century, Portugal had a small population of some one million people producing mostly wine and sugar cane. For a trading empire, it looked east, and in particular to strategic locations such as Goa in India, where it hoped to control the spice trade. In a world that was still dependent on marginal subsistence, spices were ideal for preserving food. Because Europe was unable to grow sufficient food to feed all its animals over the long winter months, Europeans habitually slaughtered a large proportion of their herds at the beginning of winter, and stored the meat as best they could. Spices helped to overcome the taste and odour of spoilage; often they also weakened viruses and bacteria.

Consequently the trade in spices was immensely profitable. Nutmeg bought in the East Indies rose in value 1,000 per cent by the time it hit European markets. During Elizabethan times, £1-worth of nutmeg in the East Indies fetched £60,000 in London. It was so valuable that crews unloading ships were made to wear canvas clothing with no pockets.[33] No wonder the Portuguese grabbed Goa and the 40 per cent of the spice trade they believed it represented. But ambition did not always pay, particularly when it intersected with intolerance. Landes claims that Portugal initially prospered because of tolerance. Its people intermarried with foreigners, and they were prepared to learn from them. This openness served them well in the fifteenth century.

But after 1497 Portugal came under great pressure from Rome and Spain to be less tolerant, and the effects of their new-found intolerance were profound. First, they introduced anti-Jewish pogroms, which eventually caused the departure of most Portuguese Jews. With them went their wealth, skills and knowledge; all Portugal was impoverished. Landes comments: 'in matters of intolerance, the persecutor's greatest loss is self-inflicted. It is this process of self-diminution that gives persecution its durability, that makes it – not the event of the moment or of the reign – but of lifetimes and centuries'.[34] Portugal became more inward-looking. It failed to send its students abroad. It discouraged originality, with disastrous consequences for its science and economy. Agriculture and industry stagnated. Only the church grew wealthy. Because of Portugal's self-imposed closure, it lost competence in areas that it once dominated.

Second, emboldened by religious bigotry, the Portuguese determined to replace the Arabs as the main spice traders in the rich market port of Malacca, which the Chinese had originally founded on the Malay coast in 1403. Malacca was a truly multicultural trading centre, with over 84 different communities represented. But its attraction for the Portuguese lay in the cost of its spices – one third of the price for which they could be purchased in India. When Alfonso de Albuquerque seized Malacca in 1511, he drove out its Islamic traders, much to the delight of neighbouring cities eager for their business. In addition, he looted the city of some sixty tons of gold and carried away over two hundred chests of diamonds and rubies. But the Portuguese reaped no short-term benefit. Albuquerque's ship sank off the coast of Sumatra. 'By the time the city fell to the Dutch [in 1641], only a few thousand inhabitants remained', Simon Elegant writes. 'The Portuguese strangled their golden goose almost as soon as they had gained it'.[35]

Portugal never monopolized the pepper trade as it had hoped. Most of the trade still journeyed across the Indian Ocean or overland into West Asia. Most Portuguese profits came instead from tolls or from its role in brokering Japanese trade with China.[36] The Portuguese experience mirrored that of other European nations as they struggled to insert themselves into the vast and profitable intra-Asian trade. Chinese vessels continued to dominate trade into southern China at the end of the seventeenth century, carrying two hundred thousand tons of goods compared with five hundred tons on European ships. It took nearly another century before European ships began to equal Chinese tonnage.[37]

Europe's expansion was not planned. It was haphazard, uneven and opportunistic. It possessed no goal other than the acquisition of wealth. If it can be argued that vastly increased trading networks helped to produce future industrial societies, it was certainly not something foreseen by European nations. Indeed, although we continue to talk about Europe, Europe at this time is really a figment of the imagination. There existed no European unity, certainly not in terms of responses to opportunities; no one model of development that would allow us to say, 'this is the European way'. Such lack of unity provided some European capitalists with an advantage over many of their Eurasian colleagues. It enabled greater geographic mobility and risk-taking.

The Commercial Strategy

The Netherlands proved the point. A small state of thirty cities, the Netherlands had ended the fifteenth century dominating the North Sea trade and specializing in land reclamation, windmills, brewing, sugar refining, and wood technology. By the mid-seventeenth century it had gained its independence from Spain and nearly doubled its population to just under two million people. Its trading networks were global. It traded Baltic grain, naval stores, and English cloth for oil, and fruits and silks from the Mediterranean for sugar from the Americas and spices from the East. In addition it created a vast East India trading company (VOC, to use the Dutch acronym), which set out to replace the Portuguese and to dominate the Spice Islands in South-east Asia. It succeeded, but also established factories in east India, Ceylon and Taiwan, and traded successfully with Japan. For many years the VOC posted annual dividends of 18 per cent.

Like the Portuguese before them, the Dutch needed tradable commodities if they wished to insert themselves into the profitable intra-Asian trade. Japan was crucial in this regard. Japanese silver bought Indian cloth with which to purchase spices, much of which were sold in Europe. But spices and silver also helped to secure Chinese goods and gold, and Chinese goods were the lure for Japanese silver. The VOC Director Jan Pieterszon Coen boasted in 1619, 'All [this] can be done without any money from the Netherlands and with ships alone'.[38]

From this base, a financial empire followed and Amsterdam soon became the financial centre for Europe. The Netherlands was not a democratic society, but it was a tolerant one, and its tolerance attracted people with skills and money who were elsewhere persecuted because they were Protestant or Jewish, or who simply wished to escape war. Many merchants fled north when the Spanish sacked Antwerp in 1576. In Europe, political disunity gave capital a mobility that it did not always enjoy elsewhere in Eurasia. It could relocate to cheaper and safer environments.[39] In many respects, tolerance was simply a practical strategy for survival in a land where so many people of different faiths and backgrounds lived. Having survived the centralizing dictates of the Spanish, the Dutch had no wish to inflict the same on their own people. But their ability to get larger neighbours to accept this proposition was less successful.

England, too, was a small nation, although larger than the Netherlands and with a population of five million by 1500. It thrived on the new markets generated by American money surging through Europe. For the moment its conquering tradition was successfully redeployed by the state against Spanish, Dutch and French commercial rivals. It targeted the convoys of bullion that crossed the Atlantic to Spain or which journeyed across the Pacific to Manila. Sir Francis Drake returned in 1580 from circumnavigating the world with over £1 million-worth of captured Spanish treasure, rewarding his investors with a dividend of 4,700 per cent.[40] In 1592, England captured a huge Portuguese ship laden with some £1.5 million-worth of treasure, equivalent to half the money then held by England's exchequer.

England was fixated with the wealth of its neighbours and determined to establish its own commercial empire. It established a merchant navy to rival the Dutch and, using loot derived from the activities of its state-sponsored pirates, set up trading companies to target the Baltic, the Levant, Africa, the East Indies and North America. Colonies were also established in North America and the Caribbean, and trading centres founded in India. If anything, English traders were determined, and they had the full weight of their state behind them. In the mid-seventeenth century the state formally permitted its own traders to monopolize trade with its colonies. The state assisted in other ways also.

In 1616 the English captured one of the Banda islands, the sole source of nutmeg. But it brought them little profit, because the Dutch blockaded the island. In 1623 the Dutch launched an offensive which wiped out the small English population on nearby Ambon. The English government protested strongly at Dutch tactics. A face-saving solution was sought. The Dutch desperately wanted to retain the Banda islands and their nutmeg monopoly, and agreed to hand over insignificant New Amsterdam in North America as compensation. New Amsterdam we know today as New York. The English handed back Banda island, but they also smuggled out the nutmeg plant. Thus they both broke the Dutch spice monopoly and gained New York.[41]

However, England's immediate ambitions lay elsewhere. In the late sixteenth century the subcontinent of India possessed over one hundred million people. By 1750 its population had grown to 160 million. In the north, the cities of Agra, Delhi and Lahore each possessed over 500,000 inhabitants. India thrived on the increased trade generated by the first wave of globalization, enjoying a trade surplus with Europe, Africa, and West Asia. Only to China and South-east Asia did silver, cotton and other export commodities flow to cover deficits.

India's prosperity had expanded under the Mughals; it became more urbanized and commercialized. Trade networks extended deep into the countryside. Centres traded among themselves, with the most productive regions being Gujarat, Malabar, Coromandel and Bengal. Fifteen per cent of the British East India Company's imports came from Bengal in 1670, 66 per cent in 1740. Until the 1770s, Bengal was a major supplier of food to the rest of India.[42]

India excelled in the craft production of textiles. Flexible systems of organization, low production and food costs, and a long history of cotton production enabled it to dominate world cotton markets.[43] With Europe alone, India had a thriving trade in silks and textiles worth an annual £800,000 in silver by 1700. This trade increased phenomenally during the eighteenth century, and by 1800 Britain imported annually £26 million-worth of goods.[44]

The British certainly wished to turn the balance of trade in their favour. Since India had little practical use for European commodities, the British could not rely upon increasing their own exports to India. Accordingly, opportunities to redress the balance by other means were sought. When the Mughal Empire began to decay in the eighteenth century, the East India Company quickly secured the support of rival provincial factions and transformed itself into an Indian empire. Its first major battle against local rulers north of Calcutta won it £2.3 million in reparations (over US$1 billion in today's terms), together with rental and political rights. By collecting the land revenue that normally went to the state, the Company was able to finance its trade deficit and, after 1760, slowly drain India and its merchants of their wealth. Over the next fifty years some £5 billion made its way to Britain.[45]

England realized that Asia meant more than just spices. In any case, during the seventeenth century pepper declined in value as new areas of production increased supply. India had cotton and textiles, and the East India Company made huge profits selling Indian calico to Europe. Indian cloth transformed the dress of Europeans. Cheaper, lighter, and easier to clean than European woollens, cotton was a commodity for the mass market, not a luxury item.[46] Its social and economic effects went deeper also. Cotton replaced wool. The social disruptions caused by land enclosures in the eighteenth century were no longer necessary.

For the moment only West Asia and China avoided direct European commercial intervention in their trading networks. In West Asia that independence was due largely to the strength of the Ottoman Empire, with its vast trading network centred on Istanbul, the largest city in all West Asia and Europe, with 700,000 inhabitants. The Ottomans derived income from the silk trade with Iran and the porcelain trade with China. Closer to home, they traded regionally in a vast range of agricultural products, cottons, textiles and metals. They too enjoyed a surplus with Europe and Africa, but paid for their East and South Asian deficits with silver. They were aggressive traders, incorporating market centres such as Cairo wherever they perceived commercial advantage.[47]

New Global Dynamics

The first wave of globalization was always about much more than European dynamics, even though one of its consequences was to reconstruct Europe as 'the epicentre of a revolution that transformed global relations'.[48] Europe helped to connect the world in a way that had not been possible earlier, and the effects of that first wave were tremendous. Again these effects were often unplanned and undirected. Europe exerted less direct influence than it later supposed.

For the first time, foods were exchanged globally. The barriers that had once constrained the movement of foods now no longer existed. Europeans potentially gained more varied diets thanks to North American potatoes, corn, tobacco, squash, beans, tomatoes, and turkeys. Of course the benefits did not trickle down to all classes. In Antwerp at the end of the sixteenth century, for example, four-fifths of family incomes were spent on food, but most of it on bread.[49] American sugar also provided calories that Europe did not have to produce itself. Later the same applied to imports of wheat and meat. They enabled Europe to utilize scarce land for other uses, just as the importation of cotton had earlier done.[50]

The first wave of globalization devastated the aboriginal populations of the Americas. The Caribbean peoples entirely disappeared within fifty years. Across the whole of the Americas aboriginal populations fell from approximately one hundred million to five million, a devastation far greater than anything the plague ever imposed on Eurasia.[51] But for the rest of the world, the impact was exceedingly different. American crops helped populations to expand rapidly.

Europe only had five cities with over 100,000 residents in 1500. One hundred years later it had twelve, and London's population had grown from 50,000 to 200,000, nearly 5 per cent of England's total inhabitants. By 1700 it contained 11.4 per cent – 575,000 people.

China had always had large cities. The Song dynasty's capital in Hangzhou already had over one million people in the late thirteenth century. But the country's population began to grow rapidly after the seventeenth century, from 150 million in 1700 to around 450 million at the beginning of the nineteenth century. Over 20 per cent of the world's population lived off only 7 per cent of its arable land. American corn, sweet potatoes, white potatoes, as well as chillies and tobacco, entered China during and after the sixteenth century. These fed a fast-growing population, provided new sources of revenue to needy farmers, and doubled agricultural land usage. Today 37 per cent of Chinese food is of American origin, and China is the second-largest producer of corn.[52]

But these changes, like those of earlier agricultural expansions, had tremendous social and ecological costs. In south China, farmers rapidly increased silk production to meet new demand and removed forest cover to cultivate mulberry trees. On the lowlands they produced cotton and sugar in addition to rice, growing corn and sweet potatoes for food on higher land.[53] Many new crops made use of more marginal land, with the result that forest cover and grassland declined further. Soil erosion increased. Rivers began to silt up. Flooding became a near-annual event. Rising populations and ecological disasters provided stresses for which the Chinese government was ill-prepared. Competition for resources increased. Inter-village rivalry escalated. So too criminal behaviour. During the nineteenth century these problems brought the Qing dynasty close to collapse and made it easy prey for more ambitious imperialist forces.

China was not the only country so affected. The first wave of globalization lived up to its name ecologically. Because of Chinese and West Asian demand for spices and peppers, South-east Asia increased production rapidly after 1400. By 1600 the region supported 23 million people and contained six major trade centres, each with over 100,000 people. By 1800 its population had increased nearly 40 per cent, its agriculture had doubled in size, and its economies were monetized and globally integrated. Manila already claimed 30,000 Chinese residents in the early seventeenth century to assist in the silver and porcelain trades.[54] After the seventeenth century, increased pepper production for the world market saw the soils of vast tracts of forest in Sumatra and Borneo impoverished. Often forests were transformed into permanent grassland. Forests were similarly destroyed in Sumatra and Malaya to make way for rubber plantations, and for rice in the deltas of the great rivers of South-east Asia.

But as the former engine of world trade, China remained the elusive focus of attention during this first phase of globalization. In Europe, a new fascination with China emerged. French philosophers became impressed with Daoism and with a system of government that enabled a well-educated public service to run the country with little government interference. This contrasted with their own highly stratified society, which, like many European countries, suffered from a lack of trained, loyal administrators. European governments normally sold offices of state. Their law was cruel and civil law confused. In addition they possessed a host of regional, local, and class privileges, internal customs posts and tax exemptions which impacted negatively on economic growth, trade, and social harmony. When the French surveyed the unity and order of China they could not help but be impressed.

When visitors to China asked mandarins how they achieved this, they were told that the state practised the Daoist ideal of *wu wei*, which meant, 'Practise not doing and everything will fall into place'. Back home the French Physiocrats translated this into *laissez-faire*, the belief that government policy should not interfere with the operation of natural economic laws. It became the cornerstone of Adam Smith's *Wealth of Nations* in 1776, the basis for modern free-market economics.[55]

The establishment of global trade had other unintended consequences. The Americas produced 87 per cent of the world's silver and 70 per cent of its gold between 1500 and 1800. During the sixteenth century the Americas produced 17,000 tons of silver, 420,000 tons during the seventeenth century, and 740,000 tons in the eighteenth century. By this time 74 per cent of the silver went directly to Europe, where 40 per cent was redirected to Asia. Ten per cent went directly from Acapulco to Manila. These figures obviously exclude contraband. Nonetheless, the picture is clear. Between 1600 and 1800 over 40 per cent of the world's silver entered Asia.[56]

Inevitably this had a huge impact on its regions. In 1597 alone twelve million pesos of bullion crossed from Acapulco to Manila, at the time more than the value of the entire transatlantic trade. All of Asia reacted to this influx. Chinese tea plantations expanded. Spice production increased. Textile workshops expanded in India.[57] The huge surge of silver had an impact on the fiscal systems of both India and China. During the seventeenth century so much silver entered India that its money supply of silver rupees increased threefold, with the inevitable result that prices rose as the value of silver fell.

In China, the effect was different because production kept pace with money supply and the economy was increasingly commercialized. China's policy of encouraging its growing population to migrate into new areas also served to extend agriculture and commercial settlement. But there were occasions when China experienced severe difficulties.

In the mid-seventeenth century, silver supplies became erratic as American mine production slumped. Cold weather and problems of money supply disrupted trade across Eurasia. Japan restricted silver exports to China the better to weather the economic storm at home. In Manila, Chinese merchants were not so fortunate. Twenty thousand were massacred when they were unable to meet their financial obligations. In China poor harvests and silver shortages saw rice prices rise. In this climate the Ming struggled to gather its taxes and to equip its armies against a new Manchurian conqueror on its northern borders. In 1644 the Ming dynasty fell.[58]

Another aspect of the silver trade also deserves mention. Because China preferred silver to gold, European traders began to exploit its preference. Silver was worth more in China than in Europe. In 1570 the ratio of the value of silver to that of gold was 12:1 in Spain, but in China it was 6:1; in other words silver bought twice as much gold in China. Foreign traders quickly took advantage of the difference, shipping vast amounts of silver to China and buying gold, some of which they re-exported to Japan. But as silver production once more increased during the eighteenth century, the focus shifted to Chinese commodities. Such was the demand that between 1760 and 1780, imports of silver into China increased fourfold.

European nations such as Britain were clearly worried about the constant depletion of their silver stock, particularly when global supplies began to decline again. They looked for new ways to purchase what they wanted from China. The commodity they found to replace silver was opium. Opium could be grown by the East India Company in India's Bengal province and shipped to China. As an addictive drug, it soon developed a growing dependent market. Opium was sold for silver and the silver was used to buy, among other things, Chinese teas, porcelain and silks. By this means also, an increasing amount of silver left China. Indeed by the 1820s the amount leaving had increased fivefold. Soon it affected the ability of merchants and farmers to pay taxes. Taxes were always paid in copper coins and the scarcity of silver pushed up the value of copper. Inflation now destabilized the Chinese Empire.

Instability

Inflation also destabilized Europe. The huge influx of gold and silver from the Americas increased the supply of money in circulation. Europe imported about the same amount of silver as China, but given that its population was only half the size of China's, its effects were greater. Moreover, Europe got its silver more cheaply. China, in contrast, had to pay for much of its silver with exports.[59] Yet, without a commensurate increase in production and in trans-actions, inflation grew more in Europe, by as much as 400 per cent over the course of the sixteenth and seventeenth centuries, according to some estimates. Predictably, deflation and unemployment soon followed. Erratic bullion pro-duction in the early seventeenth century did not help. Bullion imports into Spain fell by two thirds; when they again increased in mid-century, Spain's tax receipts, like China's, suddenly devalued, weakening further its efforts to carve out a continental empire.[60]

As a strategy for security and well-being, conquest had never disappeared. It formed an important function in support of commercial strategies. In the mid-seventeenth century, England went to war with the Dutch (1650–74) and with the French (1672) to extend its role as a major commercial rival. Britain and the Netherlands fought together against the French to safeguard the North Sea for themselves (1689–97), an alliance which was consolidated further when the English invited the Dutch William of Orange to be their king. Together the two countries fought the Spanish (1702–13) to break the Spanish monopoly on trade in South America and to gain additional bases for England in the Mediterranean and in North America.[61]

Indeed, during the eighteenth century Britain (now the combined forces of England, Wales, Ireland and Scotland) used warfare against the French (1740–48 and 1756–63) to gain additional advantage in North America and India. Warfare brought Britain new territories and huge profits in bullion, slaves and commodities. Britain believed that it had an opportunity to monopolize world trade for greater profit.[62] Not so the Dutch. Size and resources now told against them. Their neighbours were too large. By the time its war with France was over in 1713, the Netherlands was financially exhausted and unable to resist invasions by Prussia and France later in the century.

The uneven consequences of globalization on Europe provided yet another motivation for conquest; indeed for elites who found dynastic aggrandizement more satisfying than commerce it was extremely appealing. Spain's ruling Habsburg family struggled against the French to control north Italian terri-tories (1495–1560) and to create its own Holy Roman Empire (1618–48). Only the combined forces of the Netherlands, France, north German states and Sweden stopped the Habsburgs. The English parliament, already facing serious price deflation as a result of the bullion crisis, wanted the Stuarts to support its commercial interests against Spain, but Charles I wished to further his own dynastic ambitions by marriage diplomacy with Spain and by reasserting control over parliament. Civil war soon erupted, but the consequences of civil war in many German states were greater. War disrupted their economies and agriculture, and cost the lives of 40 per cent of the population.[63] To make matters worse, plague returned with a vengeance in the early–mid-seventeenth century, causing one fifth of all deaths in London and costing one sixth of the city's population in 1665 alone. In Europe it was the same even during the eighteenth century, when it killed 20 per cent of Moscow's population in 1772 and half of Marseilles's in 1721.[64]

The eighteenth century brought no certainties. Britain sought to extend its colonial territories, but agricultural technology did not allow them to act as anything other than sources of raw materials or markets for manufactured commodities. Thus the Americas continued to provide cotton, sugar and monopoly access for its traders, and India the wealth upon which the East India Company fed. But problems loomed.

Britain had participated with Prussia in the Seven Years' War against France and Austria (1756–63) to good effect. But it had also acceded to Virginian demands for expansion into the rich Ohio valley. Britain had no desire to follow the whims of its American settlers, no matter how enticing they were for the settlers. The war had been expensive and Britain's national debt now ballooned to £130 million. Consequently it imposed a stamp tax in 1765 to recover some of its costs from the settlers, and set about making its empire more responsive to British needs. But westward expansion was too great a prize for the colonists simply to abandon. Having tasted the dislocation and violence of war, they were emboldened to demand greater responsiveness from Britain.[65]

India too experienced severe difficulties. In Bengal, food production had slumped to accommodate export production and the result was a massive famine (1770–71). This cut the East India Company's profitability and it petitioned the British parliament for relief. In 1773 parliament passed the Tea Act which allowed the British East India Company to dump its tea on the American market. American colonists objected and within three years unilaterally declared independence. Britain's rival, France, saw a fresh opportunity to steal a march on Britain by supporting the rebels. But French involvement contributed to a major financial crisis that took France suddenly to the brink of revolution, and over it in 1789.

The politics of recession created disorder. The commercial strategy had reached its limits. Technology did not permit colonies to contribute more than they currently did to the wealth of their owners, and the manner of Europe's insertion into Afro-Eurasian trade networks generated inflation and instability. During most of the eighteenth century Britain's annual per capita GDP grew only 0.31 per cent; from 1760 to 1780 a dismal 0.1 per cent.[66] Poor relief consumed as much as 2 per cent of GDP, and the crime wave generated by hunger and destitution drove Britain to house its growing prison population in harbour hulks and to plan penal settlements in distant Australia.

Across the Channel, European nations had none of the fat that gave Britain a measure of relief. In the middle of the century, Austrian Habsburgs had attempted to carve out for themselves a new European empire. But they enjoyed none of the success that awaited the French army after it seized power from revolutionaries who had toppled the old French aristocratic order in 1789. Under Napoleon Bonaparte (1792–1815) a continental conquest strategy now promised better rewards than global engagement.

Notes

1. Thomas D. Hall, *The World Systems Reader: New Perspectives on Gender, Urbanism, Cultures, Indigenous Peoples and Ecology*, Lanham and Oxford, Rowman and Littleford, 2000, pp. 4–5.

2. David Landes, *The Wealth and Poverty of Nations: Why some are so rich and some are so poor*, London, Little Brown and Co, 1998, pp. 37–9.

3. Peter J. Taylor, *The Way the Modern World Works: World Hegemony to World Impasse*, Chichester, John Wiley and Sons, 1996, p. 19.

4. Landes, *The Wealth and Poverty of Nations*, p. 32.

5. Ibid., pp. 41–2.

6. Ibid., pp. 43–4.

7. Stephen K. Sanderson, *Social Transformations: A General Theory of Historical Development*, Oxford, Blackwell, 1995, pp. 174–6.

8. Landes, *The Wealth and Poverty of Nations*, pp. 43–4.

9. Sanderson, *Social Transformations*, p. 176.

10. Landes, *The Wealth and Poverty of Nations*, pp. 169–70; Sanderson, *Social Transformations*, pp. 4–28.

11. Quoted in Sanderson, *Social Transformations*, p. 170; see also Landes, *The Wealth and Poverty of Nations*, pp. 177–8.

12. Massimo Livi-Bacci, *The Population of Europe*, Oxford: Blackwell, 2000, p. 119.

13. Graeme Donald Snooks, *The Ephemeral Civilization: Exploding the Myth of Social Evolution*, London and New York, Routledge, 1997, pp. 327, 336–7.

14. Robert J. Holton, *The Transition from Feudalism to Capitalism*, London, Macmillan, 1985, pp. 176–80.

15. Ibid., pp. 188–205.

16. Andre Gunder Frank, *REORIENT: Global Economy in the Asian Age*, Berkeley, University of California Press, 1998, pp. 105–7; Livi Bacci, *Population of Europe*, pp. 36–7. However, some north-western European countries tended to be more urbanized: in 1800 20 per cent of England's population was urban, 29 per cent of the Netherlands'; see also Michio Morishima, *Why Has Japan Succeeded? Western Technology and the Japanese Ethos*, Cambridge University Press, 1982.

17. Livi Bacci, *Population of Europe*, p. 61.

18. The analysis in this section draws heavily on Graeme Donald Snooks, *The Dynamic Society: Exploring the Sources of Global Change*, London and New York, Routledge, 1996, pp. 189–92, 253–9, 301–21, 343–404; and Snooks, *Ephemeral Civilization*, pp. 274–337.

19. Snooks, *Ephemeral Civilization*, p. 288.

20. Ibid., p. 328.

21. William H. McNeill, *The Pursuit of Power: Technology, Armed Forces and Society since AD 1000*, Oxford, Blackwell, 1982, p. 108.

22. Frank, *REORIENT*, pp. 56–7.

23. Ibid., p.48.

24. Ibid., p. xviii.

25. Taylor, *The Way the Modern World Works*, pp. 192, 206.

26. Snooks, *The Dynamic Society*, pp. 192, 373, 389.

27. Janet Abu-Lughod, 'Restructuring the Premodern World', *Review*, XIII (2: 1990), pp. 273–386.

28. Frank, *REORIENT*, pp. 206–22.

29. John Larner, *Marco Polo and the Discovery of the World*, New Haven, Yale University Press, 1999.

30. Frank, *REORIENT*, pp. 72–3, 222.

31. Landes, *The Wealth and Poverty of Nations*, pp. 65–6.

32. Ibid., p. 173.

33. Giles Milton, *Nathaniel's Nutmeg: how one man's courage changed the course of history*, New York, Hodder and Stoughton, 1999.

34. Landes, *The Wealth and Poverty of Nations*, p. 134.

35. Simon Elegant, 'A Pyrrhic Victory', *FEER*, 10 June 1999, p. 45.

36. Frank, *REORIENT*, pp. 135–6.

37. Ibid., pp. 180–1.

38. Ibid., p. 281.

39. McNeill, *The Pursuit of Power*, p. 106.

40. Ibid., pp. 102–3. McNeill claims that together the English, French and Dutch privateers almost drove Iberian merchant ships from the seas and forced Spain and Portugal to rely instead on state galleons financed by bankers. See also Landes, *The Wealth and Poverty of Nations*, pp. 151–2.

41. Milton, *Nathaniel's Nutmeg*.

42. Frank, *REORIENT*, p. 91.

43. Ibid., p. 175.

44. Anupam Sen, *The State, Industrialization and Class Formations in India: a neo-Marxist perspective on colonialism, underdevelopment and development*, London, Routledge and Kegan Paul, 1982, pp. 38–9.

45. Ibid., pp. 52–3; Landes, *The Wealth and Poverty of Nations*, p. 161.

46. Landes, *The Wealth and Poverty of Nations*, p. 154.

47. Frank, *REORIENT*, pp. 78–81.

48. Giovanni Arrighi, 'The World According to Frank', *Review*, XXII (3: 1999), p. 342.

49. Livi Bacci, *Population of Europe*, p. 48.

50. Frank, *REORIENT*, pp. 55, 295.

51. Ibid., p. 59.

52. Ibid., p. 60.

53. Ibid., p. 161.

54. Ibid., pp. 93–101.

55. Michael Vakikiotis, 'Capital Idea', *FEER*, 10 June 1999, p. 51; see also Elegant, 'Gorufu, Anyone?', pp. 66–70.

56. Frank, *REORIENT*, pp. 143–50; see also Immanuel Wallerstein, 'Frank proves the European Miracle', *Review*, XXII (3: 1999), p. 361.

57. Nayan Chanda, 'Early Warning', *FEER*, 10 June 1999, pp. 46–8.

58. Frank, *REORIENT*, pp. 237–48.

59. Wallerstein, 'Frank proves the European Miracle', p. 361.

60. Frank, *REORIENT*, pp. 245–6; McNeill, *The Pursuit of Power*, pp. 109–10. McNeill also believes that the cost of Spain's wars also drove inflation.

61. Snooks, *Ephemeral Civilization*, p. 291.

62. Ibid.

63. Ibid., p. 329; Taylor, *The Way the Modern World Works*, p. 27; Snooks, *Dynamic Society*, p. 374.

64. Livi Bacci, *Population of Europe*, p. 82.

65. Fred Anderson, *The Crucible of War: The Seven Years War and the Fate of Empire in British North America, 1754–1766*, New York, Alfred A. Knopf, 1999.

66. Snooks, *Dynamic Society*, p. 373.

. . . .

PART THREE

The Second Wave of Globalization

CHAPTER 5

. . . .

Globalization's Industrial Child

§ IF the eighteenth century was a time of uncertainty for Europe's leading commercial nations, the nineteenth century could not have been more different. By the start of the century Britain had begun to transform its technology in such a way that it was able to extract much more productive capacity from natural resources than in the past. This was a revolution every bit as momentous as the agricultural revolution which had similarly permitted hunter–gatherers to derive more benefit from their environments. In both instances the results were the same. New technologies enabled environments to carry larger populations. Larger populations created new political and social dynamics, which in turn demanded different institutional responses. Even now, more than two centuries after the start of the Industrial Revolution, the process of transformation is far from complete and has itself become a subject of intense study. Some people call it modernization, others development. Because of the nature of its history, it is sometimes also called Westernization. But all these descriptions fail to capture the dynamic global process that lies beneath the transformation.

The Neolithic Revolution transformed human societies. They grew larger and more complex. They globalized. They more systematically utilized a range of different strategies to maintain security and well-being. They conquered neighbours, they traded, they innovated. These strategies increased their own capacity to exploit the resources around them. But the strategies and the paradigm under which they operated established limits. Conquest and trade were zero–sum strategies. They did not create a basis from which all peoples might mutually benefit. Conquest extracted loot, tribute and slaves but had no means to sustain extraction once resources or conquerable territory ran out. At first sight trade might appear to be entirely different. It is based on the comparative advantage one area has over others in terms of geographical location, resources, technology or the cost of labour. But as with conquest, the lure of big profits exerted powerful influences. Consequently trade also assumed zero–sum characteristics. With state muscle, it created monopoly trading privileges, colonies, and production systems based on slavery.

Until the nineteenth century, technology never enjoyed the same status as commerce or conquest precisely because it lacked the ability to generate such vast profits. It remained a secondary strategy, although an extremely important one for extending military and trading capabilities as well as the range of tradable commodities. On many occasions technological developments seemed to incorporate principles of mass production similar to later industrial manufacturing. The use of movable type, particularly in Western Europe, is a case in point. And yet, undeniably, it remained craft-based. Of course craft production could and did reach massive proportions. Chinese silk and pottery production and Indian cotton textile manufacturing expanded rapidly to meet the demands the first wave of globalization generated. Given more favourable circumstances, they might have expanded further. They might even have crossed the same threshold as Britain's craft industries, though it is unlikely. As we shall see later, China and India were already the world's largest and cheapest producers of a range of highly sought-after commodities. They faced none of the pressures to reduce costs that new market entrants like the British struggled with. Consequently, neither country independently industrialized. Culture played no part in this result. Chinese or Indian peoples were no less capable intellectually or organizationally of making the transition than anyone else. Indeed they have done so since.

In fact the crucial element in determining the course of events was globalization, principally for two reasons. First, globalization is a consequence of human actions. It connects peoples and their communities in new ways. But interconnections do not necessarily generate equal opportunity. Indeed, more often than not, the niches that globalization creates generate inequalities. Consequently, what most determines opportunity or inequality is the dominant strategy driving globalization. The first wave assumed mercantilist forms, seeking profits from monopoly access and conquest. These forms increasingly disadvantaged China and India during the eighteenth and nineteenth centuries and drained them of the resources they required to innovate or respond to innovation.

Second, quite simply, the speed of diffusion during the nineteenth century made independent transformations impossible. When the Neolithic transformation occurred, it did so gradually over several thousand years in at least seven different places quite independently of each other. Human populations then were very small and less interconnected. But even under those very different circumstances, agriculture still spread to most parts of the globe through diffusion. Ten thousand years later in an already globalized and highly connected world, there was never going to be time for independent transformations, no matter how close to change countries were or might conceivably have been one or two hundred years later. On this occasion diffusion was too rapid to permit independent transformations. And it was rapid precisely because of the first wave of globalization. Indeed, it could not have occurred without it. The Industrial Revolution was its child.

Europe Alone

This is not how we normally view the Industrial Revolution. We are taught that it is a British invention. We may trace its origins through the history of the simple technology it employed, most importantly James Watt's 1765 steam engine and, twenty years later, his rotative engine which drove machinery. But as we already know, inventions have little impact unless they meet a demand. What then might have created the demand for mechanization? Many scholars believe that the answer lies in the complex changes occurring within England during the early centuries of the second millennium CE, in particular the transformation of feudalism and the creation of responsive market economies. Mechanization, therefore, was a logical market response to key factors: the scarcity of resources, the availability of capital, and the cost of labour.

But scholars are undecided as to the importance we should place on England. Both Sanderson and Landes argue that regions, rather than countries, make the crucial difference. And of all Europe's regions, it is the north-west that is most important. Britain and the Low Countries, the Rhineland, Bohemia and Switzerland were important trading states linking the northern Baltic and southern Mediterranean regions. What assisted them then and later, these authors argue, was the fact that they were among Europe's first states to remove the impediments of feudalism.[1] The Dutch were particularly fortunate. Their lands had never been subject to the same degree of feudalization as the rest of Europe, in part because of their swampy character, in part also because so much of the country was the result of subsequent land reclamation.[2]

We criticized this explanation in Chapter 4. Feudalism did not deny communities a commercial future. That depended largely on other factors, in particular the opportunities that trade presented for enhancing economic growth. Certainly, as communications across the subcontinent improved, Europe's north-western peoples exploited their location to form important trading communities. But the riches that flowed their way from the Americas outstripped all their previous gains. This wealth reinvigorated their economies and enabled them to ride the wave of globalization. In time it also enabled them to transform the interconnections that globalization produced and to generate a new reservoir of riches from which to launch another expansion.

Nonetheless, to their very institutional explanation, historians often add another dimension that widens the territory under consideration. Landes, in particular, believes that when it comes to the Industrial Revolution we are not just talking about England or north-west Europe, but all of Europe. The Industrial Revolution is a European phenomenon. It drew deeply from a peculiarly European autonomous intellectual tradition of inquiry whose results were also diffused across the whole subcontinent.

He claims two factors most assisted this development. First, Latin existed as a common language for the educated and enabled intellectuals of many different languages to communicate ideas to each other. Second, rising urban literacy standards were equally important.[3] Wright also gives particular importance to the printing press. It lowered the cost of mobilizing an audience. It promoted dissent. It organized communities of interest and provided a new means to outdo the powerful connections of the church. If commerce demanded an end to feudal barriers to trade, then the printing press provided the tool to unify countries culturally and produce nations.[4] Landes agrees. Competition between church and state, and the growth of dissenting religious beliefs ensured that no one dogma – including the authority of classical views – smothered research and inquiry. At the same time, inventions such as the telescope and the microscope, as well as the development of mathematical measures, undermined dogma and faith in magic.[5]

Griffith adds a different perspective to this argument. Protestants were fundamentalists who sought to replace the authority of the church with that of the Bible. They launched an internal crusade against the Roman Catholic Church and enlisted kings to their cause. But their war on organized religion for the sake of doctrinal purity also undercut their own authority. After years of bloodletting, the subsequent disenchantment enabled a new climate of scientific inquiry that the weakened churches had little choice but to adapt to.[6]

The development and accumulation of knowledge is not a sudden process. Knowing something does not imply an ability to use that knowledge. Water-powered machines were employed in Italy during the fourteenth century to spin silk. But since silk is a luxury cloth, it could never generate the kind of demand that might encourage technological improvements and their application to new fields.[7] Inventions, ideas or knowledge do not drive human destiny. As we saw in Chapter 2, they facilitate change once it has begun.

But for Landes, and indeed for many analysts, the significance of Europe's intellectual traditions lay in their contribution to the decentralization of authority. This empowered people and is the key to Europe's later success. It enabled increased freedom and security, greater mobility, greater social roles for women, and fewer religious or ethnic constraints on immigrants.[8] Yet as a subcontinental contribution to paradigm change, it is hard to take Europe's political decentralization seriously. Landes is the first to admit the cost of prejudice and hatred to Europe's decentralized nations. Spain and Portugal are classic examples. He argues that zealotry made more difficult the establishment of an educated population and economic diversification. As late as 1900, 48 per cent of Italy's population was illiterate, 56 per cent of Spain's, and 78 per cent of Portugal's. In contrast only 3 per cent of Britain's population was illiterate.[9] Decentralized power structures did not necessarily make for strong civil societies and power-sharing in Europe. That derived also from the mix of strategies nations pursued for security and well-being. Consequently, Landes is left with Britain as his shining example.

Certainly the British were more tolerant. It suited their commercial interests. In the seventeenth century Jews escaping Spain brought with them their skills in banking, and Huguenots escaping France brought valuable weaving skills. Here was a society that had sidelined its former aristocratic leaders, reducing them – in Landes's words – 'to vanities and appearances'. Parliament ruled. There were no strong, charismatic leaders. Britain's people were not serfs; they were citizens, and its middle classes were very wealthy. Consumption at all levels promoted technology and prosperity.[10]

Certainly agricultural commercialization and greater productivity freed labour for a range of different activities. Specialized market gardens grew up around major centres during the sixteenth century. By the eighteenth century, Britons enjoyed a more varied diet than many of their continental counterparts, with the exception of the Netherlands. Ideas on water management, fertilization and crop rotation entered Britain with Dutch immigrants. A tolerant society enjoyed many unexpected advantages and, in Britain's case, it produced a culture that emphasized improvements and made possible greater specialization. Communications improved. Roads and canals linked farms to markets and integrated mines and industry.[11]

But tolerance did not generate a paradigm shift. Tolerance and, perhaps more generally, wider power-sharing flowed from the dominant strategies adopted by nations. Europe's decentralization did not make Britain tolerant. Its reliance on trade rather than conquest did. For a more appropriate cause that sets the north-west apart, Landes returns to three specific 'medieval' legacies.

First, its nobles' taste for luxuries had monetized its economies, including labour services. Nothing of this order happened in Eastern Europe; if anything, serfdom re-established itself and no free cities existed for peasants to escape to. Serfdom reduced consumer demand. Its survival depended upon resistance to change and innovation. Consequently, where industrialization did take place, as in Russia, it tended to be disconnected from the rest of the economy, inefficient and uncompetitive. Totalitarian empires had other priorities. At the start of the eighteenth century Russia spent only 0.5 per cent of its government revenue on education and health, but 40 per cent on its army. Not that this largesse implied a modernizing army. During the Crimean war in 1854, Russia armed its soldiers with bayonets; 600,000 of its soldiers were slaughtered.[12]

Second, north-western merchants were able to bypass the restrictive practices of urban guilds by employing workers in the countryside. This had not happened in Italy, and it eroded Italy's competitiveness. But exploiting poorer rural communities could not last forever as a viable strategy; eventually another region would offer cheaper alternatives. Italy's problem was later a Dutch problem, although the Netherlands was better positioned for an industrial future. Nonetheless, as a short-term strategy the use of cheap rural labour clearly had important if unintended consequences. In Britain it industrialized the one sector that held the largest number of people and that still generated most of the country's wealth.[13]

Other writers argue that rural manufacturing's bottom-up process of learning shaped the Industrial Revolution. Griffith claims that it was driven initially by a desperate rural need to make ends meet. Part-time craft production supplemented farm work and gradually became full-time. It produced more skilled and flexible people, able to adapt to changing economic demands, and to live off a more diversified range of resources.[14] On the other hand, failure to integrate rural communities made industrialization a much more difficult and uneven process, as we shall see later.

Third, the smaller countries of north-west Europe were already internally unified and had developed common national practices and standards. Elsewhere in Europe, insular local principalities retained archaic barriers to trade and the movement of people. In France, revolution eventually swept away these internal tolls and duties, but in Germany and Italy they remained until the late nineteenth century.[15]

Landes's three legacies were important in establishing social and economic changes that facilitated economic growth, and certainly contributed to laying the foundations upon which a technological paradigm could flourish. But by themselves they were insufficient.

We should not assume that failure to benefit from such legacies prevented change. Change still occurred, but assumed different forms. Countries like France, Germany and Italy did transform themselves. Not because they were European and shared a common heritage with Britain but because Britain became too great a model for them to ignore. Most of them, Landes concedes, looked at industry and saw only power, especially nations such as France and Spain, which had dealt with Britain in the past and were inclined to regard it as little more than a nation of shopkeepers. They did not want Britain to have that power alone, and the idea of Britain as the world's first superpower troubled them. They had no choice but to beat Britain at its own game.[16]

But herein lay the rub. They were not equally positioned to compete with Britain. They had different resources, different capabilities, and different handicaps. Their economies were not as integrated as Britain's. France, far from removing peasants from the land, actually consolidated their precarious hold on small and ever more fragmented plots of land. This made agriculture less productive, raised food costs, reduced the available non-agricultural workforce, and diminished the markets available to manufacturers. Thus, to survive, peasants and capitalists alike were forced to rely more on the state to protect them from international competition. Without a complete transformation of agrarian relations, the transition to a technologically dominant strategy remained tortuous, uneven, and potentially destabilizing. Indeed, it made compensation by alternative strategies much more tempting.

Britain Alone

However, important changes occurred in Britain during the eighteenth century that did set it apart. In 1700 and 1721 Britain introduced the Calico Acts. This legislation protected Britain's woollen and linen industry from foreign imports, but coincidentally had the unintended effect of also protecting its small cotton industry from imports of cheap Indian cloth. The woollen industry was under pressure from cotton and tried to develop a water-powered spinning machine to reduce the costs of producing cloth and make it more competitive. But as an old established industry, says Landes, it possessed too many vested interests that regarded mechanization as a threat to their livelihood. The younger cotton industry had none of the vested interests associated with wool.[17]

But what gave cotton cloth producers – many of whom put out work to rural workshops and homes – the incentive to change the way they produced? The answer lies in the huge demand for cotton goods in the late eighteenth century, already evidenced by the large private investment made in canals to move raw materials around the country and thereby reduce costs. Manufacturers wanted to satisfy that demand, but they had to ensure that the goods they produced were priced competitively. Simply contracting more work out might increase production but not necessarily in ways which guaranteed lower costs and lower prices. Sending work to a greater number of small workshops in the countryside cost time and raised transportation expenses. In addition, the more workshops producers used, the harder the task of maintaining quality control. Producers might instead insist on raising worker productivity, but how could that be achieved without also raising costs or risking quality?

The only effective means to overcome competition and remain profitable was to alter the way cloth was produced. Put larger numbers of workers together where they could be supervised. Reduce a worker's role to that of a simple repetitive task in a chain of tasks performed by a chain of workers. Do away with the need altogether for skilled labour. If workers complain, replace them. There were always plenty of destitute women and children in Britain's poorhouses who needed jobs, and they were certainly much cheaper to employ than men. Men were deemed to be family breadwinners; their wages sustained families. 'Family' wages were unnecessary when women and children worked.

Machines also helped to maintain the cost-saving momentum gained through changing methods of production. The nature of work had so changed that machines could be devised to undertake the simple repetitive tasks of employees. The result was a cheaper product. Cheaper products meant more sales and more sales meant greater profits.

There are two points to note from this description of change. First, demand for cheaper cloth drove change. Demand existed because commercialization had privately empowered more people and because agricultural transformation had continued the process by creating a growing, more specialized and prosperous workforce dependent on the market for its survival. The change anticipated the consequences that deepening markets would generate 150 years later during the third wave of globalization. After 1780, per capita incomes grew more rapidly; by 1800 England had urbanized faster than any other European country. One fifth of its population lived in urban communities, compared with one eighth a century before.[18]

Second, centuries of agricultural development meant that Britain no longer had the timber available to supply its growing population with fuel.[19] Consequently the country turned to coal, but even then demand quickly outstripped supply. Mines had to be dug deeper. Hence the demand for steam engines to pump water from deep mines. Between the late eighteenth century and 1850, Britain's coal production expanded tenfold. Such power generation also stimulated factory production, as well as iron production. And factories stimulated urbanization, which further raised demand for manufactured textiles and market-purchased food. Mechanical weaving stimulated new chemical processes for bleaching and dyeing. Greater production and trade, together with the desire to reduce costs, saw communications improve further. Ports were upgraded; steam transport was developed; railways were created; telegraph systems were invented. The process self-generated.

So too did the process of staying ahead in this highly competitive game. By investing in more and more machines, industrialists risked over-capitalizing.[20] They risked placing more investment than could ever be recouped from the market, at least in the short term. Declining returns on investments meant declining profits. To overcome this dilemma, businesses streamlined production further. They introduced shift work to make better use of otherwise idle machinery. They employed more women and children. They demanded greater productivity from workers. They insisted that government end its protection of local farming so that cheaper food could be imported. Cheaper food meant lower living costs. Lower living costs justified reduced wages.

Business also demanded greater support from the state. The state had always backed mercantile activities; now its war-driven initiatives did the same for industry. Recruitment for the Napoleonic Wars and its system of Poor Relief helped to stabilize British society and prevent the sudden rush of rural populations to cities that Paris experienced in the late 1780s. Naval needs stimulated commercial agriculture and spread market relations more widely. Military demands made viable the development of new technologies that later contributed to increased iron production. They also created new markets for industry. Indeed Britain funded much of the European alliance against France. During the quarter-century after the French Revolution, Britain's population increased by 25 per cent, yet it maintained full employment. The secret lay in the sixfold increase in public expenditure that war necessitated during the same period.[21]

After the war, trade issues provided a major test of the continued political clout of Britain's new industrialists. During the late eighteenth century they pressured the British parliament to impose higher duties on Indian-manufactured cloth in order to reduce competition with their own product. Their victory signalled the eclipse of mercantile power, in this case represented by the British East India Company. But traders in general were not their target. Technology represented a much more inclusive strategy than mercantilism; this is one reason – Snooks argues – that it never produced the same domestic turmoil that commercial dominance had in mid-seventeenth-century England.[22] Traders participated in the boom, but it was a boom now generated by the products of technological innovation and production efficiencies, not monopoly access to markets. For the first time, technology generated massive profits.

Industrialists and the expanding middle classes who now rode the industrial boom had little sympathy for Britain's land-owning elite. Urban food shortages made the issue of agrarian monopolies a subject of intense public debate in the early nineteenth century, particularly in the wake of the brutal suppression of food rioters in 1819.[23] A political change brought the middle classes the vote in 1832, and they used their new access to parliament to overturn what were known as the Corn Laws. These laws placed tariffs on imported wheat, oats and corn to protect local production, chiefly from large enclosed estates and landed interests. Industrialists argued that these laws unacceptably raised food prices and hence their costs. If Britain abolished tariffs, cheaper imports would reduce production costs and enable Britain to win more customers for its manufactured goods. By 1846 their drive for free trade had not only been successful, it had entered into the canons of economics as an article of faith capable of bringing peace and prosperity to the world. Certainly this was a period of almost unprecedented prosperity for Britain. From 1830 to 1870 Britain's per capita GDP grew 1.4 per cent annually, the highest growth since the boom days following Europe's discovery of the vast resources hidden within the Americas.[24]

The alliance-building that 1832 and 1846 represented continued throughout the century. In 1867 the vote was extended to include all male householders, in 1884 all county householders, in 1918 men without property, and in 1928 all women over 21. The changes were not inevitable, and they did not always come easily. Nonetheless, they were made possible, as Snooks persuasively argues, because technology as a dominant strategy places very different demands on societies than commerce or conquest. Technology requires mass participation in employment and in consumption. Indeed it heralds the age of the masses. By the late nineteenth century, shorter working hours, higher real incomes and better and cheaper communications saw new forms of public entertainment generated, especially mass sports. Increasingly sports reinforced the dominant strategy; they engaged whole working communities and suburbs in activities that bound them together and celebrated their newly won prosperity. So too the music hall, whose creativity became an important foundation for a new form of mass entertainment in the twentieth century – the cinema. Religion also transformed itself; Methodism and evangelism celebrated the new-found power and satisfaction of a burgeoning middle class.[25]

Herein lay an important feature of modernity. Taylor argues that, like the Dutch before them, the British symbolized their technological era by celebrating its impact on middle-class domesticity. Whereas genre paintings of peaceful home life were the form that Dutch celebration assumed, in Britain it became the novel, in particular the images of ordinary lives in a changing world that novelists such as Jane Austen painted with words. In presenting to the world such ordinary faces, Britain widened the appeal of its modernity and reinforced comfort as the reason for being.[26]

Hence technology also demanded a more equitable distribution of wealth in order to create these new domestic worlds. It demanded greater investment in human capital, in education, training and public health. At first the results were slow in coming. Life expectancy rose from 37 years in 1750 to 40 years in 1850 to 53 years by 1910. Although Britain's population quadrupled during the nineteenth century – a demonstration, if ever one needed it, of industrialization's capacity to accommodate higher populations – the average number of children born to a woman declined from 5.5 in 1800 to 4.9 in 1850 to 3.4 in 1900.[27] However, what did rise much more rapidly – and with it the sense of greater change – was the proportion of people who no longer depended on agriculture for their livelihood. Seventy-five per cent of the population had depended on agriculture in 1688; by 1850 26 per cent; by 1913 only 9 per cent.

The imperatives of the technological strategy were not always well understood at first. Old attitudes died hard. New classes evoked fears. And new competitors provoked the return of less inclusive strategies, as we shall examine later.

Globalization's Child

In the late eighteenth century the clothing industry remained the one bright star for a nation facing revolt in North America, social unrest at home, and turmoil in Europe. We have traced the explanations that historians provide for the transformation that the industry underwent and its radical impact on Britain's economy and global pretensions. Indeed, integrated and monetized growing home markets were extremely important in enabling Britain to make the transition to a new industrial paradigm. So too the space that political systems created for initiative, and for the consequences of such initiatives on the division of labour. There can be no doubt as to the self-generating processes that followed.

But can we in all honesty say that this was a process indigenous to Britain or to north-west Europe, or even more generously a product of the culture that Europe itself had generated during the second millennium? Consider the commodity upon which the process most depended. Britain did not grow cotton. Raw cotton came from plantations in its southern colonies in North America and from India, itself in the process of being colonized and transformed from a producer of manufactured cloth to a producer of raw cotton only. Britain enjoyed no comparative advantage as a textile manufacturer.

A complicated exchange system incorporating Indian Ocean commodities such as cowrie shells and textiles enabled slaves to be bought and exported from West Africa. They produced the North American cotton on which Britain's alleged comparative advantage rested. The incomes that Britain derived from its sugar plantations in the Caribbean and its tobacco farms in North America, both similarly staffed by African slaves, together with the supply of cheap cotton from its colonies, enabled Britain to weather the economic difficulties of the mid-eighteenth century. Further, the European populations of its colonies also provided important additional markets for its cotton products, at the very least in terms of their impact on economies of scale. Add to that the huge profits emanating from Britain's looting of India (as much as £150 million in gold alone between 1750 and 1800)[28] and the growing profits that came from its opium trade with China. Indeed one historian goes so far as to declare Bengal Europe's greatest prize after Peru.[29] Frank puts the case very plainly: Britain's involvement in the wider world enabled it to consume and invest far beyond its means.[30]

Britain's advantage derived from its assertion of monopoly control. Long before free trade became the mantra Britain bestowed on the world, the words possessed a hollow ring. Free trade was based on conquest, trade monopolization and slavery. It derived not from indigenous features (important though they were) but from what Britain had gained from the first wave of globalization. The real question that needs to be asked is whether the

Industrial Revolution could have occurred without the Americas and without Asia.

Frank certainly believes that the Industrial Revolution would have been impossible without globalization. For that reason alone the roles of other regions need to be reconsidered. There is no doubt that industrialization broke China's and India's relative advantage, although even by the mid-nineteenth century Britain was still not strong enough to subjugate China in the way it had India.[31] Nonetheless, until industrialization, European countries like Britain had been unable to compete with Asia. This is the often unstated background to Britain's demand for labour-saving technology. Its labour was more expensive than Asian labour. Its population was smaller and it possessed a small colonial escape valve. But the cost of labour was not the only cause of British disadvantage. India had a much longer tradition of textile production and its craft producers were extremely efficient. Food costs were lower. Transportation networks worked cheaply and efficiently. Its craft producers were also extremely innovative: for example, importing skilled workers from as far afield as the Ottoman Empire and Persia to introduce new techniques for dyeing.[32]

Many historians seem to suggest that competition among British suppliers to meet demand for a growing market alone impelled the transition to mechanization. But suppliers were not just British suppliers. They included Indian manufacturers. Although Britain protected its home market from Indian competition, it could not do so in the external markets that its growing industry coveted. Since Britain already exported half of its cloth production by 1800, such competition was keenly felt. Until India could be prevented from participating in the trade altogether, mechanization remained its only chance to maintain growth. It succeeded, but not until 1815 did British exports exceed Indian imports in its major markets.[33]

Globalization made the Industrial Revolution, just as globalization made Britain a powerful trading nation. Britain's industrial transformation is meaningless without this global dimension. Historians – often unconsciously – have long sensed this; it is one reason why the origins of modernity are said to lie in the changes that took place after 1500. But instead of confronting the advantages that European nations suddenly gained through accessing American wealth, historians have argued that post-feudal developments internal to Europe were primarily responsible. Or, where they do concede the existence of non-European actors, that other peoples were clearly less responsive, less innovative, less modern, less rational, perhaps even less intellectually skilled.

Taylor, for example, claims that China did not understand a world of multiple sovereignty, where nations regarded themselves as equals, not vassals.[34] This argument suggests the importance of nation states in heralding European superiority. But this too is reading history backwards. We could always make the case that China was the original nation state. It possessed many of the features we have come to regard as essential for nation states: a largely homogeneous population, a common alphabet, a dominant language of communication, and a unified system of internal communications. Certainly it was ruled as an empire and did not decentralize its structures of governance in the same way as Britain. But then neither did Prussia. In any case, even if Europe established for itself a way of reducing warfare among its many states and territories after 1648, it was never able to prevent the conquering urge manifesting itself among these honourable nation states in the centuries that followed. It is more likely that the instability of post-1648 Europe stimulated the search for new means to gain security and well-being.

Associated with this argument is the view that Europe's decentralization of power gave Europeans the opportunity to innovate and to explore in very different ways. It enabled a culture of innovation and questioning to develop, and a market to reward success. No political monopolies prevented initiative. When Columbus wanted to raise capital for a small expedition into the unknown, there were always other political leaders who could be approached after his first efforts to get Italian support failed. Merchants enjoyed more freedom, often behaving like local lords themselves, creating companies which employed their own military forces. To gain even more concessions for themselves, they also networked effectively with the wider decision-making bodies emerging within parts of Europe. In this regard, the contrast with China could not have been greater.

This really is at the heart of Landes's argument. China had been extremely inventive; indeed many inventions adopted by European countries derived from China. But China's rulers – dominated by foreigners content with the proceeds of tax farming – failed to maximize their country's potential. Their all-powerful state stifled initiative and freedom of thought whenever it believed that these conflicted with its own interests.[35]

At the start of the second millennium CE, China had a population of some 100 million people, most of whom were skilful farmers managing imported food strains to raise productivity. Unlike fragmented and self-destructive Europe, China sustained an extremely rich mental and material life. While Europeans struggled to recopy church writings on parchment, the Chinese enjoyed widely distributed printed literature. Its craftsmen produced flawless porcelain. Its commercial workshops mass-produced silk. Its merchants moved along well-developed communications networks employing credit facilities and paper money. In addition, a powerful bureaucracy that was well educated and recruited through competitive examinations aided its imperial leaders.[36]

But this bureaucracy was also subject to factional alliances that rarely compromised with each other. Consequently, as the state became more pervasive in China, no accompanying rise in national strength necessarily emerged. The Song dynasty's defeat at the hands of the Mongols proves the point.

Historian Wang Gungwu argues that rulers in both China and India became so fixated by the threat posed by their neighbours that they neglected the sea. When they dealt with merchants, they tended to regard them as a class whose wealth and foreign links made them potentially untrustworthy. For the purpose of maintaining order at home, they preferred that their bureaucrats deal directly with foreign merchants. Certainly they did not encourage their own merchants to create long-distance trading empires and take advantage of the free flow of sea-going commerce.[37] And when traders did establish important trading networks in South-east Asia, they had to survive without state support.

Much is made of China's huge expeditions around the Indian Ocean in the early fifteen century, and in particular their failure to generate the same consequences that European voyages were to do half a century or more later. The *Far Eastern Economic Review* introduced a series of articles on Asia in the second millennium CE by asking:

> What if? What if the great Chinese Admiral and explorer Zheng He had continued his voyages, rounded the Cape of Good Hope and headed north to Europe with his fleet of junks? In the mid 15th century when Zheng reached as far as the [West Asian] port of Aden, China was technologically, economically and politically centuries ahead of a Europe still mired in the Middle Ages.
>
> What if the factional battle in the Ming court hadn't resulted in the banning of such sea voyages and the closing of the country to trade? Zheng's arrival in Europe – especially if it had been followed up by similar expeditions by Chinese merchants – could have created a world almost completely unrecognizable. One where it was China – energized and enriched by trade – that stumbled into the industrial revolution, then dazzled the semi-feudal, bickering, hidebound rulers of Europe with its technology and military prowess.[38]

This never happened, Simon Elegant argues, because the voyages were not designed to push the boundaries, to explore trade opportunities, or to promote Chinese enterprise. They were designed solely to affirm the Ming dynasty's desire to monopolize all foreign trade and to keep it out of the hands of private traders. Political power, China's leaders believed, made trading wealth possible. The reverse could never be true. This triumph of politics over trade stifled economic growth and the cultural and scientific efflorescence that accompanied it.

What the *Review* does not concede, however, is that even if China had exhibited the same spirit as Europeans and had made it to Europe, the result would not necessarily have been an industrial revolution. The world may have been different, but trade with Europe could never have provided China with the same huge injections of bullion that flowed from Europe's stumbling into America.

We need to approach China differently. Historian Jonathon Spence argues that it was the sheer wealth of China that proved in retrospect to be its greatest disadvantage. Agriculture was productive, water-borne transportation was convenient, natural resources were sufficient, and an abundance of muscle power made labour-saving devices unnecessary.[39] Historian Mark Elvin also believes that having such a large economy meant that it was more difficult for something like an increase in foreign trade to surge through the economy and raise overall demand in the same way that trade had in smaller European economies. China was constrained by its success.[40]

Frank agrees that the issue is not what China's leaders wanted, but the signals that the Chinese economy itself sent to its own people. He agrees that China was immensely successful. Until the nineteenth century it always re-tained its surplus from trade and remained competitive. But because trade contributed less to its GNP, China's income distribution tended to be more polarized than in some European countries. When combined with greater population pressures on resources, it conspired to reduce demand for consumer goods. Consequently, no price incentive existed to invest in labour-saving technology. During the eighteenth century, as China's population expanded, agricultural land became scarce and animal feed more expensive. But rather than mechanizing, China made greater use of its cheap labour and equally cheap water transport systems. It rationally economized.[41] The supreme goal of the state, says Spence, became measured prosperity. Elites frowned on anything that could upset the social balance on which such prosperity was based. Merchants were not encouraged to seek new boundaries.[42]

Something of this spirit exists in China's reaction to European nations during the eighteenth and nineteenth centuries. China had no tradition of isolationism, hostility to innovation or xenophobia, as some historians argue. Waley Cohen's recent study of China makes exactly this point. The Chinese were passionately interested in the scientific achievements of Europeans, but they distrusted the exclusivity of Europe's messengers, in particular its Jesuits. When the Qing emperor feigned indifference to Europe's manufactures in the late eighteenth century, Europeans misread the diplomatic message.[43] China's elite was open-minded. It knew China was not superior. But its goals of measured prosperity and social stability differed from those of Britain's elites, and certainly the manner in which they were to be achieved.

Something of the same dynamics also affected India, a subcontinent whose population exceeded 100 million, and whose standard of living was never surpassed by Europe until Elizabethan times. Like China, it too was a region of great social and economic stability, despite chronic political instability, which in the end would make India susceptible to colonization in a way that China was not.[44] Deepak Lal makes the case that when Eurasian nomads first cleared the forests of the Gangetic plains in northern India, they confronted a major economic problem. Labour was scarce and land plentiful, but the method of plough-based farming they had developed was highly labour-intensive. Societies were not so technologically advanced that they might seek mechanical labour-saving solutions as they would two thousand years later. Nor were political states stable enough or administratively centralized enough to impose slavery, indenture or bureaucratic limits on the movement of people. Instead, they solved their labour problem by developing a caste system, which divided society into separate hereditary classes based on employment, and enforced the divisions by means of local social ostracism. As in Japan, war became the monopoly of professionals, with the result that while states feuded with monotonous frequency, the lives of their masses were left largely unaffected and they continued to provide rulers with a steady source of revenue.

Such resilience did not encourage rural innovation. Nor did it encourage India's growing mercantile classes. The rural surplus siphoned off by India's rulers certainly stimulated a vast trade in luxury handicraft production. But merchants enjoyed no social and political status, and their wealth could be confiscated at any moment, particularly if rulers felt that it might be used to generate rival power bases. Consequently, only elite conspicuous consumption prospered, not productive investment.[45] What demand such consumption did generate locally never sufficed to lower labour costs. In this way India's workers were marginalized and unable to act as a rising market for consumer goods, and their cheap labour benefited only production for export.[46] The entry of the British in the eighteenth century changed little in this regard.

Global Development Futures

Marx once claimed that whenever countries looked at Britain they saw their own future, or at least the power and self-confidence they desired for themselves. Certainly the British equated industrialization with progress. They made industrialization a stage in historical development and endowed it with faith in a bountiful future. Britain's scientists ensured that nature conformed also to this new purposiveness. After Darwin, evolution and progress became synonymous.[47]

But replication was never possible. Once one country industrialized, it changed forever the global circumstances facing all countries, would-be in-dustrializers included. Britain had no industrial competitors, an advantage that quickly enabled it dominate global markets for industrial products, and later even the home markets of competitors. The first countries to emulate Britain did not enjoy the advantage of scale that its market dominance bought. If they produced the same commodities as Britain, they faced ruinous com-petition. Nor did they possess the wealth that Britain extracted from its colonies in order to launch themselves into this brave new era.

We sometimes use terms such as 'Westernization' to imply a single Western model of development, but there was no uniform sequence of change that followed Britain's industrialization; no single way which suggested a cohesiveness that was decidedly European. Britain demonstrated the power of industrialization, but with that demonstration came no guarantee that similar changes could occur elsewhere as effectively and as rapidly.[48] If anything, the general context of the changing global economy dictated different methods and procedures for industrialization. It also tempted countries to adopt alternative strategies to overcome weaknesses that threatened the successful pursuit of technological change. Under these circumstances, replication was never possible.

For a start, the cost of technology rose sharply. In the nineteenth century, no World Banks and International Monetary Funds existed to provide bridging loans to governments facing balance-of-payments difficulties or a lack of investment funds. Britain's early industrial endeavours had been funded from the wealth of its colonies, and when the cost of technology rose along with the sophistication of factory systems and transport networks, its technology earnings continued to generate sufficient windfalls to fund investment in improvements and new technologies. But for countries wishing to purchase those technologies and establish the basic infrastructure they required, costs had to be met by alternative means. Some old trading houses in Europe, such as the Rothschilds, rose to the challenge, but most banks shunned the long-term risks that industrial investment involved. Sometimes special development or investment banks mobilized capital for new enterprises but, more often than not, the state had to step in and provide the resources needed for investment.

Security provided an important motivation, but so too did the increasing differentiation between European societies. West European incomes were already 20 per cent higher than East European incomes by 1800. Sixty years later they were 64 per cent higher; by 1900 80 per cent.[49] Even within Western Europe, divisions were sharp. French and German incomes were only 69 per cent of Britain's in the early nineteenth century. By 1913 German incomes had risen to 73 per cent, but Italian incomes were still only 50 per cent of British levels.[50] Industrialization might promise a homogenized future, but in the real world division and fragmentation ruled, with political consequences for Europe as elsewhere. To reduce disparities and to fashion technologically driven societies, states had at the very least to create space for industries to develop. Just as Britain provided domestic protection for its cotton industry, so states in newly industrializing countries stepped in to legislate tariffs and duties and to coordinate the planning that industrialization necessitated.

Although Britain's success had initially been in a consumer sector (cotton still made up half of its exports in 1850),[51] the development of machinery to drive production and transport soon became an industry in its own right. To this new sector – heavy industry – most newly industrializing countries turned.

Through such specialization, they hoped to develop a global niche for themselves. With the wealth thus generated, they hoped also to begin integrating the rest of their economies (in particular agriculture) into the so-called modern or industrial sector.

Sometimes this trickle-down strategy worked. But invariably industries found it more profitable to perpetuate economic distance between sectors. It kept wages low. It enabled them to compete more favourably in external markets. Interest in the difficult task of integrating long-neglected rural communities waned. Industrial power alone seemed much more important. It offered states military resources to suppress any social unrest generated by internal polarization. It also offered states the means to seek the elusive quick fix by deploying resources against neighbouring countries or overseas territories. In old strategic remedies and novel nationalist distractions, new vistas opened.

Who were these industrializers? By and large they were European, and that fact alone is said to lend weight to the assertion that, no matter what differences existed between individual European countries, they all shared a common heritage and possessed similar advantages over other world regions. Certainly Europe existed as an interconnected set of smaller regions. Many writers believe that since the end of the disastrous Thirty Years War in 1648, it has existed as 'a society of sovereign states'.[52] The post-Napoleon accommodation reached in the Concert of Europe strengthened that community and created a security framework that enabled development. In addition, Europe's interconnectedness ensured that all of Europe benefited – even if unevenly – from the first wave of globalization. Spanish bullion, trading prosperity and colonialism generated regional multiplier effects.

We should not be surprised then that the countries lying closest to Britain, which formed important markets for British products, should also be among the first to wake up to the threat that an industrial Britain presented to their economies and to their regional status. Nor should we be surprised that they were among the first countries to grasp the opportunities that industrialization presented for their own future well-being. Culture and heritage did not make the difference; geographical proximity, economic distance, interconnections, market value, and autonomy did.

These values did not apply to China. Britain's technological machine regarded China only as a source of revenue, derived increasingly from the colonial opium trade. It did not figure as a market for British products. For its part, China did not grasp soon enough how the global economy had changed and would continue to change. Its past success told against it. No longer the engine of global growth, it entered a period of painful decline. The environmental consequences of past economic and demographic expansion now bore more heavily on the country, as did the destabilizing consequences of the opium trade. China's institutions were ill-equipped to deal with these mounting difficulties. The more that silver drained from its economy, the fewer resources the nation possessed for either reinvestment or defence. In any case, China's rulers, paralysed by the fear that transformation would cost them leadership, could no longer contain local responses to imperialism, 'nor digest their full implications'.[53] For the first time in centuries, China found itself poorly positioned to respond to changing global dynamics.

Nonetheless, China did resist. It succeeded in thwarting British efforts to 'Indianize' the nation. Despite two disastrous wars over opium sales, China emerged with a Treaty Port system that denied Britain and other industrialized countries the access to its vast hinterland that they coveted.[54] It bought time only, but the competence of the Qing dynasty did not inspire confidence. Japan's reactions were more successful. Smaller, more unified and without China's handicap of a foreign governing elite desperate to cling to power at all costs, Japan too bought time with a series of unequal treaties. But it quickly embarked on exactly the same kind of nation-building activity that soon absorbed all Europe.

Elsewhere across Asia, the old empires that had once provided security and strength in the agrarian age found the challenges that a technologically driven age presented difficult to meet. Invariably conflicts of vested interests made rapid change difficult, and their empires became captive to raw-material demands of new industrial markets elsewhere. In colonized India the trans-formation was more complete. By 1816 it had become a net importer of textiles.[55] Africa had no access to investible capital, and South America, despite formal independence early in the nineteenth century, was constrained by its continued colonial economic status. Only the United States, which had won its freedom from Britain by 1783, and Britain's Canadian and Australasian colonies were able to retain sufficient surplus for internal investment and pursue independent industrial futures. Of all the colonies or former colonies, the United States was the most successful.

Technological success required the development of new markets for the products of industry. It required access to resources to develop technology and its industrial base. Indeed, many of the features that historians have read backwards into the historical record as crucial for the emergence of 'capitalism' or industrialization now did assume new importance. Technological success did require more organized and coherent state systems than previously existed, less hierarchical or polarized social structures, huge investments in communica-tions infrastructure and above all in human capital. Feudal structures did not help; nor did narrowly based systems of governance, illiteracy, large rural communities unable to participate in the new economy, or sectarian or ethnic divisions that threatened to tear communities asunder. The industrial era drove this change.

Although never fully understood until the nineteenth century, industry demanded a completely different form of economic growth from that generated by conquest and commerce. Conquest and commerce thrived on exclusion; technology on economic inclusion. It is in this context, and only this context, that the rationalizing, centralizing, homogenizing nation state came into its own. It is why nation states have been held up as the supreme example of modernity, why it is sometimes suggested that modernity itself flows from them, and why tracing the origin of nation states is equated with tracing the origins of modernity.

But unified states, whether nation states or not, were a product of industrial change, not its precursor. Certainly unified states existed before industrialization, but never with the same imperative that technology imposed. Consequently, the nature of all states gradually changed. Again proximity, interconnectedness, market value and autonomy most influenced the nature and speed of change. In Europe, the conquering Napoleon facilitated much of the reorganization that industrialization required from the French state – in particular standardized laws and language. German states also reorganized themselves, first as a southern customs union and later as part of a greater Prussian state in 1871. Italian states also united. Many European nations deliberately adopted aspects of Britain's parliamentary system of checks and balances. They emulated and rebuilt themselves in the image of the most successful pioneer of industrial technology.[56] In Eastern Europe old regimes persisted, but invariably their hold on power became so tenuous that crises quickly pushed them aside. By the end of the First World War, the same forces for coherence and responsiveness had swept the subcontinent and were poised to break over the whole Afro-Eurasian continent.

Britain, too, could not escape these industrial consequences. It began the nineteenth century as the predominant industrial nation. It possessed a massive trading system based on the import of cheap raw materials and food, and the export of manufactured goods. But by the end of the century two countries challenged its dominance: the United States of America and Germany.

The United States was in the process of converting itself from being an exporter of raw materials to an import-substitution industrializer, focusing on its own market. And this market was certainly growing. Thirty-two million people migrated from Europe to the United States between 1821 and 1914, during which time the country's population grew from a modest 10 million to 94 million. Despite this influx of people, labour remained relatively scarce and expensive, providing an incentive to substitute capital for labour. The USA's area of cultivated land increased by 2.6 times between 1860 and 1910, and far exceeded Europe's farming capacity.[57] The US became a society of small landholders, and – in Landes's words – 'a seedbed for democracy and enterprise'. An immigrant society expected change, innovation and openness. None of the old world's class barriers or landed estates thrived here.[58]

By 1870, the US contributed 23 per cent of global industrial production, less than Britain's 32 per cent, but it enjoyed the world's largest economy. By 1913 its output was 2.5 times that of Britain or Germany (Britain's proportion of global industrial production had fallen to 14 per cent, the US's had risen to 38 per cent) and its output was 4 times that of France. In addition, its per capita GDP was 20 per cent higher than Britain's, 77 per cent higher than France's, and 86 per cent higher than Germany's. By 1930, when Britain's global industrial output had collapsed to 9 per cent, the US's had risen further, to 42 per cent.[59] It ushered in a new world of insatiable consumerism, where ordinary people could own what previously only the rich had enjoyed.

Germany faced greater difficulties. It selectively developed an industrial base focusing on industrial chemistry, and in time led the world in this field. But it was too narrow a base for the same kind of growth as the US. Agricultural change had been slow, and did not enable an integrated economy to sustain rapid consumer growth. Furthermore, Germany was not free of the territorial ambitions that earlier characterized Europe's old agrarian empires; in time this would divert investment and cost the country dearly.

Britain did not surrender to German and US expansion into its markets. At first it retaliated by exporting capital to foreign businesses and governments, loans that could be used to purchase British goods such as railway stock. Between 1850 and 1874, Britain exported £15 million of surplus capital each year and reinvested its earnings overseas. In this way it still profited from capital when direct investment in production itself was less profitable. But the strategy held dangers. By the mid-1870s many of its borrowers faced financial difficulties. Spain became bankrupt, Turkey and Greece defaulted on their debts, and the economies of Russia and Australia slumped. To complicate matters, at the same time as the once profitable loan market collapsed, Germany and the US began erecting tariff barriers to exclude British competition.

Britain had no alternative but to reinvest its surplus capital at home. That shift homeward became an important ingredient in transforming technology further, particularly in steel production and in the use of electricity, oil and chemicals. Some people refer to its effects as a second industrial revolution, but to do so is to misread the nature of technological change. Technology thrives on innovation. Change is to be expected. Further, the changes that now began did not produce a new paradigm, rather they signalled the consequences of greater competition and continuing innovation, and the need for constant adjustment. But they also signalled to Britain that without further social change its industries were unlikely to remain competitive, and economic growth would falter. The steel industry was a case in point.

To offset competition from the United States and Germany, Britain invested in new production facilities that cut the cost of production and allowed prices to fall 60 per cent in the 1870s and 1880s. Lower prices should have increased profits, but on this occasion they did not because by now a new and again unplanned dynamic was at work within industrial societies, albeit one that flowed directly from the levelling impulse of the technological strategy. Unskilled workers, who at one time were treated as expendable factory fodder, became as organized as the corporations they worked for. They demanded higher wages and were prepared to organize pitched battles with recalcitrant employers. At the same time improved transportation reduced the cost of food imports, giving workers a real increase in purchasing power. Immediate returns on industrial investments, then, fell short of expectations.

In some respects, the situation was temporary. Rising incomes provided the basis upon which further technological change would ultimately depend. But Britain's industrialists had little consciousness of this global feature of technologically driven economies, and it ultimately cost Britain the opportunity to stay ahead of competitors such as the United States, where mass consumption based on leisure and spending became more quickly entrenched. As long as the majority of workers struggled to survive, the potential for telephones, electricity, cars and a host of household consumer goods lay well in the future. Cars were developed in the late nineteenth century and mass-produced by the 1910s, but outside the United States their manufacture never took off until the 1950s. Britain focused instead on luxury models that suffered from short production runs and costly techniques. When it did begin mass production after 1918, it failed to copy the American example and buy workers' cooperation with higher wages. Instead it economized and became uncompetitive. Britain, says Landes, became 'caught in the net of habit [and] fell behind'.[60] But more importantly, it forgot that technology could not thrive with restricted markets and that workforces needed to be empowered as consumers.

Industry's initial response to greater competition in the late nineteenth century was to restructure itself, and the result was a form of organization quite different from the small competitive enterprise envisaged by Adam Smith a hundred years earlier. To overcome greater competition and survive leaner times, to provide more capital for investment in vastly more expensive technologies, and to remain profitable, companies began to merge or reach agreements to divide the market between themselves, even to fix profit levels. Not only industries merged; financial institutions joined forces with industry, as did trading companies. Now one giant corporation could control all aspects of production, from capital mobilization to retail.

This transformation is often referred to as monopoly capitalism, and the large corporations it spawned were the forerunners of today's giant transnationals. But large corporations heralded no instant era of prosperity; rather they raised the stakes in a game in which the goal remained unchanged.

Instead of competition between many small companies, competition now existed between fewer industrial giants. And because a nation's economic health came to depend more and more on fewer and fewer companies, states were even more inclined to treat their businesses as representatives of their nations. Tariffs were increasingly used offensively. They no longer served just to protect home markets as before. Corporations encouraged tariffs because they guaranteed high profits in their home markets. With those profits they subsidized exports and undermined competition.

Colonies fitted into this strategy also. The creation of monopoly capital at the same time as the last wave of colonial imperialism is no coincidence. Both were exclusive strategies designed to keep nations and their industries ahead of the competition. New colonies were grabbed and made appendages of metropolitan home markets, captive reservoirs for cheap labour and raw materials, and outlets for export capital. Indeed, as competition drove Britain further and further from free trade, it came to rely more and more on its own empire as a market of last resort. In 1880, 46 per cent of Britain's foreign investments were empire-bound; by 1929, 81 per cent.

Indeed the export of capital in general again assumed importance. British foreign investment stood at £82 million in 1872; by 1913 it had reached £225 million. This was still far less than Britain's export of manufactured goods, but even the composition of its exports changed dramatically. Increasingly Britain exported capital goods – machinery, systems of production. Capital goods exports increased in value from £263 million in 1890 to £430 million in 1910, over half the value of all exports. Mass consumption goods no longer dominated.

The extent to which deeper markets assisted industrialization was poorly understood in the nineteenth century. Deeper markets empowered citizens, but they also produced unsettling social and political changes. Consequently, as the second wave of globalization enveloped them, states sought stability through monopolies. However, this was not an option open to all societies, with the result that exclusion rather than inclusion again characterized globalization.

Notes

1. Stephen K. Sanderson, *Social Transformations: A General Theory of Historical Development*, Oxford, Blackwell, 1995, pp. 171–4; David Landes, *The Wealth and Poverty of Nations: Why some are so rich and some are so poor*, London, Little Brown and Co, 1998, pp. 169–76.

2. Peter J. Taylor, *The Way the Modern World Works: World Hegemony to World Impasse*, Chichester, John Wiley and Sons, 1996, p. 88.

3. Landes, *The Wealth and Poverty of Nations*, p. 205.

4. Robert Wright, *NONZERO: The Logic of Human Destiny*, New York, Pantheon Books, 2000, pp. 176–184.

5. Landes, *The Wealth and Poverty of Nations*, pp. 201–4, 52.

6. Brian Griffith, *The Gardens of their Dreams: Desertification and Culture in World History*, Nova Scotia, London and New York, Fernwood Publishing and Zed Books, 2001, pp. 314–22.

7. Landes, *The Wealth and Poverty of Nations*, pp. 206–7.

8. Ibid., pp. 217–22.

9. Ibid., pp. 223, 250.

10. Ibid., pp. 219–24.

11. Ibid., p. 223.

12. Ibid., pp. 230–43, 254.

13. Ibid., pp. 242–4.

14. Griffith, *The Garden of their Dreams*, pp. 326–8.

15. Landes, *The Wealth and Poverty of Nations*, pp. 244–7.

16. Ibid., pp. 233–5.

17. Ibid., p. 207.

18. Massimo Livi-Bacci, *The Population of Europe*, Oxford: Blackwell, 2000, pp. 36, 128. The Netherlands was the most urbanized at nearly 29 per cent but that was down from 34 per cent a century before. French urbanization was stagnant at 9 per cent. European per capita incomes rose 20 per cent 1785–1820.

19. Forest cover in West Europe declined from 95 per cent during the first millennium to under 20 per cent in the 1800s (Griffith, *The Garden of Their Dreams*, p. 324).

20. Snooks (Graeme Donald Snooks, *The Laws of History*, London and New York, Routledge, 1998, p. 53) denies this and claims that technological change does enable profits to keep pace with both labour and capital costs.

21. William H. McNeill, *The Pursuit of Power: Technology, Armed Forces and Society since AD 1000*, Oxford, Blackwell, 1982, pp. 206–12.

22. Graeme Donald Snooks, *The Ephemeral Civilization: Exploding the Myth of Social Evolution*, London and New York, Routledge, 1997, pp. 339–45.

23. Ibid., p. 346.

24. Ibid., p. 300; Growth during the period 1492–1561 had been 1.6 per cent.

25. Ibid., pp. 356–62.

26. Taylor, *The Way the Modern World Works*, pp. 197–211.

27. Livi Bacci, *Population of Europe*, pp. 129, 134–6.

28. Andre Gunder Frank, *REORIENT: Global Economy in the Asian Age*, Berkeley, University of California Press, 1998, p. 296.

29. Felipe Fernández-Armesto, *Millennium: A History of Our Last Thousand Years*, London, Black Swan, 1995, p. 367.

30. Frank, *REORIENT*, p. 295.

31. Ibid., pp. 175, 177, 294.

32. Ibid., p. 201.

33. Ibid., pp. 286–91.

34. Taylor, *The Way the Modern World Works*, p. 16.

35. Landes, *The Wealth and Poverty of Nations*, pp. 337–48.

36. Jonathan Spence, 'Paradise Lost', *FEER*, 15 April 1999, p. 40.

37. Wang Gungwu, 'Long Path to Power', *FEER*, 10 June 1999, pp. 40–4.

38. Simon Elegant, 'Trade Triumphant', *FEER*, 10 June 1999, p. 38.

39. Spence, 'Paradise Lost', pp. 40–6.

40. Mark Elvin, 'The X Factor', *FEER*, 10 June 1999, pp. 66–9.

41. Frank, *REORIENT*, pp. 300–2.

42. Spence, 'Paradise Lost', pp. 40–6.

43. Waley Cohen, *The Sextants of Beijing*, New York, Norton and Co., 1999, pp. 4–7, 287.

44. Samir Amin, 'History conceived as an eternal cycle', *Review*, Fernand Braudel Center, XXII (3: 1999), p. 314.

45. Deepak 'Golden Chains', *FEER*, 10 June 1999, pp. 50–54.

46. Frank, *REORIENT*, pp. 303–305.

47. Taylor, *The Way the Modern World Works*, pp. 119–20, 133–4.

48. Gilbert Rist, *The History of Development: from Western Origins to Global Faith*, London and New York, Zed Books, 1997, pp. 122, 137.

49. Landes, *The Wealth and Poverty of Nations*, p. 194.

50. Livi Bacci, *Population of Europe*, p. 128.

51. Frank, *REORIENT*, p. 202.

52. David Held, Anthony McGrew, David Goldblatt and Jonathon Perraton, *Global Transformations: Politics, Economics and Culture*, Oxford: Polity Press, 1999, p. 37.

53. Spence, 'Paradise Lost', p. 45.

54. Snooks, *Ephemeral Civilization*, p. 477; Cohen, *The Sextants of Beijing*, p. 287.

55. Frank, *REORIENT*, p. 315.

56. Taylor, *Way of the World*, p. 112.

57. Livi Bacci, *Population of Europe*, p. 162.

58. Landes, *The Wealth and Poverty of Nations*, p. 297.

59. Ibid., p. 307.

60. Ibid., pp. 284, 461–4.

· ·

CHAPTER 6

Empires of Disadvantage

§ THE discovery of the Americas at the end of the fifteenth century enabled dynamic and competitive West European societies to insert themselves into previously separate but interconnected regional trade networks. The resulting exchanges radically altered European fortunes; in some countries they deepened markets sufficiently to enable the emergence of a new technological basis for production. Certainly, the new exchanges transformed global diets, world demography, and regional ecologies. But above all they instituted new global networks of production, trade and finance. Consequently, within three centuries, the global context in which most societies operated had changed. China began as an engine of world growth, buoyed by trade surpluses that rippled through its large economy; by the end of the first wave, its surpluses were threatened and its economy was under stress. But nothing prepared it for the second wave of globalization, unleashed by the irruption of the industrial era and the collapse of yet another conquering ambition.

What made this second wave so different? Its global impact was much deeper and more rapid. It inherited the networks of the first wave but was driven instead by technology, not trade. Improved communications and systems of transportation reduced distances in time and enabled the new movements of goods and people on a scale never before possible. Europeans benefited most. Over sixty million left for the Americas, Australasia, and southern and East Africa between 1815 and 1914; one million went to North Africa. But they were not alone. Nearly twenty million Chinese and Japanese migrated, as did some two million Indians.[1]

Industrial systems of production also connected with new sources of raw materials, again on scales that seemed constantly to escalate. They generated wealth that surged through industrial economies much more impressively than Spanish bullion; indeed there seemed no end to its production and reproduction. From these effects derived the second wave's most significant characteristic: it transformed societies, and in very distinct ways.

Europeans did not describe these changes as globalization; they preferred to regard them as progress. Industrialization's initial success may have been based on the inclusion of more and more people in the commercial economy, but as far as many Europeans were concerned, progress applied only to the fittest; it had no universal application. Many Europeans thought it applied only to them. When Japan successfully challenged Russia at the beginning of the twentieth century, the Russians damned the Japanese as upstarts, 'monkeys' acting in defiance of 'the rights of man'.[2] Yet even the Japanese transformation, still not accepted as of the same stuff by many Eurocentrics nearly one hundred years later, did nothing to alter the one feature of the second wave that both energized it and doomed it. Its diversity was built upon fundamental inequalities that denied inclusion. Thus transformation coalesced around two basic forms.

First, it took an industrial form in societies whose proximity, interconnections, market value or autonomy enabled them to respond to Britain's industrialization. Over the course of the nineteenth century their populations increased, and became more urbanized and less dependent on agriculture. As these societies industrialized, new social and political dynamics emerged. How they handled these dynamics determined their future success. In most industrializing societies the stresses were nearly overwhelming. The United States massacred 600,000 of its own people in a bitter civil war in the 1860s. Revolution convulsed much of Europe in 1848 and France in 1871. Japan's fractious elite rebelled during the 1870s, and Russia's government collapsed in 1917, sparking a long and bitter civil war, and a much longer division among industrial nations over the nature of change required by modernity. Still the landscape changed.

Second, societies unable, unwilling or unaware of the need to respond urgently to the industrial era very quickly found themselves captive to a new international division of labour; they assumed colonial forms. Some, like European settler states, became self-governing and retained a margin of autonomy with respect to the income their economies generated. They invested in social and economic infrastructure, and created communities that shared in the wealth and culture of the countries from which they were derived. Others, such as China, managed to retain the semblance of autonomy, but increasingly lost control of their economies. Haiti won its independence from France in 1804 but at the cost of an indemnity, the equivalent of France's total annual budget, which denied it investment funds for development.[3]

For the majority of the world's peoples, however, globalization meant only one thing: colonialism. They were incorporated into the economies of industrializing nations to supply raw materials and cheap labour; nothing more. The effects were diverse. In Asia, colonial authorities built on existing structures of power and transformed local economies into plantation industries. In southern and eastern Africa, Europeans settled and established large estates.

In central Africa, they looted; when their forces eventually pulled out some seventy-five years later, they left behind shattered communities with no infrastructure beyond that required for colonial dependence.

The colonial experience was harsh and brutal, and often resembled multiple holocausts. It trapped future generations in legacies of bitterness and disadvantage. It refashioned systems of governance that disempowered the subjects whom colonialism claimed to civilize. In doing so, colonialism not only weakened globalization but created difficult handicaps for the next wave to overcome.

The Industrializing Impulse

Off the coast of Eurasia, and dwarfed by its Chinese neighbour, Japan had undergone substantial transformation since the seventeenth century. Its intensive agriculture became commercialized and its market-oriented economy fed off large and well-connected urban populations, whose homogeneity provided cohesion at a time of great national stress. Furthermore, its royal family – like Britain's – remained safely cocooned from government.

But in 1853 the United States came knocking. It wished to become a Pacific power. Having expanded its frontiers along the North American Pacific Coast, it now cast greedy eyes at the opportunities for trade being forcibly created in China. Japan provided an ideal refuelling spot en route to Shanghai. Accordingly, its fleet sat menacingly in Tokyo Bay while emissaries demanded open access for its merchants and ships. Within five years, Japan had signed Unequal Treaties with the United States, the Netherlands, Russia, Britain and France. By denying Japan the right to impose tariffs to protect its own producers from foreign competition, the Unequal Treaties started a process designed to strip Japan of its autonomy. They failed in this regard, but by the time the treaties lapsed in 1911, they had given special shape to the Japanese response.

To begin with, the sudden insertion of European traders into the Japanese economy precipitated severe inflation and debased the currency. Peasant unrest grew. For capitulating to foreign pressure, the Tokugawa Shogunate bore the brunt of public shock and anger, particularly in the southern districts of Satsuma, Hizon and Choshu, where local traders were far more aware of the dangers Japan faced. They knew of China's fate after the Opium Wars, and had themselves experienced American retaliation when foreigners were expelled from Kagoshima in 1863. Discontented, they united against the Shogunate and overthrew it in a short civil war in 1868.

Taking the name of a new emperor, the Meiji revolutionaries now set about to meet the Western challenge by building a strong, wealthy nation. They ended the feudal privileges of the samurai; they created a modern army; they removed caste barriers. The changes did not come easily. For much of the 1870s samurai elements fought pitched battles against the Meiji revolutionaries. Nor did the changes come cheaply. Paying off the samurai and their warlords, suppressing the discontent that change generated, establishing the basic infrastructure for industrialization (rail, telegraph, port and banking facilities) and instituting compulsory primary education nearly bankrupted the government.

Not surprisingly, conquest overseas tempted Japan. It promised quick returns for investment at home, and a welcome distraction for malcontents. Taiwan and Korea became its first targets, then the rich resources of Manchuria. At the same time, Japan also eased the state burden at home by selling many of its enterprises in the 1880s. The buyers were wealthy merchants and high officials whose resulting large enterprises (*zaibatsu*) soon dominated Japanese industry but remained loyal to the Meiji objective of a strong, wealthy nation. Japan's corporatism was not unique; indeed the partnership of state and business interests became a defining feature of the second wave of globalization, just as mercantilism had defined the first wave.

Undeniably, the Meiji Revolution saved Japan from colonialism, but could not so easily overturn the effects of the Unequal Treaties. Unable to protect its own industries, Japan promoted instead a low-wage economy. In addition, because the external economic threat remained overwhelming, the Japanese did not believe they had the luxury of time to enable all their various economic sectors to develop evenly. Consequently, their government decided on a policy of selective development; only certain sectors would receive government assistance. The rest would be integrated later.

Japan's resultant uneven development came in two forms. First, within the labour force itself. The large *zaibatsu* represented the sectors most favoured by government and closest to it. Because of the incentives in wages and conditions of employment that they were able to offer, *zaibatsu* gained the best workers, and, by sheer dint of their superior resources, remained far in advance of smaller, non-government-supported companies. Economic duality resulted and contributed dangerous internal pressures, as the expected better life failed to materialize for the majority of Japan's citizens. Lacking a strong and integrated internal economy, Japan searched instead for foreign markets and raw materials that would provide it with the kind of economic expansion that its own sacrificed internal markets could not.

Agriculture, once the engine of the Japanese economy, now also suffered. State resources poured into industry, and Japan relied more and more on food imports to feed its rapidly urbanizing population. The cost manifested itself in different ways. Over six million Japanese left, seeking alternative pastures in the Americas, South-east Asia and Hawaii. But rural backwardness also affected Japan's capacity to act as a market for its own industrial products and reinforced its decision to seek external markets that it could secure from competition.

Being weaker than Britain or the United States, it knew it could not compete on the basis of open-door policies, as these two countries now insisted, at least with regard to China. Only aggressive military pressure, it believed, could do that. Between 1868 and 1945 Japan went to war on ten different occasions. The early wars against Taiwan (1874), Korea (1876), China (1894) and Russia (1904) quickly demonstrated the advantages of aggression: Japan's military forces were strengthened, raw materials and cheap labour were seized, and access to new markets was guaranteed. When the First World War began in Europe, Japan declared war on Germany in order to grab the German colonies of Shandong, and the northern Pacific Mariana, Caroline and Marshall Islands. It dressed up its own imperialism as liberation from European dominance. It also made use of Europe's preoccupation with war to pressure the weak Chinese government to concede economic rights over Manchuria and Fujian. 'It is my belief', one nationalist argued, 'that Heaven has decided on Japan as its choice for the champion of the East. Has this not been the purpose of our three thousand long years of preparation? It must be said that this is a truly grand and magnificent mission'.[4]

Japan was not alone in reacting to globalization in this manner. The United States also felt that it had to expand in order to secure a strong economic base for itself. In 1822, President Munroe told Congress that 'Extent of territory ... marks ... the difference between a great and small power'.[5] Expansion fostered prosperity and permitted the absorption of vast numbers of immigrants fleeing poverty and unrest in Europe. It also promised future growth. 'Our destiny', claimed one senator, 'is to grasp the commerce of all the seas and sway the sceptre of the world'.[6] Indeed, by the end of the nineteenth century it had made a good start in that direction, having seized lands from North American Indian tribes and from neighbouring Mexico (Texas, California and New Mexico in the 1840s). By 1860 half of its population lay in the western states.[7]

Disagreements over the need for an industrial future for the whole of the country, in particular the new western states, were resolved in a bitter Civil War in the early 1860s. The defeated South's plantation economies now declined and were incorporated into the industrial machinery of the North. Civil war stimulated industrial growth and the integration of the western states. Rail networks more than trebled during the late nineteenth century. Into this vast US market poured another influx of European migrants. But after the 1880s land for settlement dried up. Migrants and disillusioned farmers began moving instead into cities for work. Urbanization doubled in the late nineteenth century; by 1910, 46 per cent of the population lived in cities and manufacturing absorbed 22 per cent of the workforce, compared with 14 per cent fifty years before. By 1913, the US produced nearly 13 per cent of world trade in manufacturing. Cities became the new frontiers, acting both as consumer stimulants to industry and as sources for cheap industrial labour. Annual per capita GDP growth rose 2.1 per cent between 1870 and 1900, one third higher than in the years before the Civil War, and nearly as high as the boom years which would follow the Second World War.[8]

As in Japan, industrialization produced large industrial monopolies that squeezed out small property and business people, and justified their dominance on Social Darwinist premises. The powerful exemplified the survival of the fittest. By 1892, the US had four thousand millionaires, who regarded themselves as the nation's elite. The poor were poor, they said, because they lacked industry, piety and thrift. If the US was to prosper, it had to be led and governed by those who were successful. In time the benefits of their actions would trickle down to those below them. Indeed, for the most part, US governments were content to let business have its way, particularly when it came to dealing with its urban masses. In 1903 it formed state National Guards as elite militias of the middle class to combat rebellious workers.

Social Darwinism also provided justification for external expansion similar to Europe's civilizing missions and Japan's liberating service. It was the duty of the 'fittest' races to rule in order to guarantee progress. 'God has not been preparing the English-speaking and Teutonic peoples for a thousand years for nothing', thundered a US senator in 1903. 'No! He has made us the master organizers of the world to establish system where chaos reigns'.[9] But expansion was never predicated solely on moral arguments. Expansion would sustain national economic and social well-being. The wealth it yielded would trickle down to provide prosperity for all Americans, and the patriotism it generated would dissolve the divisions of town and country, native and immigrant.

By the end of the nineteenth century, the US had its own colonial empire: Cuba, Puerto Rico, Guam and the Philippines. The Philippines gave the US access to Asia, the focus of a second major initiative, the declaration in 1899 of an open-door policy towards China. Already Hawaii (and half of Samoa) had been annexed in 1898 to facilitate US power and commerce in the Pacific. In 1904, President Theodore Roosevelt extended the open-door principle: henceforth the US would act as the policeman of the world. To demonstrate US determination, he financed Panama's revolution against Colombia and seized control of the Panama Canal. Increasingly the US now intervened in the affairs of Latin America to promote its own economic interests. 'Our surplus energy is beginning to look beyond our own borders', Roosevelt's successor, Taft, explained, 'to find the opportunity for the profitable use of our surplus capital and for markets for our manufactures'.[10]

Russia also responded to industrialization, by expanding across Eurasia to the Pacific. Siberia's population increased fourfold, to ten million people, in the half century before 1914, perhaps some four million alone in the years following the opening of the Trans-Siberian Railway in 1890. Because of this migration, Russian land under cultivation more than doubled to 31 million acres.[11] But Russian reluctance to transform old feudal structures undermined its efforts at industrialization. Although it did finally abolish serfs in 1861, it could not bring itself to remove communal systems of tenure and taxation. Consequently peasants were not permitted individual title to land, but were tied instead to villages whose elders decided on land distribution. Peasants were also made to pay for their emancipation with a special tax that went to the nobility. The tax kept the nobility from revolting, but it retarded agricultural reorganization.

Fearful of change and fearful too of peasant revolt, the autocratic Tsarist regime resisted all efforts to introduce universal education, to decentralize political control, and to democratize Russian society. But it did support industrialization after the 1870s, and in particular financed railway and military expansion. Both helped to maintain control over the vast empire. The state also raised new protective duties to encourage capital investment.

But Russia's industrialization bore all the hallmarks of semi-colonialism, being financed largely by foreign capital (mostly French). It was also highly focused, large and capital-intensive, with few linkages to the rest of the economy. Most of the small industrial workforce was still employed in archaic workshops which produced as much as 30 per cent of Russia's industrial output. In fact, development tended to be both geographically and industrially uneven, which also contributed to unrest in the country. Government slowness in adjusting to demands for change merely added fuel to an already raging fire.

When Japan defeated Russia in 1904, thwarting the latter's ambitions to expand further in East Asia, land riots swept the country and forced the Tsar to revise his land tenure laws and concede a measure of parliamentary rule. He had little room to manoeuvre. Dependence on foreign investment produced high profit remittances, interest charges and loan repayments. Russia needed to convert its annual surplus from the land into foreign currency to pay these costs. This required both land reform and a measure of rural harmony. Accordingly, some peasants were allowed to consolidate their holdings and to modernize agricultural production. But this option was still not open to most peasants. Instead, they were impoverished by crippling taxes imposed by a state impatient to cover the cost of industry's growing import bill.

Peasants formed the bulk of Russia's population at the turn of the century. Their exploitation meant that they could never become consumers of the products of industry. Unrest simply brought fresh waves of repression upon them, with the result that even the small gap between peasants and *kulaks* – Russia's modernizing peasants – fostered resentment.

Thus Russia's agriculturally driven export production failed to finance industrialization and produce a stronger nation. When the First World War broke out in 1914, Russia was ill-equipped with the kind of administrative and industrial skills war demanded. It mobilized fifteen million soldiers, but could supply only three million rifles. In the slaughter that followed, the Tsarist regime collapsed. With it went its fledging parliamentary experiment, the Duma. Instead, a new revolutionary group of radicals seized power, determined to pursue a path of modernization that they believed would place Russia ahead of the world in a new, post-capitalist stage.

Japan and Russia reacted differently to the global impact of industrialization in the nineteenth century, but each retained a degree of autonomy. Other countries were less fortunate. Unable to determine their own fate, they became colonies or semi-colonies that provided raw materials and cheap labour to augment the wealth and power of industrializing nations. In 1800, European countries exercised control over nearly 35 per cent of the world. By 1878, the proportion had increased to 67 per cent; by 1914, to 85 per cent. Such incorporation assumed many forms but, for the vast majority of people caught in this web of imperialism, the end result was always the same: powerlessness.

Prisoners in Other People's Futures

Something of this fate awaited China. China had always tightly monitored European access to its resources. Until the nineteenth century, foreign merchants were permitted to operate only in the southern Chinese ports of Macao (already in Portuguese hands) and Guangzhou (Canton), but the smuggling of opium resulted in further restrictions. When the Qing dynasty finally moved to end the trade, the British government retaliated with its successful First Opium War (1834–42). Humiliated, China was forced under the terms of the 1842 Unequal Treaties to open four more ports to merchant activity. By 1860, France, Germany, Russia, Japan and the US had extended this number to eleven, and by 1899 to forty-five. The American John Adams justified their actions in this way:

> The moral obligation of commercial intercourse between nations is founded entirely ... upon the Christian precept to love your neighbour as yourself. ... But China, not being a Christian nation, its inhabitants do not consider themselves bound by the Christian precept. ... [Therefore] the fundamental principle of the Chinese nation is anti commercial. ... It admits no obligation to hold commercial intercourse with others ... It is time that this enormous outrage upon the rights of human nature, and upon the first principles of the rights of nations should cease.[12]

China's refusal to trade in opium was an unacceptable affront to the march of civilization.

The presence of new centres for foreign trade and the introduction of foreign-owned and controlled factories had a disastrous effect on China's traditional economy. Vast numbers of porters, boatmen and coolies were thrown out of work in southern China as Guangzhou lost its dominance as a trading centre and as the use of steamboats increased. Opium sales burgeoned, and China lost its silver income. This loss, combined with the huge indemnities forced on China for not immediately capitulating to Britain's demands concerning opium, precipitated a major monetary crisis. Unable to pay their rents or taxes, many peasants fell into debt and were forced to sell their land and become wage-labourers. Twelve million Chinese chose to migrate during the nineteenth century. New methods of production, particularly in the treaty port enclaves, also destroyed the traditional handicraft industries on which many peasants depended to supplement their incomes.

This gradual transformation of the Chinese economy, while making China increasingly dependent on global trading empires, did little to help the Qing dynasty, which barely knew how to manage the changes confronting it. Its prestige fell with every concession made to foreign interests. As government corruption and ineptitude increased, and as natural disasters combined with foreign economic penetration to worsen the position of peasants, large-scale revolts erupted throughout the provinces in the mid-nineteenth century. The largest of these – the Taiping Revolution – came close to toppling the Qing dynasty.

But foreign competition now made it impossible for Britain or any other nation to take control in China as Britain had in India. Nor was it possible for European imperialists simply to divide China among themselves as they did Africa after 1870. By the late nineteenth century a new player had to be considered: Japan.

In the end, the Qing dynasty went the way of Japan's shogunate and Russia's tsars. But even after the 1911 Revolution, no united administration emerged to meet the challenges that China faced. Instead, the country collapsed into warlord factionalism. Foreign government control increased to include China's postal services, taxes, customs, and – because of the heavy debts and indemnities imposed on China whenever it tried to stand up to foreign powers – its financial services as well.

Something different was happening here. The historian Geoffrey Barraclough explains it this way:

[In the late nineteenth century t]rade was no longer the issue: it was, in the American idiom, 'peanuts'. What mattered now was property rights, mineral rights, mining rights and above all else financial control, for loans meant the right to control the wherewithal to repay the loans, which usually was customs duties, and this meant ... foreign control of customs finances, and perhaps also the right to insist on new taxation to provide the means to service the loans.

And if, as was only to be expected, new taxation produced unrest and even revolt, that also would create a pretext for intervention which could only be welcome.[13]

Little wonder China lost its ability to respond. For similar reasons, so too did many other countries. Egypt tried to industrialize in the 1860s and even sought its own empire in the south. But it ran out of money, faced an Islamic revolt, and was conquered by Britain. Morocco tried to claim the Sahara, but a rebellion gave Spain and France the opportunity to intervene. Zanzibar tried to build an empire for itself in central and eastern Africa based on slave networks, but Belgium, Britain and Germany soon overwhelmed its creation.[14]

Despite the increasing attractiveness that colonies held for industrializing countries, they ultimately contradicted the levelling impulse of the new technologically driven era. This was not immediately apparent. Colonies had always satisfied the desire of their masters to extract profits. Indeed they existed as part of the zero–sum strategies of conquest or monopoly trade, cogs in machines that produced profit for someone else, never themselves. Industrial technology, however, created new potentials for profit, but its success depended on markets for its products. Imperialism satisfied industrial demands for cheap raw materials with which to offset competition from rivals, but ultimately it denied industry additional markets or growth potential. In all probability, industry leaders judged the potential too distant to be of immediate concern, or allowed racial attitudes to dismiss it out of hand. Nonetheless, the cost of sustaining empires of disadvantage eventually exceeded their value. Indeed the political and social instability they contributed to not only doomed the second wave of globalization but created powerful destabilizing legacies that reached far into the future.

Empires of Disadvantage

At first there was logic to imperial expansion. To keep ahead of competition, industrializing nations sought access to new resources and cheap labour, or to extend supplies of existing commodities. Australia and New Zealand were developed as British farms; the discovery of precious metals there was an unexpected boost for projects already begun. In reality, of course, much empire-building was based on speculation. One British prime minister described it as 'pegging out claims for the future'.[15] It raised morale and confidence. And for industry it provided all-important horizons and promised expanding futures. Confidence, after all, sustained enterprise.

But empire-building was also a game of strategy. In 1840 France decided to launch a full-scale war to capture Algeria. It wished to position itself in North Africa to take advantage of any crisis that threatened to weaken Ottoman dominance in the region. Most particularly it wished to exclude Britain. At the same time Britain seized New Zealand, in part to thwart French designs on the South Island. Much later Britain seized East Africa and Egypt to protect its lucrative route through the Suez Canal to India. A well-placed competitor such as France could create havoc, or so it was assumed.

Sometimes pride determined action. Empires made nations seem great, and greatness was a prerequisite for big-power status, the reward that industrialization had bestowed on Britain. Old conquest and technological strategies became hopelessly conflated. 'To remain a great nation or to become one, you must colonize',[16] declared French statesman Leon Gambetta. In 1830 the French crown captured Algiers in a futile attempt to restore its prestige. Ten years later it tried to deflect internal unrest by launching its invasion of Algeria. The French Revolution and the Napoleonic Wars had cost France 1.5 million deaths. The massive death toll, together with falling birth rates, meant that France could no longer sustain the massive 30 per cent growth in population that it had experienced during the previous century.[17] Many French commentators believed that France needed more people to stimulate economic development and to compete with other industrializing countries. France's defeat by the Prussians in 1870 brought the issue to the fore in a dramatic fashion. If it could not achieve size naturally, then it would have to do so by empire. Empire would salvage national pride and demonstrate greatness. It would prevent France becoming a second-rate power.

With the Germans also casting about for symbols of greatness, a scramble for Africa began.[18] Across the Channel, public intellectual John Ruskin implored the youths of England similarly to rise to the new occasion. 'Will you make your country again a royal throne of kings, a sceptred isle for all the world, a source of light, a centre of peace, a mistress of learning of the Arts; faithful guardian of great memories in the midst of irrelevant and ephemeral visions.' Their first duty, he said, was to advance the power of Britain by sea and land.[19]

Sometimes the actions of settlers and businesspeople forced the hand of governments. In 1874 Britain assumed control in Fiji after settlers had so destabilized the country that it feared a repeat of New Zealand's costly land wars. In southern Africa the same impulse for land drove settler expansion. Cecil Rhodes boasted in the 1890s that,

> When I began this business of annexation, both sides were very timid. They would ask one to stop at Kimberley, then they asked one to stop at Kharma's country. ... Now, sir, they won't stop anywhere; they have found that the world is not quite big enough for British trade and the British flag; and that the operation of even conquering the planets is only something which has yet to be known.[20]

Of course imperialist actions also helped to distract from the many tensions that industrialization created at home. With the rise of political parties at the end of the nineteenth century and the advent of mass electorates, some politicians found colonialism a useful way to appeal to the masses for support. In 1911, Germany intervened in France's attempt to control Morocco in order, in the words of its own Foreign Secretary, 'to change the views of many disaffected voters' and produce 'a significant effect upon the outcome of the pending Reichstag election'.[21]

Finally, for some imperialists, colonialism was a duty they owed humanity. One French publicist argued in 1874 that 'Colonialism is one of the highest functions of societies that have reached an advanced stage of civilization'.[22] Another declared that: 'Providence has dictated to us the obligation of knowing the earth and making the conquest of it. This supreme command is one of the imperious duties inscribed on our intelligence and on our activities.'[23] Colonialism was a moral responsibility. The people colonized were like children; industrial nations their mothers. What could be more natural than mothers caring for their offspring?[24]

With such a variety of explanations used to justify colonialism, it is not surprising that there is no consensus as to its impact. Many accounts dismiss colonialism. Landes somewhat defensively reminds us that colonialism was never a Western or modern invention.[25] Snooks similarly downplays its significance. Colonies were only an insurance against the threat posed by increased industrial competition. Colonies produced much lower returns than technological innovation.[26] Taylor suggests that Britain used its empire to mask its decline.[27]

Imperialists regarded colonization as an important adjunct to the technological strategy. It was conquest writ large, a demonstration of the global power that industrial nations had achieved. It also served to illustrate their transformative power. Although politicians carefully exploited imperial campaigns, particularly successful ones, to demonstrate their nationalistic credentials, they also appealed to this wider transforming dimension. Just as industry had transformed their own societies, so imperialism in turn would beneficially transform the world.

Schools, churches and mass circulation newspapers and magazines spread the word far and wide. So too music, theatre, literature, the visual arts, even postcards. Imperialism became part of the popular culture. Always portrayed as positive and progressive, it brought order where there was chaos, and light where there was darkness. With it emerged a triumphant imperial narrative – Gordon of Khartoum, Rhodes of Rhodesia, Raffles of Singapore, Livingstone of Africa, Scott of the Antarctic, and Lawrence of Arabia. Accounts of the exploits of soldiers, explorers and missionaries became the regular diet of newspaper and magazine subscribers and helped to spread the belief that imperialism was part of a God-given 'civilizing' mission, a crusade, the duty of all people towards the less civilized; Kipling's 'white man's burden'.[28] When the League of Nations established mandates to replace the colonies of the First World War's defeated powers, it too did not hesitate to accept imperialism's civilizing mission.[29]

But in the rush to legitimize colonialism, to portray it as the equivalent of technology's power to transform, its publicists made no mention of forced labour, heavy tax burdens, population displacement, the destructive imposition of cash crops, racial segregation, and political suppression. Nor did they explain the context for Britain's abolition of slavery; namely, its desire to make life more difficult for the French in the West Indies. These matters contradicted the positive image that imperialists wished to convey to their own people. Instead a convenient forgetting took place.

Mussolini's invading soldiers massacred thousands of Ethiopians in 1935; mustard-gas attacks on villages and concentration camps were weapons 'to annihilate cultures deemed inferior'. Says Italian historian Giorgi Rochart, 'There remains in Italian culture and public opinion the idea that basically we were colonists with a human face'.[30] Australians regard their history similarly. The use of the word *genocide* by some historians to describe the actions of nineteenth-century settlers or the assimilation policies of twentieth-century governments to eradicate Aboriginality is not widely assented to.[31]

Imperialism's 'civilizing mission' sustained public support for colonialism, and retains a powerful hold to this day. It has become the stuff of films and books that continue to distance belief from reality. David Cannadine's *Ornamentalism* invites us into a world of 'antiquity and anachronism, tradition and honour, order and subordination; glory and chivalry, horses and elephants, knights and peers, processions and ceremony, plumed hats and ermine robes; … chiefs and emirs, sultans and nawabs, viceroys and crowns, dominions and hierarchies, ostentation and ornamentalism.'[32] Nostalgia for the remnants of former ruling classes more comfortable with the conquest tradition and its affectations served and serves still to mask colonialism's most important contradiction.

Despite all its pretensions to civilize and modernize, colonialism's goal was the opposite. It set out to prevent the very kind of transformations then convulsing Europe. In a sense, Cannadine is correct. Empire was about conquest, domination and theft. It was about recreating inequalities and traditions then disappearing in Europe. It was about creating difference. The record spoke for itself. During the early eighteenth century, the ratio of wealth between Europeans and their future colonies was often no more than 2:1. By 1900 it stood at 5:1; by the time colonialism ended in the 1960s, 15:1.[33] This factor, more than any other, proved colonialism's undoing. In a technological era based on empowerment, it was unsustainable. 'We now know', writes one of Cannadine's reviewers, 'that the British Empire was essentially a Hitlerian project on a grand scale, involving military conquest and dictatorship, extermination and genocide, martial law and "special courts", slavery and forced labour, concentration camps and the transoceanic migration of people'.[34]

Imperialism unleashed a terribly destructive, destabilizing force upon the world. Its propagandists held that only the peoples of industrialized nations could achieve any meaningful form of development. The British writer Rudyard Kipling dismissed the 1854 Indian Mutiny against British rule as madness; how could inferior peoples ever think of ruling themselves?[35] At a banquet to celebrate the abolition of slavery, the French novelist Victor Hugo declared:

> To fashion a new Africa, to make the old Africa amenable to civilization – that is the problem. And Europe will solve it. … Pour out everything you have in this Africa, and at the same stroke solve your own social questions! Change your proletarians into property owners! Go on, do it. Make roads, make ports, make towns! Grow, cultivate, colonize, multiply![36]

The distinction between civilized and uncivilized peoples contained other consequences also, as the philosopher John Stuart Mill explained: 'The sacred duties which civilized nations owe to the independent nations of each other are not binding towards those to whom nationality and independence are certain evils or at best a questionable good'.[37] Imperialists did not regard all peoples as equal; rights were not universal and colonies were not countries. They existed only as a modern form of medieval estate. The public intellectual Thomas Carlyle described West Indians as 'two legged cattle' for whom slavery and the whip were preferable to self-help or upward mobility.[38] No colony bestowed the same rights, privileges and opportunities on the colonized as they did on the colonizer. To do so would have made colonies impossible to control and to loot. Colonies were never intended to be mirror images of their 'mother' country.

Justifications for the distinctions drew on an armoury of ideas about race. In France, phrenologist Gustave le Bon measured the sizes of people's heads and declared West Europeans more intelligent than American natives and Africans. Other anthropologists observed head shapes. Doctors declared that some races were more prone to illnesses than others, hence the need for racial purity. Theories of colonial assimilation, racial types, and systems of colonial practice became subjects for academic study. Universities and their new disciplines of anthropology, history, economics and sociology reinforced notions of Western superiority and moral right, and made the concept of racial segregation acceptable.

The promoters of these developments never for a moment envisaged the tremendous long-term consequences of their actions and beliefs. Their understanding of globalization excluded the technological paradigm offering benefits to all humanity. By their actions they transformed racism into both a science and a system of political administration. This added a new level of complexity to the changes that all societies faced, including their own. It induced deep psychological barriers between colonized and colonizer that perpetuated distrust and violence.

In the United States, African-American activist W.E.B. Du Bois lamented the absence of a shared culture. Segregation created a 'sense of always looking at oneself through the eyes of others, of measuring one's soul by the tape of a world that looks in on it in amused contempt and pity. [It produced] two souls, two thoughts, two unreconciled strivings; two warring ideals in one dark body.' 'The secret of Europe resides in what makes it different from us', the Cameroonian Marcien Towa wrote. It is necessary to 'deny ourselves, cast doubt on our innermost being and become fundamentally Europeanized, ... aim expressly to become like the Other, similar to the Other, and thereby uncolonizable by the Other'.[39] Sometimes these feelings induced a militancy which paralleled that of the colonizer. In the United States, Marcus Garvey fashioned a fascist movement 'to purify and standardize' his race. When he met members of the Ku Klux Klan in 1922, he applauded them for having 'lynched race pride into the Negroes'.[40]

The pain of colonialism lingered and festered. It was all-pervasive. In the 1950s, Frantz Fanon observed that 'Colonialism is not satisfied merely with holding a people in its grip and emptying the native's brain of all form and content. By a kind of perverted logic, it turns to the past of the people and distorts, disfigures and destroys it.'[41] Colonized peoples had no history. History began only when their modern conquerors arrived. Again Fanon:

> The settler makes history; his life is an epoch, an Odyssey. He is the absolute beginning ... [and the] unceasing cause of the land. Without him there would be nothing. Yet the history [that the settler writes] is not the history of the country he plunders but the history of his own nation in regard to all that she skims off, all that she violates and starves.[42]

Colonialism 'turned men and women into things', claimed sociologist Simione Durutalo. It divested them of their humanity. By means of force, tyranny and psychological emasculation, it perpetually reinforced feelings of inferiority. It developed ignorance, because it did not want natives to learn the reality of colonialism. Durutalo continued:

> During the greater part of British rule knowledge – except that provided in carefully limited doses by the missionaries – was disdained. The people were discouraged from thinking for themselves; a thirst for knowledge was considered dangerous and subversive. Trained to obey and follow, and mindful of the misfortunes that befell the poor native who, using his or her reason,

questioned however timidly the decisions of someone in authority, the people later transformed this training and fear into a conviction that one should always allow one's social and economic superiors to do the thinking for the community. … This passivity was gradually transformed into and glorified as tradition.[43]

Racism had other poisoning effects also; globalization ensured that it spread with the vast migrations of people. Slavery might be officially dead, but the British created indentured labour and sent Indians to farm sugar cane in Caribbean, Indian Ocean and Pacific islands. In Durutalo's Fiji, Indians and Fijians were segregated. They lived apart, were schooled apart, and worked apart. They were encouraged to see their differences as irreconcilable. Racial differences were explained by reference to grand narratives of civilization. Children were raised on the resultant stereotypes. The British encouraged this: subjects who hated each other were unlikely to combine against colonialism. But racism had other consequences also. Many Fijians believed deeply in the rhetoric and used it to account for their backwardness. They were less civilized. Indians were smarter. A victim mentality developed from which it was difficult to escape, and which, long after colonialism ended, added fuel to flames of disadvantage that continued to engulf the country in collective calamity. Race produces its own prison, as the philosopher Rabindranath Tagore once wrote.[44]

Hatreds are easier to manufacture than to eradicate. So too are feelings of inadequacy. They also have unexpected consequences. Stripped of their identities, colonized peoples often developed new heroes, new myths and new religions. They accepted much of the logic of colonialism. If colonists insisted on imperialism's ethnic divisions, so did they. People were different. Their characters, their natures, their beliefs were different. Edward Said strongly believes that such essentialisms, such stereotypes, do turn people against each other and create chaos.[45] Globalization might have brought the world closer together, but through imperialism it created multiple conflicting worlds and holocausts on a scale never before experienced.

In the late nineteenth century, Joseph Conrad wrote a famous novel, *The Heart of Darkness*, perhaps the greatest of all books written about colonialism. Since then it has been the basis for a number of films, the most notable being *Apocalypse Now*, set appropriately in Vietnam, the mid-twentieth century's Congo. Conrad played on ideas of lightness and darkness, and suggested that darkness lay as much in London or Paris or Brussels as on the upper reaches of the River Congo. The Congo had indeed been a place of unspeakable darkness. But the darkness lay with Belgium's King Leopold, who from the late 1870s had treated the country as his personal fiefdom. Under the pretext of ending slavery, he looted it for ivory, diamonds and rubber. His brutal soldiers, and the starvation and disease which followed their actions, slaughtered half the population, eight to ten million Congolese.[46]

When France colonized Algeria with a vengeance in the early 1840s, Alexis de Tocqueville, the aristocrat still remembered as a great democrat and liberal, wrote: 'I believe the laws of war entitle us to ravage the country and that we must do this, either by destroying crops at harvest time, or all the time by making rapid incursions, known as raids, the aim of which is to carry off men and flocks'.[47] One sixth of the population perished in the carnage that followed.

In British India, the transformation of agriculture for commercial purposes induced a famine in Bengal, which by 1770 claimed ten million lives. A similar famine in 1944, induced this time by wartime shortages and colonial policies, took four million lives.[48] In British Ireland, official neglect and agricultural transformation similarly caused potato blight and typhus to destroy close to 1.5 million people in 1846.[49]

Colonists in the late nineteenth and twentieth century – like many Americans in Vietnam – were blinded by their own 'light'. The only 'darkness' that existed was one that they themselves created: an inability to acknowledge popular resistance movements and initiatives for sovereignty in the non-European world. They forgot that 'colonial' people existed before colonialism, that power had been seized, and that a struggle against domination would eventually occur regardless of what they did. The Italian defeat at Adowa in Ethiopia in 1896 foreshadowed one possibility. Within a generation, the rise of Indian middle-class agitation for independence foreshadowed another.

Historian Felipe Fernández-Armesto likens imperialism to 'a confidence trick'.[50] It survived as long as there were local collaborators. It survived as long as the colonizers confronted their horrors, injustices and contradictions with a stiff upper lip.[51] When the empires of disadvantage finally unscrambled, their traumatized peoples were abandoned with only their schooling in the politics of division, privilege and greed to sustain them.

For this reason, Fanon feared that peaceful transitions from colonialism to self-government would not break the stranglehold of colonial thinking. Whenever natives stepped into colonial shoes, colonial traditions and structures were maintained, replicated by the colonized to suppress their own people. Even if suppression did not occur, new post-colonial structures rested on old hierarchies ill-equipped to meet the challenges a very different wave of globalization now imposed. Consequently, Fanon called on formerly colonized peoples to accept the past and turn away from it: to seek liberation and empowerment, not neocolonialism.[52]

However, past experiences of colonialism haunted transitions in other ways also. They created a deep suspicion of the motives of former colonial powers and of the policies they pursued. The former colonial powers claimed to be the home of capitalism, born of their exceptional individualism and competitiveness. They claimed also to have transferred it to the world through colonialism. They even called it Westernization.[53] Now the word has entered vocabularies as something to be resisted, in much the same way that colonialism had been resisted. Accordingly, the ex-colonies treated the development advice of their former masters with suspicion. They turned to indigenous models that they believed enabled their societies the better to accommodate the demands of a technologically driven age, or at least to demonstrate indigenous initiative – something colonial authorities had believed impossible. In some instances they embarked on alternatives that sought to motivate their people through non-capitalist means.

But for many countries, these options at the end of colonialism were never open to them. The crippling hatreds generated by colonialism and war simply escalated. Fed by Cold War paranoia, they enveloped some countries in further terrors. In Cambodia the rural Khmer Rouge generated a holocaust against its own colonially alienated elite and its new urban populations. In Rwanda, colonially intensified divisions escalated into a genocide of over three million Tutsis. Neighbouring war-torn Congo similarly never rose above its crippling hatreds. It fell easily to the corruption and vanities of former colonial powers, and regional politicians and military leaders prepared to exploit divisions for personal gain or national aggrandizement.

Not all former colonies remained prisoners of their past. Hong Kong, Singapore, Taiwan and South Korea found strength and inspiration in their indigenous cultures, and did not allow past violence to consume them.[54] They fashioned highly competitive industrial societies themselves. But they did so only within an environment markedly different from that generated by the second wave of globalization.

The Technological Imperative

The second wave of globalization enabled a small group of autonomous nations, such as Germany, Japan and the USA, to emulate Britain and incorporate themselves into the new technologically driven era. The vast majority of the world's peoples, however, were incorporated into empires of disadvantage instead. Both forms of incorporation demonstrated weaknesses that imperilled the second wave. When faced with uneven internal development or with the need to maintain existing levels of growth under more competitive circumstances, industrializing nations tended to reach for alternative strategies to strengthen their technological impulse and to overcome the stresses that industrialization generated. Hence corporatism and imperialism deepened. But neither strategy provided long-term solutions. Imperialism denied its captives the same opportunities for economic growth that many Europeans and Japanese enjoyed. That above all made it unsustainable. But so too did internal inequalities. They stifled demand and created discontent that had the potential to destabilize the new nation states or the old empires that survived.

Imperialism also posed another, even more destabilizing, threat. Global empires did not provide security. They did not guarantee greatness. If anything they increased risk. Some might say that they represented old ways of thinking, born of the days of conquest; but they also perfectly reflected the insecurities that the second wave of globalization generated. Countries that scoured the world to demonstrate imperial greatness were invariably also willing to resort to war rather than risk subjugation to a rival. And the brutality that industrializing countries like Britain, Germany and Japan practised abroad soon found expression closer to home.

The technological imperative did not thrive on inequalities. It necessitated inclusiveness and the dismantling of barriers that bred disadvantage. A strategy for security and well-being now existed that for the first time in human history had the potential to benefit everyone. The impulse for technological growth came from innovation, and innovation required demand. Maintaining supply and demand now became a central feature of the industrial era. Conquest or monopoly trade had shaped pre-industrial societies. But these strategies did not seek to sustain growth by sharing wealth. Consequently they did not sit well with a process of globalization that increased human interactions and made the well-being of one community increasingly dependent on the well-being of others. Overwhelmed by conquest and monopoly during the first half of the twentieth century, the second wave faltered and collapsed.

Notes

1. P. Hirst and G. Thompson, *Globalization in Question: The International Economy and the Possibilities of Governance*, Cambridge, Polity, 1999, p. 22.

2. Anatole France, *Sur la pierre blanche*, Paris, 1905, pp. 188–91; quoted by Serge Latouche, *The Westernization of the World: The Significance, Scope and Limits of the Drive towards Global Uniformity*, Cambridge, Polity Press, 1996, p. 14.

3. *Guardian Weekly*, 18–24 January 2001, p. 30.

4. Okawa Shumei, in R. Tsunoda *et al.*, *Sources of the Japanese Tradition*, New York, Columbia University Press, 1958, pp. 288–9.

5. William Appleman Williams, *Empire as a Way of Life*, New York, Oxford University Press, 1980, p. 70.

6. Ignatius Donnelly of Minnesota, in Williams, *Empire as a Way of Life*, p. 99.

7. Graeme Donald Snooks, *The Ephemeral Civilization: Exploding the Myth of Social Evolution*, London and New York, Routledge, 1997, p. 376.

8. Ibid., pp. 384–7.

9. Albert Beveridge in H. Alavi and T. Shanin (eds), *The Sociology of 'Developing Societies'*, London, Macmillan, 1982, p. 74.

10. Williams, *Empire as a Way of Life*, p. 132.

11. Snooks, *Ephemeral Civilization*, pp. 444–6; Massimo Livi-Bacci, *The Population of Europe*, Oxford: Blackwell, 2000, p. 163.

12. Harry Magdoff, *The Age of Imperialism: The Economics of US Foreign Policy*, New York, Monthly Review Press, 1969, p. 174.

13. Geoffrey Barraclough, *From Agadir to Armageddon: Anatomy of a Crisis*, London, Weidenfeld and Nicholson, 1982, p. 37.

14. Felipe Fernández-Armesto, *Millennium: A History of Our Last Thousand Years*, London, Black Swan, 1995, pp. 411–16.

15. Lord Rosebery, 1893, quoted in Bernard Porter, *The Lion's Share: A Short History of the British Empire, 1850–1970*, London, Longman, 1975, p. 133.

16. Gilbert Rist, *The History of Development: From Western Origins to Global Faith*, London and New York, Zed Books, 1997, p. 51.

17. William H. McNeill, *The Pursuit of Power: Technology, Armed Forces and Society since AD 1000*, Oxford, Blackwell, 1982, pp. 197, 213, 220.

18. Fernández-Armesto (*Millennium*, p. 598) declares that 'imperialism is like an appetite: it comes with the eating'. This is the logic of the conquest drive.

19. Edward Said, *Culture and Imperialism*, London, Chatto & Windus, 1993, p. 124.

20. Alavi and Shanin, *The Sociology of 'Developing Societies'*, p. 72.

21. Barraclough, *From Agadir to Armageddon*, p. 37.

22. Paul Leroy-Beaulieu, 1874, cited in Rist, *The History of Development*, p. 54.

23. Le Noury, 1875, cited in Said, *Culture and Imperialism*, p. 205.

24. Rist, *The History of Development*, p. 54.

25. David Landes, *The Wealth and Poverty of Nations: Why some are so rich and some are so poor*, London, Little Brown and Co, 1998, pp. 63–4.

26. Snooks, *Ephemeral Civilization*, p. 300.

27. Peter J. Taylor, *The Way the Modern World Works: World Hegemony to World Impasse*, Chichester, John Wiley and Sons, 1996, p. 161.

28. Said, *Culture and Imperialism*, p. 131.

29. Rist, *The History of Development*, pp. 61–2, 65, 69.

30. Rory Carroll, 'Dirty Secrets', *Guardian Weekly*, 5–11 July 2001, p. 23.

31. Henry Reynolds, *An Indelible Stain*, Viking, 2001.

32. David Cannadine, *Ornamentalism: How the British saw their Empire*, New York, Oxford University Press, 2001.

33. Rist, *The History of Development*, p. 45.

34. Richard Gott, 'Whitewashing the real evil empire', *Guardian Weekly*, 17–23 May 2001, p. 45.

35. Said, *Culture and Imperialism*, p. 178.

36. Rist, *The History of Development*, p. 51.

37. Said, *Culture and Imperialism*, p. 96.

38. Ibid., pp. 121–2.

39. Latouche, *The Westernization of the World*, p. 60.

40. Paul Gilroy, *Between Camps: Race, Identity and Nationalism at the End of the Colour Line*, London, Penguin, 2000, p. 232.

41. Said, *Culture and Imperialism*, p. 286.

42. Ibid., p. 324.

43. Simione Durutalo, 'The Liberation of the Pacific Island Intellectual', *Review*, Suva, University of the South Pacific, 10 (September 1983), pp. 10, 14.

44. Said, *Culture and Imperialism*, p. 259.

45. Ibid., p. 275.

46. Adam Hochschild, *King Leopold's Ghost: A Story of Greed, Terror, and Heroism in Colonial Africa*, London, Houghton & Mifflin, 1998.

47. Alexis de Tocqueville, *Travail sur l'Algérie*, 1841; quoted in Oliver le Cour Grand-maison, 'Liberty, equality and colony', *Le Monde Diplomatique*, June 2001, pp. 12–13.

48. Gideon Polya, *Jane Austen and the Black Hole of British History: Colonial Rapacity, Holocaust Denial, and the Crisis in Biological Sustainability*, Melbourne, 1998.

49. Livi Bacci, *Population of Europe*, p. 140.

50. Fernández-Armesto, *Millennium*, p. 438.

51. Ibid., p. 426.

52. Said, *Culture and Imperialism*, p. 323.

53. Latouche, *The Westernization of the World*, p. 35.

54. Landes, *The Wealth and Poverty of Nations*, p. 438.

CHAPTER 7

· · · · · · · · ·

Implosion

§ GLOBALIZATION demonstrated the limitations that old strategies for security and well-being had for human societies. In the late eighteenth and early nineteenth centuries, philosophers began to debate these limitations, and attempted to formulate new ways of understanding the world and economic activity. But the nature of human responses to the industrially driven second wave of globalization changed only slowly. Corporatism, nationalism and imperialism certainly differed as responses to those generated earlier by mercantilism, but they were still driven by the same zero–sum logic. Yet, as long as they positively helped capital to survive competition, they endured. They protected markets, and gave space for technological innovation and economic expansion. The resulting high growth rates served also to minimize the instability generated by rapid urbanization and population growth. Thus a sense of wonder and optimism pervaded many industrial societies by the mid-nineteenth century and obscured the fragility that these strategies bestowed on globalization.

But growth did falter during the nineteenth century, and internal tensions did flare dangerously. By the end of the century, class warfare had trans-mogrified into large union confrontations and mass political action. Many governments tried to reduce internal instability by introducing legislation designed to improve the housing, health, employment and wages of their expanding working classes. But it was never enough. Political franchises were also gradually extended to enable working-class agitation to assume parliamentary forms, but with renewed economic crises at the turn of the century, larger and larger union and syndicalist responses still resulted.

Hence the continued attractiveness of nationalist and imperialist strategies. They helped to offset division at home. They bought time. But colonial adventures could be dangerous distractions, and the veneer of superiority that they relied upon for success difficult to sustain. The empires they forged experienced unspeakable horrors and injustices, but they were safely distant from Europe. Even if colonial officials occasionally murmured discontent, ideas about racial hierarchies usually reduced the impact of any discomfort. Yet the world was not so vast that conflicts could always be safely localized and resolved. Indeed, after the turn of the century, imperial frontiers dried up and Britain's jealous rivals cast about for empires closer to home.

From this fractious competitive treadmill, industrializing nations seemed incapable of escaping, and the second wave began to falter. War accelerated the process. Europe's old autocracies – Germany, Austria–Hungary and Russia – collapsed in 1918, but no sustainable democratic regimes took their place. During the 1920s and 1930s, even the reforming zeal on which internal harmony depended also collapsed as a new economic crisis enveloped industrial economies. Globalization ended. International economic and political co-operation declined. Exclusivity reigned, but remained unsated until the whole of Europe became Hitler's Congo, and eastern Asia became Japan's new 'sphere for co-prosperity'.

The Second Wave Falters

Between 1800 and 1914 Europe's population more than doubled, growing from 188 million to 458 million. Incomes per person had increased 300 per cent, with Germans now receiving about 76 per cent of Britain's rate and the French 69 per cent. But north, east and south Europe still lagged behind. Italy's income per person represented only half of Britain's, Russia's 30 per cent. In Russia, as in Ireland, life expectancy averaged only 32 years.[1]

Such differences, after 100 years of industrialization, created frustration and fear; frustration that despite all the effort, the results seemed so dismal; and fear that the goals might never be achieved. Symbols of greatness became even more important to convince populations that the technological strategy could and would work for them. Imperial expansion – mastery of space – some reviewers argue, became necessary to maximize national power and security, and to stabilize fragile domestic social orders.[2] Industrialization produced huge urban working-class populations that became increasingly well-organized both politically and industrially. Most states developed mechanisms to deal with them; Germany in particular regarded its army as a bulwark against revolution.[3] With the onset of another recession after 1907, they became more sensitive to the threat to the established order posed by rising proletarian militancy.

Such internal tensions gave rivalry between industrialized nations a new edge, particularly after the possibility of unrestricted global expansion had ended. Japan halted Russian ambitions in the east. Germany also became frustrated. United under Prussia since 1871, it lacked the kind of empire France and Britain had acquired. Its small overseas territories did nothing to satisfy German capital, which focused instead on Europe's periphery. But

Germany did build a powerful navy in the 1890s to project a proper image as a major world power. And Britain, sensitive to changes in its own relative status, reciprocated with a costly naval arms race.

Historians and political scientists make much of Europe's inter-state system. The Treaty of Westphalia in 1648 had tried to reduce the chaos of dynastic warfare by recognizing the sanctity of national sovereignty.[4] But to little avail. Mercantilist and dynastic demands ensured that Britain, France and the Habsburgs continued their struggles for ascendancy in later decades. After 1793, Napoleon's imperial ambitions further demonstrated Westphalia's limitations. When his victorious foes met after 1815, their subsequent Concert of Europe re-established a kind of stability which, despite periodic breakdowns, endured because of Europe's preoccupation with industrialization.

But the principles associated with the Concert of Europe did not apply to societies outside Europe. Indeed many contemporaries did not even regard them as countries. The philosopher John Stuart Mill declared that most non-European societies were simply 'outlying agricultural or manufacturing estates belonging to a larger community'.[5] Consequently the Concert did not represent the basis for a new global order of sovereign states. Rather it represented a kind of honour among thieves that permitted antagonisms to be played out globally and distantly. Like all gangland agreements, it was inherently unstable.

Britain's naval superiority in the aftermath of the Napoleonic wars permitted it to act overseas with impunity. By the middle of the nineteenth century this was no longer the case. First France, then Germany, challenged Britain's dominance by industrializing their navies and armies. By the end of the century, the Concert of Europe had transformed itself into two hostile alliances. Now Britain, France and Russia in a Triple Entente confronted Germany allied with the old Central European empire of Austria–Hungary. But no alliance system – even one confined to Europe – could work if its members were unwilling to make it work. Consequently, the alliances brought anarchy not security.

The historian Geoffrey Barraclough argues that any form of 'stability based on fear, suspicion and an illusory balance of power [is] essentially unstable, at the mercy of any incidental shock or tremor'.

> The complex interlocking network of secret treaties and agreements which regulated the relations of the powers and which was supposed to ensure a balance, meant that any change in the status quo at any point was bound to have repercussions along the whole line and, needless to say, it did.[6]

What caused the equilibrium to change was the gradual dismemberment of the old Ottoman Empire in West Asia and North Africa. Here were fresh opportunities to create colonies.

In 1911 France seized Morocco. Italy, fearing that the whole of North Africa might become French, annexed Libya and sought other advantages by attacking Ottoman weak spots such as Beirut. Thus Europe precipitated the revolt of the Balkan states against their Ottoman rulers. If this had been a sub-Saharan conflict, some deal would have been reached between the major powers. But the closer conflicts occurred to Europe, the harder it became to localize them without unbearable loss of national prestige and honour, and without equally unacceptable consequences for the European balance of power.

In any case, Barraclough tells us, by 1914 the willingness of the European powers to find peaceful solutions had been eroded by a growing sense of crisis and by the emergence of problems at home to which there were no traditional solutions.[7] In particular, the ruling classes feared democracy. They feared conceding to working-class demands, and above all they feared impending recession and its implications. Democracy made governments more sensitive to the demands of new constituents. Britain's budget in 1909 taxed the rich in order to mobilize more resources for public purposes, in particular social welfare provisions.[8]

This politicization of economics troubled many conservatives and liberals alike; after 1910 Europe's armies quietly prepared for war. Britain increased its military expenditure by 30 per cent, Russia by 50 per cent, Germany by 70 per cent, France by 80 per cent. War at least fostered national solidarity. It provided welcome relief from internal unrest and fears of recession. It also enabled a demonstration of state glory and power, which went far beyond what education systems could achieve. And it enabled the absorption of disaffected rural masses into military forces.[9] Feeling that their whole society was at risk, Europe's major powers were prepared to go to the brink of war in 1914, and over.

The trigger was simple; as historian Filipe Fernández-Armesto concedes, a momentous war did not need profound causes.[10] In July 1914 Serbs assassinated the heir to the Habsburg imperial throne, and Austria–Hungary felt that the time had come to punish troublesome Serbia, which had constantly frustrated its efforts to incorporate the Balkans into its empire. Accordingly, it turned to its ally, Germany, which calculated that no time could be better for decisive action. Germany's industrialization had made great strides, but it still lost capital and labour to the larger British and US economies. With linkages between military and industrial innovations sustaining industry, Germany's leaders were prepared to consider the European theatre its space to drive future economic growth.[11] They calculated that once Anglo-Russian naval co-operation improved, Russia would become stronger and more difficult to control. Britain was presently preoccupied with union discontent and Irish rebellion. France was in the process of reorganizing its military forces. The timing was right. Consequently, Germany warned Russia not to interfere when Austria–Hungary retaliated.

Serbia turned to Russia for support, and Russia gave it. It could hardly have done otherwise, unless it wished now to reject its self-declared role as protector of Slav peoples and abandon its own plans for big-power status. Austria–Hungary's aggression threatened Russia's control of the Bosporus strait between the Black and Aegean Seas, vital for future expansion in the region, vital for the passage of its ships into the Mediterranean, and vital also as an outlet for south Russian wheat exports. Because of German commercial and military influence in Turkey, the Balkans remained one of the few areas still open to Russian influence. And there, only Austria–Hungary stood in Russia's way. In late 1914 Russia mobilized its forces.

Germany declared war on Russia and asked France – Russia's ally – to hand over its northern defences as a guarantee of neutrality. France refused and Germany declared war on France. One by one the European powers succumbed to a momentum they had neither the will nor the power to resist. Mobilization in Germany involved the timetabling of eleven thousand trains. Four million troops were marshalled within six days. Planning for just such a war had been going on for years, and Germany had long determined that to avoid a war on two fronts it would need to defeat France instantly.[12] But to avoid French defences, it had to strike through Belgium. That violated Belgium's neutrality, and Britain – as its guarantor – chose to declare war on Germany. Britain knew that German hegemony in Europe threatened its own international economy.

But the quick war that Germany envisaged against France, which it had accomplished three times in the past (against Denmark in 1865, Austria in 1866 and France in 1870), failed to go according to plan, and the Germans were left with a prolonged war on two fronts. The Western Front stretched from Switzerland to the English Channel, but in three years neither side moved more than sixteen kilometres from their trenches. Casualties were massive; one battle alone cost France 120,000 troops, and at the end of it the French gained a mere five hundred metres of land. France lost 690,000 soldiers during the first four months of the war. Altogether the war, which saw 58 million men mobilized (half of Europe's male labour force), cost 38 million lives, and its effects scarred Europe terribly.[13] The ruling families of Russia and Germany fell; Austria–Hungary disintegrated.

But this was not the war to end all wars, despite wishful rhetoric to the contrary. The war brought no lasting peace, only retreat, and a stubborn determination to press on regardless. Germany re-embarked on a drive for imperial greatness, increasingly cloaked with 'nostalgia' for an agrarian and Aryan age that had never existed. Britain and France clung tenaciously to their older empires, believing that they could still be sheltered from competition and desires for independence. Russia also retreated. Behind its borders as the Soviet Union, it tried to achieve in ten years the same industrial transformation that had taken Britain a hundred years to achieve. Across the Atlantic, the United States, now the wealthiest nation in the world and financier of the allied war effort, retreated to its pre-war position. Behind their respective borders, the industrialized nations remarshalled their forces for a new wave of competition.

The Shock of Uncertainty

At the end of the First World War, leaders of the major industrialized countries demonstrated their continued lack of global consciousness. They failed to understand the extent to which both technology and globalization demanded changes to the world in which they lived. Neither could flourish if the world remained little more than a series of independent, competing imperial nations. This was no basis for a stable, interactive global order. In addition, empires implied immutable inequalities between peoples. They denied the commonality of humanity. If inequalities were immutable, there could be no future change; no expanding and changing markets with which to stimulate technological innovation and empower more and more people. Consequently, when the world's industrial powers closed in on themselves, they caused globalization's second wave to collapse.

In 1919 a new Europe lay before the victors when they met at Versailles, the old royal palace near Paris. The German and Austria–Hungarian empires had collapsed. To the east, the Russian Empire had also collapsed, its Tsarist regime replaced in 1917 by a Communist one that declared itself hostile to capitalism as the means to industrialize. Nothing better illustrated modernity's crisis than a revolution that unleashed great energy in new and totally un-expected directions.[14] Allied forces invaded Russia after the war but were unable to defeat the Bolsheviks. But they did encourage a bitter civil war that added a further five million deaths to Russia's already high war toll. In addition, the Allied intervention left a legacy of hatred and mistrust between East and West that poisoned international relations for decades to come, and paralysed Western responses to the rise of fascist Germany.

With Germany down and Russia out, the war's victors decided to create a series of new nation states in Eastern Europe. These nations were to be part of a quasi-international system overseen by a new League of Nations, head-quartered in Geneva. Like the system it replaced, the new order remained largely Europe-focused and did nothing to alter the structures of subordination introduced during the second wave of globalization. Not surprisingly, it re-mained highly unstable, and from the very beginning began to break down.

In the United States, President Woodrow Wilson failed to convince his country that it should continue its involvement in Europe and guarantee the peace. Congress refused even to endorse the League. Britain, fearing the instability a Soviet Russia now seemed to present, decided that Germany should be allowed to resume great-power status in order to act as a buffer to Russia. But France had no intention of allowing Germany to regain its former status, and determined that the newly created East European nation states would act as a durable buffer to any future German or Russian ambitions.

No one power possessed the strength or willingness to impose order on this new, more fragmented inter-state system. Thus divided, the League of Nations achieved little. It represented no more than a coalition of like-minded industrial states hobbled by their respective national ambitions and fears. When the League criticized Japan for invading Manchuria in 1931, Japan abandoned the League. So did Italy, after its 1935 invasion of Ethiopia provoked a similar response from the League. Hitler took Germany out in 1933.

After such a disastrous Great War, nothing better illustrated the failure of industrialized nations to acknowledge the hollowness of nationalism than the terms of its settlement. France and a slightly less enthusiastic Britain forced Germany to accept a humiliating peace. First, Germany lost its colonies; they were redistributed to the victors. No industrial leader considered independence or a new economic deal for colonies in general, although within a very short time Britain was forced to move uneasily towards a degree of self-government for India. War had destroyed the foundations of Western pretensions, but few Western leaders were prepared to acknowledge the change. Only force now held empires together, and that too was more apparent than real.[15] Britain's self-governing settler dominions gained the right to self-government in 1931, but elsewhere neglect and indifference reigned, even after US agricultural overproduction made colonial systems of food production less viable.

Second, Germany lost 13 per cent of its land, which was absorbed into the territory of new neighbouring states. The redistribution cost Germany three quarters of its iron output, one third of its coal and nearly one sixth of its cultivated land. Third, the Allies demanded that Germany pay reparations for the damage it had caused: US$40 billion in money and goods over 30 years as well as 26 per cent of its annual exports.[16] Germans regarded this as enslavement. In any case, they had no ability to pay.

France seized Germany's coal-producing Ruhr district in 1923 to force the issue, and the fragile German economy collapsed. The German mark, which had earlier been worth four to the US dollar, fell in value to forty-two trillion to the dollar.[17] Briefly, Britain, France and the United States patched up their differences to reduce Germany's debts and to provide loans to resuscitate its economy. For a time it looked as if a new spirit of international co-operation might hold. League members renounced war as an implement of state policy in 1928. They even considered a United States of Europe. But neither France nor Britain was committed; their own empires came first.

Failure to cooperate undermined economic recovery. None of Europe's countries wanted to admit that economic interdependence contradicted national goals of self-sufficiency and made nonsense of the value of empires. Britain and France were heavily indebted to the United States, which had financed their war against Germany. Their repayments depended on access to US markets for their products, and reparations from Germany. In turn, German reparations depended on short-term American loans to revitalize its economy. But in 1928 much of that capital fled back to the US to take advantage of a huge stock-market boom, and when the stock market crashed one year later, remaining US assets in Europe were quickly liquidated. Most governments responded to the crisis by tightening belts, reducing public expenditure and waiting for investor confidence to return.

Contradictory post-war policies made rational responses difficult. In the 1920s Britain restored the gold standard as the means to determine currency relativities. The measure represented little more than a nostalgic attempt to restore pre-war stability. The gold standard had never worked as well as economists now argued that it had, and with Britain's financial weight greatly diminished, it worked even less well. In fact, the restoration of the gold standard made more difficult state responses to the emerging economic crisis, and increased state tendencies to manipulate interest rates in order to attract capital or cover deficits. The working public bore the cost as economies shrunk.

During the nineteenth century, industrialization had expanded the size and role of middle classes. As the engineers and managers of industry and commerce, they formed important markets for the products of industry. They also gained important political rights and came to wield increasing political power. But the incorporation of the more numerous impoverished working classes proved more difficult. Nonetheless, by the turn of the century working-class agitation and unionization had succeeded in winning important social and economic legislation that improved working-class living conditions and demonstrated the importance of the working classes to the health of the economy and society as a whole. Working-class agitation tapped into middle-class concerns about the fitness of the nation as it prepared for an age of intense competition. Consequently, in the early twentieth century they continued to win additional education rights and an expanding range of social services. Of course much more was needed, and, when war broke out in 1914, governments very quickly promised their working public a better life in return for war support.

Delivering on the promises proved more difficult. Many politicians now viewed the pre-war period as one of great stability, at least in contrast with the uncertainties that war had generated. To restore that stability required tempering demands for improved public services. Public debt had to be minimized in order to restore investor confidence in their economies. If governments succumbed to labour pressures to introduce relief schemes to assist the growing armies of unemployed, recovery would be delayed further. They had no choice but to sacrifice their working populations' well-being.

In the past, migration had always offered populations a measure of relief. Between 1880 and 1914 Russia had exported six million people to Siberia and four million to the Caucasus. During the nineteenth century North America, and to a lesser extent Australasia, had offered a similar escape for Europe's dissatisfied masses. After 1906 some 1.4 million people left Europe each year, but during the early 1920s the United States drastically cut its intake. Emigration from Europe fell 55 per cent; by the 1930s only 100,000 left each year.[18] With the safety valve gone, the consequences of weakening public confidence in political systems could not be so easily contained.

Government belt-tightening precipitated the Great Depression. In Germany, industrial production fell 46 per cent and the proportion of its unemployed workforce hovered between 30 and 40 per cent during 1931 and 1932. In Italy output fell 33 per cent, in France 28 per cent. Britain's unemployment stood at nearly 18 per cent in 1932. In the US, unemployment rose to 15 million, one quarter of its workforce. By 1935 world trade was only one third of what it had been in 1929. British earnings from foreign investments fell by more than one third. US imports alone fell two-thirds, representing at least 13 per cent of the global decline in trade. In 1930 the US introduced a vast range of tariffs to protect its domestic producers from foreign competition. Now debtor nations could no longer trade their way out of debt. A debt moratorium in 1932 confirmed what was already reality; reparations stopped altogether.

As the global economy shrank, capitalism seemed to offer no means by which to rebuild shattered economies. Most international money markets ceased to exist. Not surprisingly, states turned in on themselves and produced inward-looking economic policies that provided much-needed short-term relief. Higher tariffs and non-convertible currencies succeeded in stabilizing prices and ending the desperately high levels of unemployment. Guaranteed prices for rural commodities provided a measure of relief for farmers, and in time domestic markets slowly expanded again. But now domestic sources of capital replaced international capital, and rearmament resumed to drive growth. Free trade was gone; so too were the virtues of open competition. The second wave had unravelled.

Corporatism's New Deals

In the United States these policies were introduced under Franklin Roosevelt's New Deal programme, a corporate alliance of big business, unions and government designed to break the back of unemployment and restore public confidence in the political system. Economic growth, Roosevelt reasoned, was too important to leave to the vagaries of the market.[19] Loans to businesses and agriculture helped to stimulate recovery. Welfare eased poverty. Federal expenditure exceeded revenue by 231 per cent in 1933.[20] But Roosevelt did not intend to depart permanently from orthodox economic ideas. Once recovery began, he moved to cut spending, raise taxes and bring his federal budget into balance. The result was a fresh economic crash in 1937. Two years later unemployment still stood at 17 per cent of the workforce. Forty-five per cent of white households, and ninety per cent of black households, lived below the poverty line.[21] Only war gave the United States the opportunity to reorient its economy internationally and to reinforce the Great Depression's main lesson, that economic success depended on governments managing their economies. Economies did not manage themselves. Consequently the United States rode the war wave into an unprecedented boom. By 1944 unemployment stood at 1.2 per cent.

Britain's decline since the late nineteenth century had fostered a reactionary public-school elite scornful of science and technology. Its solution to Britain's problems was the creation of a unified empire behind tariff barriers. The construction of this façade had been long in the making, but Queen Victoria's Diamond Jubilee in 1897 and the Boer War shortly afterwards were important stages.[22] Briefly, the Great Depression brought it to fruition. In 1932 Britain officially abandoned free trade and introduced a system of reciprocal trade preferences with its Empire to guarantee markets for itself. In reality this was no solution. Most colonies were not geared to purchasing consumer or heavy industrial products; they existed solely to feed raw materials into Britain's industrial machinery.

Settler colonies could provide something of a market, but the low prices they received for their primary produce (50 per cent below pre-war levels) made purchasing more manufactured goods from Britain difficult.[23] By the 1930s they too toyed with ideas of self-sufficiency and adopted import-substitution strategies to foster independent industrialization. These policies further weakened demand in Britain. Consequently, by 1939, British unemployment still stood at 13 per cent, testimony to the sterility of the colonial vision and to Britain's failure to transform its workforce into consumers. Although lumbered with the added burden of upgrading its technological base, Britain's lack of success in exploiting the technological transformations of the late nineteenth century drew principally from this failure. Social empowerment had met deep institutional barriers; the result was the Great Depression.

Ironically, the only economies that presented themselves as dynamic were those belonging to fascist or soviet regimes. In fact neither was what each seemed. Communism demanded faith, 'a psychological investment that rendered it impermeable to rational refutation'.[24] Yet at the time, the Soviet experiment did seem to demonstrate what one nation could do by shaking off the West; that it was possible to build a new society that repudiated the values of modernity.[25]

In the late 1920s the Soviet experiment took a more nationalist turn. Stalin instituted a massive programme of rapid urbanization and industrialization. This required greater state procurements of food to feed urban populations and to produce sufficient surplus to pay for industrialization. Initial procurement and collectivization experiments seemed promising, but in 1931 and 1932 farmers rebelled. Stalin was unmoved. 'We are fifty or a hundred years behind the advanced countries', he warned his party's congress in 1932. 'We must make good this lag in ten years. Either we do it or they crush us'. Collectivizing small peasant farms into large state units sparked a horrendous civil war with Stalin's own peasantry. Famine swept the Ukraine and Russia as peasants destroyed food, cattle, and tools rather than hand them to their government. Nine million peasants perished. To make matters worse, government grain demands rose 44 per cent, largely to finance breakneck industrialization, but poor harvest yields reduced output by 12 per cent. Ten million recalcitrant peasants were exiled to Siberia, and forced labour became a permanent part of the Soviet economy. By the end of the 1930s, nearly three million prisoners languished in brutal labour camps across the country. When his party revolted, Stalin ruthlessly purged it, executing 680,000 people between 1937 and 1938. He deified himself as a new Augustus,[26] and cleverly exploited the growing anti-fascist struggle to excuse Russian atrocities as fascist propaganda.[27]

Stalin's urban workforce trebled during the 1930s, but this was a low-income economy. It had no room for consumerism. The command system fed a national war machine; it could not sustain economic growth and innovation. Hitler also produced a low-income economy, but unlike Stalin ruled through a large party devoted to his leadership. Unlike Russia, Germany was a major industrial power with a highly skilled workforce. Hitler came to office on the back of mass disillusionment with the record of democratic government in post-war Germany. Once in power he quickly ended the parliamentary system and began a programme of rearmament that increasingly fuelled economic growth. Large-scale public works also stimulated recovery, among the more impressive results some four thousand kilometres of autobahns linking Germany's major cities. By 1939 German unemployment stood at only 3 per cent.

Both fascism and communism transferred the lessons of the First World War to politics; 'familiarity with violence, the simplicity of extreme passions, the submission of the individual to the collectivity, and the bitterness of futile and betrayed sacrifices'.[28] However, fascism's appeal also lay in its claim to offer dynamic rebirth after 'periods of national weakness' and in its exultation of war.[29] In many respects, the illusions of both communism and fascism fed off each other; they saw themselves as the mirror images of their adversaries.[30] In fact fascism derived in part from communism. Mussolini began his political career as a socialist, and much of fascism's traditional conservative hostility to modernity was cloaked in Marxist rhetoric.[31] This made fascism also attractive as a model for the disaffected around the world. But it was not revolutionary; if anything, it was reactionary, a cancer that ended forever the West's claims to superior enlightenment, which – among other things – it had used to justify colonialism.[32]

Hitler's solution, like Stalin's, was part illusion. While economic growth rates during the late 1930s were impressive in comparison with those of Britain or the United States, Germany's strategy possessed flaws. Inefficient and chaotically bureaucratic, fascist Germany stressed manual labour and folk crafts, not machinery, technology and mass production. It meant that – in the end – Germany would never be able to match the production of its rivals. But in the short term, the bluff worked.[33]

The Hitler phenomenon was an exercise in propaganda and the manipulation of state power. New technologies such as radio and film, which the Nazis promoted, became a means to control and direct the popular will. So too did contrived mass rallies, the exploitation of anti-Semitic, anti-communist and anti-Versailles sentiment, and the resurrection of folk myths and concepts of racial superiority that bestowed historical legitimacy to the Nazi mission. But to sustain propaganda, more and more successes were needed. When opportunities presented themselves Hitler felt compelled to grasp them. In doing so, he fuelled expectations still further. But few people outside Germany anticipated just how terrible his gamble would become.

Hitler did not intend to conquer Western Europe. But, as his biographer Ian Kershaw argues, Hitler failed to realise that he could not just do what he wanted in Eastern Europe.[34] Yet Eastern Europe was essential to his plan. He declared: 'For me the object is to exploit the advantages of continental hegemony. ... When we are masters of Europe, we will have a dominant position in the world. 130 million people in the Reich, 90 in the Ukraine. Add to these the other states of New Europe and we'll be 400 millions as compared with the 130 million Americans'.[35] Hitler wanted Germany to become a megastate, like the United States and the Soviet Union. He did not want a scattered empire such as Britain possessed. Instead he looked east. 'What India is for England', he argued, 'the territories of Russia will be for us'.[36]

Each gamble took Hitler closer to his goal: rearmament, his defiant re-militarization of the Rhineland, and the return of the Saar. Each success fuelled expectations for more, and when opportunities presented themselves Hitler felt compelled to grasp them. When local Nazis revolted in Austria, Hitler seized the opportunity to join his homeland with Germany in early 1938. In September Britain sought to prevent further tension by forcing the separation of the German-peopled Sudetenland from Czechoslovakia; instead it precipitated the collapse of the strongest Versailles state. When Britain and

France similarly tried to address the separation of Danzig from Poland, Poland refused to become involved. To allay Polish concerns, Britain offered to guarantee their territorial integrity. Hitler gambled that Britain would never honour its commitment, and invaded Poland in September 1939. His gamble failed. The invasion brought both Britain and France into war with Germany. This was not his goal, but when faced with war, he accepted his fate and revelled in his role as warlord, conquering all of Western Europe except Britain. But like all conquerors, he needed to maintain the momentum of conquest. Consequently, he turned his attention to the Soviet Union and his dream of a German empire west of the Urals.

Stalin, like Hitler, was in awe of the British Empire, so much so that he believed that the real threat to Russia's future would come through backdoor deals between Germany and Britain. He never for a moment imagined that Hitler would act alone. When German forces began amassing on his border, Stalin believed Hitler simply sought to pressure him to make further concessions on the Balkans. Consequently he waited for Hitler's ultimatum. It never came. Instead Hitler launched an invasion of the Soviet Union.[37]

What most differentiated Hitler from other leaders of industrial nations was his attitude to race. For him, politics was simply a racial struggle and the state an expression of the racial *Volk*.[38] He did not believe that all peoples – and by extension their states – were equal. In fact, those he deemed inferior to Germans he treated in exactly the same way that most imperialists treated their subjugated colonial peoples. It was something that Europe had not expected, but which the First World War should have taught its people.

Hitler represented the absurdity of the post-war 'one people one nation' Versailles policy at a time when multiculturalism more accurately represented Europe's reality. One third of Europe's population lived as minorities within countries. To argue for pure nations based on ethnicity alone was always going to raise difficulties, especially in Eastern Europe, which held nearly three quarters of Europe's minorities. The Soviet solution was more durable; a federal structure which, despite the all-pervading presence of the Kremlin, offered non-Russians some semblance of political power and cultural autonomy. Ukrainian children were taught in their native language. That never occurred in Poland.[39]

Instead, assimilation demanded compliance to a national standard. Democracy could not survive with anything less, it was claimed. But of course assimilation invariably meant incorporation into a dominant ethnic group. The League of Nations was supposed to protect minorities, but could do nothing because it prioritized the sovereignty of nations. It refused to interfere in the internal affairs of states. Ironically the Polish constitution had been put together with the rights of minorities in mind; it stressed national citizenship rights, though not individual rights. Without individual rights, minorities had no protection if the definition of citizen ever changed. The priority of community rights over individual rights eventually cost minorities dearly.[40]

Non-citizens, the argument went, were separate people who could not be assimilated. As the multinational Ottoman Empire collapsed during the First World War, the Turkish state embarked on a programme of homogenization. One million Armenians were exterminated. Religion also provided a basis for exclusion. Turkey expelled Turkish-speaking Orthodox Christians. But Jews and gypsies had no 'alternative' home. Since the US had closed its doors to migrants at the end of the First World War, there was no longer a refuge across the Atlantic for Europe's growing number of stateless peoples.[41]

Ideas about the purity of nations coincided with ideas about social health. Across Europe states intervened to provide welfare services to their masses, improve housing and schooling, and institute health and physical fitness programmes. Contamination of any kind became a scourge to be addressed scientifically. Asylums isolated inferiors. Sterilization ensured that they did not contaminate the national stock. Of course in colonies these views had a much longer history. Academic disciplines such as anthropology helped colonial administrators to decide which races should be preserved for the benefit of the Empire, which races should be allowed to interbreed, and which races should die out. These views had never been applied to Europe's peoples, but they were under the Nazis. They undertook investigations into different racial types, but their focus was on Jews.

Jews had long been targets for persecution, but during the nineteenth century they came also to represent a danger to the ethnic purity of new nation states. The French noble Comte Arthur de Gobineau described them as 'bacilli', dangerous to the purity of French blood. The German composer Richard Wagner claimed that they undermined German modernity. They were not part of the *Volksgeist*, the spirit of the race.[42] The Nazis followed this tradition, but with a ruthlessness not previously seen. At first they excluded Jews from citizenship, subjected them to economic boycott, and then deprived them of protection under the law. These were a people who comprised only 1 per cent of the German population.

But Jews were only part of a much broader picture of racial reorganization that Hitler had in mind for a Nazi Europe. Europe to Hitler was a racial entity, not a geographical one. Germans were scattered across the continent, in Italy, Yugoslavia, Latvia, Estonia, Soviet Poland, and Russia. He would resettle them; and Poland would be the first European site for Germanization. But despite all the rhetoric, there was little thought of how the idea might be translated into practical reality. When 25,000 Germans were settled in one Polish district, they met with resistance from local Poles and Ukrainians and had to be given costly police protection. The whole scheme quickly became economically unviable. In fact, not many Germans really wanted to resettle, certainly not under these conditions, and certainly not as peasants. Here the Nazi world was out of touch with reality. It idealized a rural German world that no longer existed. When Hitler outlined his vision for Eastern Europe, he anticipated a feudal and ethnically purified farming belt. Perhaps no more than half a million German settlers participated in Hitler's reconstruction of Europe; by early 1945 they were all retreating to Germany as refugees.[43]

Germany's empire was hierarchical. Germany ruled Europe to benefit Germany. This brutal reality eventually cost fascist Germany support from the many peoples who initially welcomed the German presence. And their resistance cost Germany the economic benefits that Hitler had promised. To compensate, he introduced slavery. Between ten and twelve million Europeans were forced to work for the Reich, many of them for large German manufacturers. By 1944 in Germany alone over one quarter of the workforce were slaves. This enabled the Nazis to cushion Germans from the economic consequences of war. At least 250,000 slave labourers were worked to death. In France, Germany confiscated 50 per cent of industrial output; all in all as much as 30 per cent of German war production was pillaged from occupied or allied European countries. In the end, Mazower asserts, Hitler's primitive economics of conquest made winning the war impossible. He lost the hearts and minds of his subjects. Each labour drive simply increased resistance.[44]

For Hitler, race was the organizing principle for Europe, not rationality. People could be rearranged, resettled, enslaved or killed. Hitler toyed with the idea of expelling Jews to Madagascar or herding them into Poland. Ultimately genocide – a new term for the 1940s – became the favoured option; 100,000 in 1940, one million in 1941. By the end of 1945, six million Jews – close to half the world's Jewish population – had been exterminated in specially established death camps. In Poland and Greece whole communities disappeared. With the invasion of the Soviet Union in 1941, the madness escalated. By now the genocide of Jews was only part of a much wider holocaust. Three million Soviet prisoners of war died of starvation. Half a million gypsies entered the gas chambers; Serbs, Poles, Ukrainians and Russians too, in all another eight million people. Often local authorities helped the Nazis to round up their racial enemies, although in some countries, such as Greece, the Netherlands, Denmark and Italy, authorities successfully resisted.

Death on such a scale presented huge opportunities for pillage. Houses, land and property were looted. Hitler's private army, the Waffen SS, took 674 trainloads of household goods out of West Europe; 72 trainloads of gold from the teeth of Auschwitz victims were collected in Berlin.[45]

If these statistics are depressing, so was the reality of Hitler's imperialist crusade in Europe. Its greatest achievement was to end Europe's two-century-long population crisis.[46] By 1945, six years of war had left sixty million people dead: nearly 60 per cent of them civilians, 40 per cent of them Russians, 13 per cent Poles and 11 per cent Germans. There were over eleven million displaced persons, ten times the number generated by the First World War, and in Eastern Europe alone, forty-six million refugees.[47]

Hitler's racial war was not his alone. On the other side of Eurasia, Japan felt keenly the European racism that barely acknowledged its considerable achievements as an industrializing nation. In 1919 it asked that the League's Covenant specifically affirm racial equality. The victors refused. Britain and France had no desire to grant equality to its colonial subjects. Nor did the United States, which still practised segregation and separate development at home. Racial equality was not possible. Japan very quickly understood that the League did not represent a new global order, only the same club of industrial powers that had always frustrated its ambitions in Asia. Nothing had changed. The race for empires, each with their own international community and rules, continued.

Thus Japan determined to go it alone. In 1931 its army forced the issue by invading Manchuria in northern China and declaring war as the means to fulfil Japan's historic destiny. Most Japanese politicians and bureaucrats adjusted their views accordingly. Two points pushed them to support their military. First, they feared that inactivity might worsen social chaos and class upheaval, and thereby risk sundering Japan's social fabric. Second, imperialism was not a subject for debate. All major industrial powers were imperialists. The only subject for debate was whether Japan could get away with it without antagonizing those powers which still wanted an open-door policy for China. During the 1930s it seemed as if it could, and in 1937 it began a full-scale invasion of China, the first stage in plans for its own Japan-centred international zone. The massacre of 300,000 Nanjing residents soon followed, perhaps demonstrating both Japan's desire to shock China into submission and the ill-discipline of its peasant troops. But China was not shocked into submission.

Like Germany and Italy, Japan decided that trade was not enough to prevent it from becoming a third-rate power. It required an empire. With Europe distracted by Hitler's war, Japan seized the opportunity to launch an ambitious attack on American and European colonies in South-east Asia. They would supply the necessary oil and iron that its war machine required, and which the United States now refused to supply. To buy itself time to secure those much-needed colonial supplies before the US could retaliate, Japan made a surprise attack on the US fleet in Hawaii in late 1941. Thus began Japan's Pacific War.

But the strategy was flawed. The very problems that prompted Japan to go to war limited its capacity to sustain war. Its industrial base was weak. The South-east Asian and Pacific theatres of war overstretched its forces. They were difficult to supply. Dependence on shipping to maintain Japan's industries left it vulnerable to counter-attack. China tied down the bulk of its forces. And of course, when the US did finally move in for the kill, it did so in a way that dramatically highlighted the technology gap between itself and Japan.

The Manhattan Project, a massive Allied project involving 120,000 people and costing US$2 billion, now bore fruit.[48] The Japanese emperor's delay in ending the war in order to secure an exit plan for himself gave the US the opportunity to use its new atomic weapons.[49] Consequently, 92 years after US forces first demanded that Japan open its doors to Western trade, two atomic bombs obliterated Hiroshima and Nagasaki. By the time Japan surrendered, three million Japanese were dead, and 40 per cent of its urban areas were destroyed. At only 5 per cent of the total war dead, Japan's costs were comparatively light; certainly far less than the 16 per cent that China bore as Japan's main theatre of war.[50]

Empires were not a stable response to industrial globalization. The primacy they gave to power and conquest, and their infatuation with racial hierarchies, not only denied them the industrial future they craved but precipitated the very social and political collapse they sought to avoid. Certainly they ended the second wave of globalization. In 1945, after two world wars and one great depression, it was time for lessons to be drawn.

Notes

1. Livi Bacci, *Population of Europe*, pp. 128–9.
2. Held *et al.*, *Global Transformations*, p. 94.
3. McNeill, *The Pursuit of Power*, p. 246.
4. Taylor, *The Way the Modern World Works*, p. 36.
5. Mill, quoted in Said, *Culture and Imperialism*, p. 68.
6. Barraclough, *From Agadir to Armageddon*, p. 111.
7. Ibid., p. 154.
8. McNeill, *The Pursuit of Power*, pp. 288, 294.
9. Ibid., pp. 307–12.
10. Fernández-Armesto, *Millennium*, p. 396.
11. Giovanni Arrighi, 'The Seven Hegemonies', *Review*, XIII (3: 1990), p. 347.
12. McNeill, *The Pursuit of Power*, pp. 305, 254. Germany developed the Schlieffen Plan in the 1890s to frustrate French and English rapprochement and prevent a war on two fronts. But once the plan was set in motion, there was no stopping it. McNeill calls this an example of the 'irrationality of rational professional planning', and considers it an irony that such triumphant commandism emerged at the same time as the market economy pushed in the opposite direction.
13. Livi Bacci, *Population of Europe*, p. 173; McNeill, *The Pursuit of Power*, p. 317.
14. Fred Halliday, *Revolution and World Politics*; London, Macmillan, 2000; see also Andrew Gamble, 'When Manifest Destinies Conflict', *Times Literary Supplement*, 24 March 2000, p. 11.
15. Latouche, *Westernization of the World*, p. 16.
16. J. Kenneth Galbraith, *The World Economy Since the Wars: A Personal View*, London, Sinclair-Stevenson, 1994, p. 35. This equated with about $400 billion in mid-1990s' values.

17. Mark Mazower, *Dark Continent: Europe's Twentieth Century*, London, Allen Lane, 1998, p. 110.

18. Livi Bacci, *Population of Europe*, p. 169; McNeill, *The Pursuit of Power*, p. 312.

19. Taylor, *The Way the Modern World Works*, p. 148.

20. Galbraith, *The World Economy since the Wars*, p. 105.

21. David Kennedy, 'A Tale of Three Cities: How the United States Won World War Two', *Background Briefing*, 21 October 2001, abc.net.au

22. Taylor, *The Way the Modern World Works*, pp. 163, 169.

23. Galbraith, *The World Economy since the Wars*, p. 83.

24. François Furet, *The Passing of an illusion, the Idea of Communism in the 20th Century*, Chicago, Chicago University Press, 1999; see also Mark Lilla, 'An idea whose time has come', *New York Times Book Review*, 25 July 1999, p. 12.

25. Latouche, *Westernization of the World*, p. 15.

26. Snooks, *The Ephemeral Civilization: Exploding the Myth of Social Evolution*, p. 456.

27. Mark Lilla, 'An idea whose time has come', p. 12.

28. Ibid.

29. Gilroy, *Between Camps*, p. 146.

30. Mark Lilla, 'An idea whose time has come', p. 12.

31. Stevan Sherman, 'Hegemonic Transitions and the Dynamics of Cultural Change', *Review*, XXII (1: 1999), p. 102.

32. Latouche, *Westernization of the World*, p. 16.

33. Mazower, *Dark Continent*, pp. 132–6.

34. Ian Kershaw, *Hitler, 1936–1945: Nemesis*, London, Penguin, 2000.

35. Alan Bullock, *Hitler: a Study in Tyranny*, London, Penguin, 1962, p. 657.

36. Ibid., p. 656.

37. Gabriel Gorodelsky, *The Grand Delusion: Stalin and the German Invasion of Russia*, New Haven, Yale University Press, 1999.

38. Mazower, *Dark Continent*, pp. 69–70.

39. Ibid., pp. 49–50.

40. Ibid., pp. 65–8.

41. Ibid., pp. 57–62.

42. Colin Tatz, 'The bitter truth behind the ban on Wagner', *smh*, 2 August 2001.

43. Mazower, *Dark Continent*, pp. 68–72, 150–1.

44. Ibid., pp. 150–2; *Guardian Weekly*, 23–29 December 1999, p. 5; Snooks, *The Dynamic Society: Exploring the Sources of Global Change*, p. 314.

45. Mazower, *Dark Continent*, pp. 143–76.

46. McNeill, *The Pursuit of Power*, p. 313.

47. Kennedy, 'A Tale of Three Cities'. US deaths amounted to only 405,199 or 0.7 per cent of the war's total, and Britain's to 350,000 or 0.6 per cent.

48. McNeill, *The Pursuit of Power*, p. 356.

49. Herbert Bix, *Hirohito and the Making of Modern Japan*, London, HarperCollins, 2000.

50. Kennedy, 'A Tale of Three Cities'.

PART FOUR

The Third Wave of Globalization

. . . .

CHAPTER 8

American Globalism

Strategies for Globalization

The collapse of the second wave of globalization demonstrated the necessity for specifically global strategies to enhance international co-operation and deepen prosperity. Indeed, the architects of the post-war third wave of globalization knew that they had been awarded a rare opportunity to provide for a future vastly different from the disastrous past from which they had just emerged.

Much of the initiative for change came from the United States of America which, alone of all the industrialized nations, emerged from war confident and economically rejuvenated. Its consumer economy had been protected by a deliberate government decision in 1942 to slow its rate of mobilization. This delayed the Allied invasion of Western Europe, but it enabled the US standard of living to rise 15 per cent during the war. Its British and Soviet allies enjoyed no such advantage. Their living standards fell by one third.[1]

In addition, American wartime losses were comparatively slight; from an army of 8 million, only 400,000 soldiers died. But most importantly, the United States emerged from war with its industrial stock undamaged and its economy booming. Its gross national product (GNP) had more than doubled between 1939 and 1945, and within another four years its per capita income would be twice that of Britain, three times France's, five times Germany's and seven times the Soviet Union's.

In contrast, Germany and Japan were shattered shells of their former selves, their peoples starving, and subject to the demands of their new occupiers. At the close of war, Germany contained 6.5 million displaced persons. Forty per cent of its factories were destroyed, and industrial output struggled to make 34 per cent of 1936 levels. Japan was similarly affected. One quarter of its national wealth had been destroyed. Nine million of its people were homeless. In addition some six million Japanese, repatriated from their former empire, strained further the resources available for recovery.[2]

Although by no means as severely affected, Britain also struggled to restore its pre-war economy and head off dependency on its new American creditor. But the Soviet Union, where the bulk of the war had been fought, bore the largest damage bill (in both capital and human terms) of any nation: 27 million people dead, 30 million injured, 1,700 cities and 70,000 villages razed, and 65,000 kilometres of rail and 100,000 large farms destroyed. By 1948 the Soviet Union's GNP was one third of its pre-war level.[3]

Economic superiority bestowed on the US unprecedented opportunity to establish a new international order. War had taken it out of depression and created mass employment for the first time within a generation. During the 1930s proposals for increased state expenditure and deficit financing had been regarded as unsound; but the laissez-faire cure imposed had been worse. By insisting that the economy be left to correct itself without state intervention, governments induced depression and social unrest, and encouraged the very nationalistic responses that strangled global trade and eventually brought war.

In contrast, the experience of war vindicated deficit financing and state planning as strategies for reconstruction. But these tools required global co-operation to be effective. Thus was born a two-tiered strategy: state planning at home to redistribute wealth and foster political stability, and international trade liberalization to prevent nationalist economic competition.[4]

Accordingly the third wave of globalization began with a sense of globalism that earlier waves had lacked. The long first wave had seen the wealth of the Americas inject new global dynamics into still largely regional economies, but its key protagonists, the European Atlantic seaboard countries, possessed no sense of a whole greater than the sum of its parts. The second wave was little different in this respect. Invigorated by the Industrial Revolution, itself a product of the first wave's global dynamics, Britain exploited the exhaustion of its European competitors after the Napoleonic Wars to create and dominate a new world order. Only after industrial competition had intensified during the mid- and late nineteenth century did the limitations of that order become apparent. No mechanism existed to manage its global dynamics, and in particular prevent its degeneration into yet another mad scramble for monopoly and other forms of exclusion. Thus the second wave sank into an abyss of nationalism and empire building, and destabilized Eurasia.

Nineteen forty-five, in contrast, offered the possibility of a fresh start. In the final years of the Second World War, Allied planners proposed a new era of global decision-making and international co-operation to prevent the disasters of the inter-war years. In mid-1944, at Bretton Woods in New Hampshire, US Treasury Secretary Henry Morgenthau told a special UN Monetary and Financial Conference called by President Roosevelt that laissez-faire economic policies had deepened the depression's impact and rendered many countries susceptible to nationalistic reactions.

All of us have seen the great economic tragedy of our time. We saw the worldwide depression of the 1930s. We saw currency disorders develop and spread from land to land, destroying the basis for international trade and international investment and even international faith. In their wake, we saw unemployment and wretchedness – idle tools, wasted wealth. We saw their victims fall prey, in places to demagogues and dictators. We saw bewilderment and bitterness become the breeders of fascism, and finally, of war.[5]

Fortunately, the application of Keynesian[6] economic policies – although for war spending not social welfare – had ended the economic threat for the United States.[7] It dispelled the misery of depression and finally restored full employment and health to the US economy.

Something similar was now required to prevent the US economy from returning to its pre-war state once war expenditure ended. Its share of world manufacturing had stagnated at 20 per cent during the inter-war years. To increase that share, the government had to refocus on internationalizing the American economy. Accordingly, it came up with a plan to quadruple US exports.[8] But to succeed, the US required access to new markets that were themselves prosperous and stable. And access depended on nations acknowledging a community of interest and agreeing to behave co-operatively.

'[A]ll countries big and small, victorious or defeated [should] have access on an equal footing to the markets and the raw materials of the world necessary for their economic prosperity', the United States had argued in its 1941 Atlantic Charter with Britain.[9] Britain had been in no position to disagree with the terms of the Atlantic Charter. It desperately required war finance. Any lingering hopes it possessed of salvaging its empire and returning to its system of imperial preference vanished over the course of the decade as the weight of global power and finance shifted swiftly to the United States. By 1947 the erstwhile centre of world trade and finance was on the brink of financial collapse.

In fact much more than trade liberalization was required. Somewhat belatedly, in 1947, the United States awoke to the importance of domestic state planning for prosperity, and pledged reconstruction funds to help restore well-being and stability to European countries. At stake was not just European recovery, but the maintenance of American prosperity. An understanding of common interests shaped American globalism.

Yet the sense of globalism that the United States bestowed on the post-war settlement remained deeply influenced by its desire to seize the moment and secure future national advantage from its hegemony. An American Century was its manifest destiny, and few American officials saw anything wrong in the United States using its economic power to internationalize its own economy. Everyone would benefit from the more stable order it produced.

In any case, US global intervention was hardly a new phenomenon, even if its scale now promised vastly different rewards. During the nineteenth century, the US had succumbed to imperialist pressures for an overseas empire and spheres of influence in Asia, the Pacific, the Caribbean and South America. Yet its wealth came principally from growing internal markets spurred on by continental expansion, large-scale immigration, and production for mass consumption. An opportunity now existed to expand the involvement of its companies in international markets. And like Britain in the nineteenth century, it could do so without high domestic tariffs. As the dominant economic power, the US stood to gain most from free trade.

In 1944 Secretary of State Dean Acheson told the House Special Committee on Post-war Policy and Planning that American domestic markets could never absorb everything the US was capable of producing. Without foreign markets, the US would never know 'full employment and prosperity'.[10] By internationalizing its economy and by insisting on global free trade, the United States could access the very markets from which its expanding businesses had once been excluded by competitive imperial and national policies. To that end the United States began to plan a new set of international regulatory authorities charged with creating the global economic environment it required.

Regulation represented a compromise between the demand of social democrats for planning and that of free traders for deregulation.[11] Made necessary by the perilous state of domestic economies after the war, the compromise eventually produced the defining two-tiered feature of post-war American globalism. But that was not at first apparent when its regulatory institutions were foreshadowed at Bretton Woods in 1944.

To ensure the liberalization of trade, the US administration proposed a supervisory International Trade Organization to co-ordinate the simultaneous reduction of tariffs and quotas. But while 'the Americans saw trade as the engine for growth, Europeans believed that investment was the key'. Europeans, economist Barry Eichengreen argues, gave precedence to the popular post-depression priority of full employment.[12] Consequently the US Congress rejected the new organization, fearing harm to American economic interests. Thus the stillborn International Trade Organization became the first victim of tensions between the two post-war strategies for recovery. The US government had to rely instead on nations pledging to reduce tariffs and accepting a code of practice that minimized the potential for harm. The 1947 General Agreement on Tariffs and Trade (GATT) also committed industrialized nations to promote free trade by means of multilateral bargaining rather than by preferential agreement, the cornerstone of most industrial empires in the early twentieth century.

The US reduced its tariffs by one third after 1947, but few participating nations followed the American example. Subsequent rounds had more success;

during the course of the century, average tariffs on manufactured goods fell from 40 per cent to 4 per cent. But tariffs on agricultural products and textiles, the primary concern of many developing countries, remained stubbornly high (as much as 40 per cent on agricultural products). Indeed, industrial countries continued to subsidize their farmers on average by US$11,000 each every year, a grand total of US$300 billion each year, the equivalent of the entire GDP of sub-Saharan Africa.[13]

The International Monetary Fund (IMF), established in 1946 to stabilize exchange rates, also suffered from the same tensions. It provided nations with loans to overcome balance-of-payments deficits. Nations no longer needed to engage in competitive devaluations to redress deficits. In addition, currencies would be convertible and exchange rates fixed. Private capital would not enjoy free rein. Indeed, as Eichengreen argues, pegged but adjustable exchange rates were possible only because countries employed capital controls to insulate themselves from destabilizing capital flows. They also directed private capital to sectors that fulfilled post-war objectives, namely reconstruction and economic growth.[14]

The IMF could do hardly anything about this. In any case, the US tied its hands by refusing to provide sufficient funds to finance deficits. The leader of the British delegation to the Bretton Woods conference, the economist Maynard Keynes, had proposed a fund of US$26 billion; the IMF eventually got US$9 billion, of which the US contributed only US$3 billion. This proved a mistake, which immediately threatened American interests. Europe could not pay for imports from the United States and was reluctant to finance deficits through an export plan that would require devaluation to produce competitiveness. Devaluation would lower living standards, hardly the recipe for reconstruction and political stability.

Britain's sterling crisis in 1947 demonstrated the absurdity of the US position. During the war, sterling bloc countries had accumulated some £3.5 billion. This represented approximately one third of Britain's GNP, and seven times its reserves. Britain had good reasons for refusing immediately to follow the American dollar and make its pound convertible. But the US preference for trade liberalization took precedence. It wanted American exporters to compete without disadvantage in British markets. Consequently it imposed convertibility as a prerequisite for a US$3.7-billion loan that Britain desperately needed to pay off its war debts and assist with reconstruction. Within one month of Britain's reluctant accession to US demands in June 1947, holders of overseas sterling had nearly exhausted the loan in their rush to convert to dollars.[15]

The United States had to recognise the difficulties European countries faced. After all, their inability to purchase US goods affected the American economy, and already there were signs that the US might be heading for a recession. Demand for European goods in the United States had declined, further impacting on Europe's dollar deficit. Some recognition of the conundrum had appeared earlier from the US administration. Secretary of State George Marshall announced in June 1947 a plan to encourage European economic co-operation. The US would extend credits worth US$22 billion (more than US$200 billion in contemporary values) over four years, much of which would finance its dollar deficits, thereby indirectly assisting US recovery.[16] But Congress remained unconvinced and approved a paltry US$4 billion instead. Only the Plan's incorporation into an anti-Soviet strategy during 1948 persuaded Congress to endorse it in its entirety.

The existence of the Marshall Plan demonstrated the IMF's failure to deal with problems that it had been established to resolve. But the failure also derived from the huge imbalance in strength between the American economy and those of its European partners, most of whom were in any case eventually forced to devalue in 1949. US trade objectives conflicted with European desires for domestic stability. The Europeans required credit to promote growth, not increased taxes, higher interest rates or currency devaluation. They also required currency stability to restore the prosperity that American traders hoped to tap into. Above all, they required a breathing space for reconstruction.

The Marshall Plan provided the right environment to achieve these goals. Growth resumed, trade balances strengthened, and investors returned. US global monetary reserves fell from their 66 per cent high in 1948 to 50 per cent two years later.[17] By 1958 most European currencies were convertible, although not because of US pressure, but because European economies had strengthened sufficiently for them to gain from convertibility.

The European example encouraged developing countries to pursue a similar path; by pegging currencies and limiting capital flows, they hoped to create a similar stable environment for development. Indeed, South American per capita incomes grew 73 per cent and Africa's 34 per cent between 1960 and 1980. But as the number of countries floating their exchange rates increased, international capital became both more active and more mobile. The IMF, which had never had sufficient funds to finance imbalances, began to encourage greater private capital flows and to discourage currency fixing. With no Marshall Plan to provide alternative finance, Third World countries had little choice but to accept the new conditions the IMF attached to its loans. It made resolving domestic problems impossible. Accordingly, over the next twenty years, per capita incomes in South America fell 6 per cent; in Africa, 23 per cent. This collapse cost the third wave much of its legitimacy.

The origins of this disaster for globalization lay in the nature of America's globalism. When the architects of the third wave met at Bretton Woods in 1944, Keynes urged the conference to develop a level playing-field for international trade by instituting a new global trading currency. This would ensure that countries possessing hard currencies would not be advantaged over those that did not. To level the playing-field further, Keynes also proposed an International Clearing Union that would charge the same interest to creditor and debtor nations alike. By this means Keynes hoped to promote a culture of transient debt; to encourage wealthier countries to invest in poorer countries or improve their terms of trade, rather than sit back and idly profit from compound interest on debt.[18]

However, the financial status quo suited American interests more. They had no wish to lose the leverage and wealth their creditor status bestowed them. In addition, power over American-proposed regulatory bodies related directly to the credit that countries invested in them. As the largest investor, the US exercised the greatest power. In contrast, Keynes's proposals were too altruistic for the United States. Thus the world got the IMF and a second Bretton Woods institution instead.

Established as the International Bank for Reconstruction and Development, the Washington-based World Bank had as its goal to stimulate and maintain demand through the provision of private credit. During the 1950s it focused largely on supplying capital for basic infrastructure projects in the Third World. But like the IMF, it dispensed little funding; only US$10.7 billion between 1947 and 1967. Robert McNamara's presidency in the late 1960s provided new impetus to the World Bank. Between 1968 and 1973 alone, it dispensed US$13.4 billion on 760 projects.[19] But this new-found largesse soon came with strings attached. Increasingly, loans conformed to a new American determination to open Third World economies to international capital and to effect debt-induced growth. In addition, only a select few countries benefited, usually those that offered strategic advantage to the United States.

The primary goal of all these initiatives was to create a single international environment for co-operation. US predominance as the world's leading industrial nation helped to achieve that goal; it explains also why each new organization (with the exception of the weaker GATT) was headquartered in the United States. This was true also for the New York-based United Nations Organization (UN), which replaced the moribund League of Nations. Its goal was to facilitate international peace and security, and to promote human rights. At one level it existed as an international forum of equal nations, but at another level five permanent members of a select Security Council held the power of veto. The UN was not a democratic, accountable institution. Nonetheless, its multi-centred character did provide space for policy diversity in a way unattainable within Bretton Woods institutions. Increasingly, specialized agencies, programmes and funds became involved in promoting development, and intervened in the internal affairs of nations to prevent disorder or protect human rights.

The UN's growth represented a momentum of its own making. So too the persistence of the post-war boom. It derived from the transformation of many societies into consumer-driven democracies. Paid for by increased productivity and innovation,[20] the boom persisted because industrial and social planners succeeded in placing domestic recovery ahead of capitalist freedoms, and in investing in the infrastructure necessary for recovery. They ensured that the American strategy for its third wave remained two-tiered. Eichengreen believes that

> Controls loosened the link between domestic and foreign financial conditions; they granted governments freedom to alter domestic financial conditions in the pursuit of other goals without immediately jeopardizing the stability of the exchange rate. Controls were not so watertight as to obviate the need for exchange rate adjustments when domestic and foreign conditions diverged, but they provided the breathing space needed to organize orderly realignments and ensure the survival of the system.[21]

The consequences of this were far-reaching, as we shall see in the next chapter. But so also were the consequences of another post-war change, also part of the drive to effect a single world environment for co-operation. The second wave had enveloped the world's non-industrial peoples in colonialism. The third wave undid that legacy. Decolonization represented another important new feature of American globalism.

Decolonization

During the first two waves of globalization, protagonists had established colonies as markers of success. They were also forms of monopoly that denied other trading nations or corporations access, part of the same exclusive strategy for growth that ended so disastrously in war and depression in the twentieth century. But with the collapse of the second wave, colonies were no longer sustainable, either economically or politically.

Nonetheless, colonial powers were reluctant to decolonize. Britain argued that colonialism was simply a form of trusteeship designed not to exploit its subject peoples but to develop their resources. Yet the values of post-war trusteeship barely differed from those of nineteenth-century colonialism. Both implied that superior peoples were civilizing backward peoples. Trusteeship only added self-government to the features of 'civilization' to be attained. It gave no timetable and no uniform set of steps by which it might be achieved. In the end trusteeship became a device to enable Britain to save face, to transform the collapse of its empire into a triumph of Western values. Britain could argue that it had transformed disparate territories and tribal groupings into independent democratic nations. Thus honour was restored to empire and loss transformed into triumph.

Other colonial powers were equally determined to cling to their empires, despite the growing resistance of their subjects. The Dutch tried desperately to hold on to Indonesia. France fought bitterly to maintain its empire in Algeria and Vietnam. On the other hand, Britain's perilous finances forced it to accept Burma's post-war declaration of independence and to bring forward India's independence. In these circumstances lay a truth that colonial powers rarely wished to concede. Once colonial peoples resisted, no amount of 'civilization' could maintain imperial control. The solution – expensive endless military occupation – was hardly an action appropriate for a new era of co-operation, democracy and equality.

Nonetheless, until the 1970s Britain continued to project itself as a major global power through its remaining territories. In the immediate post-war years, it depended heavily on its colonies to survive economically. Indeed, as industrial consumer economies grew, tropical regions assumed new importance as suppliers of vital metals and primary produce. With the development of cheap mass transportation, they offered new opportunities for further investment in tourism. But none of these activities required colonial control.

In reality the cost of maintaining colonial rule far outweighed the benefits, especially if colonial elites demanded independence and gained a mass following, as they clearly had in India at the close of war. Not that this experience stopped Kenya, Cyprus, Egypt and Malaya becoming costly theatres of British resistance to decolonization, or Rhodesia and South Africa becoming similar theatres of settler resistance. In reality of course Britain no longer possessed the power to sustain an extensive empire. It might turn to the Commonwealth as a face-saving alternative, but it was no substitute. After the 1960s, when British capitalists became more interested in the possibilities that Europe and its new Common Market presented, Britain abandoned much of what was left of its empire. Its last significant colony, Hong Kong, returned to China in 1997. Most former colonies of the industrialized powers had become independent nations by the 1980s.

But integrating these former colonies into the world economy in a way that realized the much-heralded goals of development proved more difficult. Colonial strategies had provided little in the way of infrastructure and human capital suitable for anything other than colonialism. Few colonies had experienced sustained, meaningful democratic practices, except perhaps in the last frantic years before decolonization. Such minimalism lacked indigenous ownership and served only to enable exiting colonial authorities to save face. More often than not, the democracies they produced were unsustainable.

Colonial economic development was similarly unimpressive. 'The vast majority of Africans went into colonialism with a hoe', the academic activist Walter Rodney declared, 'and came out with a hoe'. Zambia, for example, a country of four million people, became independent in 1964 with only one hundred university graduates and one thousand secondary school students.[22]

In many instances, also, the newly independent countries possessed no unifying sense of national identity to carry them through difficult times ahead. The Congo contained over two hundred different tribes and ethnic groups, few of whom were effectively linked together by communications networks. Zimbabwe faced the added difficulty that 4,500 white settlers continued to farm one third of its cultivated land. These lands had been seized from tribes during Rhodesia's colonization during and after the 1890s, leaving some 700,000 peasant families to exist on lands much less suitable for farming. Britain's failure to provide a buy-back programme or to compensate the dispossessed when Zimbabwe became independent in 1980 allowed the issue of resettlement to simmer, and twenty years later to become an ugly and destructive feature of a desperate power struggle in the country.[23]

Unfortunately the process of decolonization also became tragically entangled in Cold War tensions between the United States and the Soviet Union. Korea, a former Japanese colony, retained its Soviet and US occupation zones as independent but warring entities. Another former Japanese colony – Taiwan – became home to the Guomindang regime fleeing the successful advance of the Communist Party in China. Along with South Korea and Japan, it became part of an American protectorate in East Asia. The US also replaced France in Vietnam's war of independence, in order to prevent its south from becoming communist. The United States had already seized Japanese colonies in Micronesia after the war to further its nuclear and military goals. France similarly clung to French Polynesia in the South Pacific in order to develop its own independent nuclear capability. And in Africa, US and Soviet tensions shaped conflicts in Angola, Ethiopia and Somalia.

Cold War entanglements were not always negative. During the Korean War, the US military expended over US$3.5 billion in the region. Much of this assisted Japan, but it also benefited South Korea and Taiwan. Most importantly, these countries were able to use Cold War investments and rare access to US markets to fuel highly successful development drives. They demonstrated what was possible when countries were given space and substantial resources to develop infrastructure and human capital. Usually Cold War entanglements had a very different impact.

British and American fears that a democratically elected Patrice Lumumba would drive the newly independent and mineral-rich Congo to the left led their leaders to conspire to murder him in January 1961. They were far happier with the pliable Mobutu Sese Seko, whom they sustained in power until his death in 1997. Mobutu practised a policy of development by theft which – although hard to imagine given the Congo's past – left his country even worse off than it had been under colonialism. After twenty-five years, 141,000 kilometres of rudimentary roads dwindled to 19,300 km.[24] Mobutu's 'vampire elite' presided over an empire of decay in which, according to one commentator, the only absolute law was Mobutu's eleventh commandment –'Fend for yourselves'.[25] By the time of his death, 80 per cent of the Congo's fifty million people were reduced to subsistence lifestyles.[26]

Most leaders of newly independent countries accepted industrialization as the way their peoples could achieve equality in the future. The lessons of history were plain. But after years of colonial servitude, they also wanted to distance themselves from their former rulers. Only by breaking free from their colonial pasts could they regain lost confidence and become truly independent. When Mao Zedong seized power in China in 1949, he declared that never again would the Chinese people be enslaved. All links with former imperialist powers in China were cut, and China embarked on a massive programme of social reconstruction. Over the next two decades it groped for a development strategy that would break the shackles of the past and establish a pattern of balanced development where industry catered for local needs and drew on local resources and abundant labour. In China, communism became an ideology to enable the fallen giant to catch up with other industrial nations, but the costs were high.

Possibly thirty million lives were lost between 1950 and 1975 as Mao and members of the Communist Party fought over development strategies. Neither enjoyed the overwhelming power exercised by Stalin in the Soviet Union, and once détente opened the way for China to rejoin the community of nations, the differing factions quickly accommodated themselves to integration with the global economy.

Unlike China, not all newly independent countries had the resources to protect themselves or to end their colonially induced relationships with the world. Not even the determination of Castro to take the Soviet path in 1961 could reduce substantially Cuba's dependence on sugar exports. Radical social and agrarian reform could not overcome the fact that there were scant resources for independent industrialization. In addition, if independent industrialization meant self-sufficiency, then it would have as much chance of success as economic nationalism had had in the 1930s. The US blockade of Cuba after the 1950s simply reinforced that point.

India's Prime Minister Jawaharlal Nehru thought that it might be possible to take a third path of development by using the state to develop an economy that was neither wholly capitalist nor wholly communist. Thus India did not withdraw from the world economy like China; nor did it embark on a programme of social reconstruction. Instead it built up a powerful state-owned industrial sector and became, by the 1970s, the tenth-largest industrial nation. Yet 80 per cent of India's population remained poor peasants. Their landlords dominated India's parliaments and refused to countenance changes that might weaken landlord control over the social, economic and political life of the Indian countryside. Consequently, the inability of the vast majority of the population to consume industrial products acted as a brake on industrial development and forced India to depend heavily on export markets. By the late 1970s India's third way of development was in tatters.

Keynes had foreseen these difficulties. In 1944 at Bretton Woods, he argued that post-war recovery depended on more than just post-war reconstruction. The new post-war order, he said, had specifically 'to develop the resources and production capacity of … less developed countries, to [raise] the standard of life and the conditions of labour everywhere, [and] to make the resources of the world more fully available to all mankind everywhere'.[27] But his advice went unheeded, drowned out by the exigencies of Cold War and by America's determination to profit most from its new global strategies.

This failure to extend to the Third World the social and economic privileges enjoyed by the First World engendered fierce debate on the priorities of development and the purpose of globalization by the close of the twentieth century. But equally it created a global divide just as threatening to the well-being of the whole as the divides that had crippled the second wave in the early twentieth century. These had reflected the inability of industrialized nations to create domestic environments capable of benefiting from and furthering the second generation of industrialization.

At the start of the twenty-first century the third wave's global dividedness possessed a similar potential to frustrate a third generation of industrialization. The era of supermen might have gone, but other dangers now replaced them. Reflecting in 1966 on his country's disastrous war in Vietnam, US Defence Secretary Robert McNamara argued that a relationship existed between violence and economic backwardness that could only be healed by removing 'the causes of human suffering and deprivation'. 'Violence anywhere in a taut world threatens the security and stability of nations half a globe away', he warned, and it 'could not be cured by counter-insurgency alone'.[28] That much had been acknowledged at Bretton Woods back in 1944, but it had been subsumed by other priorities in the decades that followed. The US failure not only weakened the third wave of globalization, it also contributed to the demise of US globalism's two-tiered strategic character.

Modernization

Despite decolonization, the 'civilizing' zeal of former imperialists was far from dead. In Britain and the United States a new mantra emerged: Western values, Western institutions, Western capital and Western technology. Only by Westernizing could former colonies hope to achieve a modern future. The American political economist Walt Rostow declared that only one path produced modernization. It involved five stages and at the end of it former colonies would take off into self-sustained growth as mass consumer societies.

There is 'a tendency in the modernization process', sociologist Robert Bellah concluded, 'which leads to the sort of society which American society is'.[29]

Something else was involved here also. Rostow took the anti-communist unity of the US order and implied a common trajectory of development for which there was no historical basis. The First World – the West – was presented as a homogeneous set of countries that had already made the transition to industrial modernity; they were the developed world. In contrast the former colonies – the Third World – were portrayed as still in the process of catching up; they were the developing world. The only example they should follow was that presented by the already developed world. For this reason Rostow called his path to modernization 'a non-communist manifesto'. Yet, like the Communists, Rostow emphasized production[30] and a final stage towards which all history inexorably moved. But he never made clear what drove this change; certainly not class conflict or the capitalist spirit.[31] But Rostow implied that the engine for growth for developing countries had to be external to themselves; in other words, the already developed countries. No precedent justified this argument, certainly not British and American industrialization.

Why then an external agent for the Third World? The answer lies in the perceived differences between First and Third World societies. The First World saw itself as homogeneous in its modernity and innovation, and the Third World as homogeneous in its poverty, backwardness, and undevelopment. The reason, Rostow argued, lay in the persistence of tradition in Third World countries. Static, unchanging tradition differentiated the Third World from the dynamic modern First, and held it back. Hence the need for an external agent of change.

Rostow's arguments were hardly novel, but coming from one of President Kennedy's New Frontiersmen, they represented a powerful restatement of the West's civilizing mission. 'Our frontiers are on every continent', Kennedy intoned after assuming office in 1961, and those frontiers included the Third World. Hence the importance of Rostow's message. Traditions could never be adapted for the purposes of modernization. No alternative to Westernization existed.

Thus was born a concept of duality that excluded so-called traditional economic sectors from assistance, denied them integration into national economies, and regarded them as static and beyond redemption. Economists assumed that traditional and modern sectors had nothing in common and forgot that what had made Britain so successful as an industrializing nation was the role that its dynamic rural society had played as a motor for growth. They forgot also that the failure to incorporate traditional agricultural sectors in many continental European nations had denied industry the consumer base it required for growth and generated terrible inequalities. But above all they failed to acknowledge that in reality there were no contradictory two sectors, no dualism.

Modern sectors fed off traditional sectors and kept them alive. Traditional sectors ensured a plentiful supply of cheap labour, kept costs low, and reduced political pressures for change. They also provided a conservative base from which old ruling elites might maintain power and recruit military support. Fernando Henrique Cardoso, later Brazil's president, declared the relationship of modern sectors with traditional sectors to be a kind of internal colonialism. It produced dependent development,[32] which generated greater inequalities and raised the potential for destabilizing unrest.

Proponents of modernization focused only on external sources of growth and had no interest in utilizing so-called traditional sectors. Growth came from trade and integration with the dynamic First World, not from sectors labelled traditional but which in reality were marginalized. Not surprisingly, during the 1950s and 1960s, South American critics began to examine the external linkages that modernization promoted. They concluded that, far from producing modernization, these linkages with the outside world produced inequalities, dependency and stagnation. Independence under these conditions simply transformed colonialism into neo-colonialism. They demanded Import Substitution Industrialization (ISI) instead, and protection from foreign competition. ISI, they believed, better reflected both the lessons of industrial history and their own wartime experiences, when isolation had encouraged rapid industrial growth. Instead of importing manufactured commodities, Third World countries should now manufacture the same commodities themselves.

Economic historian David Landes is scathing in his condemnation of this failed experiment. In South America, he says, the cocooning of economies fostered a morbid propensity to blame others; it promoted only economic impotence.[33] Certainly Import Substitution Industrialization had flaws, but in many parts of the world, such as Australia, it succeeded in promoting industries that might otherwise have collapsed under competition from larger, better-resourced foreign competitors. South America's problem was not protectionism but its failure to reform social structures. Without social reconstruction for the rural and urban poor, most industries in South America lacked the necessary mass market to become sustainable, and eventually turned to export production to survive, as modernizationists had always argued they should.

Nonetheless, many people in newly independent countries were deeply influenced by these critiques of capitalism during the waves of decolonization. Powerful classes and military groups that prospered from the status quo often encouraged such analyses because they distracted attention from their own contributions to national problems. All problems could be blamed on the West or on the nature of linkages with the West. During the 1970s, the Third World was able to use its numerical strength in the United Nations to gain greater representation in multilateral institutions. They formed a UN Conference on Trade and Development (UNCTAD) to press for trade reform, and argued for a New International Economic Order to address the dependency generated by external linkages. No new order materialized, but the debate did generate a climate more conducive to amending the terms of trade with First World countries.

In 1975 the Lomé Convention and associated protocols gave former European colonies preferential access to European markets for selected commodities at subsidized prices. The more regionally focused US Caribbean Basin Initiative and Australasia's SPARTECA performed the same function. In addition, UNCTAD succeeded in gaining further access for some manufactured goods to First World markets through its Generalized System of Preferences.

The debate had come full circle. Third World leaders now sought Western markets as the engine for growth. Dependency analysis had questioned external linkages and their ability to generate modernity. That debate had been transformed into trade reform, and its principal beneficiaries were the non-national actors of the global economy – transnational corporations (TNCs). By the end of the 1970s, Export Oriented Industrialization (EOI) had transformed the third wave and threatened the two-tiered basis of American globalism.

The War of Globalisms

All globalizations have been contested, although during the first wave no one nation possessed the economic strength to exercise overwhelming dominance. The second wave differed in this respect. Industrial Britain emerged from war with no strong competitor to constrain its global ambitions. The United States was not so fortunate in 1945. Certainly it possessed the only thriving economy, and its wealth had been critical for reinvigorating the Allied struggle against Germany and its Axis partners. But the Soviet Union, and not the United States, drove back the bulk of Germany's military forces and won the war in the European theatre. At the end of the Second World War, Soviet forces occupied Eastern Europe and a considerable part of Germany. Consequently, in devising a post-war settlement for Europe, the United States had to accommodate Soviet interests.

This was no easy feat, given the nature of past European and American relations with the Soviet Union. That the Soviets cloaked their industrial catch-up strategy in the garb of nineteenth-century international Marxism created an additional ideological hurdle. Add Stalinist paranoia born of decades of internal struggle, and it is not difficult to see why the third wave quickly evolved characteristics that frustrated goals of global co-operation.

Both powers had different immediate post-war goals. The United States wanted barriers to trade and investment in Eastern Europe removed, whereas the Soviet Union wanted to transform that region into a compliant bloc and remove the potential for future capitalist or fascist European threats. In addition, the Soviet Union desperately required reparations from Germany, whereas the United States had no such need. When Stalin moved to effect these goals in 1947, the United States declared him a new Hitler, a new Genghis Khan. The Soviet Union in turn saw American actions as dangerously selfish. Its Washington ambassador wrote in 1946 that Eurasia's colossal post-war need for consumer goods and economic infrastructure

> provides American monopolistic capital with prospects for enormous shipments of goods and the importation of capital into these countries – a circumstance which would permit it to infiltrate their national economies. Such a development would mean a serious strengthening of the economic position of the US in the whole world and would be a stage on the road to world domination by the US.[34]

Consequently, instead of peace and global harmony, the third wave began with a new division of Eurasia, an unprecedented arms race, and a destructive Soviet–American rivalry. It was not an auspicious start.

At first the tensions that existed between the United States and the Soviet Union renewed fears of another war, and the US deliberately invoked the Munich legacy, the danger of appeasing dictators, to garner support when the Soviets extended their control over Czechoslovakia in 1948. The arms race and its potential for global destruction served similarly to mobilize (and polarize) future generations. New and terrifying weapons that could never be used safely were designed to demonstrate superiority and to undermine the opposition's confidence. This was an era of spies, of the space race, of proxy wars, and above all of hyperbole. The US threatened to 'roll back' the 'Soviet Iron Curtain' and 'liberate' oppressed people wherever they might be. The Soviet Union promised to 'bury' the United States. Neither did either. Instead they developed a psychological war, the course of which each hoped would demonstrate the superiority of their beliefs and determine which order would define the future. The war of globalisms was a cold war, not a hot war.

Nonetheless, this psychological focus did not prevent their mutual hostility from erupting into war in many parts of the Third World. These wars were dangerously destabilizing to the countries and regions in which they were fought, whether in sub-Saharan Africa, Indo-China or Central America. Certainly they haunted international relations for the next forty-five years and frustrated development initiatives long after the Cold War's end. The Vietnam War enveloped its Indo-Chinese neighbours and helped to produce the geno-cidal Khmer Rouge regime in Cambodia during the late 1970s. When oil-rich Angola in southern Africa won independence from Portugal in 1975, East–West tensions contributed substantially to a long, bitter civil war that left half a million of its people dead and displaced one quarter of its population of twelve million. In Indonesia, armed forces invoked anti-communism to defend their bloody seizure of power in 1966 and their equally bloody invasion of East Timor nine years later.

Such wars also impacted severely on the two superpowers themselves, in particular on the weaker Soviet Union. But the United States did not escape unscathed. The Cold War might have transformed it into the most militarized global power by the century's close, but its impact on US global objectives was also substantial. Certainly it contributed to the demise of America's dual post-war global strategies. It contributed to the collapse of post-war financial stability, and left the United States economically indebted and less able to weather future global recessions. But for many observers the Cold War's more dangerous impact lay elsewhere. It returned the world's main powers to the second wave's dangerous delusion that military prowess and territory were markers of success.[35] Yet behind the arms race lay a struggle for technological supremacy, in which America's economic strengths proved decisive.

Soviet Globalism

Soviet globalism had very different origins from America's. Although deeply influenced by inter-war experiences, its roots lay in the idealist philosophy of Karl Marx. Marx had sought to define the historical context of nineteenth-century industrialization in order to understand its nature and predict its future course. When he looked into the past, he saw the struggle of classes. The bourgeoisie had successfully eclipsed Europe's old landed classes and in doing so had brought into being a hitherto unknown set of classes – the urban industrial proletariat. In the nineteenth century these new working classes grew rapidly and constituted a new mass capable of being organized into a political force. Marx believed that they were the future; next in the evolutionary chain, they would inherit the world.

Marx's vision promised a dictatorship of the proletariat to create a just and classless society. He did not regard these as contradictory objectives. Industrial societies themselves were harsh and brutal. Average life expectancies for workers in industrial cities like Manchester rarely exceeded twenty years. Although conditions for workers and their families improved during the course of the nineteenth century, they did so in part because the proletariat organized itself and promoted its interests politically. Dictatorship would enable the proletariat finally to overcome the power of contending classes, transform the institutions of the state, and claim their rightful place in the sun. Consequently when a small Russian Communist Party seized power in a coup during the chaos of the First World War, many communists believed that Marx's dream of a workers' paradise could now become reality. The year 1917 would become the defining moment of human history, when global politics and social organization began a new trajectory. But few communists asked themselves how a still largely agrarian country could lead the world into a new industrial future.

Marx had been deeply influenced by the Industrial Revolution's increased focus on the production of capital goods during the mid-nineteenth century. The Soviet Union inherited this bias, even though by 1917 a second generation of industrialization heralded a more consumer-centred focus. But wartime exigencies produced their own demands, especially in an industrially backward country like Russia. Infrastructure and defence came first. During the 1930s Stalin added his own imperative – industrialization had to be rapid. 'We are on the eve of our transformation from an agrarian to an industrial country', Stalin declared. 'We are fifty or a hundred years behind the advanced countries. We must make good this lag in ten years. Either we do it or they crush us'.[36] Stalin's directive derived from national fear rather than ideology. He feared the hostility of other industrial nations, in particular Britain and Germany, and his fear drove the speed of industrialization and reinforced its bias towards heavy industry. Both features survived the Second World War, and would prove an inadequate basis from which to challenge American globalism or provide an alternative means to empower human societies.

As we noted earlier, much of the Soviet Union lay in ruins in 1945, but its armies had liberated Europe from the shackles of fascism and now occupied much of Eastern Europe. Stalin had no intention of conquering Europe. If that had been the case he would hardly have urged his allies for so long to open a second front against Hitler in the West. Nor would he have demobilized his troops: twelve million soldiers in 1945 became three million by 1948. But he did intend to use his hard-won position in Eastern Europe as a basis from which to rebuild the Soviet Union.

Soviet ideology confronted American ideology, but Stalin's obstinacy did not make him another Hitler. Despite Cold War rhetoric, which tended to conflate fascism and communism, and label them both totalitarian, there were significant differences. Like Hitler, Stalin was ruthless and responsible for millions of deaths, but Stalin also held very different objectives. Hitler's empire had space only for Germans, and sought to create an ethnically pure feudal farming landscape. In contrast, Stalin's empire had no time for ethnic purity. It supported local elites and accommodated East European nationalism, even redistributing boundaries to buy support and turning a blind eye to forced repatriations and the murder of collaborationists. This difference, historian Mark Mazower contends, ensured that the Soviet Empire endured much longer than did its Nazi predecessor.[37]

The Soviets in 1945 also offered a different future. They believed in social transformation and they promised an urbanized industrial utopia, and – above all – an end to the historical gap between east and west. Pre-war market capitalism, based largely on Western investments, had done little for Eastern Europe except deliver key industries into foreign hands. Now a new alternative presented itself. Given the weakness of democratic parties, the nationalism of most communists, and the compliance of civil servants – many of whom had wartime pasts to live down – it was accepted.[38] An accommodating Stalin established coalition governments to win broad support.

But good will between the major powers disappeared in 1947. Most of the victorious allies, including the Soviet Union, anticipated Germany's reunification after their occupying forces left. Only France refused to countenance reunification and planned to annex southern Germany to guarantee desperately needed coal supplies. Before long each of the separate occupation zones had their own social and political regimes which reflected the differences between their occupiers. Although social transformation became the Soviet Union's principal goal in East Germany, it still wanted to ensure that Germany as a whole paid for its wartime destruction.

The winter of 1946–47 put paid to that. Across Europe, 'the harshest winter in living memory' suddenly restored memories of the Great Depression and threatened the birth of America's brave new world. In Britain unemployment briefly reached levels nearly twice those of the 1930s. Coal production collapsed. Industries shut. Facing bankruptcy, Britain immediately advanced plans for Indian independence and transferred control of Palestine to the United Nations. It also signalled its inability to continue providing aid to Greece and Turkey. Even its occupation of Germany was too heavy a burden to carry.[39]

Across Western Europe, poverty and hunger threatened stability. In Germany, the US halted reparation deliveries from its zone and asserted a new goal: Germany's economy would be revived but within a united Europe. The Soviet Union objected. To end reparations threatened its security and wellbeing. The needs of a devastated Soviet Union now conflicted with a newly confident and wealthy United States, which wished instead to avoid mass starvation in a country where Lucky Strike cigarettes (one carton was worth US$2,300) had become the main currency.[40]

In June 1947 the United States responded to the European crisis with the Marshall Plan, a programme of reconstruction designed, in part, to reduce the attractiveness of communism to Europeans. Three months before, President Harry Truman had declared that the United States would never appease communism and pledged to fill the gap in the eastern Mediterranean left by Britain's sudden withdrawal. Truman reasoned that if the Soviet Union 'corrupted' Greece, it could carry its 'infection' to 'three continents' – Europe, West Asia and Africa. 'It must be the policy of the United States to support free people who are resisting attempted subjugation by armed minorities or by outside pressure', he declared.[41]

The Soviets believed that the US now threatened its own reconstruction plans for Eastern Europe. A Cold War unfolded. Coalition governments in Eastern Europe collapsed and were replaced by Communist regimes. In return for US aid, France gave up its plans for the Rhineland, and all non-Soviet zones were merged to form a new West German nation. The Soviets panicked and created a public relations disaster. They blockaded the Western sectors of Berlin, which lay 170 km inside East Germany, protesting that since the West no longer intended to unite Germany, it had no reason to retain its presence in the old capital. The polarization intensified. By 1949 there were two rival Germanies. Soon there would also be two rival defence pacts – America's North Atlantic Treaty Organization (NATO) and the Soviet Warsaw Pact.

Communist victory in the Chinese civil war in 1949, the invasion of South Korea by the Soviet-influenced North in 1950, and France's withdrawal from Vietnam by 1954 dramatically shifted the focus of the Cold War to East Asia. The US responded with a massive increase in military expenditure and developed military bases around the world in order to prevent the further spread of communism. Again it invoked the Munich legacy and declared brinkmanship a Cold War art. But there were limits to American responses. With China cocooned from US intervention by size and Soviet support, the United States could only provide protection for surviving anti-communist forces on Taiwan. US forces re-established South Korea but did not end the conflict with the North. In Vietnam it supported a permanently divided country. But when the Soviet Union invaded Hungary in 1956, it did not retaliate. In Europe at least, the status quo provided a kind of stability.

The new Democrat President John Kennedy had to relearn the lesson in the early 1960s when East Germany sealed its borders with West Berlin, and when his efforts to destabilize Cuba produced a dangerous confrontation with the Soviets over missiles. But it was a lesson only partially learned. Kennedy also strengthened counter-insurgency forces to stamp out threatening wars of national liberation, and Rostow declared 'Vietnam ... a testing ground for our policy in the world'.

Nonetheless, the goal of supremacy soon imposed costs that the United States found difficult to bear. The Vietnam War absorbed half a million US soldiers under Kennedy's successor, President Lyndon Johnson, cost US$30 billion per annum to sustain, and added another layer of internal discontent for the already socially troubled superpower to accommodate. Accordingly, by the 1970s the United States began to reconsider its relations with China and even embraced détente with the Soviet Union.

The Soviet path to the same destination proved equally tortuous. At first the Cold War made the Soviets much more assertive.[42] In Eastern Europe they demanded total conformity. In part the reason lay with Stalin, whose paranoia increased with age and ill-health. In Moscow he unnerved his closest collaborators by stalking the corridors of the Kremlin at night muttering obscenities about them. He feared losing control. Across Eastern Europe and the Soviet Union, his faithful secret police murdered thousands of suspects, and herded millions into labour camps, possibly as many as half a million in Eastern Europe alone. Forced industrialization, Soviet style, now began in earnest. Predictably, agriculture became the first casualty; peasants who resisted collect-ivization were deported or placed in camps. Unrest swelled. In 1953 even the better-off Berlin industrial workers rebelled against their conditions. But by then Stalin had died and a process of de-Stalinization enabled power to fall into the hands of a new technocratic intelligentsia. Communist parties still retained control, and their agenda remained economic growth. But the focus shifted more to administration and reform, and, as long as changes did not threaten the integrity of the Soviet bloc, Stalin's successors no longer de-manded rigid economic conformity. Indeed, they too embraced détente, hoping by the 1970s to gain from greater trade and co-operation with the West.

Meanwhile, Eastern Europe rapidly urbanized. During the 1940s, 36 per cent of its people lived in cities; by the 1950s over 50 per cent. Social services expanded, living standards improved, and income differences fell. Educational opportunities increased vastly, and upward mobility now became more than just a possibility. Economic growth, too, was spectacular, almost 4 per cent per annum; a remarkable achievement given that the Soviet Union continued to extract reparations, probably worth as much as US\$14 billion.[43] But there were serious problems.

The focus on industrial production neglected many sections of society, particularly peasants and elderly people. Prestigious construction projects took precedence over much-needed housing. Industrial growth derived from labour-intensive heavy industries that were unlikely to remain competitive in the long term.[44] Indeed they were not only inefficient but also dangerously polluting. Eastern Europe and large parts of the Soviet Union became ecological disaster areas. The 1986 nuclear disaster at Chernobyl and the death of the Aral Sea – the world's fourth-largest body of fresh water – were symptomatic of wider failures. Stalin's successor – Nikita Khrushchev – precipitated the latter crisis by creating huge new farms on the virgin grasslands of Western Siberia, Kazakhstan and the Volga, which later turned into disastrous dustbowls. Thus the gap between East and West grew rather than shrank, and faith in the communist alternative began to evaporate. Khrushchev became the first victim of this failure.

Despite the rhetoric of Cold War, the Soviet Union and its satellites were increasingly integrated into the world economy. Global recession at the end of the 1960s affected the Soviet bloc also. Some countries turned to the West for help. Yugoslavia made tourism its important growth sector, and by the 1980s two million visitors poured on to its beaches each year. When US president Ronald Reagan declared a new Cold War in the early 1980s, Poland, Hungary and East Germany were already being kept alive by Western bank loans and trade credits.

Mazower believes that what most stymied communism was its belief in a workers' paradise. By the 1960s, Western societies had transformed themselves into service-driven entities. Affluence created the basis for these transformations, an affluence that derived from the Keynesian strategies of the 1950s and the rise in real wages generated by increased productivity. Affluence also laid the basis for the next generation of industrial revolution, electronics and information technology.[45]

The Soviet Union possessed none of the affluence needed to build an information- and technology-driven society. It remained wedded to an earlier form of industrialism. Party bosses preferred declining productivity and inefficient heavy industries to sacrificing the industrial proletariat. Mazower argues that in return for job security their people got shoddy goods, and longer and longer queues for ever scarcer consumer products. In Poland the working classes rebelled.[46]

Reality and ideology, Mazower argues, had parted company. With the possibility of overtaking the West long gone, the Communist Party no longer had a mission, and its technocratic leaders no longer believed. Holding the Soviet bloc together cost too much. By the 1980s the Soviet Union subsidized Eastern Europe through cheap fuel to a sum equivalent to 2 per cent of its GNP. In addition nearly 15 per cent of its GNP disappeared into its own military machine.[47] Even this no longer matched the resources that the United States, spending only 6 per cent of a much larger GNP, poured into a new technologically based arms race.[48]

In 1979 the Soviets added to their difficulties by invading Afghanistan, for no other reason than to save face and prevent a dubious communist regime from collapsing. The United States, still recovering from its loss of face in Vietnam four years earlier and from its humiliating exit from Iran in 1978, seized on Afghanistan as the focus of its new Cold War, and channelled funds to anti-Soviet forces.

By the mid-1980s Afghanistan had become a Soviet 'Vietnam', and the problems of Eastern Europe no longer seemed as pressing. Eastern Europe had been the first major test of Soviet globalism. Now it represented simply another burden. With its globalism dead, all the Soviet Union had left was empire. And, in an age of transnational economic co-operation, empire was anachronistic.

In 1985 a new reforming Soviet leader, Mikhail Gorbachev, set out to rejuvenate the Soviet economy. Perestroika – economic reform – demanded freedom of information, and that in turn demanded democratization. Eastern Europe was already going its own way, having maintained links with the West after the breakdown of détente in the 1980s. Increasingly its leaders now sought non-Communist credentials by fomenting hostilities towards minorities in their countries.

When the workers' Solidarity Party defeated the Polish Communist Party in elections in 1989, the Soviet Union refused to intervene. When Hungary opened its borders with Austria to draw attention to the plight of Hungarians in Romania, a fresh exodus of East Germans began. One by one Eastern Europe's communist regimes fell, and the Soviet Union stood by and watched. In 1991, it went the same way itself.

Except in the Balkans, the transitions were smoother than those experienced at the close of either the First World War or the Second. But that meant little to the bulk of their ill-prepared workforces who suddenly found themselves exposed to global competition. The rush to liberalize and privatize the once centralized economies of the Eastern Bloc carried a heavy price. Unemployment and poverty (one third of all Russians were suddenly plunged below the poverty line) accompanied the withdrawal of state services. An elite of former managers and mafia bosses now inserted themselves where once Communist Party cadres ruled. The Russian population, barely half the size of the former Soviet Union, bore the brunt of the harsh transformation. Its population fell from 148 million in 1990 to 145 million ten years later. Life expectancies also collapsed, from 69 to 66 years (to 59 for men). The situation in many former Soviet republics was also bleak. Moldova's economy shrank 60 per cent and its people were forced to survive increasingly on remittances from illegal emigrants abroad. With the old Soviet Union's linkages gone, Moldova's government declared self-sufficiency its new national goal.[49]

Globalization Transformed

Soviet globalism died in the late 1980s, a victim of the changing character of the third wave of globalization. But, contrary to assertions of American triumphalism in the early 1990s, its demise had already been preceded by the slow death of American globalism. No global New Deal based on technological investment and social justice had succeeded the Marshall Plan.[50] Instead the US increasingly allowed economic self-interest to determine global policy. Its message to the world, political scientist Peter Taylor argues, became its own success as a consumption-driven society. Modernization theories in the late 1950s and early 1960s demonstrated the shift. In January 1941 Roosevelt had declared freedom of religion and speech, and freedom from want and fear to be overriding US objectives. In reality a fifth freedom took precedence – freedom of choice; and a new American existential mantra arose – 'I shop, therefore I am'. When ideals go, Taylor concludes, all that is left is pragmatism.[51]

Such pragmatism had already seen the United States support unpredictable dictators and corrupt leaders in the fight against communism, many of whom, like Saddam Hussein and Osama Bin Laden, would 'blow back' to haunt it after the close of the Cold War. Gone too were the regulatory compromises that had made the Bretton Woods system so successful. The Cold War and support for client states cost the US dearly, by as much as US$400 billion annually (in 1996-dollar terms) according to one estimate.[52] So too Japanese and European economic recovery.

US productivity increased only 4.1 per cent between 1950 and 1969, compared with 6.7 per cent for Western Europe and 13.8 per cent for Japan. America's share of world trade declined from 21 per cent in 1950 to 12 per cent in 1978. At the same time West Germany's share of world trade rose from 4 per cent to 12 per cent and Japan's from 1 per cent to 8 per cent.[53] Japan's GNP rose from 10 per cent of America's in 1965 to 40 per cent by 1980, by which time it had become a major creditor nation.[54] In contrast, the US trade deficit increased from $2.9 billion to US$19.8 billion between 1967 and 1971 alone; its total debt from US$33 billion to US$68 billion.[55] By 1984 the US trade deficit had risen to US$125 billion and its current account deficit to US$100 billion. It no longer possessed sufficient gold and currency reserves to cover its deficits. Consequently the US become dependent on capital flows from the rest of the world to stay afloat; by some US$80 billion in 1984,[56] by nearly US$400 billion in 2000 when its deficit reached a record US$435 billion.

American deficits presented difficulties for countries that now found themselves with a surplus of dollars. Fearing that the resultant rise in money supply would increase inflation, European nations traded their Eurodollars and tried to convert reserves to gold. During the 1960s US gold reserves declined sufficiently to threaten dollar convertibility, and the United States found itself in a position similar to that of West European countries in the early 1950s. Like them, domestic pressures for social programmes (and Cold War pressures for military expenditure) made the normal IMF prescription – expenditure reduction policies – politically impossible.

By 1971 the international flight from the dollar forced President Richard Nixon to suspend the dollar's convertibility, devalue the dollar 7.5 per cent, and impose a temporary 10 per cent tax on all imports to pressure European currencies to revalue. In doing so he brought down two crucial pillars of the Bretton Woods system – convertibility and stability. Worse followed as the decade progressed. When the Organization of Petroleum Exporting Countries (OPEC) raised the price of oil in 1973, all industrial nations were plunged into deficit. By 1978 the value of the dollar had fallen another 12 per cent, undermining further its role as a global reserve currency. Gold prices soared to US$850 per ounce as investors sought alternatives.

The dollar crisis demonstrated the increased difficulty of maintaining a system of pegged exchange rates in the presence of increasingly mobile capital. The capital needed to offset speculative flows did not exist. Accordingly, during the 1970s most West European countries responded by floating their currencies.[57] The US refused to consider the use of Special (IMF) Drawing Rights as an alternative international currency, arguing that nations in surplus should increase their imports from the United States and contribute more to the military costs of the Cold War. In 1976 the US had IMF regulations amended to enable currency values to reflect the balance-of-payments situations of countries. A further pillar of the Bretton Woods system tumbled.[58]

Given the susceptibility of the US dollar to domestic manipulation, the European Union established in 1979 a European Monetary System to encourage intra-European trade expansion and reduce fluctuations in exchange rates between members. However, the removal of capital controls made managed currency realignments within Europe impossible and strengthened the case for a single European currency as the remedy. In the late 1990s the Euro became an alternative reserve currency, at the start of 2002 the European Union's official currency.

Just as Europe sought to protect itself from this volatility, so American transnational corporations looked for new ways to remain competitive. Since the 1940s, Import Substitution Industrialization had enabled many countries to employ forms of protection to promote domestic industrial growth and meet domestic demand for light consumer goods without sacrificing precious foreign exchange. Import substitution rarely met all these objectives, at least not simultaneously. As we noted earlier, industrialization still required imports, only this time of raw materials and machinery, not finished products. But if the basis for mass consumption did not exist, then import substitution did no more than reinforce existing social inequalities. However, transnationals found that import substitution presented them with new opportunities. Instead of having their exports excluded by tariff walls, they shifted production into the newly industrializing countries themselves. There they enjoyed tariff protection and could make use of cheap labour. The size of the local market did not affect them because they focused instead on exports to their traditional markets.

In countries like the Philippines, martial law in 1972 facilitated the demise of import substitution in favour of transnational capital. Pressure came also from loan institutions such as the World Bank. It determined that the future of Third World economies lay in export production, and especially in export production derived from the new agricultural technology of the Green Revolution that transnational agribusinesses controlled.

But export production was not the panacea promised. Infrastructure costs produced further foreign exchange losses, and TNC-dominated production enclaves never developed sufficient linkages with other sectors to stimulate widespread economic change. Whenever export commodity prices fell or protectionist responses in destination markets increased, export-dependent countries suffered. The 1980s demonstrated their vulnerability. Export markets recessed after the second dramatic OPEC oil price rise in 1979, and debt-servicing costs escalated as petrodollars (which had been recycled as cheap loans to the Third World in the 1970s) dried up. No sizeable domestic markets existed to compensate.

How could countries accept such narrow options? Part of the problem lay in the development perspectives held by institutions such as the World Bank. For them, development consisted solely in removing technical obstacles to economic growth and efficient production. Hence, in distributing funds, the profit-seeking World Bank sought to maximize its investment returns by directing funds to projects deemed cost-effective and most likely to deliver immediate profits. Not surprisingly this approach favoured projects incorporating already wealthy, skilled personnel, whose activities were focused on already available foreign markets. This narrowed the range of clients and reduced the potential for internal market expansion.[59]

IMF demands on governments had a similar impact. When Third World governments sought assistance with balance-of-payments difficulties, they were forced to implement adjustment programmes that cut wages, retrenched public services, and increased the cost of services remaining. In most instances results were similar: real incomes fell, unemployment escalated, government revenues declined, debt servicing assumed a larger proportion of state incomes, and political instability increased. Algeria provides a useful example. When the oil boom ended in the mid-1980s, its oil revenues fell 61 per cent, crippling economic growth. By the end of the decade, two thirds of all 15–20-year-olds were unemployed, and the revenue that Algeria required to pay the interest on its loans had risen from 51 per cent of its foreign income to 87 per cent.[60]

Across the Third World the picture was similar. The rich got richer, their gains invested in real estate or foreign bank accounts rather than in employment-generating activities. Corrupt authorities also siphoned off profits that might otherwise have been invested. Invariably the only sectors that flourished were garment or footwear industries, which employed women at wage levels that little benefited the domestic economy. Tourism also flourished, but with foreign carriers bringing tourists to foreign-owned hotels. Income leakages in these industries were notoriously high, often 70 per cent of turnover.

Export strategists sometimes argue that Third World countries have no choice but to utilize their only comparative advantage – cheap labour, or lax environmental and labour laws. Others suggest that these advantages are not highly significant, that most TNCs pay better wages than local companies and implement policies for environmental and occupational safety that set standards for local companies. TNCs need skilled labour, good infrastructure, and proximity or special access to foreign markets.[61] Indeed the latter is often a crucial determinant of foreign investment, given the lack of domestic markets.

With state revenues falling, balance-of-payments difficulties worsening and commodity prices falling, many Third World countries have no choice but to rely on export production. Nonetheless, a small group of countries, often with privileged access to First World markets, did succeed in using export production to transform themselves. Dubbed Newly Industrializing Countries (NICs) in the 1980s, South Korea, Taiwan, Hongkong, Singapore, Mexico, and Brazil were able rapidly to expand production in textiles, clothing, steel, cars, shipping, and consumer electronics. But their advantage was slender, and when competition began to bite, they diversified their markets. Importantly they made their own producers consumers. Europe and North America had pursued this path, yet it was still not one advocated by the World Bank or the IMF.

Export-driven growth introduced another important change, this time an organizational one. Reduced transport costs and new automation processes assisted the change. Earlier, when we examined the origins of industrialization, we noted that a central factor in the creation of the factory system had been a new division of labour. Workers no longer produced an entire product, but discrete parts that together made the whole. A similar transformation occurred during the 1970s and 1980s, only this time its scale was global rather than factory-wide. Businesses began to fragment the manufacturing process into a number of elemental operations that could be performed at different locations depending on cost advantage or some other factor. The promotion of EOI simultaneously helped to reduce barriers to transnational investment and enabled the creation of new global production networks, a central feature of the third wave of globalization at the end of the twentieth century. Some companies have used global production networks to cease production altogether and focus solely on product design and marketing, now the most profitable components of their industry.[62]

The impact of these changes on the Third World has been complex. Along the Mexican border with the United States, for example, transnational corporations now employ over one million people, but their factories have few links with the Mexican economy, except in terms of pollution, drugs and prostitution. Indeed, far from homogenizing societies, transnationalism has produced a diversity of development. The notion of a Third World was always flawed if it implied homogeneity. By the end of the twentieth century, the diversity of development outcomes meant that all-encompassing terms such as the Third World, Less Developed Countries, or the South (a geographic alternative proposed in the late 1970s) were largely meaningless. Indeed, distinctions between former colonies were often as great as distinctions with industrial nations. Some former colonies, such as South Korea, Hong Kong and Singapore, surpassed many Western nations in terms of wealth.

The shift to EOI grew not only from a new generation of technology but also from the collapse of American globalism in the wake of transnational capital's resurgence. The Bretton Woods system had restrained global capital in the interests of domestic stability and prosperity. But the use of the US dollar as the international reserve currency created conflicts of interest that ultimately doomed the system. Consequently, during the 1970s and 1980s, First World nations gradually floated their currencies and lifted constraints on private capital transactions. These changes facilitated transnational investment in Third World economies, but also created new avenues for global profit. With this transformation came a remarkable shift in power to private capital. Nothing better symbolized the shift than the abandonment of neo-Keynesian economic policies for monetarist policies, sometimes called economic rationalism.

Although much of the inflation experienced during the 1970s had been due to financial instability and to wage growth exceeding productivity, monetarists succeeded in convincing industrial governments that they could address inflation by increasing interest rates. Effectively banks now took control of money creation and, with the twin pillars of the Bretton Woods system (stable exchange rates and capital controls) dismantled, governments surrendered their control over national well-being to the markets. Not surprisingly, capital quickly profited from the change.

Monetarists urged governments to abandon public subsidies and surrender public enterprises to private interests. With the focus on new sources of profit, monetarists were keen to ensure that inflation did not damage future profits. To that end, relentless pressure on governments to restrict spending and lower taxes mounted during the 1980s and 1990s.[63] With the growth in speculation in currencies and trading futures, financial markets became the new decision-makers. By 1989, foreign exchange transactions exceeded US$650 billion per day, a figure 40 times the value of world trade.[64] By 2000, foreign-exchange trade exceeded US$1.5 trillion per day and already speculation had created major financial crises in Mexico (1995), Thailand, Indonesia, Malaysia, South Korea and Taiwan (1997), Russia (1998) and Brazil (1999).

The emergence of this transnational economy is much more complex than our picture suggests. One of the chief beneficiaries of what we might call transnationalism has been transnational corporations themselves. Global production techniques mean that over one fifth of all world trade is simply intra-firm trade, ideal for reducing costs and preventing the diffusion of new techniques to competitors. TNCs account for 70 per cent of world trade, perhaps 25 per cent of total global output, certainly 80 per cent of information technology trade, and 90 per cent of private research and development.[65] At the close of the twentieth century, the top 200 TNCs were estimated to have a combined turnover of US$7.6 trillion, only US$1 trillion less than the world's largest economy, the United States, and 2.5 times more than in 1982. They produced a profit of US$345.7 billion. Ninety per cent of these corporations are headquartered in just five countries – the United States, France, Britain, Germany and Japan. Thirty-seven per cent are American and they control 53 per cent of all profits generated.[66]

Transnationalism has emerged as a new feature of the third wave of globalization, a far cry from the globalism projected by Roosevelt's New Dealers in 1945, and one cause of much of the angst that globalization generates today, as we shall see in the final chapter. But concern also arose because transnationalism seemed to jeopardize many of the achievements brought to industrialized countries by the third wave, to which we now turn.

Notes

1. David Kennedy, 'A Tale of Three Cities: How the United States Won World War Two', *Background Briefing*, 21 October 2001, abc.net.au

2. Richard J. Barnet, *The Alliance, America–Europe–Japan: Makers of the Postwar World*, New York, Simon & Schuster, 1983, pp. 19–20, 22.

3. Basil Dmytryshyn, *USSR: A Concise History*, New York, Charles Scribner's Sons, 1971, pp. 231–2; and Jeremy Isaacs and Taylor Downing, *Cold War*, Bantam Press, London, 1998, p. 23.

4. Mark Mazower, *Dark Continent: Europe's Twentieth Century*, London, Allen Lane, 1998, p. 209.

5. Susan George and Fabrizio Sabelli, *Faith and Credit: The World Bank's Secular Empire*, London, Penguin, 1994, p. 26.

6. In contrast to orthodox economic prescriptions, Keynesian economic policies recommended deficit financing as a means to kick-start depressed economies. The policies were named after John Maynard Keynes, the British economist who most successfully articulated them in the inter-war period.

7. J. Kenneth Galbraith, *The Age of Uncertainty*, London, BBC–Andre Deutsch, 1977, p. 221.

8. Barnet, *The Alliance,* p. 103, Graeme Donald Snooks, *The Ephemeral Civilization: Exploding the Myth of Social Evolution*, London and New York, Routledge, 1997, pp. 386–7.

9. George and Sabelli, *Faith and Credit*, p. 23.

10. Ibid.

11. David Held, Anthony McGrew, David Goldblatt and Jonathon Perraton, *Global Transformations: Politics, Economics and Culture*, Oxford: Polity Press, 1999, p. 281.

12. Barry Eichengreen, *Globalizing Capital: A History of the International Monetary System*, Princeton, Princeton University Press, 1998, p. 101.

13. *The Economist*, 3 March 2001, p. 27; 28 July 2001, pp. 24–6.

14. Eichengreen, *Globalizing Capital*, pp. 94–5. The following interpretation of the Bretton Woods institutions draws heavily on Eichengreen.

15. Ibid., p. 103.

16. Paul Ormerod, *The Death of Economics*, London, Faber & Faber, 1994, pp. 200–1.

17. Eichengreen, *Globalizing Capital*, pp. 192–4; 113–14.

18. George Monbiot, 'Global Democracy', the John Moore Lecture at the Cheltenham Festival of Literature, England, December 2001; reproduced on 'Background Briefing', Radio National, abc.net.au, 6 January 2002.

19. George and Sabelli, *Faith and Credit*, pp. 11, 43.

20. Peter J. Taylor, *The Way the Modern World Works: World Hegemony to World Impasse*, Chichester, John Wiley and Sons, 1996, p. 70.

21. Eichengreen, *Globalizing Capital*, p. 192.

22. David Pallister, 'Continental Drift', *Guardian*, 26 August 1997, p. 13.

23. Christophe Champin, 'End of the Zimbabwe model', *Le Monde Diplomatique*, May 2000, p. 3.

24. Taylor, *The Way the World Works*, p. 45.

25. Philip Gourevitch, *We wish to inform you that tomorrow we will be killed with our families: Stories from Rwanda*, London, Picador, 1999, p. 284.

26. *Guardian Weekly*, 5–11 July 2001, p. 5.

27. George and Sabelli, *Faith and Credit*, p. 30.

28. Ibid., p. 49.

29. Quoted in John W. Dower, 'E.H. Norman, Japan and the Uses of History', in J.W. Dower (ed.), *Origins of the Modern Japanese State: Selected Writings of E.H. Norman*, New York, Pantheon, 1975, p. 36.

30. Gilbert Rist, *The History of Development: from Western Origins to Global Faith*, London and New York, Zed Books, 1997, p. 101.

31. Graeme Donald Snooks, *The Laws of History*, London and New York, Routledge, 1998, pp. 122–130.

32. Fernando Henrique Cardoso, 'Dependency and Development in Latin America', in Hamza Alavi and Teodor Shanin (eds), *The Sociology of 'Developing Countries'*, London, Macmillan, 1982, p. 119.

33. David Landes, *The Wealth and Poverty of Nations: Why some are so rich and some are so poor*, London, Little Brown and Co, 1998, pp. 327–8.

34. Martin Walker, *The Cold War*, London, Vintage, 1944, p. 44.

35. Taylor, *The Way the Modern World Works*, p. 91.

36. Isaac Deutscher, *Stalin, A Political Biography*, London, Penguin, 1966, p. 328.

37. Mazower, *Dark Continent*, pp. 49–50, 254.

38. Ibid., p. 265

39. Walker, *The Cold War*, pp. 47–50.

40. Barnet, *The Alliance*, p. 40.

41. Walker, *The Cold War*, pp. 48–9.

42. The following section draws heavily on analysis by Mark Mazower in *Dark Continent*, pp. 253–89, 367–401.

43. Ibid., p. 284.

44. Ibid., p. 272.

45. See also J.K. Galbraith, *The World Economy Since the Wars: A Personal View*, London, Sinclair-Stevenson, 1994, pp. 238–45.

46. Mazower, *Dark Continent*, p. 371.

47. Ibid., pp. 384–5.

48. The US spent US$19 trillion on defence after the 1940s, including US$5.5 trillion on nuclear weapons (*Guardian*, 12 July 1998, p. 5).

49. *Guardian Weekly*, 12–17 April 2001, p. 3.

50. Taylor, *The Way the Modern World Works*, p. 80.

51. Ibid., pp. 80, 82.

52. Isaacs and Downing, *Cold War*, p. 419.

53. Andre Gunder Frank, *Crisis: In the World Economy*, London, Heinemann, 1980, pp. 25–6.

54. Fred Halliday, *The Making of the Second Cold War*, London, Verso, 1983, p. 259.

55. E.A. Brett, *The World Economy Since the War: The Politics of Uneven Development*, New York, Praeger, 1985, pp. 119–20.

56. M. Westlake, 'Where will the buck stop?' *South Magazine*, December 1984, p. 76.

57. Eichengreen, *Globalizing Capital*, pp. 131–5.

58. Brett, *The World Economy Since the War*, p. 129.

59. This topic is covered substantially in George and Sabelli, *Faith and Credit*.

60. Brian Griffith, *The Gardens of their Dreams: Desertification and Culture in World History*, Nova Scotia, London and New York, Fernwood Publishing and Zed Books, 2001, p. 233.

61. Philippe Legraine, former adviser to the WTO Director-General, 'Dump prejudice and learn to love big government', *Guardian Weekly*, 19–25 July 2001, p. 2, *Australian*, 29–30 January 2000, p. 49.

62. See Naomi Klein, *No Logo*, Flamingo, 1999.

63. Held *et al.*, *Global Transformations*, pp. 214–29.

64. Robert J. Holton, *Globalization and the Nation State*, London, Macmillan, 1998, p. 52.

65. Held *et al.*, *Global Transformations*, pp. 236, 260.

66. Frédéric Clairmont, 'When the giants play with fire', *Le Monde Diplomatique*, December 1999, p. 15.

. . . .

CHAPTER 9

Globalizing Democracies

The Democratic Divide

At the close of the twentieth century, the condition of many Third World countries stood in marked contrast to the achievements of most First World countries. Those achievements derived principally from the process of democratization that they underwent after the Second World War. Democratization radically transformed First World societies on a scale never before experienced by human societies or individuals. It generated new forms of liberation and autonomy, created the basis for further technological innovation, and spawned forms of global consciousness that reflected desires for more inclusive strategies to achieve security and well-being.

But democratization was not a strategy directly enunciated by the architects of the third wave at Bretton Woods. Only recently has it emerged as a process of change that needs to be acknowledged, fought for, and extended. It is also diffuse, unsettling, and difficult to plan and implement. No universally accepted understanding of it exists.

Because the process of democratization has been deeper in First World countries, we often associate democracy with the First World only. Thus, in the eyes of many people, the First World–Third World divide is also a democratic divide. Often we argue that democracy is culturally specific or that its origins lie deep within European culture. We sometimes argue that with the Cold War's end, the inevitability of democracy has finally been accepted globally. In 1980 only 35 per cent of the world's population lived within democracies; twenty years later 54 per cent did. In another twenty years the proportion will be higher still. Thus democracy is inevitable; it has become *the* universal modern condition. Even dictatorships have tried to claim modern legitimacy by renaming their countries 'democratic republics'.

But the democratic divide does not exist at this level of appearances. The United States might have declared its Cold War with the Soviet Union a struggle between democracy and totalitarianism, but many of its allies were as authoritarian as the Soviets. Indeed, during the 1960s American modernization theorists, such as Samuel Huntington, argued that dictatorship should be regarded as a necessary step on the path to modernity, a precondition for sustained economic growth and eventual democracy.[1] Thus Marius Jansen's famous declaration in 1961 that

> the important thing is that people read, not what they read; that they participate in the generalized functions of mass society, not whether they do so as free individuals; that machines operate, and not for whose benefit; and that things are produced, and not what is produced. It is quite as modern to make guns as automobiles, and to organize concentration camps as to organize schools which teach freedom.[2]

Modernity and democracy had no necessary association.

In the Third World, division over the importance of democratization has been just as marked. Malaysia's future prime minister Mahathir Mohamad argued in 1969 that 'authoritarian rule can at least produce a stable government'.[3] Singapore's elder statesman, Lee Kuan Yew, concurred. 'What a country needs to develop is discipline more than democracy', he suggested in 1994. 'The exuberance of democracy leads to indiscipline and disorderly conduct which are inimical to development'.[4]

China's leadership agreed also. Democracy came with economic maturity. They had only to point across their borders to the former Soviet Union for an example of what happens to a country when it attempts to run before it can walk. Efforts by the West to impose so-called democratic virtues amounted to little more than a crusade. Westernization, they declared, represented a new form of colonialism whose goal was to deny the dynamism of Asian values and Asian institutions.

China's leaders might find it convenient to characterize democracy as foreign, but the divide can hardly be characterized as between the West and the rest. Many Asians acknowledge this reality, including Burma's opposition leader, Aung Sun Suu Kyi. Why, she asks, should concepts such as democracy be regarded as alien to Asian cultures? Democracy's opponents simply denounce liberal democratic principles as alien in order 'to justify and perpetuate [their] authoritarian rule' and to claim 'for themselves the official and sole right to decide what does or does not conform to indigenous cultural norms'.[5] However it is expressed, tradition or culture becomes a mask to obscure very contemporary struggles to dominate the development agenda.[6]

Chinese physicist and dissident Fang Lizhi also challenges the idea that democracy is Western.

> From the movement for science and democracy of 1919 to the rising tide of demand for intellectual freedom of 1957, and from the protest marches of 1926 that were met with swords and guns to the demonstrations of 1989 that were

confronted with tanks, we can see how passionately the Chinese people want a just, rational and prosperous society. … [O]ur history clearly shows that the Chinese people have sought the same kind of progress and development as people everywhere, no matter (what) their race or nationality. When it comes to common aspirations, Chinese people are no different from any other.[7]

Unfortunately, in the still post-colonial late twentieth century, democracy was easily painted as Western and alien. Many First World nations themselves encouraged this view. In the wake of decolonization, it assuaged their sense of loss. Democracy was a Western gift to the world, carefully nurtured since its foundation in Classical Greece. Thus Suu Kyi and Fang found themselves assaulted from both sides of the post-colonial global divide.

But it is not a First World–Third World divide that hinders understanding. Democratization is not a Western gift; it is a dynamic of globalization. Herein lies the source of contemporary misunderstanding. If globalization is regarded solely as a creature of hegemons, it and its features will always remain things that are imposed and to be distrusted. Undoubtedly for many peoples, recent global interconnections and their products did arrive in imperial forms. But, as economist Amartya Sen argues, the acceptability or otherwise of ideas and creations should depend on their value not their origins. Should we reject electricity and penicillin because their origins are not indigenous? Sen quotes the Bengali poet Rabindranath Tagore: 'Whatever we understand and enjoy in human products instantly becomes ours, whatever might have been their origin'.[8]

To regard modernity as Westernization is to deny humanity its common heritage; it is to accept the West's appropriation of shared intellectual creations. Western science, technology and liberalism, Sen argues, emerged through the diverse efforts of different parts of the world. To see them as Western because the West influenced their later development belittles the contribution of others.[9] It induces also a sense of powerlessness or inferiority that is hardly conducive to development. Further, it encourages the idea that globalization and its by-products originate with and are directed by the West.

Democratization is also a by-product of globalization; like industrialization, it is its child. Democracy did not originate in Classical Greece. Whatever similarities exist between Greek forms of democracy and our own derive from a common reliance on commerce. Commerce- (and technology-) based societies depend for their success on a wider ownership of resources and wider political franchises than conquest societies require; in other words they necessitate democratized political and economic systems.[10] Contemporary societies share these features, but not because of any cultural or historical connection with Ancient Greece. Rather their contemporary origins lie in the social and economic changes wrought by globalization.

Globalization sustained the commercial strategies of nations such as the Netherlands and enabled wealth and political participation to be more widely distributed. Thus modernity and democracy became entwined, and together bequeathed their central contemporary goal – mass comfort. Since then, successive waves of globalization have reinforced what Peter Taylor calls its ordinary face: Dutch families in their town houses, the cluttered domesticity of middle-class Victorian Britain, and the mass consumption of American suburbia. What distinguished these societies, says Taylor, was their accumulation and ever wider distribution of wealth in order to create new domestic worlds.[11] Their attractiveness lay in their ordinariness and in their apparent attainability. But attainability never came easily.

During the first two waves of globalization, most political and business leaders were seduced by the power that new economic activities offered. That modernity and democracy might be entwined rarely crossed their consciousness; that industrialization ultimately depended on an ever wider distribution of wealth and power received little recognition in an age of imperialism. Britain gradually democratized its political structures, but its fixation with class demonstrated the difficulties that democratization faced, not least from an establishment fearful of its consequences for their own power and privileges. Hence, economic democratization flowed much more slowly and less easily. In Britain 42 per cent of income went to 10 per cent of income earners in 1760; one hundred years later 50 per cent. Even as late as 1918, 10 per cent of income earners still received 40 per cent of all incomes. Britain's relative decline in the early twentieth century and its resort to empire as compensation reflected its resistance to democratization.[12]

In the rest of Europe and North America the picture was remarkably similar. Only the United States seemed to escape the contagion, but even here there were damaging limits to its democratization, as the Great Depression quickly revealed. Roosevelt's much praised New Deal did little for the country's disadvantaged peoples, particularly rural dwellers and Afro-Americans, and failed to drag the nation from depression. In all industrial societies the message was the same. Success could be sustained only through complete democratization.

Yet, democracy was far from the minds of most twentieth-century politicians. The collapse of Europe's authoritarian monarchies provided a fresh opportunity to democratize societies after 1918. But Europe's political leaders were as uncomfortable with democracy in the 1920s and 1930s as they had been in the nineteenth century. Instead they gave weight to ethnic cohesion and blamed political instability on socialism, corruption or backwardness. They declared democracy an alien imposition of war and felt more comfortable with the dynamism and strength offered by fascism and its refashioned traditionalism. To paraphrase Suu Kyi's later observation, political and business leaders feared losing control to forces that did not conform to perceived indigenous cultural norms. Even Churchill congratulated Mussolini for saving Italy from a system of government to which it was ill-suited. Not surprisingly, within two decades unemployment and depression had transformed most of Europe's thirteen post-war republics into dictatorships.[13]

Democracy was virtually extinct in Europe by the time war erupted again in 1939, and the nations which now confronted an expansionist Germany did not place democracy and human rights high on their agendas. Hitler's racialism and anti-democratic actions simply represented a more extreme version of their own. Mazower reminds us that in 1908 Sir Harry Johnson, a British colonial commentator, had defended anthropology as a science able to help imperial rulers to decide which races should be preserved, allowed to inter-breed, or be forced to die out. Hitler differed only in that he sought to apply the same logic within Europe. '[T]he violence which Europe had found so easy to ignore when committed abroad proved harder to stomach at home'.[14]

Still it did not force the Allies immediately to reassess their own racialism. Britain entered the war to maintain its empire and all its undemocratic principles and human rights violations. The United States joined in 1941 with segregated military forces. Mazower notes, 'if the war, with its renewed stress on racial equality and human rights, did eventually contribute to the ending of European imperialism, it did not do so automatically'. Even the United Nations' Universal Declaration of Human Rights in 1948 and its Genocide Convention remained 'little more than ... pious wish[es]'. The victorious allies refused to provide for their enforcement.[15]

This historic neglect of democracy and human rights contrasts sharply with Western rhetoric. Yet it contains a contemporary resonance. Not only has the West not pursued democracy as a long-term strategic goal, it has also failed to speak with one voice on issues of democracy and human rights. The United States still refuses to sign UN conventions on economic and social rights, on women's rights, on children's rights, and the 1997 convention outlawing the use of landmines. For forty years it refused to ratify the Genocide Convention. It still refuses to endorse the establishment of an International Criminal Court, because it does not wish to subject its own people to the jurisdiction of a non-national court. Even the 1977 Protocols to the Geneva Conventions protecting civilians during times of war remain unsigned.[16] But most damningly, it refused to extend democracy and equality to all its own peoples until 1966. To say that democracy and human rights are universal norms, one commentator recently remarked, necessitates that we admit that their 'message is just as incompatible for the old imperialist nations as for the newly independent ones'.[17] Indeed, another noted, that incompatibility makes democracy extremely fragile: 'when economic growth and social democracy are seen to be incompatible, it is the latter that must go'.[18] That the relationship between economic growth and democracy is symbiotic still escapes recognition.

Nonetheless it is the basis for the democratic global divide, a divide that transcends all other divides – East–West, First World–Third World, North–South – and penetrates deep within nations. Law professor Roberto Unger sees it as a struggle between globalization and the democratic economy. The US system of checks and balances and its parliamentary system based on consensus is designed, he says, to slow down high politics and decision making while also disaggregating society and demobilizing the populace below. This provides a double protection for the continuity of entrenched interests, he claims.[19] But he is wrong to disassociate democracy and globalization.

Entrenched interests, whether at the national or international level, increasingly regard democratization as their greatest challenge. The challenge is not spoken of as such. It is couched in terms of threats to national sovereignty or to the operation of the free market. But in reality – to paraphrase Sen – the divide concerns the accommodation of a world of many institutions, and in particular of new social institutions that are the most dramatic outcome of globalization's democratic impulse. Their origins lie in the demographic and social transformations of the first two waves of globalization, which enabled the emergence of mass societies.

The Democratic Imperative

Globalization, particularly in its industrial form, not only transformed the governance of societies but also vastly altered the landscapes in which all individuals existed. Had industrialization not occurred in the late eighteenth century, globalization would never have had this impact. Colonization would undoubtedly have continued, reaping sufficient windfall profits to induce attempts at world empire. Snooks's examination of a world without industrialization concludes that even more urban-based labour-intensive craft economies would have been susceptible to dominance by aristocratic–military elites. With no means to generate new wealth, we could never have transcended 'the endless cycle of civilizations'.[20]

Industrialization broke 'the great wheel of civilization' by introducing growth-inducing technology as the engine of trade and production.[21] In doing so, the Industrial Revolution transcended the limitations of agricultural technology and contributed to a vast expansion in global population. This established a new set of dynamics for which most societies were ill-prepared. The history of the third wave is a history of unprecedented accommodation to these dynamics.

Of course population growth has long been regarded as a motor of human history. In all probability it helped to drive the transition to agriculture twelve thousand or more years ago. It enabled economic specialization and the formation of states. And it produced new social dynamics when urban-focused. In turn each of these consequences fed back and impacted on population growth. So too the environmental pressures that humans confronted as a consequence of their expanding numbers, their migrations and continual quest for security and well-being. Four million humans on the eve of the agricultural revolution suddenly doubled in number within the space of two thousand years. Within less than ten thousand years they had reached one hundred million; by the eve of the first wave of globalization four hundred million.

Globalization accelerated population growth further. New foods and the wealth generated by trade and plunder transformed the political and environmental dynamics of population. Consequently world population almost doubled to one billion by the time industrialization precipitated a new expansion that would last at least three centuries. It took but 130 years for world population to double again, reaching two billion by 1930. Within forty-five years it again doubled. By 2000 it stood at six billion, and is anticipated to reach at least nine billion by 2070.

Such unprecedented growth challenged all societies. Not surprisingly, most European nations welcomed the relief that emigration provided them with to accommodate demographic change. Until 1924 it absorbed one quarter of their natural increase in population.[22] But the nature of that expanding population presented equally pressing challenges, which remained largely unresolved until the third wave.

Britain was already 78 per cent urban by 1850, and Europe soon followed the same trend as it industrialized. At the start of the nineteenth century, three quarters of its workforce depended on agriculture; by 1850 at least one half; in 1900 only one third.[23] Also, during the course of the nineteenth century, average per capita incomes trebled across Europe. Together with improved public health and nutrition, these changes transformed the character of Europe's population. Life expectancy rose from a British average of 37 years in the 1750s to 40 years one hundred years later. By 1910 it stood at 53 years. Female reproduction rates declined accordingly. Women had on average some 5.55 children each in 1800. By 1850 this had fallen to 4.95; to 2.84 by 1910.[24] A healthier, longer-living populace, with greater resources to assist the future of their offspring in smaller families, transformed social dynamics. Their urban concentration also gave them a political importance never enjoyed by formerly dominant smaller and more scattered agrarian populations, concerned largely with the daily struggle for existence. Nobilities had dominated agricultural societies, but the rise of industrial cities changed the balance of class forces dramatically. New middle and working classes transformed ruling coalitions and reduced the power of old elites.

Consequently, industrial societies became less severely stratified than agrarian societies and less polarized. Economic productivity enabled benefits to be transferred to workers in order to reduce the potential for disorder. Self-interest governed. Diseases did not recognize class divisions; in highly populated cities improved sanitation and housing benefited everyone, although not equally. Mass education produced more highly skilled workforces aware of common interests and able to bargain. Old mechanisms of government, the sociologist Anthony Giddens reminds us, no longer work when citizens live in the same information environment as those with power over them.[25] The economist Kenneth Galbraith makes the same point: economic development creates more educated people than can be kept quiet and excluded from a role in public life.[26]

We should not imagine that these changes were easily accommodated. Indeed, during much of the nineteenth century, as industrialization intensified, the position of many working classes seemed to worsen. Agricultural crises in the early part of the century drove the rural poor into cities, where they competed for work with an already abundant workforce. Unemployment, insecurity, poor conditions of employment, and poverty created tensions that easily erupted into mass violence.

These conditions could not continue indefinitely if industrialism was to prosper. Industrial societies cannot permanently sustain industrial systems of serfs. They require social harmony. Social harmony generates the confidence required for dynamism. And dynamism requires that workers become strategists and consumers as well as producers. Exploited producers constrain consumption and growth; they limit social potentials. Hence, economic health demanded a balance of power that better favoured subordinate classes.

The second wave did move in this direction, although we need to remember that ultimately it failed. Industrial states did increasingly accept that they had a duty to act on behalf of all their citizens. They became 'nightwatchman' states, to borrow Taylor's description, ruling not for their people but in their perception of the public interest.[27] They established new administrative bodies, hospital facilities, water supply and sewerage disposal systems, and town planning. New systems of taxation enabled social insurance to provide a measure of protection for workers; so too employment legislation. Although small and inadequate, these initiatives demonstrated what could be achieved, and provided inspiration for activists.

But they could not undo the increasing segregation of industrial societies by class. Middle classes often perceived the working classes as alien, and set out to civilize them in much the same way that they sought to civilize 'backward' peoples in their colonies. Government legislation concerning housing, health, employment and wages increasingly regulated the lives of the working classes, and created physical and institutional environments in which their undesirable habits could be eradicated. New centres of civilization were established in urban working-class outposts, missions that sought to propagate new moral codes and enable philanthropic middle classes to visit the poor and influence them by example. The spread of evangelical Christianity, co-operatives, friendly associations, even unions, all aided the development of notions of self-help, self-reliance and thrift.

By these means the working classes were gradually incorporated within the industrial strategy.[28] The enfranchisement of artisans and skilled workers in the British Reform Act of 1867 singled out the working-class elite; and in 1884 the working-class male franchise was extended. These reforms provided an important legal channel for working-class discontent and transformed the nature of politics. Increasingly, democratization replaced parliament with the mass political party as the effective decision-making body. Party caucuses now made decisions; executives enacted them. The existence of mass electorates forced politicians to appeal to their masses for support; elections became party popularity polls. Political democratization also transformed state bureaucracies as power sharing dictated that the new power elites be incorporated into previously more narrowly based institutions.[29]

But the political accommodation of industrial social change did not come easily. It placed industrial states under great pressure and tempted leaders to pursue imperialist and nationalist strategies in order to divert attention from pressing problems at home or to blunt dangerous obsessions with perceived class interests. Increasingly, also, these same leaders came to believe that imperialism might help them to sustain industrial growth and thereby promote domestic harmony and their own grip on power. They justified social reform in these strategic terms. Britain's Lord Rosebery wrote in 1900 that 'An empire such as ours requires as a first condition an Imperial Race – a race vigorous and industrious and intrepid. Health of mind and body exalt a nation in the competition of the universe'.[30] Social reform suited the imperial purpose, which, together with internal insecurities, gave industrial rivalry a dangerous edge in the early twentieth century, especially once economic prosperity faltered and the safety valve of emigration ended. Indeed, insecurities propelled Europe into war and fascism, and brought forth Soviet communism as an alternative vision for social change. One consequence, therefore, was the need to reinterpret democracy, but the task had to await the close of the Second World War.

Democracy Reinterpreted

The collapse of the second wave had brought industrial nations to the brink of collapse. Even the much more democratic United States had experienced high unemployment and widespread poverty during the 1930s. As late as 1940, unemployment stood at 15 per cent. If states wished in the future to avoid domestic instability and ruinous international competition, they had to become not only more socially interventionist than in the past but also more oriented to meeting the diverse needs of their people. In other words, the state itself had to be democratized. An assistant editor of the London *Times*, E.H. Carr, wrote in 1944, 'If we speak of democracy, we do not mean a democracy which maintains the right to vote but forgets the right to work and the right to live'.[31] Social democracy, not bourgeois democracy, had to be the new focus, French politician Léon Blum argued. In Britain, economist John Maynard Keynes urged governments to tackle employment, health, and housing as the first steps towards a new democratic consensus.[32]

War and depression transformed democracy, and in Western Europe generated broader-based coalitions than the old class alliances of the past. These new coalitions brought stability for the first time in decades and generated mixed economies and welfare states that received support from across the political spectrum. The consequences were profound.

Economic democratization empowered people and their communities as never before. For the first time, civil expenditures became more important than expenditures on the military or on war. European nations spent only 11 per cent of their GNPs on social services such as education, health, and welfare before 1938. By the 1970s that percentage had more than doubled to 23 per cent. Total public expenditure increased from 30 per cent of GNP to 47 per cent in the same period.[33] The United States was less interventionist. War had seen its living standards rise by 15 per cent, not decline by one third as in Britain.[34] Until internal unrest forced the Johnson administration to introduce its 'Great Society' programme in the mid-1960s, the US focused instead on defence spending and the provision of credit facilities. Consumer debt averaged only US$6 billion during the inter-war years, but by 1959 it had expanded to US$39 billion and by 1973 to US$155 billion.[35] Nonetheless, the effect was similar. The stimulus fed economic growth, and services as a proportion of economic activity began its rapid rise from just 6.2 per cent in 1945 to 33 per cent fifty years later.[36]

Much of the success of post-war recovery derived from infrastructure changes that improved ordinary lives, and from consumerism, which had the same goal. These strategies replaced class politics with the politics of consumption management.[37] In doing so they created new avenues for growth. The car transformed urban environments and lifestyles. Motorways, shopping centres and supermarkets became central features of suburban landscapes. Consumerism also extended leisure opportunities; along with new technologies, it enabled entertainment industries and tourism to expand.

Western Europe and North America enjoyed full employment for the first time in living memory. Recovery also enabled mass education for the first time. For at least a generation prior to the First World War, most children completed only primary education. Now secondary schooling became the norm. Health systems, too, were upgraded and their social applications extended. Work, health, housing, education: the egalitarian societies these measures produced appeared to be more stable, and more prosperous. For a time it seemed – at least to a privileged global few – that the woes of the past had been finally banished to the pages of history.

Welfarism was not uniformly adopted by industrial societies. Some still emphasized voluntary insurance schemes, which tended to perpetuate existing income inequalities. Others deliberately maintained sectors of last resort which could absorb periodic economic shocks. In Japan the domestic service sector fulfilled this role; in other societies, the public sector. But in welfare states, working people generally accepted the higher tax burden that welfarism necessitated as the price for social cohesion and well-being. Not so the United States. It used its burgeoning service sector to absorb the otherwise un-employed; from the 1980s its prisons served the same purpose.

Between 1970 and 1992 the US economy grew by 76 per cent and employment by 45 per cent. The proportion of working poor doubled; incarceration rates increased fivefold. Together they wiped at least four percentage points from America's official unemployment rate of 5.4 per cent in the mid-1990s.[38] In contrast European Union economies grew 73 per cent, but few European governments sought to transform their unemployed (as high as 10 per cent in some countries) into an underclass of working poor. Consequently employment rose only 7 per cent. Despite these differences, most industrialized societies accepted that states had a role to offset the inequalities of economic practice, to prevent capitalism's tendency towards underconsumption, and – through education – to promote fresh opportunities for new generations.

The latter task had its own unintended consequences. An educated population now produced a new kind of commodity that had scarcely been recognized before – cultural capital. While it laid the intellectual basis for a new generation of technological innovation, it also revealed civil society's symbiotic link with capital. To function and to grow, civil society required resources that, in the short term, business might wish to utilize for profit generation. Yet capital's long-term prosperity depended on civil society's capacity to transform those resources into new horizons for capital.

Welfare societies, then, represented a new form of risk management. They were not focused on classes or on other collectivities, as they might have been in the past. Instead they now acted in a more egalitarian fashion to expand individual opportunities and choice. They emphasized citizenship. In many respects these changes were possible precisely because of the consensus produced by war and depression, which drove together class-based parties previously opposed to each other. Mazower argues that in Western Europe democracy was stabilized by the middle classes accepting the agendas of the working classes, and turning those radical agendas to their own ends.[39]

In the post-war industrialized world, this reinterpretation of democracy has transformed societies. Per capita incomes grew only 1.2 per cent per annum between 1913 and 1950. However, over the next twenty years they grew an unprecedented 4.3 per cent per annum, reinforcing trends already apparent since the start of the Industrial Revolution. European life expectancy rose dramatically from 69 years in 1950 to 76.8 years by 1994. The average number of children women gave birth to also fell during the same period, from 2.51 to 1.39.[40]

Obscured by these statistics is the baby boom of the immediate post-war years. Population growth rates briefly reversed; in Europe from 0.91 per cent in pre-war years to 0.98 per cent during the 1950s.[41] The pattern was even more marked in the United States, but not because of any significant change in family sizes. In the US, families did increase, but only from an average 4.4 members before the war to 5.2 after. Rather the baby boom derived from the fact that families in every ethnic, occupational and class group across all child-bearing ages decided to have children at the same time. Relative affluence made children more affordable, and the dominant popular culture continued to stress the role of the family in returning society to post-depression and post-war normality.[42]

Longer-living populations also transformed social priorities. In the 1890s the median age in most industrial societies had been 21 years; by the end of the post-war boom in the 1970s, 28 years.[43] This too helped stabilize societies. With the majority of people in the most productive of ages, greater economies of scale were possible to assist market expansion and infrastructure development.[44] Demographer Massimo Livi Bacci suggests that these changes in the profile of industrial populations helped people to stabilize interpersonal relationships and set goals for employment and careers. With fewer children, fewer illnesses, and the ability to control fertility and reproduction, people had more time for productive activities and for leisure. In addition, the post-war focus on egalitarianism – on sharing wealth and power more widely – eliminated many former barriers to mobility and enabled human resources to be allocated more wisely. Both factors further boosted economic development.[45]

Undoubtedly the most significant transformation occurred for working classes. Not only did they receive better educational opportunities for their children, but their work environments were also gradually transformed. One-time bastions of paternalism now became 'public spaces subject to inter-personal norms'.[46] In France, most working-class families lived in cramped one- or two-roomed flats, which gave family members little privacy. Homes tended to be the domain of women; men found entertainment in cafés and pubs. While most homes had electricity by the 1950s, 40 per cent had no running water, 74 per cent no indoor toilet, and 90 per cent no bathroom and central heating. The democratization of housing transformed working lives. Like the middle classes before them, the working classes moved into new suburbs away from the noise and pollution of work. Their homes were now large enough to give family members greater privacy. And although new European high-rise neighbourhoods often lacked the intimacy of older more homogeneous neighbourhoods, the introduction of walkways, cafés and squares soon domesticated their spaces.

In the United States vast new suburbs of prefabricated homes achieved the same result. Indeed, suburbs soon housed more people than cities, absorbing sixty million people between 1950 and 1980.[47] The US had adapted to the demands of the second generation of industrial technology much faster than any other industrial nation. By the mid-1920s, 60 per cent of its homes had electricity. Such economies of scale not only reduced the cost of electricity, but also stimulated demand for domestic appliances.[48] Post-war prosperity escalated that demand further. But overall, the effect was similar in most industrial societies. It re-emphasized comfort as the mass goal of modernity. In fact it added a very special quality to the idea of comfort – relaxation. Post-war modernity produced relaxed societies.

The change began in the home.[49] Nuclear families had once operated as an economic unit within a much larger family system. Parents had exerted greater control over their children, directing them into work to help sustain the family, influencing their friendships, their education, even their choice of marriage partners. Now the state also exerted control, ensuring adequate child-rearing standards, mandating that children stay longer in schooling, and promoting better health through medical services and vaccines. Many families also received child allowances from the state.

These interventions transformed family relationships. Nuclear families became units of consumption rather than production. Democratization replaced authoritarianism as the principle by which families operated. Domestic and sexual violence was no longer hidden away as family matters. Public laws extended into the home. Parental dominance declined. In a democratic family, says Anthony Giddens, the authority of parents is based on an implicit contract of legitimacy and fairness.[50]

Children expected their school environments to change similarly, or at least to mirror something of the interpersonal norms expected of adults publicly. And children left home earlier. Much of the decline in the proportion of US households composed of two parents and children (down from 45 per cent in 1960 to 23 per cent in 2000) is the result of these departures.[51]

Marriage relationships similarly changed. By the late 1960s, feminism, family planning, the pill and abortion had severed the once strong link between marriage and procreation. Increasingly marriages became a formality only. Relationships now existed because of love or sexual attraction, and they depended for their survival upon trust, not coercion or authoritarian power.

Divorces too became acceptable. In the United States, 50 per cent of all new marriages ended in divorce, although four out of five divorced persons remarried within three years. Some studies purported to show that by the mid-1980s only 15 per cent of families retained a traditional structure and that the number of unmarried couples living together had increased fourfold during the decade.[52] In 1980, 18 per cent of children were born out of wedlock; by 1999, 33 per cent.[53] The rise in single-parent households demonstrated a new independence, but it also created new avenues for poverty and bequeathing disadvantage to younger generations. By the end of the twentieth century, 42 per cent of single-mother households were poor, compared with 8 per cent of married households.[54]

The relaxation of social mores penetrated all aspects of life. Improved housing, hygiene, state health services, and generally greater prosperity extended to the masses views about health and physical appearance once confined to the elite. This coincided with the new emphasis on the individual that technology and housing afforded, and on less formality in clothing. Real life became leisure not work.[55] The decline in formality assumed many appearances. Dress became a statement of personal expression. Forms of address relaxed. Status distinctions became more nuanced. Liberalized labour laws and cheaper transport democratized holidays once enjoyed only by the middle classes. Vacations now became an escape from the earnestness of ordinary life.[56]

The media similarly mirrored these changes. Technology made radios cheap and small. They became the property of individuals, not families. Within a short space of time broadcasters responded with niche marketing. Teenagers were discovered and became a new focus for advertisers and identity makers. Television soon followed suit, blurring further the boundary between public and private life. Viewers became spectators in real-life dramas. Politicians communicated directly in private spaces. Like movies in the pre-war era, television focused on melodramas and private idylls, but it also increasingly undermined public life's seriousness with its satires and comedies, its frivolity and mocking.[57] 'It is the very tranquilizing, mesmerizing effect of a media-saturated culture', one commentator suggests, 'that is the ultimate source of contemporary political stability'.[58]

The mass media, of course, were not the cause of change; still less was the impact of change necessarily stability. Antoine Prost maintains that the result was liberated conformity.[59] But liberation also created new grounds for contestation. During the 1960s and early 1970s, contestation assumed a generational flavour, as economically empowered teenagers and young adults challenged the conformism, paternalism and consumerism of their parents. Their rebellions derived from post-war social transformations, and in particular from the opening up of education and the spread of consumerism to the masses. Despite its fragmented character, youth rebellion signalled discontent and existential crises that would grow rather than decline in later decades. Modernization had critics among those to whom it gave the most advantage.

The deepening of democracy had further unintended consequences. Better-educated and informed citizens became less prepared to accept what they were told by politicians. Giddens argues that they became less tolerant of corruption, of old-boy networks, and of secret deals.[60] Power had been devolved, constitutions reformed, and decision making made more transparent and closer to the everyday concerns of citizens. This became the age of occupational health and safety, and legislated freedom of information. Political parties had now to work with a host of non-governmental organizations and pressure groups. They had to contend with the intrusion of the media into their affairs, and with the pressure of constant public polling. They had to confront civic cultures that placed constraints on politicians in ways unimaginable decades before. Democracy itself had been democratized.

Of course none of these changes would have been possible if economies had not themselves been democratized. Democratization engenders empowerment, and in three specific areas its consequences give cause for optimism that the continued democratic divide can eventually be overcome.

First, it has generated a much more relaxed approach to sexuality. No longer dominated by reproduction, sexuality lost its formerly strong connection with marriage and legitimacy. Removing the link between sexuality and heterosexuality also enabled homosexuality to be more generally accepted.

In the first post-war decades, as in pre-war years, many homosexuals married in order to disguise their sexuality. But from the 1970s, the changing social environment and advocacy of human rights groups made it possible for homosexuals to 'come out'. They still faced hostility. In 1992 Colorado tried unsuccessfully to outlaw civil rights legislation that protected gays and lesbians. But the trend towards acceptance was undeniable. 'When people feel more secure', gay activist Denis Altman suggests, 'they are more accommodating of diversity'.[61] Australian Justice Michael Kirby also observes that the growing body of scientific evidence for a genetic basis to sexual orientation reinforces the unacceptability of prejudice and legal discrimination.

> Once the hand of criminal punishment and social repression was lifted, people came to know their gay and lesbian fellow citizens. They came to realise that … they have all the same human needs as the heterosexual majority. The need for human love, affection and companionship; for family relationships and friendships; for protection against irrational and unjustifiable discrimination; and for equal legal rights in matters where distinctions cannot be affirmatively justified.

Once people 'realise the overwhelming commonality of shared human experience', he adds, 'the alienation and demand for adherence to shame crumbles'.[62] Something of the same accommodation occurred in a second area also, and its impact would be even more revolutionary.

Gender Democratized

Despite the radical transformation of democracy, very conservative societies emerged after the Second World War. War exhaustion produced nostalgia for the home and an idealization of domesticity. War altered traditional gender roles, disrupted family ties and provided new tasks and challenges outside the home for women, but only briefly. In the United States the proportion of females employed increased from 28 per cent to 37 per cent during the course of the war, three quarters of the newly employed women being married. By 1945, 25 per cent of all married women were working.[63] But the war did not transform gender relations. Like all forms of democratization, that required changed economic circumstances.

Unfavourable economic circumstances had forced female liberation into retreat after the First World War. Fascists and democrats alike looked askance at declining birth rates and feared for the future of their nations in an era of increased competition. Nazis urged German mothers to stay at home and reproduce. Germany and France gave medals to its most productive mothers. Token payments were made to families to assist with the expenses of motherhood. Across the industrialized world, many states passed laws restricting the employment of married women. Instead they were urged to place themselves at the forefront of a new domestic science. Families were a nation's building blocks, and motherhood was its cornerstone.[64] Nineteen forty-five did not challenge this mantra.

In the rush to marriage after the war and in the consequent baby boom, patriarchy went unchallenged. For a time, material well-being appeared to sustain its dominance. David Halberstam records women in the 1950s being urged to strive for togetherness.

> The family was as one, its ambitions were twined. The husband was designated leader and hero, out there every day braving the treacherous corporate world to win a better life for his family; the wife was a mainstay on the domestic side, duly appreciative of the immense sacrifices being made for her and her children. There was no divergence within. A family was a single perfect universe – instead of a complicated, fragile mechanism of conflicting political and emotional pulls. Families portrayed in women's magazines exhibited no conflicts or contradictions or unfulfilled ambitions. Thanks, probably, to the drive for togetherness, the new homes all seemed to have what was called a family room. Here the family came together, ate, watched television, and possibly

even talked. 'When Jim comes home', said a wife in a 1954 advertisement for prefabricated homes, 'our family room seems to draw us closer together'. And who was responsible ultimately for togetherness if not the wife?[65]

Such idealization may have reflected the expanding middle class's vision of domestic bliss, but for the majority of families it represented impossibility. A single income could never achieve the American dream.

To attain the levels of consumption that previously had been the preserve of the smaller middle classes, both parents had to work. The change reinforced the extent to which families had shifted from being production units to centres of consumption. In a consumer-driven age, even the cost of raising children had escalated. For many women, then, work was not a choice, although for many others, cheaper consumer goods and the availability of new housing did provide a powerful incentive. Their work alone made it possible for working classes to imitate middle-class consumption.[66] With the American economy booming, they grabbed the opportunity that labour shortages now offered them. In 1950, 25 per cent of wives worked. Twelve per cent of mothers with pre-school children worked. By the late 1980s over 60 per cent of wives worked, and 45 per cent of mothers with pre-school children.[67]

Of course, because most women had never been raised with the same work expectations as men, they were often less well equipped for work. In addition, because they tended to focus on establishing families first, they lacked the training and experience that men had gained in the interim.[68] Nevertheless, women did gain a degree of choice previously denied them. Smaller families and the availability of labour-saving domestic appliances helped to give women more time for productive work outside the home. Indeed, so did the industries responsible for reducing the labour required for housework. The technologies that lay behind the consumer boom produced light industries that required unskilled labour. The shift to a service-oriented economy similarly provided women with new work opportunities.[69] A new symbiosis emerged: women were attracted to work that emphasized social and communication skills; employers wished to utilize the comparative advantage women enjoyed in those skills.[70]

The role of women in the economy changed, but cultural attitudes did not. Men were still considered the principal wage-earners; this attitude justified their higher wages. For a time it also justified limiting the employment of women to a very narrow range of professions, such as nursing and teaching. But gender discrimination and segregation could not survive unchallenged. Middle-class women, in particular, found themselves disadvantaged when competing against men who lacked their education and skills. Why should they not lead the sort of lives they were capable of? Why should their potential be restricted simply because they were women? Their frustration launched a social and political movement for women's liberation.

In *The Feminine Mystique*, published in 1963, journalist Betty Friedan first voiced the yearning of many suburban women for new horizons. 'As she made the beds, shopped for groceries, matched slip cover materials, ate peanut butter sandwiches with her children, chauffeured Cub Scouts and Brownies, lay beside her husband at night, she was afraid to ask herself the silent question –'Is this all?' [71] But the success of feminism did not lie in the consciousness it both articulated and engendered. Rather it derived from the post-war re-interpretation of democracy, and the economic democratization that it induced. Traditional gender roles stood in the way of self-affirmation and self-expression at a time when these became defining features of the third wave's modernity.

The demand for gender equality deepened democracy and transformed societies. Constitutions proclaimed equality, but social and legal practices muttered otherwise. These discrepancies were challenged over successive decades and altered the nature of social debate. The collective political and military needs of nation states no longer dominated as they had in the past. Marriage became a matter of choice not duty. Husbands and wives became equal under the law. Women no longer needed their husbands' approval to work. Divorce laws were reformed.

At the end of the twentieth century, prospects for women in industrial societies were decidedly better than at the beginning. They no longer left home for domestic service in their early teens. They no longer bore four to six children. They no longer died at 55. Instead they were raised in smaller families. They continued their education through their teens in secondary schools. Women made up half the university population. Fewer women now married; when they did, it was in their late 20s. They bore only one or two children, after which they re-entered the workforce. They could expect to live into their late 70s or early 80s, after enjoying greater success in a wider range of occupations and life experiences than before. Women won 40 per cent of seats in the European Parliament in 1999. In the European Union they comprised 30 per cent of all parliamentarians.[72] New Zealand entered the new century with a female prime minister, a female leader of the opposition, a female chief justice, a female attorney-general, a female cabinet secretary, and a female head of state.

These changes were neither instantaneous nor global. In Eastern Europe the collapse of communism reduced female parliamentary participation in the Czech Republic from 30 per cent to 6 per cent during the 1990s. In East Africa women comprised 80 per cent of the food-producing workforce but received only 1 per cent of agricultural loans. In West Africa their economic activities were often better recognized, but women still experienced extremely high death rates from childbirth: 980 deaths per 10,000 births compared with a First World average of 2.3.[73] Infant mortality rates were also high, especially for teenage mothers. One report suggested that each additional year spent by mothers in primary school reduced the risk of premature child deaths by 8 per cent. During the 1990s, the Indian state of Kerala had nearly universal literacy and the lowest infant mortality rates in the Third World.[74]

Nonetheless, many societies regarded female emancipation as Western-ization, an example of cultural imperialism by a still colonizing West. For them, democracy had not been reinterpreted. Nor had they experienced the kind of economic growth that facilitated revaluing the labour, talent, ambition and achievement of half their population. Denying women equality became a badge of their distance from the West, something raised to generate internal support for a new struggle against the all-engulfing West.[75]

The United States stopped performing female circumcision in 1937; the patients were said to be suffering from 'hysteria' or nymphomania. But at the close of the twentieth century, 89 per cent of Sudanese women were still circumcised. In West Asia, five thousand honour deaths occur each year as family members slaughter daughters or sisters to defend the family name against the imputation of unchastity. Attitudes are hard to change when the economic and power relations that sustain them remain unaltered.

Nonetheless, increasingly – globally – the issue of gender equality cannot be avoided, as police belatedly discovered in Dinajpur, Bangladesh, in 1995. After three policemen raped and murdered a 14-year-old girl running away from a servant's job that her poverty had driven her to, riots erupted. Across the country, women protested at the brutality of a police force that used tradition and religion to justify crimes against humanity. In the absence of economic democratization, the most important force promoting democracy in many Third World countries has been the movement for female emancipation.

Even where equality is accepted, it – like other forms of democracy – has constantly to be fought for. 'Earth's womb', the playwright Bertolt Brecht wrote, 'still teems with monstrous tyrannies'.[76] Nothing can be taken for granted, and today women are organized as they have never been before. In 1900 only two hundred international organizations worked for women's rights. One hundred years later over eighteen thousand organizations did, testimony to the global nature of the problem women still faced, and to the distance women still had to travel.

That distance has led many feminists to challenge the effectiveness of their movement and to question its goals. But in reality feminism's success has made the movement much more diverse. It is a measure of the complex world in which women now live. Political action is transformed when mass unemployment affects women in ways never realized when they remained tied to homes, or when employment itself is dependent upon the availability of day-care centres and the willingness of partners to share parental and household duties. '[I]t is women and children', a feminist recently wrote, 'who remain at the cutting edge of the contradiction between work and welfare, markets and morality'.[77]

Political action is transformed also when global poverty is feminized (today 70 per cent of the world's poor are women). Or when teenage pregnancies afflict one in sixteen girls over 15 in India, Pakistan and the US (compared with 1 in 47 in Australia or 1 in 166 in Hong Kong). Or when work and schooling continue to be organized around the assumption that mothers stay at home.[78] Or when new barriers are raised to frustrate occupational equality. Women may no longer face exclusion on the grounds that they are not 'the right stuff', as female astronauts were in the 1960s, but they encounter new glass ceilings in many former male kingdoms.

In the United States, women still earn only 76 per cent of the male wage, up from 59 per cent at the start of the 1970s, despite the fact that the 1965 Civil Rights Act outlawed employment discrimination on the basis of sex as well as race. But then the 1972 Equal Rights (Constitutional) Amendment for Women has never been ratified and made law. In the top 500 US companies, only 10 per cent of corporate officers are women. Australia is slightly better off: women earn 85 per cent of the male wage, up from 65 per cent in the 1970s. But only 8.3 per cent of its corporate directors are women, 1.3 per cent of senior management. In addition the range of occupations open to women is still narrow. And with economic restructuring, the bulk of new jobs for women remain low-paid, part-time service work.

Regardless of expectations, a revolution in gender relations has begun and it is global, differing only in degree and cultural context from country to country. It was never a war between the sexes, but a struggle for liberation from discrimination,[79] a human rights movement for equality and justice. In First World nations its success derived from its association with economic democratization. That association also benefited a third important movement for change. Like feminists, the proponents of civil rights in the United States would soon learn that successes could never be taken for granted and have constantly to be struggled for.

Democratizing Race

America's blacks, its Afro-Americans, did not share equally in the wealth generated in the post-war United States, although the participation of Afro-Americans was as central to its success as was that of women. Instead the stigma they endured from the wider community denied them equal access to the benefits of prosperity.

Afro-Americans were descendants of slaves, many of whom had been freed at the end of the Civil War and abandoned to the racism and bitterness of defeated white communities in the southern states. Promises of land never materialized. They became sharecroppers instead and remained asset-poor. States deliberately imposed high licence fees to prevent blacks escaping their poverty through business ventures.[80] They imposed toll taxes to exclude blacks from the electoral process. In the 1940 presidential election, only 2.5 per cent of blacks voted.[81] 'Separate but equal' laws further reinforced disadvantage. Afro-Americans composed. 12 per cent of the US population, and a much higher proportion of southern populations. Yet in seventeen southern states during the 1930s only 6 per cent of higher education students were black. Those same states spent three and a half times on white education what they spent on black education; in addition they denied blacks access to white schools and universities.[82]

Segregated into expensive and sub-standard inner-city apartments, urban Afro-Americans also found themselves denied access to the suburban housing subsidies offered in New Deal programmes and by post-war governments. Consequently, they lost the ability to build up equity in housing, a major means of white upward mobility after the Second World War.[83] Decades later they were still scarred by this disadvantage. During the 1990s the net worth of white families remained ten times that of non-white families. Even among the middle classes, white assets were double those held by blacks. Disadvantage trapped Afro-Americans in poor neighbourhoods with access only to poor schools and low-paying jobs. In a privatized society like the United States, author Dalton Conley writes, upward mobility requires wealth. Whites were further advantaged because they inherited over half their assets. Blacks had few assets to pass on. In addition, US pension schemes did not cover the occupations in which most blacks worked, requiring black families to support their elderly financially. Under these circumstances, accumulating assets to pass on to offspring became even more difficult.[84]

Afro-American disadvantage cut deeper than segregation. In southern states, whites employed fear 'to keep the niggers down'. Between 1882 and 1968, 4,742 blacks were lynched, often for no more than looking at white women or displaying disrespect. 'Uppity' blacks who aspired to better living conditions, who became educated, who managed to buy a farm, or who tried to enter politics were also targeted. Terror kept blacks in check, and retribution came swiftly to anyone who stood up for their rights. In Tulsa, Oklahoma, the Ku Klux Klan ripped through the black suburb of Greenwood in 1921 after locals tried to prevent a lynching. Possibly as many as four hundred people died, and up to ten thousand blacks were left homeless. During the 1950s blacks were shot for voting or for encouraging others to vote. In 1955 Emmett Till, a cocky 14-year-old Chicago boy visiting relatives in Tallahatchie County, made a playful remark to a white woman. He was murdered. A jury set his killers free.[85]

Perceptions of race imposed their own brutal logic. In the early 1920s, black activist Marcus Garvey thanked the Ku Klux Klan for having 'lynched race pride into the Negroes'. He agreed that the two races should be segregated and that they should retain their distinctiveness. Garvey wanted to purify and standardize his people and create a new strong nation from the crucible of their suffering. 'It is natural that the children of mother Africa scattered in the great diaspora will cleave together again', his son declared many years later. 'It seems certain that the world will one day be faced with the black cry for an African Anschluss and the absolute demand for an African Lebensraum'.[86] The cry for a new segregation drove the Nation of Islam in the 1960s and after.

But the most successful challenge to white supremacy came from the middle classes. Blacks such as the Reverend Martin Luther King came from privileged backgrounds and lacked the self-doubts that racism had imposed on other Afro-Americans.[87] They wanted their community to benefit from the prosperity that America enjoyed, and they wanted desperately to democratize its democracy. 'I have a dream that one day this nation will rise up and live out the true meaning of its creed', King told 200,000 civil rights supporters during a march on Washington in August 1963. 'I have a dream that my four little children will one day live in a nation where they will be judged not by the colour of their skin but by the content of their character'. Inspired by Mahatma Gandhi's non-violent decolonization struggle in India, King rejected the strategies of black militants.

Throughout the 1950s civil rights activists tested the South's segregation policies on schools, buses, universities and voting. Responding to one of their cases, the Supreme Court in 1954 finally overturned its 1892 ruling and unanimously declared 'separate but equal' legislation unconstitutional. The federal government was forced to use its army to back the court's ruling when southern states reacted angrily to the court's declaration. The Civil Rights Movement demanded greater federal responsiveness, but had to wait until the Johnson administration, empowered by the wave of political and civil violence that swept the United States in the 1960s, imposed heavy penalties for discrimination in a new Civil Rights Act in 1964. In the following year it guaranteed blacks the vote.

The Civil Rights Movement triumphed at the very moment that the United States belated addressed its earlier failure to democratize its economy. Lyndon Johnson declared war on poverty as part of a strategy to remould America into a 'Great Society'. The elderly received medical assistance, the poor assistance in kind. Federally funded community groups tackled problems associated with unemployment, health, housing and education. Project Headstart addressed disadvantage among pre-schoolers and brought into being the long-running television show *Sesame Street*.

The war on poverty reduced poverty levels by a third, but only for a short time. Expenditure on the Great Society paled in comparison with expenditure on the Vietnam War, and much of what was spent disappeared into new bureaucracies or became the basis for corrupt activities. By the end of the 1960s the exigencies of war doomed the Great Society, and riots in black urban ghettos across the country drowned out the Civil Rights Movement. A defeated Johnson resigned in 1968. Kennedy's frontiers had closed in on the nation. John Kennedy succumbed to an assassin's bullet in 1963, the militant Malcolm X in 1965, and the dead president's brother, Robert, and Martin Luther King in 1968. The moment for reform had passed.

Efforts to desegregate housing met stiff opposition from white citizens who feared increased crime rates and the loss of real-estate values. Many schools remained segregated, but education for blacks did improve and the middle classes expanded to incorporate about one third of their community. But the drive simultaneously to enrich ghettos and integrate blacks into the wider community – a goal recommended by the Kerner Commission in 1967 – never happened. Similarly, for the one third of blacks who remained victims of poverty during the rest of the century, nothing changed. By then much of the infrastructure of the Great Society had been undone and blacks faced an entirely new threat. This time they had no empowering boom to attach their cause to, and no welfare system from which to gain respite.

One of the longest periods of economic growth in American history occurred during the 1990s, but it did not translate into improved wages. Instead the wealthy benefited. Between 1974 and the mid-1990s, chief executive officer (CEO) salaries tripled in value while average wages fell 13 per cent, and 30 per cent for blacks. In the United States CEOs earned 120 times the average wage, compared with 16 times in Japan and 33 times in Britain. With an army of 15 million working poor, the United States retained low unemployment but at the cost of tremendous inequality.[88] The proportion of the private workforce covered by pensions fell from 50 per cent in 1979 to 43 per cent in 1989. By 1992, 83 per cent of people under 65 had no health insurance, and all attempts to introduce a national health scheme had been defeated by insurance and pharmaceutical companies. Unemployment insurance covered only half the unemployed.[89] The weight of democracy's collapse in the US fell heaviest on Afro-Americans.

If the working poor disguised American unemployment levels, so did its prison population. During the 1980s and 1990s US authorities abandoned goals of rehabilitation, introduced mandatory sentencing laws, and declared war on drugs. Their strategies criminalized poverty.

The US prison population had – along with crime rates – declined about 10 per cent during the late 1960s and early 1970s. By 1975 there were 380,000 prisoners. Twenty years later there were 1.6 million prisoners, or 645 prisoners for every 100,000 citizens, between six and ten times the incarceration levels in the European Union. Including individuals on parole or probation, the total US prison population stood at 5.4 million people, making the justice system the fastest US growth industry at the close of the twentieth century.

Invariably this growth came at the expense of health, education and social welfare budgets. It also came at the expense of the black community. Forty years after the passage of civil rights legislation, discrimination and poverty still traumatized black communities. Racial profiling, police discrimination, and the practices of courts and prisons determined that African-Americans suffered most as a result of increased incarceration rates: one in five of all black males and one in three blacks in their 20s. Afro-Americans comprised an estimated 13 per cent of drug users, but 33 per cent of arrests and 75 per cent of imprisonments for drug-related offences. Not surprisingly they soon made up half the country's prison population.[90]

At the close of the twentieth century, the story of the American civil rights struggle demonstrated both the possibilities inherent in democratization and its limits. Like decolonized peoples in the wider world, Afro-Americans were affected by the changing character of the third wave and the legacies of their past. Their actions, like those of feminists and homosexuals, deepened democracy, and produced communities that were much more diverse and fragmented than before. Accommodating difference now increasingly assumed centre stage, as the changing nature of global economic activities removed the certainties that welfare-oriented states and economic growth had once provided for communities. Vast movements of refugees and migrants similarly tested the strength of democratization and revealed further the limitations of the third wave. But these limitations did not invalidate Martin Luther King's plea for inclusion: 'Injustice anywhere is a threat to justice everywhere', he once declared. Like cancer, it had to be nipped in the bud before it consumed all societies. The time had come for new globalizing perspectives.

Notes

1. Samuel Huntington, *Political Order in Changing Societies*, New Haven, Conn., Yale University Press, 1968.

2. J.W. Dower (ed.), *Origins of the Modern Japanese State: Selected Writings of E.H. Norman*, New York, Pantheon, 1975, p. 48.

3. *Far Eastern Economic Review (FEER)*, 31 December 1998 – 7 January 1999, p. 108.

4. *Australian*, 3–4 September 1994, p. 30.

5. *Far Eastern Economic Review*, 9 January 1992, p. 32.

6. This argument is pursued in greater detail in a case study in Robbie Robertson and William Sutherland, *Government by the Gun: The Unfinished Business of Fiji's 2000 Coup*, Sydney, London and New York, Pluto Press and Zed Books, 2001.

7. Quoted in Linda Jaivin, 'Gentle Shoves and Secret Executions', *Australian Society*, October 1990, p. 11.

8. Amartya Sen, 'Choosing Freedom', *Far Eastern Economic Review*, 27 January 2000, p. 38.

9. Ibid., p. 38.

10. Graeme Donald Snooks, *The Ephemeral Civilization: Exploding the Myth of Social Evolution*, London and New York, Routledge, 1997, pp. 55, 207, 232.

11. Peter J. Taylor, *The Way the Modern World Works: World Hegemony to World Impasse*, Chichester, John Wiley and Sons, 1996, pp. 198–208.

12. Snooks, *Ephemeral Civilization*, p. 355.

13. Mark Mazower, *Dark Continent: Europe's Twentieth Century*, London, Allen Lane, 1998, pp. 5, 10.

14. Ibid., pp. 101, 76.

15. Ibid., pp. 198–9, 214. The following interpretation on reinterpreting democracy draws heavily on Mazower.

16. Phyllis Bennis, 'US undermines international law', *Le Monde Diplomatique*, December 1999, pp. 1–2.

17. Michael Ignatieff, 'Keeping an old flame burning brightly', *Guardian Weekly*, 20 December 1998.

18. Rikki Kersten, 'Liberalism sidelined in new Asia', *Australian*, 15 January 1997, p. 11.

19. Roberto Unger, *Democracy Unrealized: The Progressive Alternative*, London, Verso, 1999; see also A. Barnett, 'Creative Utopias', *Times Literary Supplement (TLS)*, 24 March 2000, pp. 13–14.

20. Graeme Donald Snooks, *The Dynamic Society: Exploring the Sources of Global Change*, London and New York, Routledge, 1996, pp. 424–6.

21. Ibid., pp. 415, 427.

22. Massimo Livi-Bacci, *The Population of Europe*, Oxford: Blackwell, 2000, p. 136.

23. Ibid., p. 161.

24. Ibid., pp. 140, 135–6.

25. Anthony Giddens, *Runaway World: How Globalisation is Reshaping Our Lives*, London, Profile Books, p. 75.

26. J.K. Galbraith, *The World Economy Since the Wars: A Personal View*, London, Sinclair-Stevenson, 1994, p. 242.

27. Taylor, *The Way the Modern World Works*, pp. 61–2.

28. Snooks, *Ephemeral Civilization*, pp. 349–50.

29. See R.T. Robertson, *The Making of the Modern World*, London, Zed Books, 1986, pp. 77–81.

30. Quoted in Bernard Porter, *The Lion's Share: A Short History of British Imperialism, 1850–1970*, London, Longman, 1975, p. 130.

31. Quoted in Mazower, *Dark Continent*, p. 188.

32. Mazower, *Dark Continent*, p. 189.

33. Ibid., p. 304.

34. David Kennedy, 'A Tale of Three Cities: How the United States Won World War Two', *Background Briefing*, 21 October 2001, abc.net.au

35. Lendol Calder, *Financing the American Dream: A Cultural History of Consumer Credit*, London, Wiley, 1999.

36. Snooks, *Ephemeral Civilization*, pp. 352, 417.

37. Mazower, *Dark Continent*, p. 306.

38. Loic Wacquant, 'Imprisoning the American Poor', *Le Monde Diplomatique*, September 1998, pp. 8–9.

39. Mazower, *Dark Continent*, p. 305.

40. Livi Bacci, *The Population of Europe*, pp. 178, 135.

41. Ibid., p. 164.

42. Elaine Tyler May, 'Myths and Realities of the American Family', in Antoine Prost and Gérard Vincent (eds), *A History of Private Life: Riddles of Identity in Modern Times (Vol. V)*, Cambridge, Mass., Belknap Press of Harvard University Press, 1991, pp. 571–2.

43. David Frum, 'Not young anymore', *Times Literary Supplement*, 14 July 2000, p. 12.

44. Livi Bacci, *The Population of Europe*, p. 179.

45. Ibid., pp. 178–9.

46. Antoine Prost, 'Public and Private Spheres in France', in Prost and Vincent, *A History of Private Life*, p. 45. The following analysis draws heavily from Prost's examination of change in post-war France, pp. 1–144.

47. David Halberstam, *The Fifties*, New York, Villard Books, 1993, p. 142.

48. Taylor, *The Way the Modern World Works*, p. 203.

49. For a more detailed account, see Prost, 'Public and Private Spheres', pp. 69–93.

50. Giddens, *Runaway World*, p. 63.

51. *The Economist*, 28 July 2001, p. 43.

52. May, 'Myths and Realities of the American Family', p. 587.

53. *The Economist*, 28 July 2001, p. 43.

54. Ibid.

55. Prost, 'Public and Private Spheres', pp. 85–93.

56. Ibid., p. 127.

57. Ibid., pp. 135–40, 127.

58. Charles Krauthammen, 'The Great Di Turnabout', *Time*, 22 September 1997, p. 128.

59. Prost, 'Public and Private Spheres', p. 137.

60. Giddens, *Runaway World*, p. 75.

61. *Australian*, 1–2 January 2000, pp. 17–19.

62. 'Justice for All', *Australian*, 3–4 July 1999, p. 25.

63. May, 'Myths and Realities of the American Family', p. 568.

64. Mazower, *Dark Continent*, p. 79.

65. Halberstam, *The Fifties*, p. 591.

66. Snooks, *Ephemeral Civilization*, p. 417.

67. May, 'Myths and Realities of the American Family', p. 587.

68. Ibid., p. 568.

69. Snooks, *Dynamic Society*, p. 198.

70. Stephen Buckle, 'The Second Sex', *Australian Review of Books*, April 2001, pp. 16–17.

71. Halberstam, *The Fifties*, p. 596.

72. *Le Monde Diplomatique*, December 1999, p. 16.

73. Elizabeth Lequerot, 'Africa's forgotten tribe', *Le Monde Diplomatique*, January 2000, p. 15; Collette Berthoud, 'Who would be mother', *Le Monde Diplomatique*, January 2000, p. 14.

74. Victoria Brittain and Larry Elliott, 'Educating girls is a real lifesaver', *Guardian Weekly*, 9–15 March 2000, p. 27.

75. Polly Toynbee, 'Buried under the burka', *Guardian Weekly*, 4–10 October 2001, p. 11.

76. Bertolt Brecht, *The Resistible Rise of Arturo Ui* (1941), London, Methuen, 1981.

77. Lynne Segal, 'Why we still need feminism', *Age*, 15 November 1999, p. 17.

78. May, 'Myths and Realities of the American Family', p. 585.

79. Prost, 'Public and Private Spheres', p. 127.

80. Dalton Conley, 'More unequal than others in the US', *Le Monde Diplomatique*, September 2001, p. 6; see also Conley, *Being Black, Living in the Red: Race, Wealth and Social Policy in America*, Berkeley, University of California, 1999.

81. Halberstam, *The Fifties*, p. 414.

82. Godfrey Hodgson, *The People's Century: From the Start of the Nuclear Age to the Close of the Century*, London, BBC Books, 1996, p. 64.

83. May, 'Myths and Realities of the American Family', p. 581.

84. Conley, 'More unequal than others in the US', p. 6.

85. Halberstam, *The Fifties*, p. 430.

86. Paul Gilroy, *Between Camps: Race, Identity and Nationalism at the End of the Colour Line*, London, Allen Lane, 2000, pp. 232–6.

87. Halberstam, *The Fifties*, p. 551.

88. Peter Wilson, 'The "Me" Society', *Australian*, 18–19 May 1996, pp. R1, 6.

89. *Australian*, 25–26 November 1995, p. 29.

90. This analysis draws heavily upon the research of Wacquant in 'Imprisoning the American Poor', pp. 8–9.

CHAPTER 10

. . . .

Globalizing Perspectives

§ GLOBALIZATION is a dynamic component of human experience. It is not and has never been a single event, let alone a single process of change. Far from being a technological or capitalist juggernaut, globalization reflects the material consequences of our desires for security and well-being. It reflects also the extent to which people participate in its many parts, and are able to give shape and purpose to their long-term needs. Global consciousness cannot drive globalization, but it can – by enabling better understanding of the forces that enmesh us – produce responses which ensure that our global interactions remain beneficial and empowering.

Despite the importance of technology in expanding the reach of human activity, human desires also shape the character of globalization. Indeed, for most of human existence, those desires have been satisfied – at least in the short term – by exclusivity. We should not be surprised that the hegemons which dominated the first waves of globalization did not seek to be inclusive. Globalization became their tool for national aggrandizement. But exclusion can never be the basis for sustainable global interactions; past waves of globalization faltered as a consequence.

The third wave also began under the auspices of a hegemon, but due in part to heightened awareness of the second wave's failings, it became much more avowedly inclusive. A sense of globalism emerged that both enabled and in turn was strengthened by greater democratization. But it remained poorly articulated, and susceptible to pressures for exclusion from capital, which now assumed powerful transnational forms, and from the hegemon that in a more economically interconnected world no longer possessed the absolute economic dominance it once enjoyed. With no Cold War remaining to give shape to its own goals, the United States has relied increasingly on globalization itself as an alternative mantra. But its definition of globalization is narrowly focused on upholding the economic privileges enjoyed by itself and other leading industrial societies and their transnational corporations. Consequently it has left unanswered humanity's need for existential meaning, and distorted popular perceptions of globalization at the very moment when people need most to assert ownership of globalization.

During the first decades of the third wave, 'modernizationists' preached that all futures would converge, that the third wave was really nothing more than 'a modern secular version of building the Holy Community on earth'.[1] Since then very similar theories have produced national strategies to attain modern consumer status. But these theories did not drive globalization. What gave shape to the third wave was the economic recovery it generated and the democratization that followed. Democracies enabled more inclusive societies; the empowerment they generated created new synergies and new, unplanned possibilities for economic activity. The dynamic of globalization changed. The number of players grew. A third generation of technological innovation created its own transforming effects. Globalizing processes intensified.

But this dynamic of globalization is not inevitable. Earlier waves faltered when globalizing processes were used for exclusionary purposes. That danger also faces the third wave in the twenty-first century, especially when the certainties once generated by US globalism have evaporated. Three problems particularly stand out. In their own way, they all pose severe threats to the security and well-being of humanity as a whole. They also demand a deepening of existing global consciousness and the formulation of new global strategies to address them.

The first concerns the economic challenge that now needs to be addressed before democratization can have global meaning. The lure of quick profits and the quest for monopoly wealth still deeply influence the formulation of economic policy. We like to think that we are on the verge of something new and exciting. This is the age of information technology, of flexible employment strategies, and 'the new economy'. But the inequalities this 'new age' engenders – the poverty, corruption and debt it coexists – with create dangers every bit as momentous as those that confronted people in the first half of the twentieth century.

The second problem concerns the cost of globalization to the environment. In the past, environmental consciousness rarely impacted on strategic planning, but democratization and greater human interconnections have changed that. Yet, despite their new-found global consciousness, humans still lack the means to plan and implement global environmental policies, and to override the short-term goals that transnational capital and states often present instead. Environmental degradation simply adds to the burden of inequality that the whole world has to carry. As such it represents a new element of danger confronting humanity.

The third problem is a direct consequence of the scale of human interactions today. The vast movements of people around the globe have transformed human societies and challenged notions of identity and belonging. Managing the diversity that globalization presents to human societies is in many respects the most immediate challenge that we face in the years ahead. As yet no global responses exist.

The Economic Challenge

The years of war and depression in the early twentieth century produced consensus among policy makers that unemployment should be kept as low as possible. Economists now argued that by putting money into the economy, growth could be achieved. Consequently governments spent to create jobs. The result was an unprecedented rise in living standards across the industrialized parts of the world and very low levels of unemployment – on average only 4.6 per cent between 1951 and 1973 in the United States. But at 2.7 per cent per annum, the inflation cost was high; prior to 1939, historical averages stood at only 0.5 per cent per annum.[2]

Nonetheless, despite the upheavals of the century and the battering that economic orthodoxy received because of the depression, most policy makers still believed that economies operated like predictable machines. Indeed, growth in the 1950s encouraged the idea that wages provided the mechanism to balance unemployment and inflation. The more people that were unemployed, the greater the pressure on workers in employment to moderate wage demands. And since wages formed a large component of costs across most economies, any tendency for wage rates to decline would similarly impact on inflation. In other words, unemployment had a beneficial impact on inflation. The relationship between inflation and unemployment demonstrated the existence of a natural equilibrium, which could be manipulated by policy instruments such as tax rates, public spending, and interest rates to ensure continuous growth.

Despite this new understanding, economic predictions went horribly astray in the 1970s. Unemployment and inflation – instead of balancing each other – both rose at the same time. The phenomenon became known as stagflation and it confounded economists. Into the vacuum stepped monetarists, who had been largely left out of economic debates because of their contributions to the debacle of the 1930s. Now they returned with a vengeance, arguing that Keynesian economists had misled governments into believing that they could spend their way out of recessions. The Chicago economist Milton Friedman decreed instead that spending fuelled inflation. To stop inflation governments had to slow monetary growth by raising interest rates and by reducing public expenditure. Many governments fell under the spell of monetarism, but it was no more successful than other mechanistic approaches. Britain adopted monetarism in 1976 and stressed the control of profit-destroying inflation – not unemployment – as the primary goal of economics. But unemployment doubled and growth shrank. Its economy did not work as predicted.

The economist Paul Ormerod believes that economic policies do not determine economic trajectories, only historic events and reactions to them. Until 1939 most governments accepted high levels of unemployment because they thought it economically unsound to intervene in economies to protect employment and welfare. The eruption of war convinced them otherwise, and pushed their economies into completely different trajectories. The sudden fourfold increase in the price of oil in 1973 had much the same shock effect as the war. It shifted industrial economies into new trajectories. Unemployment soared; so did inflation, although at different levels in different countries. No natural rate existed for either inflation or unemployment. Indeed, says Ormerod, no connection exists between economic growth and unemployment over time. Between 1970 and 1992, as we have already noted, the US economy grew 76 per cent and employment 45 per cent. In contrast the European Community's economies grew 73 per cent, but employment only 7 per cent. Economies do not follow a single linear path. Instead they follow many paths as communities react differently to specific events at crucial points in time. Small differences can produce vastly different outcomes.[3]

Stagflation punctured the confidence of post-war industrial economies. After more than twenty-first years of recovery the world economy had changed dramatically. West European nations and Japan had become wealthy consumer societies. Third World nations had became independent and in many instances developed infrastructure that enabled greater involvement in the world economy, although few were as successful as the oil-producing countries. They challenged the power of oil companies and demonstrated their market clout. But even before the shock of sudden oil-price increases in the 1970s sent economies into the red around the world, most of the mechanisms put in place for monetary regulation had already unravelled. In addition, the Cold War had not gone well for the United States. Its long war in Vietnam divided American opinion and ended in ignominious defeat in 1975. In addition, two years before, the president who had escalated the war to envelop all of Indo-China had been forced to resign after a bitter corruption scandal. Also, in 1979 America's staunchest West Asian ally – Iran – collapsed into revolution.

Into this vacuum stepped a remade old guard, led by President Ronald Reagan in the United States and Prime Minister Margaret Thatcher in Britain. Both wished to demonstrate Cold War determination and both supported in principle the new monetarist ideology of resurgent finance. Market failure might have produced Keynesianism after the war, but state political and economic failures during the 1970s now necessitated the return of the market.[4] A new guard assumed control of government and multilateral policy making. Consequently, monetarists dominated the World Bank at the very moment that the huge but previously cheap debts that Third World countries had been urged to accumulate in order to further modernization suddenly attracted high interest rates. As alternative sources of aid dried up in the 1980s, the World Bank found itself well positioned to insist that all clients adopt monetarist strategies. Assistance now depended on structural adjustment – winding back statism, opening up markets to private capital, and balancing budgets.[5]

But despite the rhetoric, the monetarist surge was far from revolutionary. The United States intensified its wind-back of social programmes and injected vast resources into its renewed Cold War, resources that were largely borrowed and not derived from tax revenue. Indeed Republican governments during the 1980s doled out large tax deductions to the wealthy and forgot about their goal of balancing the budget.[6] Instead of renewal, the US sank deeper into deficit.

Debt sustained the American economy, but as the costs of servicing debt rose, social services declined. Debt also sustained domestic consumer spending, jumping from US$155 billion in 1973 to US$795 billion in 1989. The widespread use of credit cards in the 1990s pushed it to record heights once more, to US$1.3 trillion in 1998.[7] Monetarism also failed to roll back the state in Britain. Public expenditure remained at 42 per cent of GDP during the 1970s and 1980s. If anything, Thatcher's authoritarianism and centralizing tendencies strengthened the state sector.

In the end, public support for the provision of state services weakened the monetarist push.[8] Even monetarist politicians faced elections, and this fact alone quickly tempered their enthusiasm. In fact, in both Britain and the rest of Europe, the maintenance of welfarism served their societies well by preventing exactly the kind of devastating social shocks that had destabilized European societies during the 1930s.

Nonetheless, state attitudes to the once powerful popular contract did alter. States now argued that they had to make their societies more globally competitive. This meant reducing wage costs, shifting the burden of tax away from businesses, disposing of state assets, and rolling back uncompetitive employment sectors of last resort, which had acted to cushion societies during recessions. State assets had to be privatized and labour markets made more flexible. Consequently workers' employment conditions deteriorated, unemployment rose, state expenditures on roads, health, housing and education fell, and in many cases the more expensive services provided by the now privatized utilities declined in quality. The two-tiered strategy of state planning at home and trade liberalism internationally, which had been the central feature of the post-war years, disappeared. Now only one strategy officially existed – deregulation for both the nation and international relations.

Monetarism reflected changing global forces in the late twentieth century. The end of fixed exchange rates heralded the rise of unfettered capital, and monetarism pressured states to reduce costs that business might otherwise bear. Modernization Mark II had arrived, based not on state planning but on the dynamics of a new information age that heralded the end of ideologies and the rise of management. In the drive to fashion a post-industrial or knowledge nation, the state was rejected. Now was the time for managers attuned to consumer needs and business desires for flexibility. The power of the message lay in the rise of international finance after the mid-1960s, in the growth of communications and information technologies during and after the 1970s, and in the position many Third World countries now occupied in transnational strategies. Above all, it presented a forward model of change that was at once universal and – like its predecessor – suggested strong Western influences.[9] Consequently, it also breathed new life into the monetarist policies that had so dramatically failed during the 1980s.[10] By the 1990s, the processes by which these changes would be achieved became known as globalization, although to observers such as Canada's former Deputy Prime Minister Paul Hellyer, 'globalization [remained] a code name for corporatization'.[11]

These changes have had far-reaching consequences for the third wave. Unregulated capital has reacted to the volatility of its own markets by increasingly emphasizing short-term profit at the expense of investment; the resulting decline in growth feeds volatility further. This reaction had its origin in the managerialism of the 1950s and 1960s, when company managers became concerned less with the product they produced than with the value of their companies. They were stock investors who used profits to drive up share prices. Consequently American car manufacturers did not innovate, preferring to pay senior executives exorbitant salaries and to maximize profits by restructuring old models. Not so their Japanese competitors. They innovated, and by the 1970s could produce for sale in the United States a more reliable and economical car for half the cost of an American vehicle. With government assistance, American manufacturers tried to limit Japanese imports, but the Japanese simply shifted production to the United States, retaining competitiveness with superautomated systems of production. US companies responded by moving production offshore to Brazil and Mexico to take advantage of cheaper labour.[12]

Competition forced car manufacturers to be more competitive, but the strategy has not always stressed innovation. Often it sought to reduce competition and to resist the constant pressure to lower prices. This has been achieved by denying competitors access to markets or by encouraging mergers and partnership agreements that straddle North America, Europe and East Asia. Mergers, share buy-back schemes, restructuring, outsourcing, and downsizing became familiar means to maintain share value and profit. During the 1990s General Electric's largest investment was not in research and development but in share buy-backs. It spent US$30 billion, paid for by slashing its payroll, its marketing budget, and its research and development.[13]

The quest for rapid profits is by no means a modern phenomenon. Rome thrived on loot long before such tactics were regarded as defining features of capitalism. Indeed, as we have seen, the spur of unprecedented wealth lay behind all three waves of globalization. But profits do not in themselves generate growth. What matters are the uses to which profits are put. As Ormerod observes, the more businesses invest in their workforce, the greater the pool of skilled labour for the economy as a whole, and the greater the competitive pressure on other companies to train their workforces and use innovation and competitiveness as sources of profit. Investment is the key to growth,[14] but investment does not come naturally. States need constantly to guide and entice businesses to respond in this way.

Information technology industries might seem like models in this regard. They are described as 'the new economy', demanding economies of scope rather than scale, and product variety at lower levels of production than older industries. Consequently they require high levels of investment, good management, and above all greater inputs of human capital.[15] Certainly many information technology enterprises possess these qualities. The New York company Corning doubled its investment in research and development and captured 40 per cent of the fibre optic market. But it took fifteen years to make the effort profitable.[16]

Still, the lure of quick profits drives many information technology companies. In the rush to build cable networks and to cash in on the internet boom, telecom companies created a fibre optic glut in the late 1990s and fell victim to their own propaganda. Hardware technologies could not handle the high-speed data processing they promised. European telecoms spent over US$7,000 annually on each customer, who returned only US$1,750. With debts of up to US$600 billion, the bubble could not last, and during 2001 share prices fell more than 70 per cent.[17]

Monopoly also figured as a major information technology strategy for profit, achieved principally by requiring customers to purchase regular software upgrades. Indeed some commentators now believe that it is monopoly power that most distinguishes 'the new economy' from the formerly dominant consumer goods industries that today face competition from cheaper imports.[18] But the difference should not be exaggerated. All industries have adopted similar strategies in the past, as of course many contemporary commercial and industrial entities still do.

Information technology boffins like to present themselves as heroic rebels opposing old-fashioned elites. Like modernizationists before them, they adopt the language of radicalism, or even the 'new age'. Iomega computer employees regard themselves as a special species – Iomegans.[19] In the 1980s, New York stock and futures traders declared themselves 'masters of the universe', and employed the newly won freedom of international capital to create a Wild West environment in which they daily faced unknown dangers in the expectation of reaping instant riches. In the 1990s hedge fund operator Long Term Capital Management regularly bet between US$45 and US$250 for every dollar they held.[20]

Kenichi Ohmae calls 'the new economy' 'the invisible continent', and claims that it thrives on skills, creativity and the ability to learn quickly. It spawns Godzilla companies that hatch fast, grow fast and consume everything they can. What matters for Microsoft, Oracle, Sun Microsystems, Dell Computers, Circo or America On Line (AOL) is the quality of strategic practice. In a diverse and borderless continent, Ohmae claims, clarity of focus is imperative if Godzilla companies are to continue doubling in size annually. To this end networking is crucial; so also the lack of distortions and internal rivalries that often mark traditional pyramid structures.[21]

In reality none of this makes information technology companies significantly different from earlier forms of management that accompanied technological change. One is reminded of the large corporations that succeeded family businesses in the late nineteenth and early twentieth centuries, and set out to use size and market control as mechanisms to reap vast rewards. By 1997 Microsoft had become a true heir to this tradition, generating an annual profit of US$3.5 billion from a turnover of US$11.4 billion, and with only 22,300 workers.[22] The nature of enterprises may change, but the goals are not dissimilar. In fact even the different nature of the companies should not be exaggerated. AOL spent US$4 billion to acquire Netscape, and will probably spend years attempting to implement its merger plans rather than focusing on its customers or staff. Mergers, as we noted above, may generate vast profits for executives, and be seen as a way of ultimately reducing costs. But they can equally create the dangerous illusion of dynamic activity.[23]

It is precisely for these reasons that 'the new economy' presents similar challenges to those proffered by the second generation of technological change after the late nineteenth century. No matter how invisible their operations, the world on which they ultimately depend is very visible. It is not a static world, but one that has changed dramatically within the space of a single generation, and not just because of information technology. The free market itself is partly responsible for this transformation because it no longer recognizes society, only self-interest, as Margaret Thatcher so aptly put it in the early 1980s.

In the immediate post-war years, profits from growth were more equally shared, with large amounts being invested in social infrastructure and capital. The result was unprecedented social cohesion.[24] In contrast, short-termism and greed have undermined public confidence. Certainly changes in employment conditions, the rise in part-time employment, and the destruction of many blue-collar jobs as consumer production shifted offshore strained popular notions of egalitarianism.

Flexible employment strategies and cheap labour do not in themselves enhance skills and training. Nor do they reduce unemployment. For many workers 'deindustrialization' promises nothing but insecurity, poverty and often homelessness. In industrialized nations like Britain and the United States, poverty rose from 14 per cent in the early 1980s to 17 per cent a decade later. Britain's industrial workforce shrank 16 per cent between 1960 and 1983, reflecting the rise of service industries and the new importance of electronics and pharmaceuticals to the economy. But the shrinkage also reflected the loss offshore of a range of once important industries, in particular textiles, ship-building, steel and car production.[25] Defensive politicians often blamed the poor for their situation. They cut benefits and tied welfare to work programmes that seemed designed to discourage access rather than encourage new skills. In many European countries prison populations doubled. Minority groups also came under pressure as work options narrowed. New divides emerged but with global characteristics that have led some observers to question the continued relevance of terms such as the First World.

One sociologist, Ankie Hoogvelt, believes that over the course of the next generation, as wages fall by up to 50 per cent, 30 per cent of people in societies traditionally regarded as advanced will be marginalized within a new, non-spatial social periphery that had once been the sole spatial preserve of the Third World. Perhaps 20 per cent of people in societies once collectively called the Third World will form part of a new globalized core. This implosion of capital and its resultant global restructuring is the real meaning of global-ization for Hoogvelt. First World and Third World will lose the geographic meanings that North and South once gave them.[26]

For *Guardian* columnist Larry Elliott the dangers are all too apparent. Unless the market delivers what people want – a living wage, job security, quality of life, a decent environment, dignity in old age, a thriving welfare state – then it stands to lose not just public support but its entire legitimacy. It is the social democratic structure that makes life worth living.[27] Economist James Galbraith makes the same point. If large proportions of the population do not believe that they have access to the wealth and privileges of the rest of the population, then society loses its legitimacy.[28]

The statistics tell their own tale. If California was independent, its per capita annual income of US$49,695 would make it one of the wealthiest countries in the world. But its wealth is based on infrastructure developed in the post-war decades, and since the 1980s annual per capita expenditure on infrastructure has fallen from US$180 to just US$20. The net result affects everyone, increasing the costs of transport and eroding the quality of life as energy and water crises escalate and old sewers pollute beaches. Over the next thirty years California's population is expected to expand from 36 million people to 50 million, with infrastructure that is barely adequate for 36 million.[29]

Galbraith's research is on a wider canvas. Inequalities declined in 45 out of

64 countries during the 1960s and 1970s, but increased in 52 during the next twenty years.[30] One in six children in the world's richest countries now live in poverty; in Sweden the proportion is only 3 per cent, but in Britain it is 14 per cent, and in the United States 22 per cent. Poverty presents these children with learning difficulties, encourages their early withdrawal from education, and leaves them more susceptible to drugs, crime and unemployment. They are also more likely to become young parents themselves. Thus their disadvantage is passed on to another generation, and the whole of society is the worst for their neglect.[31]

But the growth in inequalities is greatest outside industrial democracies, where some 20 per cent of people (1.2 billion) survive on less than US$1 per day, and 50 per cent (3 billion) on less than US$2. It is measured also in contrasts. Twenty-three per cent of America's adults are obese, and 55 per cent overweight. Treating obesity costs the United States US$96 billion each year, or 10 per cent of its health bill. Thirty-two billion dollars are spent annually on diet pills. In India, however, 49 per cent of adults are underweight, losing the economy some 9 per cent of output.[32] Aid can never resolve inequalities but, like the Marshall Plan, it can provide the basis for growth. Unfortunately, since the end of the Cold War, international aid has fallen 21 per cent; US non-military aid by 50 per cent.[33]

In sub-Saharan Africa the situation is more desperate. Some 50 per cent of the continent's 600 million people are likely to live in poverty by 2008.[34] Two decades of economic stagnation, cuts in public spending, debt servicing, civil wars, the AIDS epidemic, and demographic pressures have seen educational outlays per pupil fall one third since 1980. Half of Africa's men and two thirds of its women are illiterate.[35] Daniel Cohen believes that the gap between the world's wealthiest countries and its poorest has grown continuously. In 1800 the difference may have been as little as 30 per cent, but by 1870 the industrial powers were eleven times as wealthy; in 1995 fifty times as wealthy.[36]

Of course there are many reasons for the inequality that so marks the third wave, as the above list suggests. War expenditure alone absorbs 2.6 per cent of the world's gross national product, with devastating consequences for countries affected. During the 1980s Iraq spent eight times on defence what it spent on health and education; Somalia five times. Around the world unexploded landmines annually kill 26,000 people and the tragedy most affects countries such as Cambodia and Angola; the latter is estimated to have ten million unexploded mines, one for each member of its population.[37] Much of the money devoted to warfare could easily address the health and education needs of impoverished peoples, but politics – itself in part born of the poverty it aggravates – and human desires dictate otherwise. Ethiopia's prime minister defended his country's war with Eritrea in 2000, declaring that 'The poor have the right to wage war' too.[38]

Certainly war is not the only cause of Africa's problems. Corrupt ruling elites have played their part, even in countries where wars have not been an immediate issue. In Nigeria, the former military leader General Sani Abacha and his colleagues stole US$2.2 billion from their country. This is a country which has an airforce of 10,000 men but only 20 functioning planes, and a navy incorporating 52 admirals and commodores but only 8 serviceable ships. During the 1980s, 469 members of the Nigerian National Assembly voted themselves a US$25,000 furniture allowance. Nigeria's average monthly wage is US$30.[39] In the Congo, Mobutu Sese Seko tucked away US$4 billion from his cash-starved people. In the Ivory Coast, one long-ruling president spent vast sums of money transforming his village with motorways, hotels, a vast airport, and the world's largest Christian church.

Corruption and vanity are not unique to Africa, even on this scale, but they certainly contribute to the problems faced by many countries. Some economists argue that, regardless of corruption, people in these countries still possess huge untapped resources. The informal economy is often ten times the size of the formal economy that is measured in official statistics. If the assets possessed by the majority of people could be transformed into capital, economic activity would automatically expand.[40]

For others, debt is one of the greatest hurdles, costing the Third World three or four times as much as it currently spends on health and education. Clearly exposure to debt varies considerably, from just 5 per cent of the value of exports in the case of Singapore to 186 per cent for Indonesia and 423 per cent for Argentina.[41] In Brazil, debt is equivalent to 332 per cent of exports or 52 per cent of GDP. One third of this is payable each year, leaving the country highly vulnerable to market panics. Already its interest bill, at 9.5 per cent of GDP, exceeds state expenditure on health and education.[42]

In Tanzania, since 1985, debt has effectively transferred control of the country's economy to the World Bank and IMF. School enrolments fell by more than 60 per cent when fees were introduced as an economy measure. Since then Tanzania's per capita GDP has fallen from US$309 to US$210, literacy has declined, and poverty now encompasses more than half of the population. For much of Africa, the pattern has been similar. Before debt, sub-Saharan Africa's per capita income rose 34 per cent; after 1980 it fell 23 per cent.

In the late 1990s a remarkable 'Drop the Debt' campaign, organized by Jubilee 2000, focused world attention on the gap between rich and poor globally, and forced industrialized nations to consider debt relief. The Group of Seven industrial nations agreed in June 1999 to reduce the debt stock of 52 countries by as much as US$100 billion (one third of their total debt), if their states were prepared to channel the savings into anti-poverty measures that might help to halve global poverty by 2015. But progress has been slow. The

US Congress approved only two thirds of President Bill Clinton's US$600-million pledge in 1999, and by early 2002 only US$18 billion of debt had actually been cancelled.[43]

For those nations successful in gaining debt relief, the benefits are potentially huge. Uganda's US$1 billion in debt relief enabled school enrolments to double. Mozambique converted 60 per cent of its US$127 million annual repayments into housing and health services. Zambia, where debt repayments threatened to engulf 55 per cent of its annual budget of US$800 million, saved nearly US$220 million[44] from debt relief.

Nonetheless, these initiatives did not prevent Tanzania opting to purchase a US$40-million air defence system from Britain. Nor did they convince multilateral institutions like the IMF, responsible for at least 40 per cent of the debt of poor countries, to end their insistence on poverty-generating structural adjustment strategies as a precondition for loans. And they did not prevent hedge-fund businesses continuing to profit from debt. Elliott Associates in New York purchased Peruvian debt for US$20 million, and took the Peruvian government to court to force it to hand over US$65 million that it had transferred to other bond-holders. The company earned US$130 million in 1999 from bought debt.[45]

Corporate practices are not always so predatory. Nestlé might have peddled baby formula as an alternative to breast milk in the 1970s, but many transnationals in the 1990s began to reorient their activities to meet the needs of poorer customers. At the turn of the century, Bristol Myers Squibb cut the daily price of their AIDS drug in Africa from US$20 to US$1, Shell's South African Solar division sold affordable solar power units to isolated communities in the Eastern Cape, and Unilever developed cheaper products for its Indian customers. In Bangladesh, the highly successful Grameen Bank distributed micro-credit to some 2.5 million borrowers whose poverty and lack of assets normally excluded them from business finance.[46]

Despite the apparent failure of globalization to empower people in many parts of the Third World, there are grounds then for cautious optimism. The successes of the Asian Tigers (South Korea, Taiwan, Hong Kong and Singapore) are symptoms of change. In China, also, per capita incomes have increased 6–7 per cent per annum for the last decade (quadrupling between 1970 and 2000), and absolute poverty (which afflicts 9 per cent of the population) has fallen by 42 per cent.[47] In India between 1993 and 1999, the number living in absolute poverty fell from 36 per cent of the population to 26 per cent. Literacy rates have also improved.

The UN Development Programme's 2001 Human Development Report is equally optimistic. Life expectancy across the Third World rose from 59 years in 1970 to 66 years in 2000, and literacy rates from 47 per cent to 73 per cent. Five times as many people have access to safe water (now 8 in 10), while average annual incomes have nearly doubled from US$1,300 to US$2,500. Absolute poverty declined from 29 per cent to 24 per cent, although in sub-Saharan Africa it stands at 46 per cent and is still rising. Global infant mortality has halved: by two thirds in East Asia and Latin America, by one third in sub-Saharan Africa. Globally, most children now attend primary school, the attendance of girls being only 10 per cent lower than of boys.[48]

Although these figures are only averages, and obscure disparities between countries and regions, Canberra's Ian Castles believes that, contrary to popular opinion, the gap between the Third World and the First is neither widening nor as large as many analysts argue. If one uses purchasing power parities rather than US dollars to compare the welfare of countries, then a very different picture emerges. Dollar parity analysis holds that the one fifth of the world's population living in the highest-income countries consume 86 per cent of global income. Purchasing power analysis suggests instead only 60–65 per cent. According to dollar parity analysis, the gap between the richest one fifth and the poorest half is 74:1; purchasing power analysis places it at 16:1. Global inequalities have decreased, not increased.[49]

Assuming that these figures are correct, we should not allow them to encourage complacency. Gradual improvements do not necessarily suggest convergence. Nor does economic growth automatically remove inequality, as Amartya Sen reminds us. Improved access to literacy, education and credit are enabling factors that help the poor to participate in economies, rather than just subsist. They empower. They include. But it is not the market that provides these enabling circumstances; that result comes through political and social action. This is the lesson that the First World learned in the early decades of the third wave. But the lesson has not been applied globally since that time, although some Third World countries have produced similar results. In this regard, South Korea did better than Brazil in channelling resources into education and health care, enabling greater popular participation in economic growth, and raising the quality of life for its citizens. But South Korea neglected social security and safety nets, which left its people and economy vulnerable to sudden shocks.[50]

In many cases these lessons have still to be learned at the start of the twenty-first century. Average global conditions might have improved, but the pace of change in many countries is still far below domestic expectations. This produces its own dangers. A.M. Khusro notes that democracy and the information age give new power to the poor. They enable the poor to pressure governments to be less co-operative, particularly with First World countries. Governments may also court popularity by stoking up ethnic or religious tensions, or by embarking on military actions. This has happened in the First World before; some analysts suggest it still occurs within the First World, although on a different scale. We should not allow statistics to blind us to the fact that the same phenomenon is likely to occur again in any part of the world. Britain's post-war Prime Minister Clement Attlee put it very succinctly: 'We cannot create a heaven inside and leave a hell outside and expect to survive'.[51] The First World seemed to have forgotten this economic challenge at the close of the twentieth century. In the twenty-first century it is unlikely that it will be able to forget so easily.

The Environmental Challenge

For a long time the environmental challenge was similarly forgotten, dismissed as the trifling cost of development as the First World enjoyed the relief that economic resurgence and well-being brought in the immediate post-war years. In Cold War and post-colonial climates also, patriotism demanded acceptance of the same priorities. But such prioritization sat less easily with the deepening of democracy. Democratic progress depended on equal opportunity, and access to education, housing, medical services and employment. These achievements meant little if they did not also include access to a healthy environment. It was not a new discovery. The great stink of London in 1858 had hastened sewer development and public health reform in nineteenth-century Britain.[52] Modernization demanded a similar consciousness.

Unfortunately for democratic citizens in the late twentieth century, knowledge came in many forms and demanded responses which they were ill-equipped to provide. In addition, demands for ideological conformity confusingly implied a false dichotomy between environmentalism and economic growth, which made belief in economic democracy more difficult, or distracted attention from such goals.

Population growth serves as a first example. The third wave has experienced unprecedented demographic changes, with the result that on the one hand the world faces the prospect that its population will soar to between nine and eleven billion people by the end of the twenty-first century, placing extreme pressure on its food, water and forest resources. On the other hand, the dire warnings of mass starvation by analysts like Thomas Malthus (1798) and Paul Ehrlich (1968) have not materialized.[53] In fact food production outstripped population growth by 20 per cent after 1960. Global starvation levels have fallen from 43 per cent in 1945 to 18 per cent in 2000. In addition, the population growth rate peaked during the 1960s at 2 per cent per annum, and fell to 1.26 per cent in 2000. It is projected to fall to 0.46 per cent by 2050. In many societies populations will actually decline, and some demographers forecast the global population peaking at nine billion around 2070.[54]

Nonetheless, many biologists warn that this number is too large for the world to sustain, even in the short term. They believe that the world can support a population of only 2 billion at the levels of middle-class existence promised by modernization. An additional three billion mouths at the very least this century may be enough to break the proverbial camel's back. They will occupy land desperately needed to feed them and they will demand food derived from cereal production that has already fallen 6 per cent below its 1984 peak.[55]

Water is also in short supply. It takes 900 litres of water to produce one kilogram of wheat, 1,900 litres to produce one kilogram of rice, and 100,000 litres to produce one kilogram of grain-fed beef. Rising prosperity in populous countries such as China and India has increased meat consumption. But without central water management strategies, increased food production has simply silted up rivers and caused water tables to fall. Globally, ground water is being extracted at twice the rate at which it can be replenished, and many rivers, such as the Huanghe in China, run dry. Fifty per cent of water pumped through unlined irrigation canals and ditches from the Indus river is wasted, and irrigation is increasing salinity and causing water tables to rise. The Nile currently feeds 153 million people, but already only 2 per cent of its water reaches the sea. In less than twenty-five years it will have to support a population twice as large.[56] Only 10 per cent of the Jordan river empties into the Dead Sea, itself now one third smaller in size. Three countries depend on access to its waters, and the danger of water wars looms large. Once again management has been sacrificed to corporate greed or the demands of environmentally damaging growth.

Population growth is also an outcome of the longer lifespan of humans, itself in part the outcome of public health campaigns and the eradication of many childhood diseases. Former human scourges have either declined naturally or, like smallpox, been successfully removed. Leprosy and polio no longer present the threat they once did, and, although there are new fears that diseases such as Ebola or varieties of influenza present the possibility of new pandemic threats, the chief dangers that humans are more likely to face derive either from poverty or from their built environment. Asthmatic rates have more than doubled during the course of the third wave, while the growth in cancers has coincided with a 600-fold increase in the production of synthetic organic chemicals. Smog, pesticides, herbicides, and artificial sweeteners and hormones in foods may explain some of the increases in cancers. In the United States, it has been estimated that at least 7 per cent of all cancers are due to dioxins emitted from household appliances such as refrigerators.[57] For the 300 million people affected by malaria each year, or the 120 million affected by elephantiasis, however, other causes for the persistence of their condition have to be sought.

Malaria and elephantiasis are tropical diseases that mostly afflict people who live in poor countries. It is their poverty that discourages pharmaceutical companies from investing in solutions. A similar problem faces the treatment of AIDS, the acquired immune-deficiency syndrome derived from a human immunodeficiency virus transmitted in blood or sexual fluids. Originally a harmless disease among apes, it crossed to humans at some time in the early twentieth century and developed into an epidemic in the early 1980s, aided by the migration of men in search of work and by war. By the end of the century some 35 million people had contracted HIV–AIDS, and close to 22 million had died, 80 per cent of them in Africa, the continent on which the virus originated. In Botswana, for example, 20 per cent of the population has AIDS, and life expectancy has fallen from 60 to 40 years, and may even fall to 30 by 2010.[58]

Treatment for most illnesses is expensive, particularly because large transnational pharmaceutical companies own the patents for most useful drugs. Bangladesh claimed to save $60 million a year in drug bills after it started producing its own drugs in 1982. Local production in China and India is estimated to reduce costs by as much as 13 per cent.[59] But pharmaceutical companies have been quick to exploit the World Trade Organization's 1994 trade-related intellectual property rights (TRIPS) agreement on intellectual patents and deny countries access to cheaper generic drugs. When Thailand sought to produce an anti-meningitis drug at one quarter of its imported cost in 1998, the United States backed its pharmaceutical companies and threatened to ban imports from Thailand.[60]

Pharmaceutical companies employ their monopoly over drugs in much the same way that information technology companies use software upgrades. If Third World countries wish to treat their patients, they have little choice but to obtain supplies from the monopolists. Certainly they do not have the clout of the United States, which induced pharmaceutical companies to waive the ban on generic anthrax drugs following the terrorist attack in September 2001. They might try public education programmes to reduce their dependence on foreign drugs. Uganda's AIDS campaigns have been particularly effective in reducing rates of infection during the 1990s from 14 to 8 per cent.

But public education programmes do not address the issue of treatment. To purchase drugs for Zambia's AIDS victims, particularly the three antiretroviral drugs that can reduce mortality rates by 60 per cent, would cost over US$2 billion per annum, or 76 per cent of its GNP.[61] After the South African government refused to fund drugs for HIV patients, a small AIDS rights group tackled the issue head on. It promoted the use of generic drugs sourced from Argentina, Brazil or India. Eventually the South African government caved in, only to be sued by transnational pharmaceuticals that claimed in their defence that high drug prices were necessary to offset the high costs of development. But in fact five of the main anti-AIDS drugs had been developed and tested at the expense of the American public, not the pharmaceutical companies. In April 2001 the latter backed down and offered South

Africa their drugs at a 75 per cent discount, the same price as the generic drugs. If this is the market price, one commentator noted, why are European and American patients continuing to pay 300 per cent more.[62]

Corporate strategies are not the only factors affecting the incidence and treatment of diseases, but they are important ones, if only because they so blatantly contradict the objectives of modernization. In fact virtually every human and environmental disaster involves similar conflicts, one reason why both modernization and its successor, globalization, were so often vilified at the turn of the century. If anything, the catalogue of environmental disasters that impacted on public consciousness during the third wave contradicted goals of democratic empowerment.

In the 1950s, one chemical company in Japan discharged its mercury waste directly into Minamata Bay, and took twenty years to acknowledge its responsibility for over seventy deaths and countless ruined lives. In the United States, toxic rivers caught fire, and housing estates were built on top of chemical dumps. Across the globe, industries created similar horrors: pollution, acid rain, nuclear contamination, and erosion. In addition to human deaths and suffering, bird, animal and plant species disappeared or were endangered as natural habitats were destroyed or denuded. For a long time no one conceded that these disasters exceeded the justifiable price for progress, that there was a point beyond which enterprises should be forced to forgo the temptation of quick but environmentally damaging profits.[63]

In north-west Romania, a lake of cyanide burst its banks in 2000 and poisoned two thousand kilometres of the Danube river and its tributaries. Similar environmental standards in the west Carpathian mountains have reduced life expectancy for their inhabitants by ten–fifteen years. Pollution of a different sort lies to Romania's east and north. In 1958 Soviet authorities diverted water from the Aral Sea's tributaries to feed an experiment in cotton production in Central Asia. Since then the increasingly salty sea has shrunk to one third of its former size, and one of its main ports is now 150 kilometres inland. Many of the five million people who once lived on its shores have lost their livelihoods and suffer crippling respiratory diseases from the sea's pesticide-ridden sandy remains.[64]

Other parts of the former Soviet Union have been devastated by nuclear contamination. After 1951, nuclear waste turned rivers black around Chelyabinsk in the Ural Mountains. A waste dump exploded in 1957; ten years later a cyclone spread waste further around the region. Like the nuclear meltdown at Chernobyl on the border of Belarus and Ukraine in 1986, vast numbers of people were severely affected, and thyroid cancer cases among children rose 3,000 per cent.

We could of course cite numerous diverse forms of environmental disaster, from the American Union Carbide factory explosion in Bhopal in 1984 (which killed seven thousand residents and disabled or blinded a further twenty thousand) to the subsistence farmers of Kalimantan and Sumatra, whose slash-and-burn farming techniques have created massive fires during times of drought or delayed monsoons. In 1994 smoke from their fires engulfed neighbouring Malaysia and Singapore, and caused asthma cases instantly to double in number. Dams have had an even greater impact on the human environment, affecting whole ecosystems and food chains. Designed to support new industrial activities, they have dispossessed eighty million people worldwide and become new environmental threats wherever and whenever their lakes have silted up.

Most of these environmental disasters have been limited in their geographical impact, but their psychological effect has helped to generate a new consciousness of the dangers of unfettered modernization. During the 1970s, the United States established an Environmental Protection Agency to monitor industrial activities, Greenpeace launched itself as the first transnational environmental movement, and the United Nations held its first international conference on the environment. By the 1980s environmental parties had become part of the political landscape in many First World countries, and development now came to be qualified by the word 'sustainable'.

One of the first successes of the environmental movement grew out of a discovery in the 1970s that chlorine atoms released into the atmosphere were destroying the ozone layer that shields the earth from ultraviolet radiation. By 1985 a hole in the ozone layer had appeared over the Antarctic. Within a few years the use of chlorofluorocarbons (CFCs) in aerosol cans and refrigerators had been phased out. Less easy to address, however, was the effect that carbon dioxide emissions had on the atmosphere.

The Industrial Revolution derived from the burning of fossil fuels. Not unnaturally their consumption rapidly escalated with the third wave and provided 85 per cent of human energy needs by 2000. Each year fossil fuels release over 5.5 billion tonnes of carbon into the atmosphere. Deforestation, often for purposes of farming or logging, accounts for a further 2 billion tonnes. Not surprisingly, carbon dioxide levels today are over 31 per cent higher than they were two hundred years ago, and are now increasing by 4 per cent per decade.

The impact of greenhouse gases remained a subject of controversy during the 1990s. In 1997 an international conference on climate change at Kyoto accepted that the likely outcome of increased fossil-fuel usage would be global warming, and that First World nations should take the first step to reduce its impact. Although accounting for only 15 per cent of the world's population, they accounted for 51 per cent of energy consumption and 31 per cent of all emissions.[65] At Kyoto they agreed to reduce their emissions by 2010 to 6–8 per cent below 1990 levels. But the cost of compliance quickly proved too much for electorally sensitive governments already under pressure from oil and mineral interests. In 2001, US President George W. Bush walked away from his country's agreement.

Future rounds will include Third World countries and are likely to prove equally difficult to conclude, unless leaders recognize the growing scientific evidence of global warming. Some scientists fear that global warming may cause ice caps to melt, sea levels to rise, and slow the circulation of warm water in the North Atlantic. Certainly, more severe droughts, floods and storms have been predicted, along with more widespread outbreaks of cholera and malaria.[66]

Global warming will not be instantaneous, and humans will have time to react to it. But with growing energy-hungry populations packed ever more tightly into large, expanding and vulnerable high-rise cities and shanty towns on low-lying coastlines and floodplains, the costs of increased wind damage, and more unpredictable storm surges and thunderstorm activity will be much higher than in the past.[67] The third wave needs to be part of the solution, not the problem, but so far most states have not accepted that growth needs to be environmentally sensitive. Instead they have retreated to the short-term logic already evidenced in the business community at the turn of the century.

The same accusation might be made of large biotechnology companies that produce genetically modified (GM) foods. Although humans have been modifying the genetic composition of plants and animals ever since the Agricultural Revolution, GM technology now enables the genes of one species to be inserted into completely different species. For example, lichen genes can be inserted into potatoes to increase their resistance to disease. Betacarotene from carrots can be added to rice to increase production of Vitamin A. These features, its proponents allege, make genetic engineering an 'evergreen revolution' capable of feeding the world's burgeoning population with less land, fewer harmful pesticides, herbicides and fertilizers, and under conditions of greater stress from drought, global warming, salination and soil infertility. It is a scientific response to global environmental dilemmas.[68]

But the technology cannot be separated from the corporate strategies that promote it. Like information technology companies, biotechnology businesses tried to monopolize the production of seeds by introducing a terminator gene that prevented farmers using the seed produced from their plants. The private ownership of genes and seeds also raises fears about risks to food diversity. The famine that devastated Ireland in 1845 and 1846 derived from Ireland's dependence on just one species of potato. When blight struck, the whole crop collapsed. Dependence on a small number of genetically modified crops carries the same risk.

There are other risks also. Could introduced genes cross unintended into other crops or insects? At first the industry played down the possibility, but by the end of the 1990s a number of cases had been identified. Bees in France were reported to be dying because of GM seeds treated with insecticide. Hives fell dramatically in number from 1.4 million in 1996 to 1 million in 2000. Elsewhere genes used to modify oilseed rape were found in bacteria in the gut of bees, and scientists feared that such transferences could affect their ability to treat many illnesses such as meningitis. In addition, some new human allergies have been blamed on transgenic maize.[69]

Agribusinesses have a lot riding on the success of their GM enterprise, and much of the hype concerning, for example, the value of Vitamin A in Golden Rice for addressing problems of blindness in the Third World reflects marketing strategies. In fact the quantity of Vitamin A produced is too low to have a serious impact on people going blind. In addition, the early strains, which Syngenta sought approval to use, could be grown only in temperate zones. But the agribusinesses had cause for concern.

GM crops had been introduced around 1994, and within five years their usage had expanded 25-fold to cover 49 million hectares, mostly in North America. But by then the honeymoon was over, and public scepticism rose. Britain imposed a ban on the commercial cultivation of GM crops for three years. A large supermarket chain refused to stock GM products. In addition, European countries imposed a five-year cultivation ban and refused entry to US grain imports, normally worth US$200 million each year. American farmers took note and began to abandon GM crops. Monsanto shares fell 35 per cent in value, and the company moved quickly to regain credibility by abandoning its terminator gene.[70]

The GM businesses had hoped that their industry would herald a second Green Revolution. The first Green Revolution in the 1960s introduced new strains of rice, wheat and maize hybrids that were very dependent on irrigation, artificial fertilizers and pesticides. Behind the technology of plant engineering lay the introduction of capital-intensive farming into the Third World and the monopolization of seed and agricultural inputs. Certainly the Green Revolution succeeded in massively increasing production. It ended India's exposure to famine. In fact India produced more food than its government could distribute or adequately store.

But the Green Revolution's goal of commercializing the subsistent peasant sector failed. Peasants could not afford the technology. Richer farmers could, and social disparities increased as a consequence. These changes also had political repercussions. In the Punjab the Green Revolution precipitated the Sikh farmer rebellion against Hindu professional and commercial urban dominance. In other countries, by transforming poor farmers into a cheap supply of labour, the Green Revolution failed to stimulate an internal market for its products. In Mexico, its foods were exported to California instead. In Ethiopia, exports to Europe continued even during famines.

If the Green Revolution did not reach the poor as promised, what guarantee exists that the 'evergreen' revolution would be any more successful in transforming the lives of the rural poor. Subsistence farmers are still too poor to buy new seeds, and transnationals are much more concerned with their share value than with the health and welfare of the world's expanding population. Genetically modified foods may well offer many advantages. Indeed some geneticists believe that if GM foods were introduced without corporate farming techniques, if their technology became open to greater public scrutiny and transparency, and if corporations set out specifically to involve the poor, then gene technology might indeed offer a different future for the world's farmers. Less land would be abandoned, rural poverty might be alleviated, and soil erosion and contamination reduced.[71] But many Europeans, already rocked by the outbreak of 'mad cow' disease (the result of feeding stock with meat and bone-meal made from animal parts), treat the claims of biotechnologists with scepticism.

Some analysts, such as political scientist Graeme Snooks, argue that the only way to resolve the third wave's apparent entropy is to develop a new, fourth technological paradigm to succeed industrialism. A Solar Revolution, he claims, could distribute living standards more equitably and reduce environmental degradation. But Snooks fears that environmentalism will dampen the competition needed to generate such technology.[72]

Technology has not reduced inequality in the past, and there is no reason to believe that new technologies – by themselves – will do so in the future. Meanwhile, of course, major environmental problems continue to threaten the third wave. In the past, says sociologist Anthony Giddens, fate decided futures. Today we no longer rely on religion or superstition, but on risk management. And the risk we most face is not natural risk but manufactured risk. In other words, the hazards that we face are more likely to be ones that we have created ourselves.[73]

Nonetheless, it is difficult to convince businesses that they might profit from conservation. The response of many industries has been simply to export their pollution to countries less conscious of the risks, or to those whose leadership believes that the benefits, at least for a minority, outweigh the risks. Sustainable development, says economist Gilbert Rist, no longer means development which sustains the environment, but whatever it takes to sustain development at rates desired for political and economic goals.[74] No invisible hand guides the market towards a greater good,[75] nor the institutions of globalization. There is no issue, writes David Held, 'on which the retention of state autonomy, or even state sovereignty, is so politically counter-productive and the absence of public accountability so regrettable'.[76]

Consciousness of these problems has meant that much of the material basis associated with social progress no longer sustains the meaning of life for many people in affluent countries. But there is one issue that is equally damning of state sovereignty, equally counter-productive, and potentially far more explosive in the short term than environmentalism.

The Multicultural Challenge

In the last decade of the twentieth century, when the ideology of globalization held centre stage, some commentators argued that state responses to economic and environmental challenges were frustrated by the new levels of governance and economic activity of multilateral and transnational entities. Indeed, powerful state structures might eventually wither away. Mobile technology and capital undermined the state's once central role in redistributing income, and the resources that individuals now possessed were less amenable to state control. The age of sovereign individuals had arrived.[77]

But commentators also argued that just as the 'new economy' allowed niche marketing, so globalization gave rise to a new state phenomenon, the niche state. In 1994, the executive director of *The National Interest*, Michael Lind, argued that multinational states had had their day. Instead the future lay with small homogeneous states.[78] The veteran observer of nationalism Ernest Gellner agreed. 'Men can only live comfortably in political units dedicated to the maintenance of the same culture as their own', he wrote.[79] In fact, as we shall see, globalization made the niche state equally difficult to sustain.

Nonetheless, when the cohesion generated by the exigencies of Cold War ended in the early 1990s, the spectre of division and secession impacted on many countries: Indonesia, the Philippines, China, India, Pakistan, even the Russian Federation, itself much smaller than the former Soviet Union. Only Germany went against the trend, reuniting its two Cold War divisions in 1990. The two Koreas remained divided. Czechoslovakia split in two in 1993, and movements emerged or strengthened in Italy, Spain, Iraq and Canada for various forms of division. Size no longer mattered.

Within Europe, pressure to increase the legislative powers of regional institutions also intensified. Germany and Belgium provided early models, soon taken up by movements for change in Spain and Italy. In Britain, parliamentary assemblies were created for Scotland, Wales and Northern Ireland. Straddling four countries in northern Scandinavia, the Sami (Lapps) established a joint council to develop the interests of what they hoped would eventually become a new nation. Common law, some reviewers now argued, is emerging as the law of local and regional authorities, not the once powerful nation state.[80]

Sharing power had never been on the agendas of nation states when they rode the crest of the Industrial Revolution in the nineteenth century. Now they have not only to share power among themselves through multilateral institutions and with transnational corporations, but also with their own people.[81] Through democratization, globalization has expanded 'the horizons of individual liberty', novelist Mario Vargas Llosa argues.

A rebirth of small, local cultures will give back to humanity that rich multiplicity of behavioural expression that the nation state annihilated in order to create so-called national cultural identities towards the end of the eighteenth century and particularly in the nineteenth century. As nation states weaken, forgotten marginalized local cultures will re-emerge and display 'dynamic signs of life in the great concert of this globalized planet'.[82] Czech President Vaclav Havel told Canadian parliamentarians that states should transform themselves from powerful entities 'charged with emotion' into more rational administrative units. 'People are more important than states'.[83]

It is the contrast between power sharing and the expansion in state roles in the post-war years that now so exaggerates the degree of contemporary state 'helplessness'. Hirst and Thompson rightly acknowledge that states are still vitally important for regulating and policing the more diversified societies that are emerging, and for engaging in the growing functions of international law.[84] As national and international environments change, so do the roles of states. It is a mistake to fear this change and to declare globalization the culprit. As we shall see shortly, many of the shortcomings directed at globalization lie instead with the nation state.

In 1993 Samuel Huntington published an article in *Foreign Affairs* that suggested a very different consequence of globalization. Coming so soon after the Gulf War (1991) and the success of the *Mojahedin* in Afghanistan (1992), Huntington's thesis that globalization now made the clash of civilizations the greatest threat to world peace attracted international attention. US President George W. Bush's declaration that the terrorist attack on the New York World Trade Center threatened Western civilization kept the thesis alive at the start of the next century. Ignoring the fact that the most violent conflicts in history have always occurred within 'civilizations' and not between them, Huntington maintained that globalization brought diametrically opposed values and lifestyles into more direct contact with each otherthan ever before. Nation states now mattered less than the fault lines between eight civilizations: the West, Confucianism, Japan, Islam, Hinduism, Slavic Orthodoxy, Latin America, and sub-Saharan Africa.[85]

But how real is this threat? Islam possesses no economically successful state that threatens the West's globalization strategies,[86] and while Islamic fundamentalism – according to sociologists such as Anthony Giddens – represents a refusal of dialogue and a reassertion of ritual truth,[87] it also represents a very different scenario. Fred Halliday notes that whenever war or internal strife has weakened states, groups like Osama Bin Laden's al-Qaida network have been able to exploit expanding cultures of violence and religious demagogy to act independently of states. They have also deliberately used the West as a means to link historically distinct conflicts in Afghanistan, Iraq and Palestine in order to mobilize public support. However, their goal is not a clash of civilizations, but the overthrow of regimes within their own countries.[88]

To accept Huntington's thesis, Halliday asserts, is to acknowledge that the framework for addressing global issues is cultural rather than universal. In fact there is no distinction between the West and the rest in this respect. In all societies, no matter how we define them, the resolution of conflicts lie ultimately with economic democratization. The excluded must be brought into the fold.

This message represents the most important third-wave challenge facing states. In the past, empires were based on conquest, but the rise of nation states demanded a very different basis. Accordingly, during much of the nineteenth and early twentieth centuries, states constructed their own histories and propagated them through mass education systems and the media to demonstrate ancestral rights of possession.[89] In the drive for 'totalism', their 'one size fits all' mentality ignored local traditions.[90] It led the US Congress to declare after the First World War that the American identity would be White, Anglo-Saxon, and preferably Protestant (WASP). Of course, as novelist Salman Rushdie notes, 'the idea of pure cultures, in urgent need of being kept free of alien contamination, [leads] us inexorably towards apartheid, towards ethnic cleansing, towards the gas chamber'.[91] Equally, it creates difficulties for people who have traditionally resided in regions as minorities, such as Hungarians in Romania and Slovakia, or Nepalese in Bhutan. But the dangers are not always internally induced. Malays living outside Malaysia, Prime Minister Mahathir asserted in 1999, could never be free. Hitler once made the same claim about Sudeten Germans in Czechoslovakia.

Identities are invented. Burma's military propagate a history that stresses the ancient role of the military in defending and strengthening the nation. In Rwanda, divisions between Hutus and Tutsis were reinterpreted to suit the needs of expanding chiefdoms and colonial authorities, particularly the Belgians, whose Flemish members projected on to the Hutus their own struggle for autonomy against the Walloons.[92] In Bosnia–Herzegovina, three communities claim that the Serbo-Croat language they each speak is communally specific and unintelligible to either of the others.

The purpose of these inventions is exclusion. Sometimes exclusion involves disenfranchisement through the expansion of executive and corporate power, and through the disdain that policy-making elites express for ordinary people.[93] Some Americans feel this passionately and believe that the more predatory the forces that threaten local identities, the more pathological they become.[94] This is certainly the case whenever exclusion assumes coercive forms, such as the Magyarization of Slav minorities during the nineteenth century, Franco's repression of regional autonomy in Spain, the Bulgarization of Turkish minorities, or the Bhutanization of Nepalese minorities. It is equally the case where ethnic cleansing becomes the method of exclusion, as Jews, Germans, Gypsies, and Armenians experienced during the last century. One Turkish politician declared, 'If we had not cleansed eastern Anatolia of the Armenian militia [in 1915 and 1916], the founding of our national republic would not have been possible'. 'We took the risk of being thought of as murderers', another asserted, 'to save the fatherland'.[95]

Not surprisingly, such exclusions necessitate completely bestializing people. They also require strong state involvement. Only states possess the physical means for industrial slaughter and the legitimizing capacity to convince citizens that their fellow citizens are subhuman and deserve to die. Weak states do not possess the capacity constantly to fan hatreds in order to rally support from academics and religious groups and generate genocides. Genocides, such as those in Rwanda, become state-driven exercises in community building.[96]

The Rwandan genocide in 1994 also raises the spectre of manipulation by a Hutu elite desperate to maintain privileges and to keep itself in power. Behind many forms of nationalism lie the same pressures. In the Ivory Coast, political leaders stripped 30 per cent of their people of citizenship after a coup in 1999 in order more smoothly to manipulate future elections. In Fiji, a chiefly bureaucratic elite reinforced racial divides and utilized two coups to maintain their power and access to state resources. They also used terror as a weapon of control. Communists in Russia resorted to nationalist appeals during the 1980s to broaden their support as communism lost its ideological relevance. In Serbia and Croatia, Slobodan Milosevic and Franjo Tudjman similarly exploited nationalist sentiments to carve out greater and more exclusive territories after the collapse of Yugoslavia. In such countries, writes Michael Lind, dominant elites make concessions to the religious and nationalist sentiments of ethnic majorities in order to win 'new formulas for legitimacy to replace fading secular and social philosophies'.[97]

In India, too, right-wing politicians have employed Hindu solidarity as a means to preserve the dominance of upper castes. In countries like India, Puroshottam Agrawal notes, what makes nationalism possible is not the existence of ancient rivalries but the fact that large parts of society have been excluded from a range of economic activities and opportunities because of illiteracy, bad health care, incomplete reforms, and deliberate prejudice.[98] Many of the causes of state weakness or of exclusive forms of nationalism lie less in the nature of political institutions than in economies and their distributive mechanisms.

In the instance of Yugoslavia, economist Michel Chossudovsky draws particular attention to IMF programmes of reform imposed during the 1980s, which caused the Yugoslav economy to collapse and welfare provisions to shrink. A third structural adjustment package in 1990 drove real wages down 41 per cent and cut federal transfers to the constituent states, thereby fuelling discontent and demands for secession.[99] The genocide in Rwanda also occurred against a backdrop of economic hardship. In a country where 95 per cent of land is cultivated by families of eight, subsisting on half-acre plots of land, the profits of genocide are not hard to sell. In Rwanda, too, structural adjustment impositions – together with collapses in coffee and tea prices and inadequate rains – left the state dependent on foreign aid for 60 per cent of its budget.[100]

But nation states face not just the consequences of their own internal ideological contradictions, elite pressures or economic weaknesses. They also confront another reality. No matter how much they want to impose rigid conformity on their citizens, they cannot remain unaffected by the continued restless movement of the world's peoples. Under the third wave, these movements were greater than those experienced during the second wave. Between 1945 and 1995 the United States received 35 million immigrants, 5 million more than during the period of high immigration between 1880 and 1920. Europe also received over 60 million people; the total for the entire First World exceeded 100 million people, three times as many as left European shores between 1880 and 1920.[101] In addition a third wave of Chinese migration began, with over one million emigrating between 1978 and 1998, half to the United States.[102] The result for recipient countries is greater hybridization and variety.

In the United States about one fifth of the population in 2000 are either immigrants or the children of immigrants. Only one third claim roots back to the foundation of the republic. With the removal of post-First World War restrictions in 1968, immigrant levels rose fourfold by 1998, and their composition changed dramatically. Europeans now make up only 15 per cent of new arrivals, Latinos and Caribbeans 45 per cent, and Asians 30 per cent. Some Americans now attribute the dynamism of their society to its diversity, fluidity and tolerance of strangers.[103]

The desire for security and well-being drives the restless movement of humans. Most people, claims sociologist Saskia Sassen, do not really want to leave the familiarity of their home territory or their support networks if they can help it. Citizens of the European Union are free to live and work wherever they like in the Union, but fewer than 1.5 per cent do. Even the post-war movements north of Italians and Spaniards have ceased as the economic circumstances that once drove them have been addressed.[104] Today Turks, Arabs and Africans have taken their places.

In the United States, Mexicans form the largest single group of immigrants. High unemployment, in part the consequence of structural adjustment strategies and the North American Free Trade Agreement, fuels the desire for opportunities abroad. Every year, half a million Mexicans illegally cross the border into the United States to seek work. Every year they send back US$5.5 billion to their families at home.[105]

Most migrants are highly motivated and represent the cream of their country's workforce. They give to their host country much more value than they receive in return. They represent but a small proportion of the population of the countries they enter – 5 per cent in the case of Europe (twice as many as in 1970) and 9 per cent in the United States. And the majority of them return to their countries of origin, just as 60 per cent of Italians did after working in the United States during the second wave, or 80 per cent of the 35 million migrants who entered Germany between 1955 and 2000. 'International migrations are conditioned, patterned and bounded processes', says Sassen. 'They do not have characteristics of mass invasions'.[106]

Nonetheless, the impact of new minorities has been profound for many nations. By the 1970s foreign migrants made up 12 per cent of Paris's population, 16 per cent of Brussels's, and 34 per cent of Geneva's.[107] By 2000, ethnic minorities composed 7 per cent of Britain's population, and 34 per cent of inner London's, and were growing at a rate fifteen times that of the non-migrant population. Half are Asian and one third black. Some estimates suggest that by the end of the century people with some migrant background will comprise the majority of the population.[108] France does not identify people by race or religion, but it is thought to have some five million migrants, or 8 per cent of its population. Sixty per cent are North African. In Spain the proportion of migrants is only 2 per cent; in Germany it is 12 per cent.[109]

The impact on the United States has been equally varied. Some states are still dominated by their original settler communities – Mormons in Utah, Germans in Wisconsin, and Japanese in Hawai'i. But in states such as Texas and Florida, the return of Afro-Americans and the huge influx of Hispanics will soon turn the WASP population into a minority. Miami is already 65 per cent Hispanic, 22 per cent black, 9 per cent WASP and 1 per cent Asian. California, which was 90 per cent WASP in 1950 and 80 per cent WASP in 1970, recorded only 47 per cent of whites in 2000. Hispanics made up 32 per cent. WASPs still comprise 72 per cent of the US population, but they may be a minority by 2060.[110]

Since migrants do not form a large proportion of the overall population at the moment, since they do not represent a homogeneous bloc, and since they do not constitute an invasion, they should never present a destabilizing threat to First World nations. But this statement will hold only for as long as migrants or minorities are incorporated as full citizens in their new communities. In this respect all countries have problems. Europe does not possess a good track record for the treatment of minorities, and the Second World War did not transform European attitudes. If anything, the war fostered a great forgetting and enabled Germans to become the new victims of demonization.

At the end of the war, twelve million Germans were ethnically cleansed from Poland, Czechoslovakia, and Romania. Two million Germans died in the exodus. Seven million of other minorities were also forced to move. After it was over, Eastern Europe's proportion of minorities had fallen from an average of 32 per cent to 3 per cent in Poland, 12 per cent in Romania, and 15 per cent in Czechoslovakia. Anti-Jewish pogroms continued. In each country, the solution sought was not multiculturalism or a new overarching identity that accommodated diversity, but the reassertion of ethnic homogeneity.[111] Its effects were widespread, and not just in many of Europe's former colonies. For Jews, it enabled the birth of Israel, but even this act of nationalism left in its wake a new Palestinian refugee crisis.

This failure to confront the realities of diversity continues to this day. A report in 2000 on the future of multi-ethnic Britain argued for a redefinition of Englishness. Englishness, it claimed, had 'systematic long-unspoken racial connotations', with the result that racial groups are not accepted as common owners of the land.[112] The same dilemma faces Americans. Exclusive identities are problematic, and only an overarching ideology can overcome diversity – a unifying concept of Americanness. But what identity is that?[113] In France, the state's refusal to acknowledge ethnic or religious distinctions makes accommodation difficult. But the fear of encouraging difference to the detriment of state uniformity has even extended to a refusal to acknowledge the legitimacy of regional dialects. In the United States, similar fears have driven California and Arizona to declare that English is the only official language. But these fears are unfounded. In fact, as populations become more diverse, migrants tend to acquire the national language more quickly. It improves their life chances. But politicians and many citizens do not believe the evidence before them.[114]

Ghettoization merely symbolizes the existing divide. Ten years after the fall of the Berlin Wall, Czechs erected a street wall in Ustin to separate Gypsies from their neighbours. In many parts of Europe, Gypsies are still treated differently. Ten thousand Gypsies fled from Kosovo after its NATO liberation. Residents of the Greek town Evosmos evicted 3,500 Gypsies in 1998. Twenty-seven times more Gypsies than Czech children are placed in special schools because their Romany language disadvantages them in school entrance examinations.[115] In Germany, citizenship is still based on bloodlines. In Spain, Moroccans working in greenhouses at El Ejido are forced to live in poor conditions on the edge of the town. They are not integrated and face racial discrimination. In France, Arabs are ghettoized in high-rise housing around the main cities. In Britain, Asians in towns like Burnley are separated from their neighbours by economic and social forces; the collapse of local industries, the low value of their houses, and fears of racial harassment combine to effect ghettoization.[116]

In some countries, ethnic cleansing is the end-product of a long process of ghettoization. In the 1990s Croatia reduced its Serb population from 12 per cent to 2 per cent, Slovenia halved its Serbian population, while Croats similarly drove Serbs and Muslims from Croatia and Herzegovina. Muslims drove Serbs and Croats from Sarajevo, and Serbs drove Muslims and Croats from Republika Srpska and Kosovo; in all over two million displaced persons.

The United States recognized in 1967 the necessity to integrate minorities socially and economically into mainstream society. Yet many ghettos remain, and ethnic identifications are still strong. However, the 2000 Census allowed Americans dual identification for the first time, an option one in twenty Americans consequently chose, as indeed they should. After all, 40 per cent of third-generation Asian Americans marry people of different ethnic backgrounds, and two-thirds of Latins marry non-Latins. Intermarriage is also becoming more common with Afro-Americans.

Although proportions of so-called 'mixed race' people still remain small, perhaps because no incentive exists to acknowledge this status, identities are becoming more distinct. Historically the United States has proclaimed itself a melting pot rather than a multicultural society, although in reality it has been neither. That legacy still haunts the United States, and leaves many of its 'hybrids' confused. 'If you mix black and white you don't obliterate those categories', argues New York writer Malcolm Caldwell, 'You merely create a third category, a category that demands for its existence an ever greater commitment to the nuances of racial taxonomy'.[117] In New Zealand, the experience has been less divisive. Educationalist Ranginui Walker believes that intermarriage has been 'one of the most potent' ameliorating factors in race relations in New Zealand.[118]

Nonetheless, all multi-ethnic and multicultural societies require some overarching ideology to overcome the divisions that diversity can inspire, a new cohesive civil force to replace the narrow state nationalisms of the past and to promote common bonds of interest and affection, and a collective sense of belonging.[119] The European Union has suggested that, as a first step, all non-national residents should be permitted to vote in local elections. Few European countries have enacted the recommendation, but some commentators believe that 'the fact of "belonging to a nation" is becoming more relative as the affirmation of a basic humanity is taking place that goes beyond all exclusions'.[120]

Of course nothing is guaranteed. Whether or not Hutus were originally migrant Bantu farmers and Tutsis herdsmen from Abyssinia, by the twentieth century they both spoke the same language, had the same religion, intermarried, lived intermingled lives and shared the same social and political cultures. By itself, such cohesive forces did not prevent periodic pogroms and genocide.[121] David Landes believes that societies that disqualify outsiders or introduce policies of separation are practising forms of censorship by exclusion or indifference. In the past, such nations became refuges from change and promoted 'a dialogue of the deaf'. Diversity, he says, 'needs to be turned into a sense of common humanity'.[122] The creation of effective strategies to handle the reality of multiculturalism is humanity's greatest challenge. And the first step is not ideology but economic democratization.

Proposals for Developing Global Consciousness

The greatest achievement of the third wave lay in its early success in raising the First World from the quagmire of war and depression. But that success was never universalized, and, with the end of Cold War, much of the cohesion and purpose that US hegemony bestowed on its new order ended. Not even the transformation of its ideology from modernization to globalization in the early 1990s could overcome a growing sense of malaise, fed in part by globalization's very interconnectivity. Its multilateral institutions had become distant, soulless entities, tainted by the same short-term politicking that had helped to drive constituents from older forms of national identification into newer cultural identities. These people overlooked the mass murders and exterminations undertaken during the crusade against the 'evil empire of communism', but found the drift of the post-Cold War new world order more difficult. Disintegration, fragmentation and loss of control now replaced the unity of the former era.

Swiss economist Gilbert Rist believes that the change heralded an age of virtual reality in which 'people go on believing but they no longer believe as before'.

> Without certainty we act 'as if': as if growth will save jobs; as if liberalization and deregulation of markets will benefit everyone; as if states were sovereign; as if election promises are serious; as if ethnic differences explain genocide; as if economic rationality is universal. ... Doubt no longer paralyses action. Action restores consensus around the belief. All we have to do is act 'as if', as if development were generalizable, as if foreign debt could be repaid, that the poor can catch up with the rich, and limitless growth could continue. As if the virtual could triumph over the real.

'Once we made people believe in order to act', Rist suggests. 'Now we act to make people believe we believe'.[123]

The ideology of globalization demonstrated this need to believe. 'Sometimes it is easier to dream the old dreams – even when they are nightmares', Mazower reflects, 'than wake up to unfamiliar realities'.[124] But unlike modernization, globalization promised no brave new world. If anything it has generated the opposite, 'a pathology of overdiminished expectations ... that exaggerates our degree of helplessness', to quote critics Paul Hirst and Graeme Thompson.[125] Nothing better symbolized the third wave's unsettling transformation than the felling of the twin towers of New York's World Trade Center on 11 September 2001.

Many commentators believe that the third wave has run its course. Development environmentalist Wolfgang Sachs believes that 'Whatever has survived the rise of industrialism is now in danger of being drawn into the maelstrom of its fall'.[126] But few writers surpass the pessimism of sociologist Stephen Sanderson, who predicts turmoil. If there are solutions, he believes, they will come too late.

> It does not have to happen, but it will happen. Nothing is forever, and western capitalist civilization is rapidly running out of time. When the collapse comes, the only question will be one concerning how devastating it will be and what will follow. We are on the brink of a great historical shift. ... It is our fate. It is our destiny.[127]

Such disillusionment is understandable, says Mazower. First World nations once believed they had a world mission. Now they suffer 'ideological exhaustion'.[128]

In many respects, pathologies of helplessness are – to quote Mazower again – like 'ghosts from the past'; they 'offer a poor guide to the future'.[129] Each successive wave of globalization has been preceded by a technological breakthrough. In addition, disorder, the threat of collapse or war has precipitated each new wave and enabled the establishment of new features. But history never repeats itself with such symmetry. We may now be experiencing a third generation of technological innovation, but not a collapse into war or depression as occurred at the end of the eighteenth century and during the early twentieth century. The Cold War's threat of mutually assured destruction has gone, but President Bush's War on Terror is not its successor. Instead economic democratization, environmental action, and multicultural accommodation represent the dominant global challenges.

The fact that the United States is no longer the colossus it once was gives grounds for confidence. New voices may emerge to articulate a new global vision. 'An exciting new world beckons', Peter Taylor writes, although conceding that it may be a 'less comfortable one for the contented'.[130] 'No earlier age', historian Felipe Fernández-Armesto observes, 'had access to awareness of such comprehensive menace or of such awesome chance'. Unlike societies during earlier waves of globalization, 'we do have a sense of shared prospects and the possibility of pooled efforts'.[131]

Indeed, the institutions of the third wave may provide the instruments necessary for such a transition if they can be reformed to serve interests wider than those they currently serve, and made accountable for their actions.

The World Trade Organization may be weak and subject to TNC manipulation, but it does provide a platform from which to address continuing global trade imbalances and to end protectionism. It could also impose minimum human rights, environmental and social justice standards as preconditions for trading rights.[132] The same comment might be made of the IMF or the World Bank. If the latter could be transformed into a lender of first resort, the crippling dependence of Third World countries on private money markets might be reduced and one of the major impediments to economic convergence removed.[133]

Similarly, the United Nations, long sidelined by the exigencies of Cold War, has begun to display more signs of independence. It failed to prevent the genocide in Rwanda when it had the opportunity, but it has since acted more forthrightly to prosecute human rights violators in Rwanda and Yugoslavia. By laying the basis for an International Criminal Court, it has signalled the possible end to impunity for officials who commit crimes while exercising sovereign state functions. The detention of Chile's General Pinochet in 1999, the fall of Peru's Alberto Fujimori in 2000, and the arrest of many former rulers on charges of corruption, human rights abuses or arms trafficking may indicate that civil society is at last challenging the culture of impunity that has protected state officials in the past.[134] During the 1990s many state officials publicly apologized for atrocities committed by their nations. Of course, such recognition of past injustices and the existence of victimized groups 'cannot put an end to inequality', historian Elazar Barkan writes, but it can 'improve on existing social injustice'.[135]

These more optimistic scenarios suggest that globalization itself may create scope for interventions of an order quite different from those experienced in the past. War and depressions need not be the only circuit breakers. For this to occur, global institutions need to be democratized and made accountable. Political scientist George Monbiot recommends a world parliament of six hundred members, drawn from non-national constituencies of ten million people, to begin a process by which people might engage with global decision makers and hold them accountable.[136] Such an institution might also help to convince TNCs that a more democratic global agenda is in their long-term interest too.

Unfortunately, the world entered the twenty-first century with only nascent global consciousness. Former French President François Mitterrand dismissed concerns about rearming Rwandan *génocidaires* in the Congo in 1994. 'In such countries', he said, 'genocide is not too important'.[137] The United States continues to reject UN conventions on economic, social and cultural rights, the rights of children, and the prohibition of anti-personnel landmines. Until recently, it owed the United Nations close to US$1 billion in unpaid dues.

The needs of civil societies similarly receive short shrift from states. Italy's prime minster, Silvio Berlusconi, declared the demand by anti-globalization protesters for social accountability to be as deadly as Islamic terrorism. He appealed to Western solidarity for support. 'We must be aware of the superiority of our civilization, a system that has guaranteed well-being, respect for human rights, and, in contrast with Islamic countries', he argued with no trace of irony, 'respect for religious and political rights, a system that has as its value understanding of diversity and tolerance'.[138]

Human rights involve much more than civil and political rights such as freedom of speech, assembly and religion. They also increasingly concern social and economic rights that are much more difficult and expensive to deliver. Former French Prime Minister Jospin correctly recognized that it is in these areas that globalization restores legitimacy to states.[139] And yet these are the very areas that many states have made a great show of abandoning to market forces. If anything, the advent of AIDS, and its impact on African societies and economies, demonstrates the absolute fallacy of permitting corporate profits to take precedence over human rights. But the lesson has yet to be absorbed.[140]

Nor have First World leaders recognised the depth of resentment that still exists as a result of the legacies of colonialism and the West's political and economic domination. 'For those who have experienced colonial rule and interventions under such beautiful slogans as "humanity" and "civilization"', argues Tokyo academic Onuma Yasuaki, 'the term "human rights" looks like nothing more than another beautiful slogan by which the great powers rationalize their interventionist policies'.[141]

The debt crisis similarly reinforces a sense of rage and hopelessness in landscapes where, says Saskia Sassen, 'poverty and inequality are growing and governments [become] so overwhelmingly indebted that they cannot afford resources for development'.[142] But with debt levels reaching 123 per cent of GDP in Africa and 42 per cent in Latin America, and with the IMF expecting at least 20 per cent or more of export earnings to service debt, Third World countries have every reason to question the IMF's differential treatment of debtors. Why should Argentina resolve its debt crisis through budget austerity and deflationary measures when the world's largest debtor – the United States – is permitted to cut interest rates, expand private debt, and embark on fiscal packages to boost investment and consumer demand? After the Second World War, the Allies cancelled 80 per cent of Germany's war debt and demanded that only 3.5 per cent of export earnings be devoted to debt servicing.[143]

These differences not only create divides where none should exist, they also foster environments ripe for human rights abuses. Today, globally, some 27 million slaves exist, many of them forced to work as prostitutes, labourers in rug factories, or as farm hands picking coffee, cacao, cotton or sisal. In addition, some 250 million children work instead of attending school because they have no choice if they are to survive. Some become labourers bonded to repay family debt. Since only 5 per cent of children are employed in export industries, they are not part of some industrial strategy for international competitiveness. Rather they remain a consequence of extreme poverty, government indifference, poor educational opportunities, and civil powerlessness.[144]

Regional trade blocs have long been presented as one solution that might enable poor nations to access richer markets, while maintaining some degree of protection for domestic producers. Indeed, one feature of the third wave has been the consolidation and growth of trade blocs. It is quite possible that by the end of the twenty-first century's first decade, we shall witness the consolidation of an enlarged European Union (28 countries and 600 million people), an American Free Trade Association (34 countries and 880 million people), and an East Asian Free Trade Association (13 countries and 2 billion people). WTO director general Mike Moore believes that regional blocs help officials to prepare for global liberalization and enable them to develop the necessary negotiating skills.[145]

Despite the contemporary focus on mega institutions and frameworks for co-operation, we should remember that they are not ends in themselves, but simply means to achieve a broader set of goals. In other words, like economic rationalization, they are not themselves central to globalization. Political scientist Sandro Sideri calls for a sense of proportion in global debates. There is no evidence, he claims, that lower barriers to trade and capital flows necessarily produce sustained economic growth. Indeed there is plenty of evidence that they increase vulnerability to external shocks. There are occasions when a greater emphasis on domestic investment and temporary protection will engender the necessary competitiveness and limit the dangers generated by rapid exposure to global competition.[146] Economist Paul Krugman similarly warns of the 'dirty little secret' that in fact the cost of protection is not large while the benefits of liberalization are often 'fuzzy'.[147]

Some consciousness of these realities is also emerging as First World societies confront ageing populations. Median ages rose during the twentieth century from 21 to 38 years, while in many countries the proportion of elderly people is expected to rise from 7 per cent in 2000 to 15 per cent by 2050. Supporters of the ideology of globalization have used these projections to argue for vastly increased migrant intakes or for rolling back welfare provisions before they overwhelm state budgets. In fact neither option is realistic. Germany, for example, would require 80 per cent of its future population to be migrants or at least descendants of migrants in order to maintain its present ratio of workers to pensioners, and the slashing of welfare budgets would simply create a new destabilizing divide for democracies to accommodate. The extent to which elderly people – already more financially independent and in better health than their predecessors – will create their own solutions by postponing retirement or by relying on superannuation alternatives is unknown. But the way in which the debate has been generated has served only to suggest a system under stress.[148]

Stress does not exist in isolation. An increasingly interconnected world ensures that. Poverty similarly has a habit of biting back in ways that reach deep into all societies: increased drug usage, gun smuggling, environmental degradation, new waves of refugees, even the re-emergence of diseases once thought to have been eradicated. Already the world contains 25 million displaced persons in 40 countries, and accommodates 12 million refugees. If desperate countries default on their debts, they might set off a chain reaction and precipitate a widespread recession. Such an outcome would not only set back economic development further, it would also increase the global movement of migrants.[149] In the early 1990s, the last large wave of refugees to seek shelter in the European Union created a climate of hostility to foreigners in many countries and prompted their immigration ministers to erect a cordon sanitaire. This left refugees stranded in so-called 'safe third countries' that could ill-afford to house them.[150] The same strategy has since been adopted by Australia to isolate Central Asian refugees on small island states in the South Pacific.

All these issues cry out for global solutions. But the global consciousness needed to make this possible and to provide a framework for future growth is conspicuously lacking. It is often missing also among the demonstrators who have protested in recent years outside meetings of political and business leaders in Davos, Seattle, Gothenburg, and Genoa. Protests against globalization are mistargeted; globalization can be empowering, as NGOs that work to gain debt relief and promote better access to markets understand. As we noted earlier, people need to claim globalization for themselves and insist on its democratization.

Such failings, some commentators argue, are themselves consequences of globalization, which fragments consciousness and 'casts us into individual and single issue struggles that ... bring about piecemeal reform but not radical change'.[151] Globalization, Held notes, 'does not engender a sense of global community on which democracy can be built'. Rather it generates inequalities that reinforce differences and raise new tensions'.[152] French President Jacques Chirac believes that this is precisely why people cannot afford to be 'mere spectators of globalization'. Democracies 'must tame it, accommodate it, humanize it, civilize it', he declares.[153] Wolfgang Sachs disagrees. Calls for global consciousness, he writes, represent the same kind of universalism that formerly dismembered people from their cultures and pasts, and caused the present global predicament in the first place.[154]

But globalization cannot be so easily dismissed. If universalisms based on former particularisms are to be avoided in the future, new forms of global consciousness are essential. As we have already noted in these final chapters, many political and business leaders have put their faith in institutions and ideologies as the means to generate global consciousness. They have even found unlikely allies among biologists, some of whom argue that global institutions perform the same functions as the brain's frontal lobes. They prevent anarchy and promote higher consciousness, identity, empathy and soul.[155]

Unfortunately, all too often we allow means to take precedence, and lose sight of ends. This generates further confusion and disillusionment. Some academics, such as Snooks, put their faith in a future Solar Revolution which, like the Agricultural and Industrial Revolutions, will enable the world to pursue its empowering growth with less environmental and human damage.[156] What both approaches ignore are the distributive mechanisms needed to avoid the kinds of stress that revolutions invariably create. There is no guarantee that a future technological revolution would not similarly neglect equality, even if its environmental consequences were more benign.

Snooks does recognize that one of the consequences of empowerment has been the development of skills to manage complex societies.[157] Those same skills also make possible the development of global consciousness. Historian Richard Bosworth has described how the development of social history in the twentieth century democratized history. A similar process has taken place in many other areas of study. Rather than disciplines supplying answers, he argues, we now have disciplines asking questions.[158] Such diversity, Sachs maintains, holds the potential for innovation and opens the way for creative, non-linear solutions.[159]

But the movement from universalism to diversity has nothing to do with the demise of Western civilization or its 'Enlightenment' project, as so many Eurocentric analysts bemoan. Rather this is what globalization is all about. The empowerment it engenders causes all universalisms to be questioned, and it creates a willingness to pursue alternatives. Modernizationists, who once defined themselves in battle with traditionalists, now seek to prevent new traditions developing.[160] Landes similarly praises empowerment. There will be 'no miracles, no perfection, no millennium, no apocalypse', he predicts. Instead people need 'to cultivate sceptical faith [and] avoid dogma'.[161] People need to nurture benign rebels in their children, philosopher Jonathan Glover suggests. If children were taught to think, if moral philosophy entered class-rooms as a subject for study, children might grow into adults less susceptible to demagogues.[162]

Education must also reflect the diversity of the world and prepare children with the co-operative skills that they will require later in life. It must promote a dialogue that brings together people from different national cultures and religious backgrounds, argues law professor Martha Nussbaum. It must enable people to examine their own societies and traditions critically. It should prepare them to regard themselves as humans before all other identifications. It should enable them to understand what it is like to be someone different from themselves. To that end, education must provide students with knowledge of other cultures; it should enable them to learn other languages, to understand the histories of minorities in their countries, and be familiar with issues concerning gender and sexuality.[163]

All these proposals for developing global consciousness are extremely important, but they bypass one crucial lesson of history. Felipe Fernández-Armesto hinted at this when he noted that the Great Depression ended the illusion that colonialism brings prosperity to its masters, and wondered whether globalization would similarly prove a flawed belief.[164] Although he referred to the ideology of globalization, the question is none the less significant. When Robert Holton surveyed globalization and its impact on the nation state, he correctly identified globalization as a natural human condition, and not simply the late-twentieth-century remake of modernization.[165] In other words, it is part and parcel of the eternal human quest for security and well-being, a quest that has seen humans employ agricultural techniques for the same purpose, raid and conquer neighbours, undertake treacherous trading ventures, carve out far-flung empires, and devise get-rich-quick strategies to sustain corporate share values.

In many instances, if these strategies delivered sudden and massive wealth to their protagonists, then others quickly emulated them in the expectation that they too could obtain the same riches. What we call capitalism is part of this broad human condition. If 'comfort is the reason for being', as Taylor persuasively argues, then 'green' proposals to replace modernity with the subsistence lifestyles 'which the majority of people have lived for millennia' are unlikely to succeed.[166] Every economic refugee attests to this.

Rather we need first to direct our basic human desires into forms that can be achieved without war, and in co-operative ways. It is in this respect that ideologies, institutions and education come into their own. But second, we need to remember that our very basic material desires require equally basic material solutions. Human history, this exploratory study suggests, has demonstrated that of all the strategies experienced by people, democratization has the greatest chance of success. And quite explicitly, democratization means more than just the right to vote and hold opinions independent of church and state. It means, as post-war strategists have argued, economic democratization, the deepening of markets, and individual empowerment. It is these that the third wave or its successor must now consciously address on a global scale.

Notes

1. Robert Bellah, quoted in J.W. Dower (ed.), *Origins of the Modern Japanese State: Selected Writings of E.H. Norman*, New York, Pantheon, 1975, p. 36.

2. Paul Ormerod, *The Death of Economics*, London, Faber and Faber, 1994, p. 117.

3. Ibid., p. 147; see also Paul Ormerod, *Butterfly Economics*, London, Faber and Faber, 1998.

4. Stephany Griffith-Jones, *Global Capital Flows: Should They be Regulated?* London, Macmillan, 1999.

5. Nicolas Guilhot, 'Repackaging the World Bank', *Le Monde Diplomatique*, October 2000, pp. 10–11.

6. J.K. Galbraith, *The World Economy Since the Wars: A Personal View*, London, Sinclair-Stevenson, 1994, pp. 227–36, 254.

7. Lendol Calder, *Financing the American Dream: A Cultural History of Consumer Credit*, London, Wiley, 1999.

8. Mark Mazower, *Dark Continent: Europe's Twentieth Century*, London, Allen Lane, 1998, p. 337.

9. Armana Mattelart, 'Communication breeds democracy', *Le Monde Diplomatique*, December 2000, p. 13.

10. P. Hirst and G. Thompson, *Globalization in Question: The International Economy and the Possibilities of Governance*, Cambridge, Polity, 1999, p. 262.

11. Paul Hellyer, 'Global Finance: Dismantle or Reform?', *Background Briefing*, Radio National, abc.net.au, 30 May 1999.

12. This subject is covered in detail in David Halberstam, *The Reckoning: a tale of two cultures as seen through two car companies*, London, Bloomsbury, 1987.

13. Allan Kennedy, *The End of Shareholder Value*, London, Orion, 2000; *Guardian Weekly*, 15–21 June 2000, p. 10.

14. Ormerod, *The Death of Economics*, p. 192.

15. Ibid., p. 61.

16. Margaret Graham and Alec Shaldiner, *Corning and the Craft of Innovation*, New York, Oxford University Press, 2001; *The Economist*, 7 July 2001, p. 88.

17. *Guardian Weekly*, 13–19 September 2001, p. 15.

18. James Galbraith, 'Inequality, Employment and Growth: What are the Connections?' www.tcf.org/Press Releases/Galbraith.html.

19. Thomas Frank, *One Market under God: Extreme Capitalism, Market Populism and the End of Economic Democracy*, Secker and Warburg, 2000; *Guardian Weekly*, 15–21 March 2001, p. 16.

20. Kenichi Ohmae, 'The Invisible Continent', *Australian*, 26 July 2000, p. 36.

21. Ibid., p. 32.

22. *Le Monde Diplomatique*, September 1998, p. 16.

23. *Guardian Weekly*, 27 January–2 February 2000, p. 12.

24. Ormerod, *The Death of Economics*, pp. 201–5.

25. Mazower, *Dark Continent*, p. 347.

26. Ankie Hoogvelt, *Globalisation and the Postcolonial World: the New Political Economy of Development*, London, Macmillan, 1997, pp. 239–40. A similar divide between a hybrid

cosmopolitan world and a class-based world subject to increasing immigration controls is suggested by Zygmunt Bauman in *Globalization: the Human Consequences*, Cambridge, Polity Press, 1998, p. 100.

27. Larry Elliott, 'Markets must deliver what people want', *Guardian Weekly*, 13–19 April 2000, p. 12.

28. Galbraith, 'Inequality, Employment and Growth'.

29. *The Economist*, 28 July 2001, p. 46.

30. Galbraith, 'Inequality, Employment and Growth'.

31. Reuters, 13 June 2000.

32. *Guardian Weekly*, 9–15 March 2000, p. 7.

33. Ibid., 2–8 December 1999, p. 3.

34. *Australian*, 8–9 July 2000, p. 5.

35. *Guardian Weekly*, 9–15 December 1999, p. 13.

36. Daniel Cohen, *The Wealth of the World and the Poverty of Nations*, Cambridge, Mass., MIT Press, 1998.

37. Ramón-Luis Acuña, 'A Culture of Peace', *Le Monde Diplomatique*, November 1999, p. 16.

38. *Le Monde Diplomatique*, July 2000, p. 10.

39. Karl Maier, *This House has Fallen: Nigeria in Crisis*, London, Penguin, 1999; *Guardian Weekly*, 25–30 June 2001, p. 16.

40. Hernando de Soto, *The Mastery of capital: Why capitalism triumphs in the Eest and fails everywhere else*, New York, Basic Books, 2000; *The Economist*, 31 March 2001, pp. 19–22.

41. *The Economist*, 31 July 2001, p. 22.

42. *The Economist*, 28 July 2001, p. 51.

43. *Guardian Weekly*, 6–12 January 2000, p. 2; 3–9 January 2002, p. 14.

44. Ibid., 30 November–6 December 2000, p. 10.

45. Ibid., 3–9 January 2002, p. 14; 26 October–1 November 2000, p. 12.

46. Ibid., 5–11 April 2001, p. 27.

47. Ibid., 3–9 May 2001, p. 14.

48. Ibid., 26 July–1 August 2001.

49. *Canberra Times*, 21 December 2000, p. 10.

50. Amartya Sen, 'Globalization must be for all', Alfred Deakin Lecture, *Age*, 16 May 2001, p. 17.

51. A.M. Khusro, *The Poverty of Nations*, London, Macmillan, 1999; Timothy Lankester, 'It's hell out there', *Times Literary Supplement*, 21 April 2000, p. 30.

52. Stephen Halliday, *The Great Stink of London: Sir Joseph Bazalgette and the Cleansing of the Victorian Capital*, Sutton, Thrupp, 1999.

53. Thomas Malthus, *Essay on Population*, 1798; Paul Ehrlich, *The Population Bomb*, 1968.

54. Björn Lomborg, *The Sceptical Environmentalist*, Cambridge University Press, 2001; *The Economist*, 4 August 2001, p. 63; *Far Eastern Economic Review*, 16 November 1995, pp. 88–91; *Age*, 2 August 2001.

55. *Age*, 10 August 1998, p. 11.

56. *Guardian Weekly*, 6–12 April 2000, p. 26; *Age*, 10 August 1998, p. 11.

57. *Guardian Weekly*, 11–17 January 2001, p. 23.

58. *The Economist*, 11 August 2001, p. 51; Pilar Estébanez, 'Patterns of Infection', *Le Monde Diplomatique*, January 2001, p. 12.

59. *Guardian Weekly*, 6–12 January 2000, p. 12; *Le Monde Diplomatique*, January 2000, p. 10.

60. Martine Bulard, 'The Apartheid of Pharmacology', *Le Monde Diplomatique*, January 2000, pp. 11–12.

61. *Age*, 12 July 2000, p. 12.

62. Gregory Palast, 'Glaxo and Aids', *Guardian Weekly*, 27 July–2 August 2000, p. 14; BBC, 8 June 2000, *Age*, 12 July 2000, p. 12.

63. *The Economist*, 21 July 2001, p. 49.

64. George Monbiot, 'Romania's Dead Zone', *Guardian Weekly*, 25–31 May 2000, p. 21; ibid., 14–20 September 2000, p. 7.

65. David Held, Anthony McGrew, David Goldblatt and Jonathon Perraton, *Global Transformations: Politics, Economics and Culture*, Oxford: Polity Press, 1999, p. 396.

66. *Guardian Weekly*, 25–31 January 2001, p. 1; 22–28 February 2001, p. 27.

67. *Australian*, 1–2 January 2000, p. 16.

68. Luke Anderson, 'Genetic Engineering Foods and Our Environment', *Australian*, 22 February 2000, p. 15.

69. *Guardian Weekly*, 1–7 June 2000, p. 8; 16 April-2 May 2001, p. 23.

70. *Guardian Weekly*, 14–20 October 1999, p. 12; 15–21 February 2001, p. 5; *Australia*, 9–10 October 1999, p. 23.

71. *Guardian Weekly*, 26 April–2 May 2001, p. 11.

72. Graeme Donald Snooks, *The Dynamic Society: Exploring the Sources of Global Change*, London and New York, Routledge, 1996, pp. 427–29; *The Ephemeral Civilization: Exploding the Myth of Social Evolution*, London and New York, Routledge, 1997, pp. 19, 493.

73. Anthony Giddens, *Runaway World*, p.34.

74. Gilbert Rist, *The History of Development: from Western Origins to Global Faith*, London and New York, Zed Books, 1997, p. 193.

75. *Le Monde Diplomatique*, December 1999, p. 13.

76. Held *et al.*, *Global Transformations*, p. 412.

77. Thomas Friedman, *The Lexus and the Olive Tree*, London, HarperCollins, 1999; James Davidson and William Rees-Mogg, *The Sovereign Individual*, London, Macmillan, 1997.

78. *Australian*, 9 June 1994, p. 11; 10 June 1994, p. 13.

79. Ernest Gellner, 'From the Ruins of the Great Contest: Civil Society, Nationalism and Islam', *Times Literary Supplement*, 13 November 1992, pp. 9–10.

80. Bruno Rémond, 'Europe: the State is Us', *Le Monde Diplomatique*, May 2000, p. 7.

81. Keith Suter, 'Little to be gained by returning to a mythical nationalist era', *Australian*, 1 May 2001, p. 9.

82. Mario Vargas Llosa, 'The Culture of Liberty', Cátedre Siglo XXI Lecture to the Inter-American Development Bank, Washington, 20 September 2000, *Background Briefing*, abc.net.au, 8 April 2001.

83. James Button, 'Can the nation state survive?', *Age*, 8 July 1999, p. 4.

84. Hirst and Thompson, *Globalization in Question*, pp. 5–6, 260, 277.

85. Samuel P. Huntington, *The Clash of Civilizations and the Remaking of World Order*, London, Simon and Schuster, 1997; Jeanne Kirkpatrick, 'Change and Tradition in the New World', *Australian*, 9 September 1993, p. 9.

86. Robert Manning, 'Collision Course', *Far Eastern Economic Review*, 6 February 1997, pp. 39–40.

87. Giddens, *Runaway World*, p. 49.

88. Fred Halliday, 'It is nonsense to talk of a clash of civilizations', *Guardian Weekly*, 27 September–3 October 2001, p. 11; Review of Gilles Kepel, *Jihad: Expansion et Déclin d'Islamisme*, in Henri Tincq, 'Islam's Fundamental Transformation', ibid., 11–17 May 2000, p. 30.

89. Anne-Marie Thiesse, 'Inventing a national identity', *Le Monde Diplomatique*, June 1999, pp. 6–7.

90. James C. Scott, *Seeing like a State: How certain schemes to improve the human condition have failed*, New Haven, Yale University Press, 1999.

91. Salman Rushdie, 'A Culture of Easy Criticism', *Age*, 10 March 1999, p. 17.

92. Philip Gourevitch, *We wish to inform you that tomorrow we will be killed with our families: Stories from Rwanda*, London, Picador, 1999, pp. 48–58.

93. Eric Alterman, *Who speaks for America? Why democracy matters in foreign policy*, New York, Cornell University Press, 1998.

94. Geoffrey Hartman, *The Fateful Question of Culture*, New York, Columbia University Press, 1998.

95. Taner Akcam, 'Turkey's carefully forgotten history', *Le Monde Diplomatique*, September 2001, pp. 12–13.

96. Gérard Prunier, 'A well planned Genocide', *Times Literary Supplement*, 22 October 1999, p. 30; Alison des Forges *et al.*, *Leave None to Tell the Story: Genocide in Rwanda*, Human Rights Watch US, 1999; Gourevitch, *We wish to inform you*, p. 95.

97. *Australian*, 10 June 1994, p. 13.

98. Puroshottam Agrawal, 'Identity debate clouds India's Elections', *Le Monde Diplomatique*, September 1999, pp. 10–11.

99. Michel Chossudovsky, 'How the West wrecked Yugoslavia', *Frontline*, Melbourne, May 1996, pp. 13–14.

100. Gourevitch, *We wish to inform you*, p. 58.

101. Held *et al.*, *Global Transformations*, p. 312.

102. *Far Eastern Economic Review*, 24 June 1999, pp. 28–9.

103. Stephen Thernstrom, 'Plenty of Room for All', *Times Literary Supplement*, 26 May 2000, pp. 5–6.

104. Saskia Sassen, 'Home truths', *Guardian Weekly*, 27 April–3 May 2000, p. 13.

105. Janette Habel, 'The line that divides Mexico and the US', *Le Monde Diplomatique*, December 1999, p. 6.

106. Sassen, 'Home truths', p. 13; *The Economist*, 23 June 2001, p. 39.

107. Mazower, *Dark Continent*, p. 327.

108. *Guardian Weekly*, 27 September –3 October 2001, p. 9.

109. *The Economist*, 28 July 2001, p. 30.

110. Mirta Ojita, 'Best of Friends, Worlds Apart', How race is lived in America series, *New York Times (NYT.com)*, 5 June 2000; *The Economist*, 7 April 2001, p. 56.

111. Mazower, *Dark Continent*, pp. 219–21.

112. Runnymede Trust, 'The Future of Multi-Ethnic Britain', *Guardian Weekly*, 19–25 October 2000, p. 11.

113. Desmond King, *Making America: Immigration, Race and the Origins of Diverse Democracy*, Cambridge, Mass., Harvard University Press, 2000.

114. James Crawford, 'A Nation Divided by One Language', *Guardian Weekly*, 22–28 February 2001, p. LE3.

115. *Guardian Weekly*, 27 June 1999, p. 5; *Australian*, 18 November 1999, p. 13.

116. *The Economist*, 30 June 2001, pp. 32–3.

117. Malcolm Caldwell, 'Lost in the middle', in Claudine Chiawei O'Hearne (ed.), *Half and half: writers on growing up biracial or bicultural*, New York, Pantheon, 1998.

118. Michael Field, 'New Zealanders are all Kiwis', *Fiji Times*, 21 February 2001, p. 7.

119. King, *Making America*; Thiesse, 'Inventing national identity', p. 7; Runnymede Trust, p. 11.

120. Monique Chenillier-Gendreau, 'Should outsiders have the vote?', *Le Monde Diplomatique*, January 2000, p. 16.

121. Gourevitch, *We wish to inform you*, pp. 47–8.

122. David Landes, *The Wealth and Poverty of Nations: Why some are so rich and some are so poor*, London, Little Brown and Co, 1998, pp. 416–18.

123. Rist, *History of Development*, pp. 227–29.

124. Mazower, *Dark Continent*, p. 403.

125. Hirst and Thompson, *Globalization in Question*, p. 6.

126. Wolfgang Sachs, *Planet Dialectics: Explorations in Environment and Development*, London, Zed Books, 1999, p. 102.

127. Stephen K. Sanderson, *Social Transformations: A General Theory of Historical Development*, Oxford, Blackwell, 1995, pp. 379–80.

128. Mazower, *Dark Continent*, p. 406.

129. Ibid.

130. Peter J. Taylor, *The Way the Modern World Works: World Hegemony to World Impasse*, Chichester, John Wiley and Sons, 1996, p. 225.

131. Felipe Fernández-Armesto, *Millennium: A History of Our Last Thousand Years*, London, Black Swan, 1995, pp. 709–10.

132. George Monbiot, 'Global Democracy', the John Moore Lecture at the Cheltenham Festival of Literature, England, December 2001; reproduced on 'Background Briefing', Radio National, abc.net.au, 6 January 2002.

133. Saskia Sassen, 'Gold and Bombs', *Le Monde Diplomatique*, October 2001, p. 5.

134. *Guardian Weekly*, 21–27 June 2001, p. 29.

135. Elazar Barkan, *The Guilt of Nations: Restitution and Negotiating Historical Injustices*, New York, W.W. Norton and Co, 2000, p. 348.

136. Monbiot, 'Global Democracy'.

137. Gourevitch, *We wish to inform you*, p. 325.

138. BBC Online, www.bbc.co.uk, 27 September 2001.

139. *The Economist*, 4 August 2001, p. 26.

140. Ibid., 18 August 2001, pp. 18–20.

141. *Far Eastern Economic Review*, 27 April 1999, p. 63.

142. Sassen, 'Gold and Bombs', p. 5.

143. Ibid.; *Guardian Weekly*, 8–14 November 2001, p. 10.

144. Mark Riley, '27 million slaves', *theage.co.au*, 4 June 2001; *Guardian Weekly*, 30 March–5 April 2000, p. 3; Edward Luttwak, 'Why slavery persists', *Times Literary Supplement*, 26 November 1999, p. 3.

145. *Australian*, 1 February 2001, p. 28; *Guardian Weekly*, 8–14 November 2001, p. 10.

146. Sandro Sideri, 'Globalization, the Role of the State, and Human Rights', Address to the Institute of Social Studies, The Hague, 2000, p. 25.

147. *Guardian Weekly*, 17–23 February 2000.

148. Jonathan Steele, 'Europe's demographic crisis', *Guardian Unlimited*, 30 October 2000; Greg Callaghan, 'A family by any other name', *Australian Magazine*, 1–2 January 2000, pp. 17–19; David Frum, 'Not young anymore', *Times Literary Supplement*, 14 July 2000, p. 12; Phil Mulan, *The Imaginary Time Bomb*, London and New York, IB Tauris, 2000.

149. Sassen, 'Gold and Bombs', p. 5; *Guardian Weekly*, 8–14 November 2001, p. 10; *The Economist*, 3 March 2001, pp. 21–3.

150. Jelle van Buuren, 'Fortress Europe raises the barricades', *Le Monde Diplomatique*, March 1999, pp. 6–7.

151. Ambalavaner Sivanandan, 'Casualties of Globalization', *Guardian Weekly*, 17–27 August 2000, p. 14.

152. Held *et al.*, *Global Transformations*, p. 451.

153. *The Economist*, 4 August 2001, p. 26.

154. Sachs, *Planet Dialectics*, p. 102.

155. Oliver Sacks, 'Full Frontal', *Australian Review of Books*, May 2001, pp. 19–20, 27.

156. Snooks, *Dynamic Society*, pp. 427–30; *Ephemeral Civilization*, p. 511.

157. Snooks, *Dynamic Society*, p. 151.

158. Richard Bosworth, 'History: The Nation and the Past', *Ockham's Razor*, abc.net.au, 27 April 1997.

159. Sachs, *Planet Dialectics*, p. 106.

160. Taylor, *The Way the Modern World Works*, pp. 211–12.

161. Snooks, *Dynamic Society*, pp. 523–4.

162. Jonathan Glover, *Humanity: A Moral History of the 20th Century*, London, Jonathon Cape, 1999; *Guardian Weekly*, 18–24 November 1999, p. 23.

163. Martha Nussbaum, *Cultivating Humanity: A Classical Defence of Reform in Liberal Education*, Cambridge, Mass., Harvard University Press, 1997.

164. Fernández-Armesto, *Millennium*, p. 529.

165. Robert J. Holton, *Globalization and the Nation State*, London, Macmillan, 1998, p. 141.

166. Veronika Bennholdt-Thomsen and Maria Mies, *The Subsistence Perspective: Beyond the Globalised Economy*, London, Zed Books, 1999, p. 213.

Bibliography

Abu-Lughod, J.L., *Before European Hegemony: The World System AD 1250–1350*, New York, Oxford University Press, 1989.

— 'Restructuring the Premodern World', *Review*, Fernand Braudel Center, XIII (2: 1990), pp. 273–86.

Acuña, R.-L., 'A Culture of Peace', *Le Monde Diplomatique*, November 1999, p. 16.

Adshead, S.A.M., *China in World History*, London, Macmillan, 1995.

Akcam, T., 'Turkey's carefully forgotten history', *Le Monde Diplomatique*, September 2001, pp. 12–13.

Agrawal, P., 'Identity debate clouds India's elections', *Le Monde Diplomatique*, September 1999, pp. 10–11.

Alavi, H. and T. Shanin (eds), *The Sociology of 'Developing Societies'*, London, Macmillan, 1982.

Alterman, E., *Who speaks for America? Why democracy matters in foreign policy*, New York, Cornell University Press, 1998.

Amin, S., 'History conceived as an eternal cycle', *Review*, Fernand Braudel Center, XXII (3:1999), pp. 291–326.

Anderson, F., *The Crucible of War: The Seven Years War and the Fate of Empire in British North America, 1754–1766*, New York, Alfred A. Knopf, 1999.

Anderson, L., 'Genetic Engineering Foods and Our Environment', *Australian*, 22 February 2000, p. 15.

Angier, N., *An Intimate Geography of Women*, London, Virago Press, 1999.

Appleyard, B., 'IQ Tests', *Australian*, 30–31 October 1999, p. R5.

Arrighi, G., 'The World According to Frank', *Review*, Fernand Braudel Center, XXII (3: 1999), pp. 327–54.

Arrighi, G., 'The Three Hegemonies', *Review*, Fernand Braudel Center, XIII (3:1990), pp. 365–408.

Barkan, E., *The Guilt of Nations: Restitution and Negotiating Historical Injustices*, New York, W.W. Norton and Co, 2000.

Barnet, R.J., *The Alliance, America–Europe–Japan: Makers of the Postwar World*, New York, Simon and Schuster, 1983.

Barnett, A., 'Creative Utopias', *Times Literary Supplement*, 24 March 2000, pp. 13–14.

Barraclough, G., *From Agadir to Armageddon: Anatomy of a Crisis*, London, Weidenfeld and Nicholson, 1982.

Bauman, Z., *Globalization: the Human Consequences*, Cambridge, Polity Press, 1998.

Bellamy, D., B. Springett and P. Hayden, *Moa's Ark: The Voyage of New Zealand*, Auckland, Viking, 1990.

Bennholdt-Thomsen, V. and M. Mies, *The Subsistence Perspective: Beyond the Globalised Economy*, London, Zed Books, 1999.

Bennis, P., 'US undermines international law', *Le Monde Diplomatique*, December 1999, pp. 1–2.

Berthoud, C., 'Who would be mother', *Le Monde Diplomatique*, January 2000, p. 14.

Bix, H., *Hirohito and the Making of Modern Japan*, London, Harper and Collins, 2000.

Blackmore, S., *The Meme Machine*, New York, Oxford University Press, 1999.

Bosworth, R., 'History: The Nation and the Past', *Ockham's Razor*, abc.net.au, 27 April 1997.

Brecht, B., *The Resistible Rise of Arturo Ui*, London, Methuen, 1981.

Brett, E.A., *The World Economy Since the War: The Politics of Uneven Development*, New York, Praeger, 1985.

Brittain, V. and L. Elliott, 'Educating girls is a real lifesaver', *Guardian Weekly*, 9–15 March 2000, p. 27.

Buckle, S., 'The Second Sex', *Australian Review of Books*, April 2001, pp. 16–17.

Bulard, M., 'The Apartheid of Pharmacology', *Le Monde Diplomatique*, January 2000, pp. 11–12.

Bullock, A., *Hitler: a Study in Tyranny*, London, Penguin, 1962.

Button, J., 'Can the nation state survive?', *Age*, 8 July 1999, p. 4.

Buuren, J. van, 'Fortress Europe raises the barricades', *Le Monde Diplomatique*, March 1999, pp. 6–7.

Calder, L., *Financing the American Dream: A Cultural History of Consumer Credit*, London, Wiley, 1999.

Caldwell, M., 'Lost in the middle', in C. Chiawei O'Hearne (ed.), *Half and half: writers on growing up biracial or bicultural*, New York, Pantheon, 1998.

Callaghan, G., 'A family by any other name', *Australian Magazine*, 1–2 January 2000, pp. 17–19.

Cannadine, D., *Ornamentalism: How the British saw their Empire*, New York, Oxford University Press, 2001.

Cardoso, F.H., 'Dependency and Development in Latin America', in H. Alavi and T. Shanin (eds), *The Sociology of 'Developing Societies'*, London, Macmillan, 1982, pp. 112–17.

Carroll, R., 'Dirty Secrets', *Guardian Weekly*, 5–11 July 2001, p. 23.

Cash, W., 'No laughing matter', *Australian*, 26–27 December 1998, pp. R2–3.

Champin, C., 'End of the Zimbabwe model', *Le Monde Diplomatique*, May 2000, p. 3.

Chanda, N., 'Early Warning', *Far Eastern Economic Review*, 10 June 1999, pp. 46–8.

Chenillier-Gendreau, M., 'Should outsiders have the vote?' *Le Monde Diplomatique*, January 2000, p. 16.

Chossudovsky, M., 'How the West wrecked Yugoslavia', *Frontline*, Melbourne, May 1996, pp. 13–14.

Clairmont, F., 'When the giants play with fire', *Le Monde Diplomatique*, December 1999, p. 15.

Cohen, D., *The Wealth of the World and the Poverty of Nations*, Cambridge, Mass., MIT Press, 1998.

Cohen, W., *The Sextants of Beijing*, New York, W. Norton and Co, 1999.

Conley, D., *Being Black, Living in the Red: Race, Wealth and Social Policy in America*, Berkeley, University of California, 1999.

— 'More unequal than others in the US', *Le Monde Diplomatique*, September 2001.

Cornwell, J. (ed.), *Nature's Imagination*, Oxford, Oxford University Press, 1995.

Cosic, M., 'What's it all about?' *Australian* Magazine, 13–14 February 1999, p. 32–5.

Crawford, J., 'A Nation Divided by One Language', *Guardian Weekly*, 22–28 February 2001, p. 3.

Crawford, P., *Nomads of the Wind: A Natural History of Polynesia*, London, BBC Books, 1993.

Damasio, A.R., *Body and Emotion in the Making of Consciousness*, New York, Harcourt, Brace and Co, 1999.

Davidson, J. and W. Rees-Mogg, *The Sovereign Individual*, London, Macmillan, 1997.

Dawkins, R., *The Selfish Gene*, Oxford, Oxford University Press, 1976.

Descent of Man, The, *The Science Show*, Radio National, abc.net.au, January–February 2000.

Deutsch, D., *The Fabric of Reality, The Science of Parallel Universes and its Implications*, London, Allen Lane, 1998.

Deutscher, I., *Stalin, A Political Biography*, London, Penguin, 1966.

Diamond, J., Australian Museum Lecture, Science Show, Radio National, abc.net.au, 28 November 2000.

— *The Rise and Fall of the Third Chimpanzee*, London, Vintage, 1992

— *Guns, Germs and Steel: The Fates of Human Societies*, London, Jonathan Cape, 1997.

Dmytryshyn, B., *USSR: A Concise History*, New York, Charles Scribner's Sons, 1971.

Dower, J.W., (ed.), *Origins of the Modern Japanese State, Selected Writings of E.H. Norman*, New York, Pantheon, 1975.

Durutalo, S., 'The Liberation of the Pacific Island Intellectual', *Review*, Suva, University of the South Pacific, 10 (September 1983), pp. 10, 14.

Dyson, F., 'The Scientist as Rebel', Australian, 7 June 1995, pp, 22, 28.

Eichengreen, B., *Globalizing Capital: A History of the International Monetary System*, Princeton, Princeton University Press, 1998.

Elegant, R., 'Gorfu, Anyone?' *Far Eastern Economic Review*, 15 April 1999, pp. 66–70.

Elegant, S., 'A Pyrrhic Victory', *Far Eastern Economic Review*, 10 June 1999, p. 45.

Elegant, S., 'Trade Triumphant', *Far Eastern Economic Review*, 10 June 1999, pp. 38–9.

Elliott, L., 'Markets must deliver what people want', *Guardian Weekly*, 13–19 April 2000, p. 12.

Elster, J., *Alchemies of the Mind: Rationality and the Emotions*, Cambridge: Cambridge University Press, 1999.

Elvin, M., 'The X Factor', *Far Eastern Economic Review*, 10 June 1999, pp. 66–9.

Estébanez, P., 'Patterns of Infection', *Le Monde Diplomatique*, January 2001, p. 12

Fernández-Armesto, F., *Millennium: A History of Our Last Thousand Years*, London, Black Swan, 1995.

Field, M., 'New Zealanders are all Kiwis', *Fiji Times*, 21 February 2001, p. 7.

Fitzpatrick, J., 'The Middle Kingdom, The Middle Sea and the Geographic Pivot of History', *Review*, Fernand Braudel Center, XV (3: 1992), pp. 477–501.

Flannery, T., *The Eternal Frontier: An Ecological History of North America and its Peoples*, Melbourne, Text Publishing, 2001.

— *The Future Eaters: an Ecological History of the Australasian Lands and People*, Chatswood, Reed Books, 1994.

Forges, A. des, *et al.*, *Leave None to Tell the Story: Genocide in Rwanda*, Human Rights Watch US, 1999.

Frank, A.G., *Crisis In the World Economy*, London, Heinemann, 1980.

— *REORIENT: Global Economy in the Asian Age*, Berkeley, University of California, 1998.

Frank, T., *One Market under God: Extreme Capitalism, Market Populism and the End of Economic Democracy*, London, Secker and Warburg, 2000.

Friedman, T., *The Lexus and the Olive Tree*, London, Harper and Collins, 1999.

Frum, D., 'Not young anymore', *Times Literary Supplement*, 14 July 2000, p. 12.

Furet, F., *The Passing of an Illusion: the Idea of Communism in the 20th Century*, Chicago, Chicago University Press, 1999.

Galbraith, J., 'Inequality, Employment and Growth: What are the Connections?' www. tcf.org/Press Releases/Galbraith.html.

Galbraith, J.K., *The Age of Uncertainty*, London, BBC-Andre Deutsch, 1977.

— *The World Economy Since the Wars: A Personal View*, London, Sinclair-Stevenson, 1994.

Gamble, A., 'When Manifest Destinies Conflict', *Times Literary Supplement*, 24 March 2000, p. 11.

Gellner, E., 'From the Ruins of the Great Contest: Civil Society, Nationalism and Islam', *Times Literary Supplement*, 13 November 1992, pp. 9–10.

George, S. and F. Sabelli, *Faith and Credit: The World Bank's Secular Empire*, London, Penguin, 1994.

Giddens, A., *Runaway World: How Globalisation is Reshaping Our Lives*, London, Profile Books, 2000.

Gilroy, P., *Between Camps: Race, Identity and Nationalism at the End of the Colour Line*, London, Allen Lane, 2000,

Gleick, J., *Chaos: Making a New Science*, New York, Penguin, 1987.

Glover, J., *Humanity: A Moral History of the 20th Century*, London, Jonathan Cape, 1999.

Goldberg, E., *The Executive Brain: Frontal Lobes and the Civilized Mind*, New York, Oxford University Press, 2001.

Gorodelsky, G., *The Grand Delusion: Stalin and the German Invasion of Russia*, New Haven, Yale University Press, 1999.

Gott, R., 'Whitewashing the real evil empire', *Guardian Weekly*, 17–23 May 2001, p. 45.

Gourevitch, P., *We wish to inform you that tomorrow we will be killed with our families: Stories from Rwanda*, London, Picador, 1999.

Graham, M. and A. Shaldiner, *Corning and the Craft of Innovation*, New York, Oxford University Press, 2001.

Grandmaison, O., 'Liberty, equality and colony', *Le Monde Diplomatique*, June 2001, pp. 12–13.

Griffith, B., *The Gardens of their Dreams: Desertification and Culture in World History*, Nova Scotia, London and New York, Fernwood Publishing and Zed Books, 2001.

Griffith-Jones, S., *Global Capital Flows: Should They be Regulated?* London, Macmillan, 1999.

Guilhot, N., 'Repackaging the World Bank', *Le Monde Diplomatique*, October 2000, pp. 10–11.

Habel, J., 'The line that divides Mexico and the US', *Le Monde Diplomatique*, December 1999, p. 6.

Halberstam, D., *The Fifties*, New York, Villard Books, 1993.

Halberstam, D., *The Reckoning: a tale of two cultures as seen through two car companies*, London, Bloomsbury Publishing, 1987.

Halliday, F., 'It is nonsense to talk of a clash of civilizations', *Guardian Weekly*, 27 September–3 October 2001, p. 11

— *The Making of the Second Cold War*, London, Verso, 1983.

— *Revolution and World Politics*; London, Macmillan, 2000.

Halliday, S., *The Great Stink of London: Sir Joseph Bazalgette and the Cleansing of the Victorian Capital*, Sutton, Thrupp, 1999.

Hall, T.D., *The World Systems Reader: New Perspectives on Gender, Urbanism, Cultures, Indigenous Peoples and Ecology*, Lanham and Oxford, Rowman and Littleford, 2000, pp. 4–5.

Hartman, G., *The Fateful Question of Culture*, New York, Columbia University Press, 1998.

Hellyer, P., 'Global Finance: Dismantle or Reform?' Background Briefing, Radio National, abc.net.au, 30 May 1999.

Held, D., A. McGrew, D. Goldblatt and J. Perraton, *Global Transformations: Politics, Economics and Culture*, Oxford, Polity Press, 1999.

Hirst, P. and G. Thompson, *Globalization in Question, The International Economy and the Possibilities of Governance*, Cambridge, Polity, 1999.

Hochschild, A., *King Leopold's Ghost: A Story of Greed, Terror, and Heroism in Colonial Africa*, London, Houghton and Mifflin, 1998.

Hodgson, G., *The People's Century: From the Start of the Nuclear Age to the Close of the Century*, London, BBC Books, 1996.

Holton, R.J., *Globalization and the Nation State*, London, Macmillan, 1998.

— *The Transition from Feudalism to Capitalism*, London, Macmillan, 1985.

Hoogvelt, A., *Globalisation and the Postcolonial World: the New Political Economy of Development*, London, Macmillan, 1997.

Huntington, S., *The Clash of Civilizations and the Remaking of World Order*, London, Simon and Schuster, 1997.

Huntington, S., *Political Order in Changing Societies*, New Haven, Yale University Press, 1968.

Ignatieff, M., 'Keeping an old flame burning brightly', *Guardian Weekly*, 20 December 1998.

Isaacs, J. and T. Downing, *Cold War*, London, Bantam Press, 1998.

James, P., 'The Indigenous Dilemma', *Ockham's Razor*, Radio National, abc.net.au, 4 March 2001.

Jaivin, L., 'Gentle Shoves and Secret Executions', *Australian Society*, October 1990, p. 11.

Kennedy, A., *The End of Shareholder Value*, London, Orion, 2000.

Kennedy, D., 'A Tale of Three Cities: How the United States Won World War Two', Background Briefing, *Radio National*, abc.net.au, 21 October 2001.

Kersten, R., 'Liberalism sidelined in new Asia', *Australian*, 15 January 1997, p. 11.

Kershaw, I., *Hitler, 1936–1945: Nemesis*, London, Penguin, 2000.

Khusro, A.M., *The Poverty of Nations*, London, Macmillan, 1999.

Kim, J.W., *Mind in a Physical World*, Cambridge, Mass., MIT Press, 1999.

King, D., *Making America: Immigration, Race and the Origins of Diverse Democracy*, Harvard University Press, 2000.

Kirkpatrick, J., 'Change and Tradition in the New World', *Australian*, 9 September 1993, p. 9.

Klein, N., *No Logo*, London, Flamingo, 1999.

Krauthammen, C., 'The Great Di Turnabout', *Time*, 22 September 1997, p. 128.

Lal, D., 'Golden Chains', *Far Eastern Economic Review*, 10 June 1999, pp. 50–4.

Lankester, T., 'It's hell out there', *Times Literary Supplement*, 21 April 2000, p. 30.

Landes, D., *The Wealth and Poverty of Nations: Why some are so rich and some are so poor*, London, Little Brown and Co, 1998.

Langdon, J.C., *World History and the Eonic Effect: Civilization, Darwinism and the Theory of Evolution*, New York, Xlibris Corporation, 1999.

Larner, J., *Marco Polo and the Discovery of the World*, New Haven, Yale University Press, 1999.

Latouche, S., *The Westernization of the World: The Significance, Scope and Limits of the Drive towards Global Uniformity*, Cambridge, Polity Press, 1996.

Legraine, P., 'Dump prejudice and learn to love big government', *Guardian Weekly*, 19–25 July 2001, p. 2.

Lequerot, E., 'Africa's forgotten tribe', *Le Monde Diplomatique*, January 2000, p. 15.

Lilla, M., 'An idea whose time has come', *New York Times Book Review*, 25 July 1999, p. 12.

Livi-Bacci, M., *The Population of Europe*, Oxford: Blackwell, 2000.

Llosa, M.V., 'The Culture of Liberty', Cátedre Siglo XXI Lecture to the Inter-American Development Bank, Washington, 20 September 2000, Background Briefing, *Radio National*, abc.net.au, 8 April 2001.

Lloyd, G., 'Watching for the eclipse', *Times Literary Supplement*, London, 18 February 2000, pp. 3–4.

Lomborg, B., *The Sceptical Environmentalist*, Cambridge University Press, 2001.

Luttwak, E., 'Why slavery persists', *Times Literary Supplement*, 26 November 1999, p. 3.

Magdoff, H., *The Age of Imperialism: The Economics of US Foreign Policy*, New York, Monthly Review Press, 1969.

Maier, K., *This House has Fallen: Nigeria in Crisis*, London, Penguin, 1999.

Manning, R., 'Collusion Course', *Far Eastern Economic Review*, 6 February 1997, pp. 39–40.

Margulius, L., *The Symbiotic Planet: A New Look at Evolution*, London, Weidenfeld and Nicolson, 1999.

May, E.T., 'Myths and Realities of the American Family' in A. Prost and G. Vincent (ed), *A History of Private Life: Riddles of Identity in Modern Times* (Vol. V), Cambridge, Mass., Belknap Press/Harvard University Press, 1991, pp. 57–2.

Mattelart, A., 'Communication breeds democracy', *Le Monde Diplomatique*, December 2000, p. 13.

Mazower, M., *Dark Continent: Europe's Twentieth Century*, London, Allen Lane, 1998.

McGinn, C., *The Mysterious Flame: Conscious Minds in a Material World*, New York, Basic Books, 1999.

McNeill, W.H., *The Pursuit of Power: Technology, Armed Forces and Society since AD 1000*, Oxford, Blackwell, 1982.

Milton, G., *Nathaniel's Nutmeg: how one man's courage changed the course of history*, New York, Hodder and Stoughton, 1999.

Monbiot, G., 'Global Democracy', in 'Background Briefing', *Radio National*, abc.net.au, 6 January 2002.

— 'Romania's Dead Zone', *Guardian Weekly*, 25–31 May 2000, p. 21

Moreau, R., *Rom*, Sydney, University of New South Wales Press, 2000.

Morishima, M., *Why has Japan Succeeded? Western Technology and the Japanese Ethos*, Cambridge, Cambridge University Press, 1982.

Mulan, P., *The Imaginary Time Bomb*, New York, IB Tauris, 2000.

Nussbaum, M., *Cultivating Humanity: A Classical Defence of Reform in Liberal Education*, Cambridge, Mass., Harvard University Press, 1997.

Ohmae, K., 'The Invisible Continent', *Australian*, 26 July 2000, p. 36; 27 July 2000, p. 32.

Ojita, M., 'Best of Friends; Worlds Apart', *How Race is Lived in America* series, nyt.com, 5 June 2000.

Ormerod, P., *Butterfly Economics*, London, Faber and Faber, 1998.

— *The Death of Economics*, London, Faber and Faber, 1994.

Palast, G., 'Glaxo and Aids', *Guardian Weekly*, 27 July–2 August 2000, p. 14.

Pallister, D., 'Continental Drift', *Guardian*, 26 August 1997, p. 13.

Paris, E., *Long Shadows: Truth, Lies, and History*, London, Bloomsbury, 2001.

Pinker, S., *How the Mind Works*, London, Penguin, 1998.

Planck, R., *Seeing and Believing: The Story of the Telescope, or how we found our place in the Universe*, London, Fourth Estate, 2000.

Porter, B., *The Lion's Share: A Short History of the British Empire, 1850–1970*, London, Longman, 1975.

Polya, G., *Jane Austen and the Black Hole of British History, Colonial Rapacity, Holocaust Denial, and the Crisis in Biological Sustainability*, Melbourne, 1998.

Prost, A., 'Public and Private Spheres in France', in A. Prost and C. Vincent, *A History of Private Life: Riddles of Identity in Modern Times* (Vol. V), Cambridge, Mass., Belknap Press/Harvard University Press, 1991, pp. 1–144.

Prunier, G., 'A well planned Genocide', *Times Literary Supplement*, 22 October 1999, p. 30.

Rémond, B., 'Europe: the State is Us', *Le Monde Diplomatique*, May 2000, p. 7.

Reynolds, H., *An Indelible Stain*, Melbourne, Viking, 2001.

Ridley, M., *The Origins of Virtue*, London, Viking, 1996.

Riley, M., '27 million slaves', theage.co.au, 4 June 2001.

Rist, G., *The History of Development: from Western Origins to Global Faith*, London and New York, Zed Books, 1997.

Robertson, R.T., *The Making of the Modern World*, London, Zed Books, 1986.

Robertson, R. and W. Sutherland, *Government by the Gun: The Unfinished Business of Fiji's 2000 Coup*, Sydney, London and New York, Pluto Press and Zed Books, 2001.

Runnymede Trust, 'The Future of Multi-Ethnic Britain', *Guardian Weekly*, 19–25 October 2000, p. 11.

Rushdie, S., 'A Culture of Easy Criticism', *Age*, 10 March 1999, p. 17.

Sachs, W., *Planet Dialectics: Explorations in Environment and Development*, London, Zed Books, 1999.

Sacks, O., 'Full Frontal', *Australian Review of Books*, May 2001, pp. 19–20, 27.

Said, E., *Culture and Imperialism*, London, Chatto and Windus, 1993.

Sassen, S., 'Home truths', *Guardian Weekly*, 27 April–3 May 2000, p. 13.

Sanderson, S.K., *Social Transformations: A General Theory of Historical Development*, Oxford, Blackwell, 1995.

— 'Synthetic Materialism: An Integrated Theory of Human Society', paper to the American Sociological Association, San Francisco, 21–25 August 1998.

Schulz, D., 'The first bronzed Aussie?' theage.com.au, 26 June 2001.

Segal, L., 'Why we still need feminism', *Age*, 15 November 1999, p. 17.

Sen, A., *The State, Industrialization and Class Formations in India: A Neomarxist Perspective on Colonialism, Underdevelopment and Development*, London, Routledge and Kegan Paul, 1982.

— 'Choosing Freedom', *Far Eastern Economic Review*, 27 January 2000, p. 38.

— 'Globalization must be for all', Alfred Deakin Lecture, *Age*, 16 May 2001, p. 17.

Scott, J.C., *Seeing Like a State: How Certain Schemes to Improve the Human Condition Have Failed*, New Haven, Yale University Press, 1999.

Sherman, S., 'Hegemonic Transitions and the Dynamics of Cultural Change', *Review*, Fernand Braudel Center, XXII (1:1999), pp. 87–117.

Short, R. and M. Potts, *Ever Since Adam and Eve: the Evolution of Human Sexuality*, Cambridge, Cambridge University Press, 1999.

Sideri, S., 'Globalization, the Role of the State, and Human Rights', Address to the Institute of Social Studies, The Hague, 2000.

Sivanandan, A., 'Casualties of Globalization', *Guardian Weekly*, 17–27 August 2000, p. 14.

Smith, B., 'The Domestication of Plants', The Science Show, *Radio National*, abc.net.au, 15 July 2000.

Smith, D., 'In the beginning', smh.com.au, 12 August 2000.

Snooks, G.D., *The Dynamic Society: Exploring the Sources of Global Change*, London and New York, Routledge, 1996.

— *The Ephemeral Civilization: Exploding the Myth of Social Evolution*, London and New York, Routledge, 1997.

— *The Laws of History*, London and New York, Routledge, 1998.

Soto, H. de, *The Mastery Of Capital: Why Capitalism Triumphs in the West and Fails Everywhere Else*, New York, Basic Books, 2000.

Spence, J., 'Paradise Lost', *Far Eastern Economic Review*, 15 April 1999, p. 40.

Steele, J., 'Europe's demographic crisis', *Guardian Unlimited*, 30 October 2000.

Suter, K., 'Little to be gained by returning to a mythical nationalist era', *Australian*, 1 May 2001, p. 9.

Swan, N., 'Mastering the Control Factor', Health Report, *Radio National*, abc.net.au, 9 November 1998.

Tatz, C., 'The bitter truth behind the ban on Wagner', smh.com.au, 2 August 2001.

Taylor, P.J., *The Way the Modern World Works: World Hegemony to World Impasse*, Chicester, John Wiley and Sons, 1996.

Thernstrom, S., 'Plenty of Room for All', *Times Literary Supplement*, 26 May 2000, pp. 5–6.

Thiesse, A.-M., 'Inventing a national identity', *Le Monde Diplomatique*, June 1999, pp. 6–7.

Thornhill, R. and C. Palmer, *A Natural History of Rape: Biological Bases of Sexual Coercion*, Cambridge, Mass., MIT Press, 2000.

Toynbee, P., 'Buried under the burka', *Guardian Weekly*, 4–10 October 2001, p. 11.

Tsunoda, R. *et al.*, *Sources of the Japanese Tradition*, New York, Columbia University Press, 1958.

Tudge, C., *The Variety of Life: The Meaning of Biodiversity*, Oxford, 1999.

Unger, R., *Democracy Unrealized: The Progressive Alternative*, London, Verso, 1998.

Vakikiotis, M., 'Capital Idea', *Far Eastern Economic Review*, 10 June 1999, p. 51.

Wacquant, L., 'Imprisoning the American Poor', *Le Monde Diplomatique*, September 1998, pp. 8–9.

Walker, M., *The Cold War*, London, Vintage, 1944.

Wallerstein, I., 'Frank proves the European Miracle', *Review*, Fernand Braudel Center, XXII (3: 1999), pp. 355–71.

Wang, G., 'Long Path to Power', *Far Eastern Economic Review*, 10 June 1999, pp.40–44.

Ward, P. and D. Brownlee, *Rare Earth, Why Complex Life is Uncommon in the Universe*, New York, Copernicus, 2000.

Wertheim, M., 'Science, Magic, and the Kitchen Sink', *Australian*, 1–2 January 2000, p. 27.

M. Westlake, 'Where will the buck stop?' *South Magazine*, December 1984, p. 76.

Williams, W.A., *Empire as a Way of Life*, New York, Oxford University Press, 1980.

Wilson, P., 'The "Me" Society', *Australian*, 18–19 May 1996, pp. R1, 6.

Wright, R., *NONZERO: The Logic of Human Destiny*, New York, Pantheon Books, 2000.

Zeder, M. and B. Smith, Smithsonian Institute, 'Are Goats our Oldest Crop?' The Science Show, Radio National, abc.net.au, 3 March 2001.

Index